THE WELLINGTON REGIMENT
N.Z.E.F. — 1914-1919

THE
Wellington Regiment
N. Z. E. F.
1914————1919

By

W. H. CUNNINGHAM, D.S.O.,
C. A. L. TREADWELL, O.B.E.,
J. S. HANNA.

So they gave their bodies to the commonwealth and received, each for his own memory, praise that will never die ; and with it, the noblest sepulchre, not that in which the mortal bones are laid, but a home in the minds of men.

—*Pericles*

Dedicated

To the memory of those of the Regiment who gave their lives in the Great War;

And to our fellow soldiers of the Regiment who remain to serve the country in peace;

And to the present and future soldiers of those battalions that made the Wellington Regiment N.Z.E.F., in whose keeping is its good name.

For us the glorious dead have striven,
They battled that we might be free.
We to their living cause are given;
We arm for men that are to be.

—LAURENCE BINYON.

PREFACE.

WITH this book a history of the Battalions of the Wellington Regiment that played their part in the N.Z.E.F. in the War against Germany and Turkey appears.

For reasons with which we are not concerned the preparation of the book has been left for some eight years after the Armistice. We have, therefore, with such a long space of time since the events we record, been careful not to rely on memory, but on the more reliable, if less coloured, Official War Records.

The work of writing and compiling this volume has been so divided that Mr. Cunningham has contributed the first eight chapters, while for the rest of the book Messrs. Treadwell and Hanna are responsible. Every Army, Army Corps, Divisional, Brigade, Battalion and Company Order affecting the operations of the Regiment from the outbreak of the War until the march to Germany has been carefully noted, and the diaries of each Battalion have been examined. That the length of time that has elapsed may have resulted in some degree in robbing this book of vividness, or even interest, is recognised. What, however, cannot be affected is its being a record of the doings of the Regiment in the Great War, of which each and every member from Colonel to Private may well be proud. It is a record, too, of some of the brave acts of members of the Regiment. One difficulty that has impressed itself upon us has been that arising from the mention of the various acts of bravery by the different soldiers. We felt that these mentioned acts could have been said of most of the members of the Regiment. We have included in this book the official reports of the various acts of gallantry that have earned for members of the Regiment recognition and decorations from His Majesty the King.

Of its fighting qualities the Wellington Regiment had nothing to be afraid of in comparison with any other in the

PREFACE.

Field of France. The happy combination of a reasonable discipline—not enough to prejudice initiative, but sufficient to get a maximum team result, was one of the outstanding features in the Battalions.

We have added to this Regimental History a Graph prepared by the Defence Department, from which much useful information can be gleaned. The photographs have been selected from a large number available and were taken both by official and unofficial photographers. The maps in this book are specially prepared with a view to giving as much data and as little surplusage as possible.

Finally, we trust that those whose husbands, sons or brothers of our great Regiment whose lives were given for the Great Cause will find in this record a reminder of lives freely and gallantly given for justice and liberty. To those of the Regiment who are living we commend this book hoping it may remind them of those "bad old days" which sometimes were not so bad, while at other times were too bad to talk about. That this book may be treasured by our fellow comrades as a true record of a grand Regiment of soldiers, of which each member is proud to have helped to form part, is our earnest wish. If it achieves that object the many hours spent by us in its preparation will have been well spent.

We desire to acknowledge our indebtedness to Lieut.-Col. C. H. Weston, D.S.O., for allowing us free use of his book, "Three Years with the New Zealanders," to Captain W. Jervis, M.C., N.Z.S.C., for the great time and trouble he cheerfully took to find and lend War Diaries and Orders and for numerous other acts of great assistance; and to Mr. C. H. Clemens, of N.Z.E.F. Base Records, for compiling a host of useful information.

W. H. CUNNINGHAM.
C. A. L. TREADWELL.
J. S. HANNA.

CONTENTS.

	Page
CHAPTER I.	1
The Organisation of the Regiment—Departure from New Zealand.	
CHAPTER II.	6
The Voyage to Egypt—H.A.M.S. "Sydney" Destroys the "Emden"—Colombo, Suez, Port Said, Alexandria.	
CHAPTER III.	14
Egypt—Cairo—Training on the Desert.	
CHAPTER IV.	18
The Defence of the Suez Canal—The Regiment's Baptism of fire.	
CHAPTER V.	22
Preparations for the Gallipoli Campaign — More Hard Training on the Desert—Lemnos.	
CHAPTER VI.	27
Gallipoli– The Landing — Days of Strenuous Fighting—Walker's Ridge.	
CHAPTER VII.	36
Cape Helles — The "River Clyde"— Seddul Bahr — The Daisy Patch — An Order is Countermanded — Back to Anzac—Armistice—Courtney's Post—Monash Gully.	
CHAPTER VIII.	58
August Operations and Chunuk Bair — Outline of the Scheme and Preparations—The Special Part Assigned the Battalion—Happy Valley — The Night of the 6/7th—The day of the 7th and the Night of the 7/8th—The 8th August.	
CHAPTER IX.	78
Rhododendron Spur—Cheshire Ridge.	
CHAPTER X.	80
Lemnos.	
CHAPTER XI.	81
The Last Six Weeks on the Peninsula.	
CHAPTER XII.	84
Evacuation of Gallipoli — The Evacuation — Lemnos—Christmas Day, 1915—Alexandria—Moascar—Suez Canal Defences.	
CHAPTER XIII.	89
Formation of the New Zealand Division — Birth of the Second Battalion—Further Training in Egypt.	

CONTENTS.

	Page
CHAPTER XIV. Departure for France—France—Estaires—Armentieres—First Taste of the Trenches—Intensive Shell Fire.	93
CHAPTER XV. Patrols and Raids — Death of Capt. A. B. McColl—Gas Attacks — The Enemy Raids "The Mushroom" — The Australians Raid at Fleurbaix — We are Relieved at Armentieres.	102
CHAPTER XVI. We Go Back to Train for the Somme — Fricourt and Airaines.	109
CHAPTER XVII. The March to the Somme — The Battle of the Somme—New Zealand Division's Share — Flers — Rain, Mud and Slush—Factory Corner—Goose Alley—Gird Trench—Eaucourt l'Abbaye.	111
CHAPTER XVIII. We Return to the North—Armentieres Again—A Quiet Time—Sailly-sur-Lys.	127
CHAPTER XIX. Fleurbaix—January, 1917 — Re-organisation of First and Second Brigades—Fleurbaix—1st Battalion's Raid—Gas Alarm—An Enemy Raid—Second Auckland's Raid—Relief by 57th Division.	133
CHAPTER XX. Le Bizet—Pont de Nieppe—Le Touquet—Relief by Australians—Football at Nieppe — Bulford Camp—Working Parties.	140
CHAPTER XXI. Ploegsteert—First Time in Ploegsteert Wood—Red Lodge—Bunhill Row—Mud Lane—Prowse Point—St. Yves—The Douve Sector — Preliminary Work for Messines Offensive—Hutting Camp—Aldershot Camp—Neuve Eglise—Night Bombardments of Back Areas—Reprisals by our "Heavies"—We go Back to Train for Messines.	143
CHAPTER XXII. Formation of the 4th Brigade — Formation of the 3rd Battalion of the Regiment—1st Wellington Supplies New General—Brigadier-General H. E. Hart—Period of Training—4th Brigade Arrives in France—3rd Wellington near Bailleul.	156
CHAPTER XXIII. Battle of Messines—Plans for the Attack—Preparations at De Seule—The March up—Gas—Hanbury Support—The Explosion of the Mines — Roar of the Guns—Blauwen Molen—Fanny's Farm—The 4th Australian Division pass through us — Digging In — Death of Brigadier-General Brown—Casualties Holding On—Death of Capt. R. F. C. Scott—Relief by the Australians—Bulford Camp.	159

CONTENTS.

CHAPTER XXIV. ... 172
Rest After Battle—Brune Gaye—Rue de Sac—Inspection by and Congratulations from General Godley — 3rd Battalon's Baptism of Trench Warfare—Lieut. T. L. Ward Crosses the Lys and Reconnoitres Frelinghein.

CHAPTER XXV. ... 175
Trench Warfare after Messines—Hill 63—Mustard Gas—Exploits of 2nd Battalion's Patrols—Activity in the Air—Observation Balloons—The "Archies"—Midsummer Days—The Duke of Connaught at Bailleul—3rd Battalion at Nieppe.

CHAPTER XXVI. ... 184
A Well Deserved Spell—Le Verrier—St. Marie Capelle—Cassell—Sports at Doulieu—Hawke's Bay (2nd Battalion) go Back Early to Train for La Basseville—Kortepyp Camp—Back to the Trenches—3rd Battalion at Brune Gaye—A Brush with Enemy Patrols in Le Touquet Sector.

CHAPTER XXVII. ... 188
La Basse Ville—Hawke's Bay (2nd Battalion) Capture La Basse Ville; but are Driven Out—The 2nd Battalion Captures La Basse Ville and Holds It——Andrew Wins the Victoria Cross—Lieut. Nicol's Gallantry.

CHAPTER XXVIII. ... 202
3rd Battalion at Ponteeau—Pennefather Swims the Lys—2nd Battalion's Transport near Kortepyp Destroyed by Bombs — Inspection of 2nd Battalion by General Godley and General Russell — Boxing Tournament at Nieppe—First Australian Division on the March—St. Yves.

CHAPTER XXIX. ... 208
Training for Passchendaele — Hondeghem — Caestre—Wizernes—Billets at Selles—Lottinghem and Henneveux—A Trip to Ambleteuse—Brigade Training at Harlettes—Inspection by Sir Douglas Haig and Mr. Winston Churchill—The March up into the Ypres Salient.

CHAPTER XXX. ... 213
Gravenstafel and Abraham Heights—Plans for the Attack—Vlamertinghe — Goldfish Chateau — Wieltje — Kansas House—Korek and Boetleer—Kron Prinz Farm—Waterloo—Relief by West Riding Regiment—Back again at Goldfish Chateau—Poperinghe.

CHAPTER XXXI. ... 224
Belle Vue—12th October—3rd Battalion Move Forward to Spree Farm—Worst Farm—Kron Prinz Farm.

CHAPTER XXXII. ... 226
After Belle Vue — Holding the Line — Gravenstafel—Waterloo Road—Otto Farm—Relief by the Canadians.

CHAPTER XXXIII. ... 229
We go Back for a Rest—Senninghem and Affrinques—Bayinghem—Bouvelinghem—Henneveux.

ix.

CONTENTS.

CHAPTER XXXIV. ... 231
Back to the Salient—Polygon Wood—Butte de Polygon—Micmac Camp — In the Line — Heavy Shelling—2nd Battalion Starts Burying Cable — Canal Bank—Belgian Chateau.

CHAPTER XXXV. ... 235
Polderhoek Chateau — Preparation for the Second Brigade's Attack—Hoograaf—Work with Canadian Tunnellers Walker Camp—Reutel Sector—Christmas, 1917—Belgian Chateau—Manawatu Camp.

CHAPTER XXXVI. ... 240
New Year, 1918 — Reutel Sector — Manawatu Camp—Enemy Aeroplanes—Walker Camp—Otago Camp—Breaking up of the 4th Brigade—3rd Wellington Ceases to Exist—Bavinchove—Staple.

CHAPTER XXXVII. ... 247
The Germans Break Through on the British Front in the South—We Go Down to the Somme—Filling the Gap—Mailly Maillet—Colincamps—Some Hard Fighting.

CHAPTER XXXVIII. ... 253
The Trenches at La Signy Farm—A Dump Blows Up—We Relieve the Australians—Hebuterne—A Patrol from the 2nd Battalion is Captured — Death of Col. Cook in England — A Minor Operation Astride the Road to Puisieux-au-Mont—A Gallant Corporal—Sailley-au-Bois—Rossignol Farm — Brushes with Enemy Patrols—Horse Show at Vauchelles—1st Battalion Wins a Guard Mounting Competition.

CHAPTER XXXIX. ... 261
Midsummer in the Trenches—Relieved by the Manchester Regiment—A Welcome Spell—A Combined Church Parade at Henu—Vauchelles — Divisional Sports—Old Friends Foregather—Divisional Band Concert and Boxing Tournament — Hon. W. F. Massey and Sir Joseph Ward Attend Church Parade.

CHAPTER XL. ... 264
Rossignol Wood—Gommecourt—Couin Wood—Working Parties—the Enemy Withdraws — A Substantial Advance of Our Line—The Americans—A Platoon from the 2nd Battalion Attends Army Memorial Service at Ranchicourt.

CHAPTER XLI. ... 270
We Fraternise with the 18th Royal Irish — A Cricket Match — Gommecourt — Fish Alley — A Further Enemy Withdrawal.

CHAPTER XLII. ... 274
Loupart Wood — Grevillers — Biefvillers—A Check at Thilloy—The Envelopment of Bapaume.

CHAPTER XLIII. ... 281
Bancourt—Fremicourt—Stiff Opposition—Enemy Counter-attacks—Some Ground is Given — But is Re-captured in Hard Fighting — Sergeant J. G. Grant Wins the V.C.

x.

CONTENTS.

CHAPTER XLIV. — 287
Haplincourt—Bertincourt — Havrincourt Wood—Villers-au-Flos.

CHAPTER XLV. — 291
Thescault Ridge — Chip Lane and Snap Trench — Soot Avenue and Smut Trench—The Jaegers Fight Stubbornly—2nd Battalion Repels an Attack on Donrayen Trench—Relieved by the 5th Division—Back to Haplincourt Wood.

CHAPTER XLVI. — 295
A Spell at Biefvillers—Americans at Baseball—Football—Awaiting Orders.

CHAPTER XLVII. — 297
Welsh Ridge — Bonavis Ridge — La Vacquerie Valley—Lateau Wood—The Enemy is Demoralised.

CHAPTER XLVIII. — 301
An Attempt to Cross the St. Quentin Canal Fails — A Further Attempt is Successful—Crevecour—2nd Battalion Holds on Tenaciously—Ruahine Company Saves the Day.

CHAPTER XLIX. — 307
Further Enemy Withdrawal—We Capture Briastre—Joy of Inhabitants—Across the Selle—Ruahine Company (1st Battalion) Suffers Severely—Enemy Fires Villages—Hard Fighting at Belle Vue Station—River Crossing at Briastre Secured—Good Billets at Fontaine-au-Pire—A Visit from the Prince of Wales.

CHAPTER L. — 316
Enemy on the Run—Billets in Solesmes—Colonel Cunningham Leaves 2nd Battalion—Preparing for the Capture of Le Quesnoy.

CHAPTER LI. — 320
Le Quesnoy — Villereau — Potelle — Rhonelle River—Herbignies—Le Carnoy — Le Quesnoy Falls to the Rifle Brigade—We Push Through Mormal Forest — Sarioton Road—Major H. E. McKinnon is Killed—Relief by 2nd Brigade—Back to Villereau—Our Captures.

CHAPTER LII. — 329
Solesmes—Beauvois—The Armistice — Preparing for the March to the Rhine.

CHAPTER LIII. — 332
The March to the Rhine—Verviers—We Cross the German Frontier—The Journey Completed by Train — Cologne—Leichlingen—Longenfeld—Christmas, 1918—Demobilisation.

CASUALTIES (DEATH ONLY) IN THEATRES — 336

HONOURS AND AWARDS — 337

NOMINAL ROLL OF HONOUR — 346

List of Illustrations.

	Page
Lieut.-Col. W. G. Malone ....*Frontispiece*	
Brig.-Gen. H. E. Hart, C.B., C.M.G., D.S.O., V.D.	8
Lieut.-Col. C. F. D. Cook	8A
Lieut.-Col. W. H. Fletcher, D.C.M.	8B
Lieut.-Col. H. Holderness, V.D.	9
Suez Canal, February, 1915	40
Quinn's Post, 1915	40
Wellington Battalion digging in on morning after Landing	40A
The Sphinx and Walkers, May, 1915	40A
West Coast Coy.: Winners of Guard Mounting Competition....	40B
Looking Towards Pope's Hill, 1915	41
In Reserve on Gallipoli	41
Lieut.-Col. W. H. Cunningham, D.S.O.	72
Corpl. L. W. Andrew, V.C.	72A
Rhododendron Spur	72B
After the Landing	72B
Col. Malone at Quinn's Post	73
Lieut.-Col. C. H. Weston, D.S.O., V.D.	120
Red Lodge, Ploegsteert	152
Dugouts in Ploegsteert Wood	152A
Our First Aid Post at Messines	152A
Winter at Hooge	152B
Birr Cross Roads	153
Lieut.-Col. F. K. Turnbull, D.S.O., M.C.	168
Sergt. J. G. Grant, V.C.	168A
On the way to Passchendaele	168B
Aeroplane Photo. of Kron Prinz Farm, showing effect of shell fire	169
Major McKinnon at one of the Cookers	184
A Group of 1st Battalion Officers	184A
Pill Box at Korek	184B
Menin Road	185
Kansas Farm	224
Hooge	225
Abandoned Tank at Gommecourt	240
In the Front Line at Gommecourt	241
Support Line near Colincamps	248
Dinner at Solesmes	248A
2nd Battalion Headquarter's Officers at Estaires	248B
Our Field Kitchens near Grevillers	249
Maps—The Somme	126
Messines and La Bass Ville	192
Graph.—N.Z. Expeditionary Force	340

xii.

CHAPTER I.

The Organisation of the Regiment.

Departure from New Zealand.

LOOKING back to the stirring days at the beginning of August, 1914, it is difficult to regain a clear recollection of the strenuous weeks attending the birth of the Regiment. From the moment it became known that New Zealand would send a force to assist the Mother Country in the great struggle into which she had thrown herself on that fateful 4th August, 1914, the Defence Offices throughout the country were besieged with applicants for enlistment. The Dominion Military Headquarters lost no time in making a definite announcement as to the approximate force that it was intended to raise at once and as to the method in which it would be recruited. Major-General Sir A. J. Godley, the General Officer Commanding, showed his great confidence in the efficiency and organisation of the Territorial Force when he recommended to the New Zealand Government that the Expeditionary Force should be recruited from and through the existing Territorial units, and that the men on the strength of those units should be given preference, if willing to serve in the Expeditionary Force. So far as concerned the Infantry of the Expeditionary Force, this arrangement meant that each of the four Military Districts in the Dominion—Auckland, Wellington, Canterbury, and Otago—was to supply one battalion of Infantry. Each battalion was comprised of four companies recruited from the four battalions of its Territorial Infantry Brigade. As a battalion of the Expeditionary Force, according to existing War Establishments, would consist of four double companies each 227 strong, each Territorial battalion was given the task of recruiting one company. The company was

THE WELLINGTON REGIMENT

named after and wore the badges of the Territorial battalion from which it sprang. As, in reality, it represented the Wellington Infantry Brigade, the Infantry battalion of the Expeditionary Force raised in the Wellington district was called "The Wellington Regiment," and the four companies were called, respectively, after their Territorial battalions: the 7th Wellington West Coast Company, usually shortened to the "West Coast" Company, the 11th Taranaki Company ("Taranaki" Company), the 9th Hawkes Bay Company ("Hawkes Bay" Company), and the 17th Ruahine Company ("Ruahine" Company). To identify them with their Territorial units each company wore the distinctive badge and numeral of its own parent battalion. This organisation, which was maintained throughout the War, promoted keen company rivalry, and this rivalry was a potent factor in establishing and maintaining the efficiency of the Regiment. Though, at first sight, a somewhat cumbersome organisation, the preservation of the identity of the Territorial battalions in the units of the Expeditionary Force was a far-sighted policy, and the Territorial units of our New Zealand Citizen Army owe it to General Godley's foresight that they can carry so proudly on their Regimental colours to-day the battle honours won by their Expeditionary Force unit overseas.

As the first requirement of the new Battalion was a full establishment of officers, Headquarters of Territorial battalions were asked to furnish the names of all officers on the strength who were willing to enlist, and a splendid response was immediately forthcoming. The first selection of officers resulted as follows:—

Lieut.-Colonel: W. G. Malone.

Majors: H. E. Hart, J. W. Brunt, W. H. Cunningham, E. H. Saunders, R. Young.

Captains: J. A. Cameron, C. F. D. Cook, E. P. Cox, A. Greene (Chaplain), G. Home, M. McDonnell, J. M. Rose, W. J. Shepherd, J. L. Short, G. N. Waugh (Veterinary).

Lieutenants: D. Bryan, H. R. Cowan, A. J. M. Cross, T. A. Davidson, W. E. S. Furby, E. S. Harston, L. W. A. Hugo, L. H. Jardine, R. Lee, A. B. McColl, H. E. McKinnon, L. S.

McLernon, C. B. S. Menteath, E. Morgan, B. H. Morison, Wm. F. Narbey, F. K. Turnbull, M. Urquhart, E. J. H. Webb, G. C. Wells, E. R. Wilson.

It was decided to concentrate the forces of all arms from the Wellington district at Palmerston North and the Manawatu Racing Club placed the Awapuni racecourse, with its splendid appointments at the disposal of the military authorities for the purpose of a concentration camp. As the only military equipment in New Zealand at the outbreak of war was that on issue to the Territorial Force, this had to be used to equip the Expeditionary Force. The enlisted men were sent into camp from their districts as fully equipped as the resources of the Regiment permitted. Any shortages were left to be made up in Awapuni from the Ordnance Depot, which was quickly established there.

So far as personnel was concerned, the Regiment was completely mobilized before the end of August. Strenuous training commenced at once. Every man in camp was in deadly earnest and discipline was easy to maintain. The reason was simple. The men were told that, in view of the large number offering, those who committed breaches of discipline would be excluded from the final selection. Training and equipping proceeded steadily. About the middle of September, word was received that the transports were nearly ready at their respective ports, and it was made known that the troops at Awapuni would entrain for Wellington within a few days.

The training, like all training in camps throughout the War, consisted largely of physical exercises and route marching to get the men fit and hard, with a little musketry and steady drill, to get cohesion in the unit. There are two training days which deserve special mention, not, perhaps, for the training performed, but for happy recollections. The first was a route march to Feilding, where the troops were the guests of the people of Feilding, and were entertained on arrival at the racecourse. The Feilding ladies had gone to great trouble to provide delicacies for the troops, many of whom were recruited from the Feilding district. The troops bivouaced for the night at the racecourse, and marched early the next morning on the return journey to Palmerston North. Here a public welcome was accorded them in the Square.

On return to camp, it was found that companies were not all to embark in the same ship, and that the Battalion would be distributed in three different transports. Wellington-West Coast Company, to its great satisfaction, was detailed for the "Maunganui," the flagship of the transport fleet: two platoons of Hawkes Bay Company, under Major Young, were detailed for the "Limerick," and the rest of the battalion were to embark on the "Arawa." The move from Awapuni camp to the transports at the Wellington wharves was quietly and quickly effected on the 22nd September, and every one soon settled down to his quarters on board ship. The transports were in every case very comfortably equipped; but, as all carried a quota of horses, we were soon to realize that a horse is not a very pleasant shipmate. For one thing, his quarters are hard to keep clean and the odour of stables soon reached to every corner of the ship, and seemed to taint the very food.

Embarkation, including the shipping of horses and stores, was completed within 48 hours of reaching Wellington. A final farewell parade of all troops was held in Newtown Park on September 23, when His Excellency the Governor-General, the Prime Minister, the Minister of Defence and the Mayor of Wellington bade them farewell and God speed. Immediately the men returned from the parade the troopships drew out into the stream. The "Maunganui" was the only ship to remain at the wharf and, when she failed to move out during the night, rumour soon spread that there was some hitch in the sailing of the convoy. The "Maunganui" remained at the wharf and the other ships in the stream until the 28th September. On that day the sailing of the convoy was cancelled, and the troopships in the stream returned to the wharf, accompanied by four other transports carrying the South Island portion of the Force, which had arrived overnight in Wellington. harbour. Horses were disembarked, and all mounted units despatched to camps ashore. The Infantry remained aboard the ships and it was announced that the sailing of the Force would be delayed for several weeks awaiting the arrival of a naval escort of sufficient strength. It seemed that the Admiralty declined to take the responsibility for the convoy with the warships then available. The whereabouts of several powerful German cruisers, thought to be in the Pacific, were unknown. Imagine how all chafed at the delay!

In order to waste no time, rigorous training was the order of the day. The Regiment marched, manoeuvred and fought in miniature battles over the rugged hills on the outskirts of Wellington, a not unfitting preparation for the fighting, soon to be our lot on the steep slopes of Gallipoli.

On the 15th October, the troops once more embarked, and all ships moved into the stream. On this occasion, there was little fuss. The Infantry were thoroughly used to their quarters and ship routine, from having lived on board ship for three weeks or more, and the other troops quickly settled down.

H.M.S. "Minotaur" and the Japanese battleship "Ibuki" had arrived in Wellington harbour on the 14th October, and were to act as escort for the convoy. Their arrival occasioned a good deal of interest, as it was generally realised among the troops and the citizens of Wellington that the arrival of these ships indicated the early departure of the Expeditionary Force.

CHAPTER II.

The Voyage to Egypt—H.M.A.S. "Sydney" Destroys the "Emden" — Colombo, Suez, Port Said, Alexandria.

AT daylight on the 16th October, the whole fleet weighed anchor and the transports, ten in all, escorted by the "Minotaur," "Ibuki," "Philomel" and "Psyche" passed down the harbour and out into the straits. Although the hour of departure was kept secret, a great many people assembled that grey morning on points of vantage to catch a final glimpse of the transports.

The first few days at sea were of much more interest to the ship's master and officers, who had to learn to keep station in the convoy, than they were to the troops. Sea sickness affected a very large percentage, and rations were very plentiful for those who had any desire for them. When routine commenced, a good many hours each day were occupied in cleaning ship and general fatigues, and the rest of the time was devoted to such elementary training as deck space permitted.

After a good passage of five days, Hobart was reached and its pretty harbour, bathed in the brightest sunshine, was indeed a pleasant sight. No individual leave to go ashore was given; but a parade of all units in full marching kit was ordered immediately the ships berthed. The route of our march lay through the centre of Hobart and out across the hill to the outskirts of the town. It was an intensely hot day; but it was a relief to be ashore. The inhabitants received us with open arms. At the halts on the march, doors of houses were opened and the inhabitants, young and old alike, brought out jugs of refreshing drinks, and cakes and fruit, and handed them round to the perspiring troops. They picked flowers, making bouquets for the men. All ranks returned to the ships greatly cheered by their run ashore, and with feelings of gratitude for Hobart and its inhabitants. The fleet sailed from Hobart on the 23rd October, but not before a great many cases of apples had been shipped for issue to the troops. Most units possessed a Regimental Fund, which proved extremely useful on occasions such as this.

Albany was reached on the 28th October, the Australian Bight making matters rather unpleasant for those who had not got their sea legs. Here a great many large ships were found to be at anchor in the harbour awaiting our arrival, and we were not long in discovering that they contained the Australian Expeditionary Force, which was to accompany us to England (as we then expected). Four days were spent at Albany, the ships remaining in the stream. Route marches by ships were arranged ashore; but no leave was granted to the troops. To New Zealanders who had not seen Australia before, this glimpse of Albany and its surroundings was very interesting.

On Sunday morning, 11th November, the large fleet of troopships, thirty-six in number, accompanied by the escorting warships, "Minotaur," "Ibuki," "Sydney" and "Melbourne," the last two having replaced the "Pysche" and "Philomel," steamed out of the Sound in line ahead. It was a magnificent sight. Here on that bright, sunny morning, were the great ocean liners, black with troops, quietly taking their appointed places in a long line of ships making for the open sea.

Once clear of land, the ships formed up into proper convoy formation, the Australian ships in four lines, with the New Zealand ships in two lines immediately behind. Compared with the Australian ships, the New Zealand convoy appeared much more austere and warlike in its sombre grey. The liners of the Australian convoy, many of them fashionable passenger ships, still wore their peace-time appearance. This was particularly in evidence the first night out from Albany, when every ship in the Australian convoy appeared after dark in a perfect blaze of light. Not a glimmer appeared from the New Zealand ships, where even the lighting of a cigarette on deck was prohibited under the severest penalty. It took our Australian brothers several days to discipline their convoy to the standard of efficiency in station keeping, especially at night, attained by the navigators of the New Zealand convoy, but it was not long before initial troubles were overcome. Keeping station at night in pitch darkness, and with other ships in close proximity, was a sore trial to merchant skippers taught all their lives to give neighbours at sea a wide berth. Many a sultry message about lack of naval discipline passed from the escort to the convoy, and the need of it was soon to be brought home to us. The screening of lights after dark necessitated the deadlights being put in all portholes which were then screwed down closely. As we neared the tropics, and the nights as well as days became hot and stuffy, the experience of travelling during darkness with closed portholes can best be left to the imagination, keeping in mind that every ship had as many horses on board as could comfortably be carried.

On the eleventh day out from Albany a stir was created among those who were on deck at dawn, by seeing H.M.A.S. "Sydney" suddenly withdrawing from the convoy and steaming in a westerly direction. It was quickly passed round the fleet that the S.O.S. call had been picked up from Cocos Island, then about sixty miles away to the west. A further message from the same island stated that a strange warship was entering the harbour, and refused to answer signals. We had all read with interest the daring feats in the Pacific of the German light cruiser "Emden," and there had been a certain amount of apprehension that she might possibly cross our path. While we waited for news from the "Sydney," we all fervently hoped that the strange ship might prove to be this by now notorious raider, and that the "Sydney" would quickly make an end of her. Soon after the "Sydney" had left us, the Japanese battleship "Ibuki" took the "Sydney's" place in the escort, and with the possibility of a fight imminent, she ran her huge battle ensign to the peak. At the same time her funnels belched clouds of black smoke, as she got up a full head of steam.

Brig.-Genl. H. E. Hart, C.B., C.M.G., D.S.O., V.D.

Face p. 8.

Lieut.-Col. C. F. D. Cook.

Lieut.-Col. W. H. Fletcher, D.C.M.

Lieut.-Col. H. Holderness, V.D.

Once, indeed, during the course of the morning a wireless message reached the "Ibuki" that the quarry was making off in a north westerly direction, and she immediately swung and steamed in that direction for a short time, clouds of spray flying over her bows as she tore through the swell. However the "Ibuki" had responsibilities to the convoy, and, though she was the heaviest armed of all the escorting ships, she was not permitted to participate in the fight. About eleven o'clock definite news was wirelessed from the "Sydney" that she had caught and beaten the "Emden," which had been beached by her Commander to prevent her sinking, and that there were numerous casualties among the crew of the "Emden." Tremendous cheers and great excitement prevailed when this news was made known, and the rest of the day was devoted to discussing the great event, all drills and duties being cancelled in honour of the "Sydney's" victory.

The destruction of the "Emden" removed from the path of the convoy the greatest danger to which we were subject, as no other German ships were in Pacific waters. Nevertheless, strict convoy discipline was still enforced. As we neared the equator, the nights were very oppressive, and there was much competition for the clear space on deck where sleeping was allowed. The crossing of the equator was celebrated in characteristic sailor fashion, and Father Neptune was no respecter of rank in issuing his summons to attend his ceremonies. Very great amusement was caused on all ships, especially when some senior officer was perceived being hustled with scant ceremony by Neptune's minions towards the shaving brush and fish pond! The cheerfulness of the day was marred for the Wellington Regiment when, towards the end of the afternoon, it was reported from the "Arawa" that Captain E. J. H. Webb, of the New Zealand Medical Corps and one of the Regimental doctors, had sustained a very severe injury to his head, and was unconscious as the result of diving off the roof of one of the deck houses into Neptune's pond. Unfortunately Captain Webb had believed the tank to be much deeper than it really was, and must have struck his head on the deck. The convoy was stopped, and a specialist from one of the other ships was rowed across to the "Arawa," where the Medical Officers did everything possible for the injured man. He was landed at Colombo a few days later, but never regained consciousness, dying in hospital there. The same day as we crossed the line, 13th November, orders were received for the New Zealand ships to proceed ahead of the Australian convoy to facilitate coaling and the taking in of supplies at Colombo. Two days steady steaming brought us one morning, beautiful with tropical sunshine, within sight of Colombo. The sea was a gorgeous opal tint, and as smooth as glass. Soon a swarm of natives in their quaint canoes with out-riggers were coming to meet us. As the ships entered the inner harbour of Colombo, the water appeared to be black with craft of all descriptions, while the main jetty was a seething mass of humanity clad in all colours of the rainbow. It was our first glimpse of the East, and every man was eager to get ashore and make a closer inspection of the city.

Shortly after our arrival, the "Sydney" was signalled and, as she steamed slowly past the New Zealand ships, all stood silently at attention. We would have preferred to have given her Captain and crew the rousing cheers they well deserved; but, as her decks were filled with stretcher cases from the battered "Emden," we refrained.

Here, too, in the inner harbour was the Russian battleship "Askold." She presented a rather unusual sight with her five tall funnels, and was quickly dubbed "the packet of fags."

Leave to go ashore by companies or platoons was given shortly after our arrival and, with the aid of the ship's boats and some of the shore launches, every unit was able to avail itself of the welcome respite. Closer acquaintance with Colombo, more particularly the native quarter and the natives, left no desire to spend much time in such unhealthy surroundings. The walk ashore was a relief after the confinement of shipboard; but the atmosphere was very humid, and one soon got tired.

THE WELLINGTON REGIMENT

The convoy put to sea again from Colombo, but not before most of the ships had received a small quota of German prisoners from the "Emden." These prisoners were to be taken to prison camps in England, and were naturally a source of considerable interest. The captured officers were put on parole, and had the freedom of the ship on which they were placed. They took their fate philosophically, were proud of their ship's record, and made the best of things. The men were kept under strict guard; but they were well treated in every respect. A rather amusing incident happened on one of the ships carrying a portion of the Regiment. When placing the prisoners in their cabin a sentry's loaded rifle inexplicably went off; the bullet struck the steel roof of the cabin and ricochetted round the room in a most alarming fashion. Fortunately, no one was hurt; but the unfortunate prisoners had their nerves severely shaken. The sentry was promptly relieved, and given a spell of duller and more arduous duties.

Aden was reached on the 25th November, after a rather dull and uninteresting run of nine days from Colombo. The weather was fine, but the days and nights were gradually getting hotter, and everyone by now heartily tired of shipboard. No shore leave was granted at Aden; but a good view of its barren rocks could be obtained from the ships and a camel convoy coming into view caused a good deal of comment. Some amusement was caused when the convoy entered the harbour through the M.T. 10. The "Arawa" failed to drop anchor within the prescribed limits, and, in consequence, promptly got a shot across her bows, the shell ricochetting among the rocks across the bay. The anchor was let go with amazing promptitude, the "Arawa" men claiming the distinction of being the first contingent under fire. Some fifteen British transports conveying British territorials to India were in the harbour when the New Zealand transports arrived, and hearty cheers and greetings were exchanged as the ships passed near them. After a stay of 24 hours at Aden, the convoy was again under weigh for the Red Sea and Suez. At Aden word was received that important orders were awaiting the force at Suez, so the Australian Headquarters Ship "Orvieto" and the New Zealand Headquarters Ship "Maunganui" now speeded up and proceeded ahead of the convoy. As was only to be expected, the "Orvieto" soon left the "Maunganui" behind. Good weather prevailed throughout the run to Suez, and speculation was rife as to what orders would await us there. Information had reached us during the voyage that Turkey had entered the War on the side of Germany, and we knew there was every chance in consequence of our having to disembark elsewhere than in England.

The "Maunganui" arrived at Suez at 5 p.m. on 30th November, and definite orders were received for the whole force to disembark at Alexandria and proceed to camp near Cairo. Egypt was in a disturbed state in consequence of the state of war between Britain and Turkey, and, even now, minor skirmishing was taking place along the banks of the Suez Canal, which was protected by British troops throughout its length. In fact, each vessel, before entering the Canal, was supplied with a searchlight and ordered to mount any machine guns it had on the starboard side. The "Maunganui" proceeded up the Canal at 7 p.m., but, about 11 p.m., a very dense fog came up and the ship anchored in Lake Timsah till next morning, when it proceeded on, arriving at Port Said about 4 p.m. without further incident. The trip through the Canal was intensely interesting. The sun was just setting as the "Maunganui" arrived at Suez, and the Egyptian light and colouring, the golden sands of the desert, and the brown of the hills, made a lasting impression on those who now saw Egypt for the first time. With Suez we were destined to make a closer acquaintance in the near future, but our first glimpse was encouraging.

There was no leave at Port Said. The "Arawa" arrived there the day after the "Maunganui." Coaling operations were carried on during the night. From Suez certain of the Divisional Staff proceeded by rail to Cairo in advance of the troops, to take over the camp site and make preliminary

THE WELLINGTON REGIMENT

arrangements for the reception of the units as they disembarked.

At 5 p.m. on 2nd December, the convoy sailed from Port Said. By this time, everyone was packing up in preparation for disembarkation on the morrow at Alexandria. Daylight on the 3rd December revealed the coast line on our port side, and it was not long before we were proceeding up past the historic Aboukir Bay to the port of Alexandria. In the clear atmosphere, groups of buildings along the coast stood out in sharp relief, and eyes were strained to catch a glimpse of Alexandria.

CHAPTER III.

Egypt—Cairo—Training on the Desert.

BY 7 a.m. on the 3rd December several of our transports were berthed. The Regiment did not relish its task of remaining behind and cleaning up ship, but it had to be done, and the sooner it was done the quicker the detachment would get away.

Disembarkation started immediately after breakfast on 3rd December, and by 5 p.m. most mounted units were off their ships and bound for Cairo. The first portion of the Regiment to get away from the transports comprised West Coast Company and Ruahine Company who proceeded by one train, leaving the wharf at Alexandria about 2.15 p.m. on the 4th December. Cairo station was reached about 8 p.m., after a most interesting run through the Nile Delta.

After an hour at Cairo, the detachment departed on the short run to Helmieh siding, which was reached at 10 p.m. Here Major-General Godley and his staff met the troops, and guides were furnished to take the detachment to the camp site, about a mile and a half distant. There were no luggage carts, and, in consequence, the men in heavy marching order had to carry their full kit bags in addition on their shoulders. It was a bright, clear starlight night, and the air after the stuffy conditions prevailing on ship was very bracing. The two companies arrived in camp about 11 p.m. extremely tired and hungry. They were marched on the camp site, a bare patch of desert, and left to make the best of things till daylight. Arms were piled, kits sorted out under a friendly flare, and officers and men wrapped in their great coats and blankets lay down to rest. Much to everyone's surprise the ground was intensely cold, and the air seemed almost frosty. Sleep was very difficult, and the first ray of dawn saw a good many astir endeavouring to restore animation to limbs stiffened with cold and cramp. By 8 o'clock all ranks had had something warm to drink, and a start was made to pitch camp, in anticipation of the arrival of the rest of the battalion. The first night's exposure on the desert produced a mild epidemic of influenza colds, and some twenty men were ordered off to hospital the first day. By night tents had been pitched, straw issued and that night was one of comparative comfort. Those who were privileged to experience that first night's bivouac on the sands of the Egyptian desert will long remember it as one of the coldest of their lives.

From the 4th to 6th December, Battalion Headquarters and the Taranaki and Hawkes Bay Companies were detained at Alexandria to complete the discharge of the transports. They reached camp about 6 p.m. on the 6th December, well pleased to be away from work on the wharves. Immediately upon arrival, the Commanding Officer, Lieut.-Col. W. G. Malone, with his customary zeal and energy, had set to work to square the camp to his liking. All tents were struck, the camp and tent lines laid out and tent poles dressed and tents re-erected. A neighbouring pile of soft white stones, apparently ownerless and deserted, gave inspiration to all and sundry to beautify their lines, and mark out paths, boundaries and tent limits. The heap of stones rapidly faded from view, and the neat and tidy lines of the Wellington Regiment, with their white-edged streets and paths became the envy of the Divison. Our distinction, however, was short lived. A native owner, viewing the site of his future home, was astonished to find his treasured heap of building material gone; but his astonishment turned to anger, when he ultimately found the good-sized stones broken to tiny fragments, and spread out in rows about the camp. The sequel was a prompt order from Brigade Headquarters that the stones should be returned to the original heap, and the Commanding Officer would attend a court of enquiry into the unauthorised destruction of certain private property, to wit, a heap of building stone. Eventually the Regiment had to pay a considerable sum to reimburse the owner, in return for which the small pieces became regimental property.

Training now began in real earnest. Every morning before breakfast "physical jerks"; and, at 8 a.m., the battalion paraded, carrying lunch in haversacks, and the day was spent in training. Full packs were always carried on the march, and across the desert the going was heavy and dusty. The training grounds were usually selected at a distance three or four miles from the camp, so as to ensure a certain amount of marching every day.

Although the nights were invariably cold and the early mornings raw and misty, the sun shone from a cloudless sky throughout the day, and tunics were soon discarded. Training was never interfered with by the weather and, in fixing training schemes, weather contingencies were not considered.

Outside training hours there was much to interest and amuse all ranks. Cairo was within half an hour's journey by rail or tram. There, the great hotels and restaurants were still open. Then Cairo and its environs offered limitless scope to those who were interested in antiquities. The "Muski" gave those who wished to send souvenirs to New Zealand unprecedented opportunities for bargaining. Life was never dull, and, when work was over for the day, the camp quickly emptied of those entitled to leave.

Shortly after the battalion had settled down in camp, the Ceylon Planters Rifles, a company of Englishmen raised in Ceylon, which had been some weeks in Egypt, was attached to the battalion as a fifth company. They were from the C.O. to the bugler a fine lot of fellows, and a close friendship soon sprang up between the planters and all ranks of the battalion. They continued to serve with the battalion until March 1915, when they were almost all placed in an officer's training unit in Egypt to qualify for commissions in the British Army. The planters wore a light khaki drill tunic and shorts, and in the hot dusty marches we envied them their tropical kit. For our part, we had landed in Egypt with the warmest of clothing, equipped, in fact, for an English winter.

THE WELLINGTON REGIMENT

During training operations the battalion was for a few days *hors de combat* through vaccination against smallpox. Sore and painfully swollen arms were universal, entitling their owners to several days' light duty. The Commanding Officer rather scoffed at the Medical Officers considering that such a trifling inconvenience warranted men being excused parades, until his own turn came. The Doctor then saw to it that he received that application of vaccine to which his rank entitled him. Thereafter the Commanding Officer had no hesitation in taking his two days' light duty. Our vaccination for smallpox was the forerunner of many similar trials both in Egypt and on Gallipoli.

Christmas and New Year passed quietly. During Christmas week, training slackened; extra leave was granted, and rations were supplemented from Regimental Funds. All ranks made good use of the few days' leave.

CHAPTER IV.

The Defence of the Suez Canal—The Regiment's Baptism of Fire.

ON the afternoon of the 24th January, 1915, orders were received that the New Zealand Infantry Brigade was to proceed to the Suez Canal, to assist the garrison of Indian troops in resisting a threatened attack on the Canal by the Turkish Column, reported by the Flying Corps to be advancing across the desert from the East. Excitement in the camp ran high, and far into the night all ranks were busy sorting out their fighting kit for the move. The Company Sergeant Major of one company, a veteran of more than one campaign, was so overcome by excitement, and his many visits to the canteen, that when the "fall in" sounded in the early morning, he was the only man in the unit who could not move, and he had to be left behind. With great difficulty he managed to rejoin the company several days afterwards.

The battalion moved on the 25th January in two detachments by separate trains, leaving Palais de Koubbah station at 8 a.m. and 11 a.m. respectively. The right half battalion, West Coast and Hawkes Bay Companies, under the second in command, Major H. E. Hart, entrained on the first train, arriving at Khubri Siding, a short distance from Suez, and about 1½ miles from the Canal bank, about 5 p.m. The second half of the battalion, Taranaki and Ruahine Companies, arrived by the second train at 7 p.m. The battalion bivouaced for the night in the vicinity of the railway siding. About 2 a.m., a few shots were exchanged by the outposts in the vicinity of the Canal at Khubri Ferry, the bullets whistling over the bivouac. This was the first occasion the battalion was under fire. The battalion immediately stood to arms; but the excitement soon subsided.

After breakfast next morning, we moved out to the Canal, relieving a battalion of Indian troops on approximately a front of four miles. The Otago Battalion arrived shortly after the Wellington Battalion, and Lieut.-Col. W. G. Malone as Senior C.O. assumed command of the detachment consisting of the Otago and Wellington Battalions, and Major H. E. Hart took command of the battalion. Upon taking over the Canal bank, the work of improving the trenches and other defences was put in hand, and the troops received their training in real outpost work in war. On the right flank the battalion was in touch with the 2/7th Ghurkas, and many valuable lessons were learnt from those wonderful little soldiers.

Life on the Canal was very interesting. During the day, numerous liners passed, and many were the parcels and packages thrown to the troops. Swimming was freely indulged in, and, despite the heat and the small-winged insect pests, life was pleasant. A good many were detailed for outpost duty in the trenches by night, and sentries were extremely eager to detect movement that would give them some legitimate excuse to fire their rifles. One night at Khubri post, on the eastern bank of the Canal, a few shots were fired by the Turks, the bullets passing over the battalion front. No one was hit, and no return shots were fired by the battalion; but the trenches were manned to full strength in a moment, and the next week's letters home to New Zealand provided some extremely interesting reading.

The battalion remained in the trenches on the western bank of the Canal until the 2nd February, when certain changes were made. West Coast Company proceeded to Port Tewfik, near Suez, to relieve the company of the Ceylon Tea Planters who returned to Khubri. Taranaki Company, under Major J. W. Brunt, proceeded to the eastern bank of the Canal to garrison No. 3. post. Ruahine Company went, a half company to No. 4 post, and a half company to No. 5 post. The remainder of the battalion returned to Campimento,

THE WELLINGTON REGIMENT

near the railway line into reserve. The work of the West Coast Company at Port Tewfik consisted entirely of supplying guards for various posts, such as cable stations and Government offices in and about Port Tewfik and the town of Suez. The company was quartered in the quarantine station near one of the docks. The only event to relieve the monotony of guard duty was the arrival of 100 Arab prisoners taken by our friends the 2/7 Ghurkas at a very successful minor operation near Tor, on the Red Sea. The prisoners were landed from H.M.S. "Minerva" on 13th February, and were taken in charge by the garrison. A more heterogeneous collection of men and weapons it would be hard to imagine. The prisoners were of all ages, from boys of 14 to old men of 60. Their weapons were equally as varied and ineffective as themselves, old swords, fezails and obsolete single loading rifles. Many had neither arms nor equipment. Landing at midnight from the warships, the Ghurkas had marched ten miles, surrounded the enemy during the night and attacked at daybreak. After a short engagement, they had captured the whole of the enemy, killing 60, mostly Turks. The Ghurkas losses were one killed and one wounded. The only prisoner of any note was a Turkish officer of the rank of Bimbashi.

With the companies on the Canal, very little had happened to disturb the ordinary routine. On the night of the 23rd February, heavy firing was heard in the direction of Khubri post. It proved later to have been a half-hearted attack by a small body of Turks, coinciding with the main attack on the Canal, which had taken place in the neighbourhood of Tussoum. The Turks had been heavily repulsed and had retired back into the desert, leaving many dead and wounded behind. Their attack was made in good strength, and they carried several flat-bottomed pontoons for the purpose of crossing the Canal, three of which were captured. These they had carried across the desert in sections and put together prior to the final attack. The repulse of the Turks relieved the menace on the Canal, though vigilance remained unrelaxed for a considerable time.

THE WELLINGTON REGIMENT

Early in February, Taranaki Company furnished the detachment of infantry which with the Indian Cavalry conducted a reconnaissance in force, for the purpose of ousting a small party of the enemy which had been hovering for some days in front of Khubri post. Patrols from this enemy party were frequently a source of annoyance to the garrison at night. The company carried out its duties successfully, and the enemy was seen to beat a retreat on the approach of our troops, doubtless recognising the formidable calibre of the infantry supporting the mounted troops. On 17th February, West Coast Company returned from garrison duty at Tewfik, and the Ceylon Tea Planters took its place. The whole battalion again took up quarters in the trenches along the Canal on either side of Khubri Ferry.

On 26th February, the battalion left its trenches on the Canal, entrained at Khubri Siding, and arrived back in its old camp at Zeitoun at 5.30 p.m. Though it had not really come into close contact with the Turks in the month spent on the Canal, the battalion returned from its period in the trenches there with the feeling that the spell of dull training was now entirely broken. There was greater eagerness than ever on the part of all ranks to test their fighting qualities.

During the absence of the battalion at Suez, the 2nd Reinforcements had arrived from New Zealand. The week-end was spent in festivity in Cairo and, after four weeks of hard living and hard work on the Canal, full justice was done to the many attractions and distractions of Cairo.

CHAPTER V.

Preparations for the Gallipoli Campaign—More Hard Training on the Desert—Lemnos.

AFTER returning from the Canal on 26th February, the Regiment recommenced its hard training. Long and strenuous field days, with full packs up, brought inevitably long marches; but all ranks stood up to the heaviest work cheerfully, and stragglers on the march were rare. Twice the Division was inspected on the desert, first by General Godley and, later, by Sir Ian Hamilton, and both occasions were memorable for the quantity of dust swallowed by all ranks. When the Regiment marched into its own lines on its return from inspection, faces were so coated with dust as to be unrecognisable. As may well be imagined, when the command to "dismiss" was given no time was lost in reaching the nearest canteen to moisten coated tongues. Towards the end of March, frequent parades to check the state of the regimental equipment for war, indicated to all ranks an early participation in important operations. It was an open secret that the operations to be undertaken were against Turkey in the Mediterranean. As vacancies in strength occurred, the men of the reinforcements then in Egypt displayed the greatest keenness to be absorbed into regimental strength, and all weak men who had displayed any lack of staying power or any lack of discipline were quietly dropped in favour of picked men from the reinforcements.

Final orders were now received for the Regiment to join the Mediterranean Expeditionary Force, under Sir Ian Hamilton. With the rest of the Brigade, the Regiment left Zeitoun on the 10th April, the C.O., Lieut.-Col. W. G. Malone and headquarters, with Taranaki and Ruahine Companies, 18 officers and 550 others, proceeding by one train, and the

THE WELLINGTON REGIMENT

2nd in Command, Major H. E. Hart, with Wellington - West Coast and Hawkes Bay Companies, seventeen officers and 513 others, proceeding in a second train. The first train load embarked in the "Itonus," and the second train load in the "Achaia." The regimental transports sailed the next day for Lemnos. The "Achaia," which was a captured German tramp, proved a very uncomfortable ship. She had iron decks, no conveniences for working, and very little accommodation of any sort. Sleep on her iron decks, covered with rivets, was anything but easy; but it was all excellent training for the discomforts that were soon to follow. The "Itonus" was scarcely less uncomfortable. The two transports proceeded independently to Lemnos and the run through the Agean Sea, with its abounding isles and lovely colouring, was extremely pleasant and interesting. Very little training could be done on board, owing to the cramped and crowded quarters. The officers endeavoured to familiarize themselves with the Gallipoli Peninsula by studying the maps which had been issued, and Lieut. L. H. Jardine on the "Achaia," with the aid of plasticine, constructed a model of the portion on which we might expect to operate.

The transports arrived at Lemnos on the 15th April, and anchored in the outer harbour. Next day we proceeded to the inner harbour, where the Captain of the "Achaia" very proudly handed over to the Naval Authorities two large barges which he had safely towed all the way from Alexandria. The inner harbour at Lemnos at the time our transports arrived presented a scene of the greatest activity. The harbour was crowded with huge transports filled with troops. Many warships of the Mediterranean Squadron were there, from the magnificent "Queen Elizabeth" down to small submarines. There were French warships and French troopships. The land-locked harbour was surrounded by low hills, studded with windmills.

Our time at Lemnos was taken up with boat drill, incessant practice at climbing up and down the ship's side on rope ladders with a rifle and in full marching order, and frequent marches ashore. It was a disadvantage that the Regiment was not accommodated in a single transport as, to some extent, touch was lost between the two halves of the Regiment, and final prepartions for the first great trial in battle had to be made piecemeal.

At this stage it would, perhaps, be convenient to review the events which led up to the attack on the Gallipoli Peninsula. Turkey had declared war against the Allies on the 31st October, 1914, and, on the 3rd November, 1914, the Mediterranean Fleet had bombarded the outer forts of the Dardanelles for about ten minutes, endeavouring to test the effective range of the Turkish guns. The entry of Turkey into the war immediately concentrated attention on the Suez Canal. The strength and fighting qualities of the Turkish land forces were not fully appreciated by the Western Powers as they were subsequently. The easy way in which the Turkish attack on the Suez Canal in February, 1915, had been beaten off, while it demonstrated the determination of the Turk in the face of difficulties, did not enhance his military reputation. Save for the small demonstration by our Fleet at the Dardanelles on the 3rd November, we had not carried the War into Turkish territory. The possibility of undertaking operations against Turkey, either by an attack on some part of the coast of Turkey-in-Asia or against the Gallipoli Peninsula as a means of defending Egypt, had been discussed at the War Council in November 1914, but nothing definite had been decided. At this stage of the War on the Western Front had reached a deadlock; politicians and the War Staff in London were seeking some other theatre where a decisive blow might be struck. It was calculated that the capture of Constantinople would mean the immediate capitulation of Turkey, while at the same time the opening of the Dardanelles would give a free passage to Russia for munitions of war and allow the export of that country's harvest. It was a tempting prospect, and, looked at with the inadequate maps available in London, presented many allurements. It was not until early in January, 1915, that the proposal to launch an attack against the Dardanelles was translated from the sphere of empty discussion. At this time, the British Government received an urgent representation

THE WELLINGTON REGIMENT

from Russia that she was being hard pressed by the Turks in the Caucasus, and requesting that a demonstration against the Turks in some other quarter might be made, in order to relieve the pressure on the Russian front. A reply was sent immediately to Russia that a demonstration would be made. It was after this that the idea of attacking the Dardanelles with a view to forcing a passage for the Fleet to Constantinople was considered by the War Council. There was much discussion as to whether the operation should be a combined attack by the Fleet, supported by adequate land forces, which would land and occupy the Gallipoli Peninsula when the Fleet had silenced the Turkish Forts, or whether an attempt should be made to force a passage with the Fleet alone. Anxiety as to the position on the Western Front made it difficult to spare sufficient troops to ensure the success of land operations, and it was, eventually, decided to attempt to force the Dardanelles with an attack by the Fleet alone. The first operation by the Fleet, under Admiral Carden, in which the French squadron also participated, took place on 7th February, 1915, when the outer forts protecting the Dardanelles were bombarded at long and short ranges, and demolition parties were landed. The shore parties found that a good deal of damage had been done to the forts, but about seventy per cent. of the heavy guns still appeared to be serviceable. On this occasion, the Turks appeared to have retreated before the intense bombardment, and the landing of demolition parties must have been a surprise to them. No further operations by the Fleet were undertaken until the 18th March, when the attack was renewed. This time the Fleet lost five ships, principally from floating Turkish mines, and the attack had to be abandoned. After the attack of 19th February, the Turk had awakened to the fact that his defences against attack on the Peninsula required strengthening, and commenced to build field fortifications with the greatest rapidity. In the words of Admiral Sir John de Roebeck, thousands of Turks were at work like beavers all night on trenches, redoubts and entanglements. All landing places were communicated by lines of trenches and effectually ranged by field guns and howitzers.

THE WELLINGTON REGIMENT

Although in February the War Council had cancelled the sailing of the 29th Division, at the beginning of March, a decision was reached that, if the Fleet could not get through the Straits unaided, the Army would have to see it through. General Birdwood, who was then proceeding to the Dardanelles, was asked to report. He reported that he very much doubted whether the Navy could force the Straits unaided. Early in March, it was decided to send out General Sir Ian Hamilton to command the troops, which were being assembled in the neighbourhood of the Dardanelles. Meantime he was to get in touch with the Navy, and ascertain the extent of the operation which would be involved in landing on the Peninsula in the event of the Fleet failing to get through. Sir Ian Hamilton arrived before the bombardment on the 18th March and the reconnaissance he made down the coast on that date confirmed the report of Admiral de Robeck as regards the action of the Turks since the 19th February. After the failure of the Fleet on 19th March, General Hamilton was informed that he was to undertake, in co-operation with the Navy, the task of taking the Peninsula with the Army. He immediately proceeded to Alexandria to organise the expedition. The troops put at his disposal for the operations were:—

Naval Division	11,000
A. and N.Z. Force	34,100
29th Division	18,000
French Division	18,000
Total	81,000

The support of a Russian Army Corps of 47,600 men was promised when the attackers reached Constantinople.

The Turkish Forces expected to oppose a landing on the Peninsula were estimated at 40,000 on the Peninsula, with about 30,000 in reserve west of Rodosto. On this estimate, the attacking forces at the disposal of Sir Ian Hamilton appeared to be numerically superior.

CHAPTER VI.

Gallipoli—The Landing—Days of Strenuous Fighting —Walker's Ridge.

AT Lemnos the final details of the part the Regiment was to play in Sir Ian Hamilton's plan to take the Gallipoli Peninsula were given out to all officers. Sir Ian Hamilton had decided to divide his forces, and to land and attack the Turks on Gallipoli at two places, while the French were to land on the Asiatic shore by way of a demonstration, and to keep busy as many Turks as possible on that side to prevent their reinforcing the Peninsula. The southernmost landing was to be effected near Helles, with the idea of capturing the southern foot of the Peninsula, where suitable landing places were numerous, and from there pushing on to the commanding heights known as Achi Baba. To assist the progress of the southern force, and for the purpose of outflanking the Turks on the southernmost end and making the capture of Achi Baba easier, a force, consisting of the A. and N.Z. Army Corps, under General Birdwood, was to land in the vicinity of Gaba Tepe and push its way across to Maidos. The actual landing at Gaba Tepe was entrusted to the 1st Australian Division, the 3rd Australian Brigade being given the task of landing first and acting as a covering force to ensure the disembarkation of the rest of the corps.

The "Lutzow" with Battalion Headquarters and Taranaki and Ruahine Companies on board arrived off the Cove at Gaba Tepe about midday on Sunday, 25th April, and by 6 p.m. all had got ashore. In the actual process of landing, one officer, Captain M. McDonnell, the Battalion Adjutant, and four men were slightly wounded. The two companies were assembled under the shelter of the cliffs just above the beach and, about 7 p.m., two platoons of Taranaki Company, under Major J. W. Brunt, were sent to the assistance of the

16th Australian Battalion under Colonel Pope, fighting hard at the head of Monash Gully. These two platoons soon found themselves in a warm corner, but, by using their entrenching tools, they soon got some cover, and rendered some support to their hard-pressed Australian comrades. The two Taranaki platoons remained in line with the Australians in the vicinity of what was afterwards known as Courtney's Post, at the head of Monash Gully, until 2.30 a.m. on the 27th, when they were relieved by troops of the Otago Battalion and made their way to the beach. During the fighting, Private H. E. Hayden, Corporal W. G. Looney and C.S.M. A. J. M. Bonar were conspicuous for their gallantry. Unfortunately all three were killed. The death of C.S.M. A. J. M. Bonar was a big blow to Taranaki Company.

At 2 a.m. on the 26th, the two other platoons of Taranaki Company, under Captain E. D. Cox, and Ruahine Company, under Major E. H. Saunders, proceeded to relieve some troops in the trenches on Plugge's Plateau, but returned to the battalion next day after suffering several casualties.

The "Achaia," with West Coast and Hawke's Bay Companies, arrived opposite Gaba Tepe about 1 p.m. on the 25th and lay well out all the afternoon. No information could be gleaned as to the probable time of landing. In fact, one rumour gained currency that the troops on shore were to be withdrawn and the landing at Anzac abandoned. However, about 3.30 a.m. on the morning of the 26th, a destroyer arrived alongside the "Achaia" with instructions to take off both companies, and, by 5 a.m., both companies and the machine guns were ashore and were gladdened by the sight of the C.O. on the beach as cheery as ever, but growling at the disorder that prevailed. Probably nothing would have pleased him better than to have been detailed with his battalion to tidy up the beach. The two companies and the machine guns were assembled in a small scrub-covered gully just off the beach, and spent the day of the 26th in comparative quiet. Several of the senior officers made a reconnaissance of the ground between the beach and the firing line, and, about 6 p.m., West Coast Company was ordered to

Plugge's Plateau where it made itself comfortable for the night. At midnight the company was ordered back to the Gully.

The morning of the 27th April dawned bright and warm. Breakfast over, the battalion received orders to assemble in Howitzer Gully. After resting there for about an hour, at 9.45 a.m. orders were for the battalion to proceed to the left flank, where a strong Turkish counter attack had developed against the Walker's Ridge position held by the Australian Brigade. The move to Walker's Ridge was made in single file, West Coast Company leading, followed by Hawke's Bay, Taranaki and Ruahine, in that order. Whilst proceeding along the beach, the battalion was subjected to a considerable amount of shrapnel fire. The shells passed just overhead, bursting at the edge of the water, and very little damage was done. At the foot of Walker's Ridge the C.O., Lieut.-Col. Malone, held a consultation with Brigadier General Walker of the A.I.F., who was temporarily commanding the brigade in the absence of Brigadier General F. E. Johnston, who was unable to land owing to illness. As a result, West Coast and Hawke's Bay Companies were ordered to proceed up Walker's Ridge, leave their packs half-way, and reinforce the Australian troops holding the Ridge wherever help was most needed.

The track up Walker's Ridge was extremely precipitous; the sun poured down with its midday heat, and, after dumping their packs half-way, the two companies in single file made their way, hot and breathless, to the summit of the Ridge. As they arrived near the top, sections were hurried into the firing line by Australian officers, eager to thicken up their own part of the line. The bulk of West Coast Company made its way round to the right into the position subsequently known as Russell's Top, while Hawkes Bay Company took up position on West Coast's left, nearer the position subsequently known as the Neck. West Coast and Hawke's Bay Companies soon found themselves in the middle of heavy and severe fighting. Bullets whipped through the scrub from an invisible enemy. The Australian troops who had been fighting continuously for forty-eight hours without rest were physically exhausted, and it was very difficult to grasp the position. Practically no trenches existed, and, after the arrival of West Coast and Hawke's Bay Companies, far more men were crowded into the firing line than could comfortably be accommodated. Unnecessarily heavy casualties were the result. As soon as his company was absorbed in the line, the commander of West Coast Company, Major W. H. Cunningham, reconnoitred the position and found a deep Turkish trench about twenty yards in rear of the firing line in the scrub and on the reverse or seaward slope, in which were a number of picks and shovels. He thereupon withdrew a number of men from the over-crowded firing line and set them to work to dig a gap from this trench to the firing line. About 3 p.m. an alarm was given that the Turks were coming and the order was passed along to fix bayonets and for the whole line to charge. Unhesitatingly, the order was obeyed, with the result that a good many men charged down the forward slope of the ridge, where, being fully exposed to the Turkish trenches opposite, they fell an easy prey to the Turkish riflemen and machine guns. The charge, however, cleared the front of immediate danger. Hawke's Bay Company on the left of West Coast Company ultimately took up a position on an angle of the line which they found was being hotly contested and which was a very important point in the defence. The bayonet charge had carried the line forward a considerable distance, but it was soon realised that the best line to hold was the original one from which the charge had started, and an ordered retirement by sections to the original line took place. The digging of the sap from the Turkish trench behind West Coast Company to the firing line on the crest was completed before dark, and greatly assisted the organisation of the section occupied by this company. As soon as it was dusk, a trench line was sighted on the forward slope of the hill, and every man set to work to dig in. A second sap was dug to the old Turkish trench, and, when day dawned, everyone was under cover: machine guns were in position in the front line in well-protected emplacements, and a platoon was withdrawn into reserve in the old Turkish trench. The night of the 27th-28th for West Coast Company

THE WELLINGTON REGIMENT

was a strenuous digging one, but, except for the blowing of the Turkish bugles and shouts of "Allah Mahommed" from the slopes opposite, that company was undisturbed by any Turkish attack.

Further down to the left and near the Neck, Major R. Young, with Hawke's Bay Company, was holding the angle in the line where it turned from Russell's Top down Walker's Ridge. This position was being continuously assailed by the enemy who several times approached within a few yards of it. A few well-directed volleys were sufficient to beat off these attacks; but the continuous pressure made organised entrenching out of the question. Major Young's men, in the intervals between the Turkish attacks, did their best to deepen the shallow rifle pits they had scratched during the afternoon. When morning came they managed to secure a fair amount of individual cover; but there was no continuous trench and communication was difficult, any movement through the scrub bringing immediate fire from the Turkish trenches.

During the afternoon of the 27th, Ruahine Company, under Major E. H. Saunders, was sent forward from the foot of Walker's Ridge to strengthen the firing line, and arrived at a very opportune moment when a backward movement of the line had started, about the head of Malone's Gully. On the arrival of Ruahine Company, the situation was immediately taken in hand by Major H. E. Hart, who had been sent forward with the leading companies. He rallied the retiring troops and re-established the firing line. After dusk, Major Hart, while going round the firing line to see that the line was intact and to ascertain the situation of various companies, was seriously wounded in the leg. With great fortitude, he persisted in completing his return to Battalion Headquarters on foot and on making his report before consenting to go to the dressing station. As a result of his wound, he was unable to rejoin his Battalion until September, and his untimely departure was a distinct loss to the fighting strength of the battalion. For his services that day Major Hart was awarded the D.S.O.

When the battalion advanced to Walker's Ridge, the machine guns of the battalion were sent forward and came into action on Russell's Top, where they came under the direction of Capt. J. A. Wallingford. He was able to place the guns in very good positions, and they were fought with great gallantry and good effect by their gun crews. When the line advanced with fixed bayonets about 3 p.m., the guns moved forward as well. As it eventually turned out, it was a disastrous thing to have done, as both the machine-gun officer, Lt. E. R. Wilson, and the machine-gun sergeant were immediately picked off by the Turkish snipers, and the entire crew of one gun was killed or wounded and the gun abandoned in the scrub. The other gun was kept in action and, later, was moved back to its original position. The abandoned gun was recovered by a special patrol sent out at night from the machine-gun section a few nights later.

The action at Walker's Ridge viewed as the Regiment's first engagement as a complete unit was, from the point of view of the task it was asked to perform, a distinct disappointment. The work the Regiment did was magnificently done. It stiffened the Australian line at a critical period of the Turkish counter-attack, and soon dug an organised defensive position, and, within a few hours of its arrival, had taken over the whole Walker's Ridge position. Instead of the Regiment going into action for the first time with a well-defined task assigned to it, to his profound disappointment, our Commanding Officer saw companies, one after the other, straggling in single file up a steep line into a confused fight of other units, and being mopped up in sections and groups to fill weak places in the existing line. Casualties were numerous; but the great day of action had arrived and the supreme test was not to be long delayed, and our gallant Colonel lived long enough to see his beloved battalion emerge triumphant from such an ordeal as few battalions anywhere in the Great War were called upon to face.

At 6 a.m. on the 28th, the remnants of the Australian troops were entirely withdrawn from the Walker's Ridge position and the Wellington Regiment was left in complete

THE WELLINGTON REGIMENT

control. Lieut.-Col. Malone set to work in his usual manner to make the position ship-shape. Digging went on apace. Communications, which were here entirely non-existent, were organised between Battalion Headquarters and front line companies, and the battalion settled down to trench routine. By dint of vigorous digging, a connected front line along the whole battalion front was soon established and communication trenches were next undertaken. West Coast Company, whose position overlooked, at the seaward side, a very steep ravine, constructed a good platform along this cliff face, which made an excellent company rest and reserve position, secure from all enemy fire and commanding a splendid view of the sea and portion of the beach. Between the right of the battalion front on Walker's Ridge and the left of the nearest flank unit at Pope's Hill, there existed a gap which, up to the 27th, had been unoccupied. Rumours were always busy about Turkish snipers who penetrated through this gap and attained positions from which they sniped our men from inside our own lines, but it is doubtful whether the Turks knew that this stretch was unoccupied. In any case, to gain access to it meant that the Turks would have to leave their trenches and cross a deep gully which ran from Walker's Ridge down in front of the Turks' position to Pope's Hill with every risk of being shot by cross fire from their own trenches, not to mention the fire from our own side. The gap was finally closed during the night of the 27th/28th by the arrival of the Otago Battalion. During the action on the 27th and 28th April, the Regiment lost 2 officers killed and 6 wounded. Lieut. E. R. Wilson, the battalion machine-gun officer, was killed when the line charged on the afternoon of the 27th, while Lieut. L. W. Hugo was killed gallantly leading his platoon. Lieuts. D. I. C. Bryan and F. K. Turnbull were among the first of the West Coast Company to go into action but did not last more than an hour before each received a severe wound. Lieut. Bryan had his right arm permanently disabled, and was rendered unfit for further service; but Lieut. Turnbull was able to return to duty some 6 weeks later. Lieuts. L. H. Jardine and A. B. McColl were also wounded, but rejoined some weeks later, the former being wounded on the 28th by a piece of shrapnel from one of our own naval guns.

After the first two days the battalion had a quiet time in the Walker's Ridge position. One of the greatest difficulties was in bringing up ammunition, water and food. The track up to the hill, 500 feet above the beach, was very narrow and steep, and exposed to sniping fire from the Turkish trenches; only small loads could be carried by each man, and each trip took a long time. The days were excessively hot, and the long toil up Walker's Ridge with the ration parties was not a job to be sought after. When our front line was complete and we were congratulating ourselves on being well under cover, we were to be instructed by the Turk in the use of machine-guns for night firing. Night after night, he would skim the parapet of our front line with unexpected bursts of fire, and several men were shot through the head whilst on sentry, peering into the dark mass of tangled scrub in front of our trenches. The accuracy of his machine-gun fire was most uncanny.

On the 2nd May the Otago Battalion which had been occupying trenches on the right of the battalion from Russell's Top towards Pope's Hill, received orders that it was to form part of the attacking force in a night attack which was to be made for the purpose of improving our position by capturing a line from Baby 700 to Quinn's Post. The 4th Australian Brigade was to attack on the right and the Otago Battalion on the left. The attack was timed to commence at 7.15 on the night of the 2nd May. The Otago Battallion was to advance from the foot of Pope's Hill, and left Walker's Ridge at 5 p.m.; but, owing to the distance and the many obstructions along the beach and Monash Gully, it did not reach its assembly point till 8.45 p.m. The attack was preceded by a heavy bombardment. The Australian attack commenced on time; but the late arrival of the Otago Battalion spoilt the co-ordination of the attack. Otago attacked most gallantly when it arrived, but the Turkish fire was deadly, and, despite magnificent courage on the part of both New Zealanders and Australians, the whole operation was a failure, and nothing was gained. The Wellington Regiment gave what assistance it could in the way of covering fire both on the night of the 2nd May and during daylight on the 3rd, when small parties of the Otago Regiment and the Australians could be seen hanging on in advance positions in short lengths of trench they had managed to dig overnight. In conjunction with the Otago Battalion's attack, an attempt was made by a company of the Canterbury Regiment to advance on Baby 700 from the Walker's Ridge position, but the accurate fire of the Turks prevented the company from emerging from its trenches.

CHAPTER VII.

Cape Helles—The "River Clyde"—Seddul Bahr—The Daisy Patch—An Order is Countermanded—Back to Anzac — Armistice — Courtney's Post — Monash Gully.

ON the 5th May, we were relieved in the Walker's Ridge position by the Nelson Battalion of the Royal Naval Division and proceeded to the beach at the foot of Walker's Ridge. At 8.15 p.m. the battalion marched to the embarking piers on the beach and were taken aboard destroyers to proceed to Cape Helles with the rest of the New Zealand Infantry Brigade and the 2nd Australian Brigade of the Australian Division for the purpose of taking part in a grand attack which was pending there. Embarkation was rapidly effected and the destroyers sailed from Anzac some hours later, and proceeded to various beaches at Cape Helles for the purpose of landing the troops. The whole battalion was ashore by daybreak and proceeded to a bivouac area about two miles inland. All ranks were greatly interested on landing to see the murderous barbed wire now gathered into tangled heaps, which the 29th Division had had to face in their rushes ashore; to see the "River Clyde" which had been run ashore to enable the Hampshires and other troops to land; to see the ancient fort of Seddul Bahr all shattered and its very guns dismounted by the fire of the battleships.

Passing over the high ground through the village of Seddul Bahr, our route lay between olive groves and green trees to some green fields somewhat damp and clayey, where we bivouaced. The bivouac was well within field gun range of the Turks, but screened to some extent by the growth. The change from the scrub covered rugged cliffs

THE WELLINGTON REGIMENT

of Anzac to the green fields of Helles was a very welcome one. The fields were gay with poppies, whilst, close to our bivouacs, was a well of beautiful clear spring water. Shallow shelters against shrapnel were dug or scooped out of the clayey soil, and the battalion settled down to get a little rest. Since the 27th April the battalion had been fighting and digging hard on Walker's Ridge without relief or rest, had come straight from the Ridge to the destroyers, and had spent the night huddled up on the destroyers with practically no sleep.

In front of us severe fighting was in progress. At the time the New Zealand Infantry Brigade and 2nd Australian Brigade reached Cape Helles, the line held by the troops which had carried out the attack at the southern end of the Peninsula was substantially the same as had been reached on the 29th April. The French held the right flank with their extreme right on the eastern shore. The Royal Naval Division were in the centre, immediately in touch with the French, while the Brigades 88th and 87th of the 29th Division, with Indian troops, were on the left.

The New Zealand Brigade was in reserve on the 6th, and remained quietly in bivouac on the night of the 6th-7th. About 4 p.m. on the 7th, the brigade moved from its bivouac area, the Wellington Regiment moving across the open in artillery formation to the Gully Ravine leading inland in rear of the line held by the 29th Division. At the foot of the gully we settled down for the night. About 9 p.m., orders were issued to proceed up the gully and occupy a reserve trench some 500 yards in rear of that occupied by the 87th Brigade of the 29th Division. This move was completed by about 1 a.m. As the reserve trench was far too small to hold the battalion, Ruahine Company was sent back to the Gully Ravine, while the other three companies occupied the trench. West Coast Company was on the right, Hawke's Bay in the centre and Taranaki on the left. Battalion Headquarters were established in a stone hut about the junction of the reserve-trench with Gully Ravine. Auckland Battalion moved up on the right of Wellington, in support to the 88th Brigade of the 29th Division. At daybreak, the Canterbury Battalion moved up on Auckland's right.

THE WELLINGTON REGIMENT

At 8.30 a.m., detailed orders for the attack were received by the New Zealand Infantry Brigade Headquarters. Colonel Johnston now moved his Headquarters up to a ruined hut slightly in rear of the reserve trench, and, at 10.10 a.m., issued verbal orders to his battalion commanders of Wellington, Auckland and Canterbury to deploy in rear of the British front line and to advance to the attack of Krithia at 10.30 a.m. Rough boundaries for each battalion were pointed out by the Brigadier. At this time, Wellington and Auckland Battalions were still in the line of the reserve trench, some 500 yards at least behind the front-line trenches. The intervening ground was in full view of the Turks and exposed to shrapnel and long range rifle and machine-gun fire. Col. Malone hastily called his company commanders together and repeated the order he had received, parcelling out his frontage about 600 yards between the three companies equally as they lay, West Coast right to be in touch with Auckland Battalion, Hawke's Bay centre and Taranaki left. The battalion was to move to the attack at 10.30 a.m., which left ten minutes for company commanders to arrange the advance of their platoons. The intention of the Divisional Commander was that the advance should commence from the front line trenches at 10.30 a.m., at which hour the bombardment of the Turkish position was to cease. Through lack of time and some misunderstanding, the Wellington and Auckland Battalions did not move from the reserve lines till 10.30 a.m. and, consequently had to cover the open ground between the reserve trenches and the front line and emerge from the front line wholly unsupported by artillery. The three attacking companies moved forward in successive lines of platoons with five paces interval between the men and fifty paces between the successive lines. As the moving lines were seen by the Turks salvoes of shrapnel were poured into them while the ground was whipped with machine-gun bullets which spat up dust viciously among the advancing lines. The attacking companies moved as if on parade. Intervals and dressing were kept perfectly. At times the dust and smoke from the bursting shrapnel would appear to have swept our men entirely

THE WELLINGTON REGIMENT

away; but, when the air cleared, the line could be seen moving steadily forward. The troops of the 29th Division cheered the advancing lines as they reached the front line trench and, without pausing, pushed steadily into the thickening hail of bullets. Taranaki Company early got into a vicious cross fire from Turkish machine-guns posted on the seaward side of the Gully Ravine. Its left flank was exposed by the slope of the ground, and, after making some progress, the line was forced to lie down to escape some of the fire, and the advance of the Taranaki Company came to a standstill. Hawke's Bay in the centre made steady progress against a heavy fire; but it kept in touch with Taranaki, and when its left flank bent back the right automatically came to a halt. West Coast Company on the right made good progress for a while, until its leading platoon bore to the right to keep touch with Auckland. Then it got into a low-lying patch of ground which proved a veritable death trap. The commanders of the two leading platoons had by messages reported back to the Company Commander that it was quite impossible to move out of this ground which was known as the Daisy Patch. Two sections of the leading platoon under Sgt.-Major Woodhead had reached some high ground some 400 yards in front of the Essex front line and were digging in. Major Cunningham, commanding West Coast Company, coming forward with his reserve platoon, ascertained the position from the leading platoon commanders, and made his way across the Daisy Patch to the sections under Sgt.-Major Woodhead, directing Lieuts. C. B. S. Menteath and H. E. McKinnon to follow with as may men as they could dribble across. Major Cunningham reached the knoll safely and set the sections to dig in. Some stunted fir trees somewhat screened the rear side of the knoll from the Turkish fire and, though the Turks cut pieces off the trees with their fire, the digging progressed. While taking his turn with the pick and shovel, Sgt. F. J. Rule was shot in the head, dying some few days later on board a hospital ship. He had been recommended for a commission and was a very fine N.C.O. Lieut. C. B. S. Menteath, having given instructions to his platoons to try

THE WELLINGTON REGIMENT

and dribble across to the fir knoll, started to cross the Daisy Patch. He was badly wounded and one of his men endeavoured to crawl with him to safety; but he received a second bullet in the head which killed him. Lieut. Sandy Menteath was one of the most popular and efficient officers in the company. He had behaved with great gallantry on Walker's Ridge. Shortly after Menteath was hit, Lieut. McKinnon, who had led No. 1 platoon, received a severe wound in the head which rendered him unconscious. Both these platoons in the Daisy Patch had suffered severely and, scraping what shelter they could with their entrenching tools, they lay quietly in the grass till dusk. The Commander of the West Coast Company soon established communication with Hawkes Bay Company and Major R. Young, the Commander of Hawke's Bay Company, reported his position and inability to make further progress until the left of the line came up.

Auckland Battalion, as it emerged from the British front line, encountered the same murderous rifle and machine gun fire as had Wellington. The leading Companies got into the Daisy Patch to the right of West Coast Company, and though they made a gallant attempt to go forward, after losing heavily many of them took cover in a dry creek bed, where they sheltered for the time being from the Turkish machine gun fire. In the result, West Coast Company lost touch with the Auckland Battalion for the time being. Canterbury Battalion on the extreme right had been in the British front line ready to advance at 10.30, but waited for the other battalions to come up, and had fared no better than Auckland. Very few of the leading company got through the murderous fire, and the Turks directed such a withering fire on the British front line that it was impossible for some of the Canterbury Battalion to move at all.

By 1.30 p.m., the New Zealand Brigade was definitely held up. It had suffered very severe casualties and, though some progress had been made, there was not the slighest doubt that even more ground might have been gained by

Suez Canal, February, 1915.

Quinn's Post, 1915.

Wellington Battalion digging in on morning after Landing.

The Sphinx and Walkers, May, 1915.

Winners of the Guard Mounting Competition selected from the West Coast Coy. of the 1st Battalion, 1918.

Looking towards Pope's Hill, 1915.

In reserve on Gallipoli.

walking out in darkness and digging in. There would have been no casualties had the latter expedient been adopted.

The outstanding experience of the day was the heaviness of the Turkish rifle and machine gun fire and the invisibility of the enemy. The advance of the brigade from the reserve trenches had given the Turks ample warning of the impending attack. The invisibility of the Turks made it impossible for us to use supporting fire to assist the advance. The brigade had been rushed into the attack without the opportunity of reconnaissance, or without any clear cut objective, and there is no doubt that the whole effort was doomed to failure from the start. There appeared to have been very little in the nature of wire or protection in the front of the Turkish entrenchments, and it is difficult to understand why the attack had not been timed to commence at dawn; and the troops moved up under cover of darkness to their assembly positions in the front line. The New Zealand troops and the Australian Divisions had had considerable training in night operations in Egypt and their experiences at Anzac had prepared them to do battle with the Turk under all conditions. It can be confidently asserted that, had the New Zealand and Australian Brigades been given this opportunity, the fighting of 8th May would have had a vastly different result.

Shortly before 5 p.m., a message was despatched to the front line that a general advance had been ordered of the whole line with fixed bayonets at 5.30 p.m. It was intended that the advance should be made by the New Zealand Brigade alone; but the first order was countermanded and Sir Ian Hamilton ordered a general advance. In view of the way the British line throughout was pinned down by the excellently served Turkish machine guns, it was difficult to see how the advance was to succeed in doing other than increasing casualties. The troops in the front line realized the hopelessness of attempting to progress until the machine guns had been silenced; but the Divisional Headquarters did not appear to have appreciated it. Ruahine Company, which had lain in reserve throughout the day in Ravine

THE WELLINGTON REGIMENT

Gully, was ordered up and participated in the general advance on the right of the battalion in an endeavour to fill the gap in the line between West Coast Company and the Auckland Regiment. A section of the Company under Captain Short got well forward up the Krithia Nulla; but, finding themselves completely isolated, they took cover and, at dusk, retired to the line occupied by the West Coast Company.

The 2nd Australian Brigade was rushed into the advance at 5.30 p.m. It did not receive its orders until 4.55 p.m. The brigade was then lying in Krithia Nulla in close formation from one half to three-quarters of a mile below the front line. By heroic efforts the brigade got under weigh and extended to cover its allotted frontage and pushed forward on the right of the New Zealand Brigade. Only the barest of directions could be given by the Brigadier to his Battalion Commanders; but the Brigade got into its fighting formation with wonderful speed and was not many minutes late in crossing the front line to the attack. However, once into the front line, it encountered conditions exactly similar to what the New Zealanders had had to face earlier in the day, and it suffered much the same fate as the other attacking troops had done.

A strong protest had been made by Lieut. Colonel Malone to Colonel Johnston, the Brigadier, when the first order had been issued for the New Zealand to advance. He had pointed out the absurdity of attempting to push forward, while the troops on his left flank had no orders to move, and while his right was already isolated and farther forward than any of the units on his right. His protest was endorsed by Colonel Johnston and passed on to Divisional Headquarters. The original order was then countermanded and the general advance ordered instead. However, the difficulty of distributing the orders to the exposed front line and the fact that anyone, who exposed himself in the advanced lines, was immediately hit resulted in only a small portion of the advanced line going forward at the hour ordered for the general advance. The sections of West Coast Company with

Major Cunningham started forward with the general movement and were joined in the advance by some men of the 2nd Hampshire Battalion. After going forward for a hundred yards or more, it was quite evident that the troops on the left flank were not moving, and that the twenty or thirty men in Major Cunningham's party would achieve nothing by going forward on their own. He, therefore, made them lie down in the scrub and, as soon as it was dusk, the party of the West Coast Company returned to the partly completed trenches it had left at 5.30 p.m., and the Hampshires returned to the original front line.

Immediately darkness fell, the work of consolidating the ground gained by the advance of the morning proceeded apace. A supply of picks and shovels had been sent forward with the reserve platoon in each company, and digging proceeded steadily during the night. The Turkish fire was very active and the Turks throughout the night sent up star shells and Verey lights in front of the new lines. However, after the hand to hand conditions of Anzac, the battalion felt it had any amount of breathing space and went on stolidly digging in, without paying too much attention to the Turk. During the night the body of Lieut. C. B. S. Menteath was recovered from the Daisy Patch and buried near a fir tree at the rear of our new front line. Rations came up to the battalion after dark and, though the night was cold, the first night in the new line proved comparatively quiet.

At dawn, everyone was alert for a sight of the enemy. From the knoll on which the right of West Coast Company's trench rested an excellent view of the Turkish position opposite was obtainable, and Johnny Turk was visible strolling about in the scrub in front of his lines at a range of 500-600 yards. For close on an hour some excellent sniping was carried on by our riflemen, until the Turk realised that his former recreation area was under fire and quickly vacated it.

The battalion remained in the front line until the night of the 12th May, when it was relieved by the Manchester Brigade of the 42nd Division. It was not until daybreak that the relief was complete and the front line companies finally debouched into the Gully Ravine on their way to the bivouac area they had occupied when they first arrived at Helles. The Turk seemed to be aware of the impending relief, as he kept up an incessant fire all night and, as the orders were to proceed down the trench line to Gully Ravine and not to pass overland, filing down the crowded trenches was a long and tedious job. The exit into Gully Ravine lay through the trenches occupied by the Indian troops. The alternative was a dash overland running the gauntlet of the intermittent Turkish fire, and the risk of being shot at by our own troops. Through some oversight, the Indians had not been warned that the New Zealand troops were to pass through the trenches and, for several hours, Hawke's Bay and West Coast Companies were held up till the Commanding Officer of the Indian battalion concerned was informed of the position and gave permission to proceed.

From the 13th to the 19th May, the battalion remained in bivouac with the rest of the Brigade in corps reserve. Large fatigue parties were furnished for work on the beach, landing materials and supplies and making roads and tracks. The nights were somewhat disturbed by Turkish shells, but little damage was done, and the shelling was treated with complete indifference by all ranks. The surroundings of the bivouac with numerous shady trees, and the ground carpeted with wild flowers were very pleasant, and the battalion soon recovered from the strain of the previous four days' fighting.

On the 19th, orders were received that we were to embark after dark on the "Eddystone," a huge steel cargo steamer, to return to Anzac. Embarkation was safely effected *via* the River Clyde Jetty by midnight, and, at daybreak, the "Eddystone" was once more off Anzac Cove. All hands were safely ashore at the Cove by 8 a.m., and the battalion proceeded in single file round the beach to the north to a bivouac in a gully just below the Walker's Ridge-Russell's Top position. After rounding Ari Burnu point, Turkish snipers became very active, and bullets started to kick up the pebbles all round the troops. Several men were hit; but a new route was found clear of this fire and the battalion reached the bivouac area without further loss.

The gully in which we were to bivouac received the name of Rest Gully. The sides were extremely steep, necessitating the construction of ledges or little platforms in the face of the steep side to enable the men to lie down. It was a bright, sunny day when the battalion took possession of this delightful rest area and set to work to make it homely. Bivouacs were constructed more with regard to comfort than to durability, and few thought of a good solid downpour of rain. There was only one track up the gully which was obviously the route the water took in wet weather. All "bivvies," therefore were approached *via* this water channel, which was improved and widened so far as circumstances would permit. Wellington had its battalion area at the head of the ravine, while Auckland, Canterbury and Otago occupied area further down. On the night of 21st May it rained, and the rain continued until 1 p.m. on the 22nd. Daybreak on the morning of the 22nd in Rest Gully was a sight to behold. The rain had melted innumerable "bivvies" and, all along the hill slopes, soft muddy patches in which were inextricably mixed blankets, waterproof sheets and personal gear of all descriptions were gradually progressing down the hillside towards the central channel. The rain was not cold, and the homeless made light of their troubles, seeking consolation in watching a similar fate overtaking their temporarily more fortunate comrades still asleep in "bivvies" which had not quite reached the melting stage.

Throughout the morning, the muddy state of the central road or channel made it almost impossible to climb it, and the attempt of ration parties to clamber up provoked tremendous merriment. An Indian transport private, in charge of two heavily laden mules, essayed to reach the top of the gully with rations. He made excellent progress as far as the Wellington area, where the mules jostled one another and one pulling back turned sharply round and bolted down the narrow track. There was a quick scattering on all sides and Mr. Mule, with his load of biscuit tins and crates, was given a clear passage in his head-long charge. He reached the beach in record time minus his load. His wrathful driver, muttering unmentionable things in Hindustani, followed leisurely afterwards with the second mule. The Indian soldier is patience and perseverance personified, otherwise he would not be such an expert with mules, and, sure enough, in about an hour's time, the same driver arrived back with both mules, and this time delivered his load safely.

While at Rest Gully, the Brigade remained in Divisional reserve, furnishing fatigues and working parties daily. On the 23rd May and the following nights until the 27th, it furnished the inlying piquet in close support to the mounted brigade who now occupied Walker's Ridge position. The inlying piquet occupied each night a trench running from the beach to the foot of Walker's Ridge, blocking any attempt that might be made by the enemy to push along the beach. The battalion returned to its bivouac again each morning after daylight. Nothing occurred to disturb the serenity of the nights during the battalion's tour of duty as inlying piquet.

It would be well just here to review the happenings of Anzac during the absence of the Brigade at Helles from the 5th to the 19th May. When he was requested by Sir Ian Hamilton at the beginning of May to furnish two brigades from Anzac to assist in the projected attack at Krithia, General Birdwood had selected his two strongest Brigades in the 2nd Australian Brigade and the New Zealand Infantry Brigade. The departure of these two brigades, although to some extent compensated for by the arrival of the Naval Brigade and Marine Brigade, made it necessary for all troops to garrison the line, and even the troops employed on the beach in unloading and handling stores had to take their place at night in the inner lines of defence. On the 12th May, the 1st Australian Light Horse Brigade, approximately 1,500 strong, landed at Anzac, to be followed next day by the New Zealand Mounted Rifle Brigade. The two Naval Brigades immediately afterwards departed from Anzac and rejoined the Royal Naval Division at Helles. The New Zea-

THE WELLINGTON REGIMENT

land Mounted Rifle Brigade took over the left section on Walker's Ridge and Russell's Top, while the Light Horse Brigade proceeded to the left central section, Pope's Hill, Quinn's Post and Courtney's Post. On the 19th May, just before dawn, the Turkish Force at Anzac, which had been increased by the arrival of a fresh division, and now numbered approximately 42,000, attacked along the whole Anzac front. The Turkish plan was to get the assault and attacking troops into position immediately in rear of his front line in the hours of darkness, and to rush the Anzac lines just before daybreak, driving the defenders into the sea. Fortunately, the arrival of the Turkish reinforcements became known at G.H.Q., and the Anzac Commander was warned on the 18th May of an impending attack in force by the Turks, and extra precautions were taken on the night of the 18-19th May. Stand-to was ordered half an hour earlier than usual, 3 a.m. instead of 3.30 a.m., while all troops were warned to make everything ready to repel attack. The trenches had scarcely been manned when the Turks were seen in the clear light crowding with fixed bayonets into a depression in front of the Australian lines in the right central sector, and fire was immediately opened on them, thus giving the alarm. The Turks at all points now attempted to assault the Anzac lines. They came on bravely in mass formation, but were mowed down by rifle and machine-gun fire and scarcely a man reached the parapet of our trenches. Before day dawned, the grand attack had been broken with appalling losses to the Turks. Becoming confused in the darkness and the maze of their own trenches, their attacking lines had in many places moved obliquely across our front exposed to a withering enfilade fire. Daybreak found many confused and scattered groups of Turks scrummaging about in No Man's Land endeavouring to reach the shelter of their own trenches, all that was left of the main attack. The troops of the new Turkish Division, who were unfamiliar with the locality, suffered very heavily.

As the result of the fighting, a great many more dead were added to the numbers lying out between the lines at

Anzac and these unburied corpses threatened a very serious menace to health. Overtures came from the Turks for an armistice and, after some parley, this was finally arranged from 7.30 a.m. till 4.30 p.m. on the 24th May. The dividing line was marked out down the centre of No Man's Land with flags and burial parties worked on either side of the central line. The opportunity was seized by many of the officers of high rank to have a peep at their opponent's lines. The day passed without unpleasant incident, both sides loyally observing the terms of the truce. At 4.30 p.m., everybody was back in his own lines, and hosilities recommenced.

The intermittent rifle fire, both night and day was one of the peculiarities of the Anzac zone. Approaching Anzac from the sea the continuous "pop," "pop," "pop" of the rifle shots followed one right in shore and up to the front line trenches. It was the dominant note of Anzac, like the thud of the ship's engines in a ship at sea. The very few periods when the trench lines were absolutely silent were periods of uncanniness. At night, to troops in the reserve and rest areas, it was music which lulled them to sleep. If it ceased absolutely they waked wondering what the peculiar stillness foreboded; what had happened while they slept. With the return of the two brigades from Helles, the Anzac Corps felt once again its full strength, and the men who had faced the Turkish fire at Krithia were delighted to learn of the splendid defence put up during their absence, and viewed with amazement the piles of Turkish dead in front of our trenches.

The battalion passed on now to a period of garrison duty in the trenches alternated with periods of supplying working parties in the trenches and on the beaches and in rear areas, designated *periods of rest*. The period is interesting in one respect in that it marked a great personal triumph for our Commanding Officer, Lieut.-Col. Malone. He was a man to whom untidiness was anathema. He disliked it as much in war as he had done in civil life. His first desire on landing was to tidy up the beach a bit. On Walker's Ridge he quickly brought order out of chaos, and made the sector habitable. At Helles, when reinforcements arrived, he quickly set them to work to tidy up the battlefield. Had he lived to see the battlefields of France and Belgium, he would have made an ideal Director of Salvage Operations. Lieut.-Col. Malone believed implicitly that men could fight better in clean and orderly surroundings than in dirt and disorder, and there was no reason why dirt and untidiness should be tolerated in the front line trenches any more than anywhere else.

On Friday, 29th May, orders were received for the battalion to take over Courtney's Post in the Left Central Section, one company to proceed there each day until the relief was complete. Next day, West Coast Company, under Major W. H. Cunningham, proceeded up Shropul and Monash Gully to Courtney's Post. The passage up Monash Gully was not without incident. The valley was well commanded by Turkish snipers, and the Australian units furnishing the garrison at the head of the valley had suffered a great number of casualties in using the valley which was the only route to Quinn's, Pope's and Courtney's Posts. To minimize the risk of being hit, large sand bag traverses had been built out on either side of the valley and these gave a limited amount of cover. It was necessary to move briskly from one traverse to the other because the Turks watched very carefully the points where there was most traffic and, probably using a machine-gun carefully laid, would snipe half a dozen in as many minutes at the same spot. West Coast Company went into the support trenches at Courtney's Post on the 30th May. They arrived in the afternoon whilst a raid was in progress at the next door post, Quinn's, and the activity had naturally communicated itself to the neighbouring posts. On the 31st, Taranaki Company arrived, to be followed next day by the C.O., Battalion Headquarters, and the other two companies, the battalion on the 31st May furnishing the complete garrison of Courtney's Post. On arrival of Battalion Headquarters, Lieut.-Col. W. G. Malone became the Post Commander, Major W. H. Cunningham taking over command of the battalion while the command of West Coast Company devolved on the second in command, Captain A. J. M. Cross.

THE WELLINGTON REGIMENT

The first act of the new O.C. Post was to build, or rather dig, a decent Post Commander's Headquarters, and make a home where he could work and fight, free from flies, and clean and tidy. Plans also shaped themselves for the provision of more comfortable quarters for the garrison when not in the front line. Courtney's Post, like many of the Anzac sectors, was a trench line running along the top of a steep bluff. Behind the front line trench ran a support trench a few yards back, and then the ground started to slope more or less steeply towards Monash Gully. To reach the front line from Monash Gully it was a very steep climb up a zig-zag path with numerous steps. The garrison had lived in little holes scooped out of the hillside, each man making himself as comfortable as possible wherever he could. This gave the post a very higgley piggley appearance, and left much to be desired in case of emergency. Col. Malone, therefore, proposed to dig several deep terraces in the hillsides behind the support lines, obtain overhead cover and so ensure a greater degree of comfort for the men, better organisation for defence, and above all, order and tidiness. During the first week, these matters were attended to and the whole place was well cleaned up.

The dispositions in Courtney's Post were two companies in the front line, one in support, and one in reserve in Monash Gully. Companies did a turn of 48 hours in the front line and 48 hours in support or reserve. The system on which the line was held involved the presence of a strong garrison in the front line, both by night and by day, ready to repel any sudden attack. During the 48 hours of front line duty the men got practically no rest. Immediately after the arrival of the battalion at Courtney's Post, Brigade Headquarters of the New Zealand Infantry Brigade organised a special snipers' detachment composed of picked shots from the various battalions in the brigade to deal with the Turkish snipers, who were causing such loss and inconvenience in Monash Valley. The command of the detachment was given to Lieut. T. M. P. Grace of the Wellington Regiment. The snipers were supplied with special rifles fitted with telescopic

THE WELLINGTON REGIMENT

sights; powerful telescopes, and were struck off all other duties. Lieut. Grace handled his small command with marked success. Special sniper posts were selected in the scrub on the hillsides facing the Turkish lines, the scouts working in pairs. They lay in their posts all day, coming out at night to rest and returning before dawn. So well did they deal with the Turkish snipers that within two days after they had started operations the Turkish snipers had been almost completely silenced, and, within a week, Monash Gully became a safe route at any time of the day. The superiority thus gained by the brigade snipers was never lost, and was one of the measures which did much to make the positions at the head of Monash Gully the quiet and peaceful homes they afterwards became.

On the 3rd June, Lieut. J. R. Cargo (Taranaki), who had received his promotion in the field, was fatally shot while on duty in the trenches by enfilade fire from a Turkish sniper.

On the night of the 4th June, the Canterbury Battalion, who were in occupation of Quinn's Post on the left of Courtney's Post, carried out an attack on the Turkish trench in their immediate front. The attack was timed to commence at 11 p.m., and was preceded by an intense bombardment. Our battalion in Courtney's Post was assigned the role of looker-on. It was a dark night and, when the artillery opened intense fire, it was an awe inspiring spectacle for the onlookers on the seaward slopes of Courtney's; flashes and reports of rifles and machine-guns on all sides: shells appearing in the darkness to be red hot, coming straight at us from our own guns and passing just over our heads; every now and then one with a burning fire leaving a trail of sparks in its path. Then the report of the guns and howitzer; the scream and crash of the counter-bombardment by the Turks; the star shells, the bombs, all combined to make a weird impression on the onlookers in Courtney's. The Canterbury Battalion's operation was entirely successful, resulting in the capture of 28 Turkish prisoners and the taking of the trench opposite Quinn's, though later it was found impracticable to hold it, and the trench was vacated before morning broke.

THE WELLINGTON REGIMENT

On the night of the 4th June, the Canterbury Battalion, was not to go into reserve at the end of its eight days' tour of duty in Courtney's Post; but was, instead, to relieve Quinn's Post. This latter position at the head of Monash Gully was considered the key of the sector. Situated on the fringe of the hillside, the approaches to it were steep and the whole position narrow and congested. Although a vital spot in the line, it offered very little facility for the accommodation of troops, and the reserve for the post had to be posted in a gully in rear of Pope's Hill.

The continuous fighting which had been going on in the vicinity of the post throughout May, had resulted in the demolition of a considerable portion of the front line trench which was unoccupied, while the sally points and tunnels which had been constructed for the use of raiding parties, gave the front line a weak and unstable appearance. Major Cunningham visited the post on the 7th June, to report on its condition to the C.O. and, after the well ordered and clean condition of Courtney's, he found that the prospect of the occupation of Quinn's as an alternative to a spell in reserve presented little attraction. A great number of Turkish dead in a highly decomposed state lay out just in front of the front trenches. Large fat maggots from these fly-blown corpses dropped with a gentle thud into the bottom of the trench, where they writhed uncomfortably in the dust. The stench from the corpses was most offensive and generally the post bore the marks of the strenuous conflicts that had been waged around it and stood very badly in need of first of all a good clean up, and then thorough re-organization.

With his work at Courtney's fresh in mind, the Divisional Commander must have concluded that Colonel Malone, with his Battalion, was the man to take charge of Quinn's and clean it up, and he was to act as the permanent Post Commander. To save his Battalion whatever work was possible, Colonel Malone immediately interviewed Lieut.-Col. Young, in command of Auckland, with a view to getting his battalion to do some cleaning up before being relieved. However, Auckland had had a hard gruelling in the fighting of the 4th June, and was in no mood for straightening things up on the eve of relief, and it was with feelings of disgust that the battalion found itself housed in the insanitary and battered trenches of Quinn's Post after having made such a comfortable home for itself and its successors in Courtney's.

At 9 a.m. on the 9th June, Hawkes Bay and Ruahine Companies relieved the Auckland Battalion in Quinn's Post, West Coast and Taranaki Companies remaining at Courtney's till next day. As soon as the relief of the Auckland Battalion was complete, Lieut.-Col. Malone took over the command of the post, and found it all that it had been reported to be and a bit more. An entry in his diary of this date says "a more dirty, dilapidated and unorganised post it is hard to imagine. Still I like work and will revel in straightening things up. There are no places for men to fall in. The local reserve is posted too far away and yet there is at present no ground prepared on which they could be comfortably put. I selected a new Headquarters Shelter for myself and gave orders that every rifle shot and bomb from the Turks was to be promptly returned at least tenfold. We can and will beat them at their own game." This was the spirit in which Lieut.-Col. Malone tackled the task of straightening up Quinn's Post and the period from the 9th June, until the end of July, is largely the story of how the Colonel converted the most dangerous and insecure post on the Anzac Position into the safest and most impregnable, and turned a higgledy piggledy collection of battered and insanitary trenches into a clean, well-organized post. In justice to previous garrisons it must be said that timber and iron for trench work were more easily obtainable in June and July, than they had been previously; but, in any case, Colonel Malone had a way of getting things quite his own and was never satisfied to take "No" for an answer.

When the battalion took over Quinn's Post, the Turks had a complete superiority over our men in bomb throwing and sniping, and the front trenches were continually sending back casualties. An extract from Bean's Official History reads as follows:—"At Quinn's on the night of his arrival, Col. Malone caused to be opened up in the front parapet a number of loop-holes which had been closed by previous garrisons. The following day the two companies that were not on front line duty, were employed in what he termed 'tidying' the slope behind the post and in cutting terraces on the sheltered side near the summit. Within a short time, these, neatly roofed with iron and sand bags, made a clean and comfortable bivouac for the supports. Below was headquarters, looking on to a small terrace, on which the Colonel occasionally entertained at tea some of the frequent visitors. On the walls of headquarters were a few pictures and he spoke of obtaining others for his men. If he had had roses, he used to say he would have them planted on the terraces. 'The art of warfare,' he would add 'lies in the culture of the domestic virtues.'"

On the 10th June, West Coast Company and Taranaki Company were relieved in Courtney's Post and, in turn, relieved Hawkes Bay and Ruahine Companies in the front line in Quinn's Post. The battalion remained in Quinn's Post as the garrison until June 18th. During this period, the whole post underwent a complete transformation. The abandoned portion of the front line was gradually recovered. The parapets were repaired and the trench deepened: overhead cover was erected in lengths to the front line to provide bomb proof shelters, and wire-netting on a framework was placed in position in front of our front line trenches to catch and throw back the Turkish bombs intended for the front line. It proved most effective for this purpose, the bombs catching in it and rolling back into No Man's Land and exploding harmlessly there. Proper terraced shelters for the supporting companies with overhead cover were constructed on the rearward slopes of the hill. Wide paths were dug to enable the supporting troops to get rapidly about the position and definite alarm posts

THE WELLINGTON REGIMENT

were allotted to all troops forming the garrison. Frequent practices by day in forming up on their respective alarm posts familiarized the garrison with problems involved in the defence of the post. These practice alarms were usually held about dusk and Colonel Malone took a delight in timing the various units in getting into position and getting one battalion to create a record for another to beat. The period of garrison duty in Quinn's Post was eight days alternating with eight days of nominal rest in Brigade reserve in Canterbury Gully. Actually the duties in the trenches were less arduous than the duties in rest. The battalion or the battalions in reserve furnished very large fatigue parties for work on the beach and for construction work under the supervision of the Engineers both by day and by night and these fatigues commenced immediately the battalion arrived in reserve.

At the beginning of June, the heat by day became oppressive. All ranks reduced their clothing to a minimum. Discarding tunics, a shirt and shorts became the accepted uniform for the trenches. With the advent of hot weather, flies made their appearance in swarms and the sick rate in most Regiments began to mount at an alarming rate. The most prevalent trouble was an epidemic in the nature of dysentery, medical opinion differing as to whether it was true dysentery or merely diarrhoea arising from unsuitable diet. Very few individuals who had been a few weeks in Gallipoli escaped this infection. However, the policy of the Medical Corps and the inclination of the officers and men themselves was to keep on duty to the last possible moment. No one would go sick or allow himself to be evacuated sick unless he were very near the collapsing point. The direct effect of this epidemic on the troops was that their physical condition became greatly lowered. Men lost weight rapidly, and became thin and gaunt. Despite all the sickness, no change was made in the diet of bully beef, usually very salty, biscuit and thin apricot jam. A few issues of bread were made, but these soon ceased. Assisted by the heat and dust in the trenches and by the

THE WELLINGTON REGIMENT

fact that the scarcity of water made it impossible to wash clothes or bodies, vermin spread among the troops. The only chance of a wash was by getting leave to visit the beach for a swim. Owing to the large number of men constantly on duty, this was not easy to arrange and as it meant a hot and dusty walk of a mile or more men soon lost the desire to undergo the exertion. No provision, such as later obtained in France, existed for the purpose of de-lousing the men's clothing.

On the 15th June, Lieut. McColl and twenty-five selected other ranks proceeded to the Island of Imbros to act as Body Guard to Sir Ian Hamilton at his headquarters there, returning to Anzac on the 30th June. They thoroughly appreciated the rest and change and the kindly interest displayed in their welfare by General Hamilton.

On 7th July, Lieut. Jardine had been wounded by a bomb in the leg and was evacuated to Lemnos. A few days later, Major Brunt (Taranaki Company) was evacuated with acute pneumonia and, though he eventually recovered, he was never fit enough to return to the post and was invalided back to New Zealand.

On 15th July, Major W. H. Cunningham, temporarily commanding the battalion, was invalided to Lemnos and the command of the battalion passed temporarily to Major E. P. Cox, while Lieut. Carrington and Wells were wounded and sent to Hospital.

On 2nd August, Major Cunningham returned to duty and resumed command of the battalion and Lieut. Jardine also returned from Hospital. A few days later, namely, on 5th August, the battalion was finally relieved in Quinn's Post by part of the 2nd Australian Light Horse Brigade and moved into Happy Valley, immediately north of Walker's Ridge, where it was to remain till the offensive operations which had been planned commenced, thus ended the battalion's occupation of a memorable post which in the history of the Gallipoli campaign will always be associated with the name of Lieut.-Col. Malone, under whose guidance and organizing force it passed from being a source of anxiety to its garrison to being a position of rest and quiet.

During June and July, both the Turks and ourselves went in for mining and counter-mining at Quinn's Post. The position lent itself to this uncomfortable type of warfare, each side occupying a slope of the hill. The mining was done by a special mining company drawn from various units and composed of men who had been miners in civil life. It was difficult and dangerous work and there was always the feeling of uncertainty as to which side really had the upper hand or rather the lowest tunnel. On the 30th July, about 4 a.m., the Turks fired a huge mine about ten yards in front of our fire trench and beyond our defensive mine gallery. It blew the earth above it right over all our trenches on to the terraces where the supporting troops bivouaced. The descending lumps of earth and debris killed 4 men and wounded 8 in the support lines, but no one was hurt in the front line. An attack by the Turks following the explosion of the mine was expected and an immediate stand to arms was ordered but no attack came. The men were cool and steady despite the alarming explosion and Johnny Turk would have got a hot reception had he attempted to leave his trenches. During the two months the Turks fired 3 or 4 mines, while we fired no less than twenty-eight. On handing over the command of Quinn's Post, Lieut.-Col. Malone resumed command of the battalion and Major W. H. Cunningham undertook the duties of 2nd in command.

CHAPTER VIII.

August Operations and Chunuk Bair.

Outline of the Scheme and Preparations—The Special Part assigned the Battalion—Happy Valley—The Night of the 6/7th — The day of the 7th and the Night of the 7/8th— The 8th August.

AFTER the second Battle of Krithia, 6-8th May, it became apparent to Sir Ian Hamilton that, without very considerable reinforcement, the enterprise of forcing the Dardenelles by a land force was doomed to failure and a withdrawal from the Peninsula, with its bad effect on British prestige in the east, would become inevitable. The War Council in London was anxious to see the campaign made decisive and as a result of communications from Sir Ian Hamilton detailing the situation on the Peninsula he was, early in June, promised three fresh divisions and later in the month another two divisions, making five, the new forces to be available for operations on the Peninsula by the end of July and the 1st week in August. As soon as he was assured by the War Council of the new troops Sir Ian Hamilton set to work to formulate his plans. Ever since the first week's fighting had developed into trench warfare both at Anzac and Helles, the higher commanders had devoted much thought to the problem of making further substantial progress towards the main objective, still so far away. At Helles very little prospect offered except to "hammer away" at the Turkish positions until something gave way. Every advantage was with the Turk and "hammering away" had proved mighty costly and

THE WELLINGTON REGIMENT

never more so than in an attack in strength on June 10th. Other alternatives were a landing at Bulair or on the Asiatic Coast. At Anzac, General Birdwood and his Chief of Staff had been busily working out a plan for an advance from the Anzac position to capture the heights of "Sari Bair" on the main ridge overlooking the narrows and affording a position from which the Turkish communications to the south both by land and sea, could be successfully cut. As Sir Ian Hamilton says in his despatch of the 11th December, 1915, "the Australians and New Zealanders had rooted themselves in very near to the vitals of the enemy. By their tenacity and courage they still held open the doorway from which one strong thrust forward might give us command of the narrows."

A great deal of reconnaissance work had been done by scouts from the mounted troops from Anzac towards the Sari Bair heights during June and July, and the positions definitely occupied by the Turks were fairly accurately known. The Turks were reported to have no continuous line on those heights but apparently were content to occupy outpost positions on all commanding points and had the approaches to the heights up the various gullies also well picqueted. To open the way for the main attack it was necessary that these forward positions should be first seized so that the attacking columns could enter the gullies leading to the main Ridge.

Sir Ian Hamilton finally decided to use his fresh Divisions. First to reinforce the Australian and New Zealand Army Corps, so as to enable that Corps to push out from the old Anzac position and to attack the heights of the Sari Bair Ridge. The crest line of this ridge ran parallel with the sea and its occupation would give command over the Turkish line of communications running south to Helles and would enfilade the Turkish lines facing Anzac.

Secondly to effect a surprise landing with a force at Sulva Bay in conjunction with the attack on the Sari Bair Ridge and to use this force to push rapidly inland to assist the progress of the main attack from Anzac.

The plans for the operations from Anzac were left to Lieutenant-General W. R. Birdwood, commanding the Anzac Corps, who was allotted the following reinforcements:—
13th Division
1 Brigade 10th Division
29th Infantry Brigade
Certain additional artillery and transport

The extremely difficult nature of the ground, over which the proposed attack on the Sari Bair Heights was to be carried out, was early recognized by General Birdwood and his staff. Three narrow and steep gullies lead at intervals from the foot of the ridge towards the summit. That nearest Anzac was known as the Sazli Beit Dere, then came the Chailak Dere and, further north, ran the Aghyl Dere, leading towards the highest point of the Ridge Koja Chemere Tepe. The entrance to the gullies was commanded by features on either side, which were known from the reports of scouts to be occupied in some strength by the Turks. As a necessary preliminary to an advance against the Heights, it was essential that the lower features commanding the entrances to the gullies should be captured and held. In view of the narrow and difficult approaches leading to the Ridge of Sari Bair, it was also necessary that the attacking force should be divided so that all three routes could be used. General Birdwood's detailed plan therefore provided for two main assaulting columns, the right to approach the Ridge via the Sazli Beit Dere and the Chailak Dere, and the left to use the Aghyl Dere. Each of these assaulting columns was to be preceded by a covering force, whose task was to seize and hold the ground covering the entrances to the gullies and so to clear the way for the assaulting columns and cover the rear and flanks of the columns after they had entered the gullies. In order to give occupation to the Turks in front of the Anzac position and to distract his attention from the operation and to attract his local reserves at the critical moment to another part of the line a demonstration was to be made by the Australian Division from the right central sector against the Lone Pine Trench, which was a vital spot in the Turkish lines. An attack in force against Baby 700 from the Nek on Walker's Ridge was also planned to coincide with the capture of Chunuk Bair. The attack on Lone Pine though regarded as a demonstration was very carefully planned and in the event was most determinedly carried out by the 1st Australian Infantry Brigade. It not only wrested from the enemy a portion of his trench system of vital importance to his line, but drew towards Lone Pine the whole of the enemy's local reserves and inflicted on him exceptionally heavy losses.

For the assault on the Sari Bair Ridge the columns were detailed as follows:—
Right Covering Force to seize Table Top, old No.3 Outpost and Bauchop's Hill, thus opening up Salzi Beit Dere and Chailak Dere:—
 The New Zealand Mounted Rifles Brigade including the Otago Mounted Rifles.
 The Maori Contingent
 The Field Troop New Zealand Engineers
Under the Command of Brigadier-General A. H. Russell.
Right Assaulting Column to seize the ridge at Chunuk Bair:—
 The New Zealand Infantry Brigade
 Indian Mountain Battery (less 1 section)
 1st Field Company New Zealand Engineers
The Left Covering force to march along the flat ground and seize Damakjelik Bair and to assist in covering the right flank of the force landing at Suvla Bay:—
 4th Battalion South Wales Borders
 5th Battalion Wiltshire Regiment
 Half 72nd Field Company
Under Brigadier-General J. H. Travers.
Left Assaulting Column under Brigadier-General H. V. Cox:—
 29th Indian Infantry Brigade
 4th Australian Infantry Brigade
 Indian Mountain Battery (less 1 section)
 2nd Field Company New Zealand Engineers

This Column was to proceed up the Aghyl Dere to the assault of Koja Cheme Tepe and to occupy a line from Koja Cheme Tepe to connect with the right assaulting column towards Chunuk Bair.

The attack at Lone Pine was timed to commence at 5.30 p.m. on the afternoon of the 6th August, while the covering forces were timed to move on at 8.30 p.m. By this arrangement, the Turks would have committed a number of their reserves to the Lone Pine fight long before they would have received any warning of the impending attack on the Sari Bair Heights. In the Right Assaulting Column the Canterbury Battalion had been detailed to proceed by the Sazli Beit Dere to attack Rhododendron Spur from the west and thence to advance on Chunuk Bair. The Otago Battalion was to proceed by the Chailak Dere and to attack Rhododendron Spur from the north-west and then supported by the Wellington Battalion to proceed to the assault of the Chunuk Bair Ridge. Auckland Battalion was to follow Wellington in Brigade reserve.

The day of August 6th, was spent very quietly in Happy Valley. All movement was forbidden, no fires were permitted, and the day which was beautifully fine was spent in quiet rest, many seizing the opportunity to write letters home. The impending operations were discussed at a Conference of Company Commanders with the Commanding Officer. White patches for the backs and bands for the arms were issued to all ranks to be worn in the attack on Chunuk Bair. The Battalion was well up to strength. The men, the greater number of whom had seen considerable fighting on the Peninsula, were pleased at the prospect of a change from the dust and flies of the Anzac trenches and its wearing routine. Physically the majority were far from fit and at least 30 per cent., who had been suffering for weeks from the prevalent dysentery, were more ready for hospital than an offensive operation. However, Anzac spirit carried them on and, in fact, the news of the projected attack had brought back from Lemnos a number of men who were still far from well but who scorned to remain in hospital while their Regiments were going into attack.

At 8.30 p.m. the battalion quietly assembled in Happy Valley preparatory to moving out to its appointed place in the right assaulting column. Each man carried 48 hours rations, two water-bottles, and 120 rounds of ammunition. The night was clear and fresh and cool, making movement a pleasant reaction after our day of enforced inactivity. The battalion took its place in the column in rear of Otago Battalion immediately it was reported that the Otago Battalion was clear of Happy Valley.

The route lay along the new Long Sap past No. 2 Outpost to the mouth of the Chailak Dere. Lieut.-Col. Malone moved with the foremost company, Major Cunningham being with the Machine-Gun section in the rear. Progress was very slow and there were frequent long delays due to the difficulty experienced by the Right Covering Column in opening up the mouth of the Chailak Dere which it found blocked by a heavy barbed wire entanglement, flanked and enfiladed by fire trenches on the spurs on either side. With the assistance of a section of the Field Troop of New Zealand Engineers, who displayed great dash and bravery in face of heavy fire, the obstruction was removed and the mouth of the Chailak Dere opened and the covering force pushed on to complete the capture of its objectives, Table Top and Bauchop's Hill, the two features flanking the Chailak Dere, up which it was impossible to move until these two features were firmly held by our troops. It was expected that all would have been clear for the assaulting column to move up the Chailak Dere by 11 p.m.; but it was past midnight before word came for the battalion to move from the shelter of No. 2 Outpost, where it had been waiting for close on two hours, and to press on up the Chailak Dere. The Otago Battalion which had preceded the Wellington Battalion was expected to clear the country on either side of the Chailak Dere as it pressed forward, so as to ensure the passage of the Wellington Battalion, which, as soon as it debouched from the Chailak Dere on to the lower slopes of the Sari Bair Ridge, was to proceed to take the summit by assault. The task of clearing the passage up the Chailak Dere proved a longer and more difficult one than had been anticipated. Scattered parties of Turks, sheltering in the scrub and quite familiar with the ground, opened fire on the advancing infantry, frequently throwing the leading troops into confusion. The Dere itself, as it ascended towards the hill, grew gradually narrower, steeper and more broken, in places it being extremely difficult for one man at a time to push through the narrow defile. In addition, many subsidiary gullies and ravines led off it, making for confusion and delay in selecting the right track up which to advance. The Wellington Battalion found the precious minutes after midnight rapidly passing, while it was obviously far from approaching the ground from which it expected to launch the assault on Chunuk Bair.

After midnight, the chill air struck the lightly clad men and at every halt there was not lacking ample proof of the extent to which the prevailing epidemic of dysentery had its grip on the force. Lieut.-Col. Malone, at the head of the battalion, after nearly two hours had been spent in traversing a few hundred yards, began to chafe at the delay, realising that, once daylight came, all chance of successfully surprising the Turkish troops on the summit of Chunuk Bair would be gone. He used every means in his power to expedite the advance, but one man could do little to assist the progress of a battalion now strung out in single file pushing its way up the mile long bed of the Dere past the boulders and overhanging foliage. It was just breaking dawn when the leading companies of the battalion, Taranaki and Ruahine, got clear of the Dere and debouched on to Rhododendron Spur in the vicinity of the position afterwards known as the Apex. With quick soldierly instinct, Lieut.-Col. Malone recognised that he was still a long way from the summit of Sari Bair where by the operation orders he was timed to be within assaulting distance at 2.30 a.m. and that the original scheme to seize the summit under cover of darkness had failed. It would be broad daylight before the whole battalion was clear of the Chailak Dere and, meantime, the Spur which he had now reached with its semicircular rim appeared to offer a position worth securing as a jumping-off place for a further advance, and with the edge held would enable reorganisation to be effected. The Spur formed a shallow basin which appeared to afford cover from view and from fire from the summit where Turkish observers could now be plainly seen silhouetted against the growing light. The three leading companies were ordered on to the ridge to take up outpost positions covering the exit from the Dere and the fourth Company was held in reserve. The Auckland Battalion arrived shortly after the outpost dispositions were completed and took up a position lower down the Spur under cover of the outposts thrown out by the Wellington Regiment. By six o'clock, the Apex position was thoroughly secure and the men seized the opportunity of the lull in operations to scramble a little breakfast. During the forward advance, the Otago Battalion had become very scattered, isolated parties picqueting various ridges flanking the upper parts of the Chailak Dere. Shortly after daylight small parties of the Canterbury Regiment filtered across from the Sazli Beit Dere to the Apex position, but, as any movement from the Sazli Beit Dere to the Apex immediately drew machine-gun fire and shrapnel, the troops on the Apex were ignorant of exactly what fate had befallen the Canterbury Regiment. Shortly after six o'clock, the position was that two battalions of the Brigade were intact on the Apex position, Otago Battalion were scattered amongst the ridges surrounding the Chailak Dere, while Canterbury were apparently pinned down on the eastern slopes of Rhododendron Spur. The long and tedious journey up the Dere and the long night without rest or sleep had told on the troops in their low physical condition and they were tired and weary men who settled down on the Apex position at 6 a.m. Shortly after Col. Malone had picqueted the ridge, a British officer and a party of Ghurkas from the left assaulting column appeared from the direction of the farm and conferred with him. No signs of the advance of the left assaulting column were then visible from the Apex, from which a good view was obtainable.

When the men of the Auckland Battalion debouched on to the Rhododendron Spur, they still had their white patches and armlets on and the Turkish observers, clearly visible on Chunuk Bair, must quickly have concluded that a formidable thrust was in progress against that part of the ridge. Although the troops in some exposed part of the Spur offered a tempting target, the Turks on Chunuk Bair did not commence firing at the Apex until a couple of hours later. It is just possible that Chunuk Bair at that time was very lightly held and the Turks refrained purposely from attracting our attention to the weak state of their defences there. No regular trench line existed but merely here and there on the seaward crests short lengths of trench for observation post. There was a chance that, had the Wellington Regiment advanced with Auckland in close support, the ridge of Chunuk Bair might have fallen an easy prey into our hands. On the other hand, the night's operations had lasted long enough to have convinced all ranks that the original scheme had underestimated the appalling difficulties of the country: that the progress of the assaulting columns had been much delayed, and that the movements of the attacking troops now required co-ordinating. Units were hopelessly out of touch with one another and there was little information available for anyone, even for the staff. Great faith had been pinned to the anticipated rapid advance of the Suvla Bay force which was to take the pressure off and assist the progress of the Centre at Sari Bair. Earlier experiences on Gallipoli had warned commanders of the danger of isolated attacks on the Turks with flanks in the air, and weighing all the possibilities, Col. Malone took it upon himself to occupy the Apex position. Major Temperley, the Brigade Major, arrived as companies were getting into position and was anxious for Col. Malone to push on with

THE WELLINGTON REGIMENT

the attack, as Otago and Canterbury were, apparently, too scattered and out of touch as a result of the night's operations to effectively carry out the assault. Col. Malone held the view that much had been gained and, while the chance offered, it was better now that daylight had intervened that what had been gained should be secured. The heights were within easy assaulting distance, but the troops were tired and weary and in no mood for a rapid advance in broad daylight up a steep hillside. About 8 o'clock, Brigadier-General Johnson arrived and there was a conference between him and Cols. Malone and Young. Neither the Brigadier nor his battalion commanders were optimistic at that hour of the chances of a successful assault against Chunuk Bair. The approach from the Apex was along a narrow saddle with steep sides, fully exposed to enfilade fire from the main ridge. Chunuk Bair, by that hour, was occupied in some force by the enemy. Sniping and machine-gun fire had commenced and casualties were constantly occurring among the troops on the hillside. However, the matter was referred to the Divisional Commander, who ordered an immediate assault. The Auckland Battalion was detailed for this operation, to be supported by two companies of Canterbury, and, at 11 a.m., it moved out through the outpost line.

Immediately the leading troops debouched from the Apex, they were met by a withering fire from Chunuk Bair, where the Turks were in force with rifles and machine-guns. With magnificient bravery, platoon after platoon pushed on across that fire swept saddle; but the advance finally came to rest in an enemy trench about 200 yards from the Apex leading up from the valley of the farm below, which the New Zealanders immediately occupied. It soon became evident that no further progress could be made in daylight and the rest of the day passed with the position on the Apex unchanged. As soon as it was dusk the outpost companies on the Apex were ordered to dig in. The ground proved most difficult. It was full of boulders and to obtain a depth of a few feet involved tremendous exertion. However, by midnight, a trench line had been constructed, the machine-guns were distributed along the trench, and the Battalion, with sentry groups on duty, endeavoured to settle down for a few hours' rest.

About 1 a.m. the Brigade Commander sent for Lieut.-Col. Malone and gave orders that the battalion was to attack Chunuk Bair at 4.15 a.m. and that the attack would be preceded by a heavy bombardment of the enemy position on the ridge lasting three-quarters of an hour from 3.30 to 4.15. The advance of the battalion was to be timed so as to reach as near to the crest as the shelling would permit before the bombardment ceased. The 7th Gloucester Regiment, which during the night had moved up the Chailak Dere and was lying in rear of the Wellington Battalion, was to move out in line with the Wellington Battalion and attack on the left, prolonging the line towards hill 971. After returning from Brigade Headquarters, Lieut.-Col. Malone conferred with his second in command, Major Cunningham, and the necessary orders were drawn up for the attack. West Coast Company on the left, and Hawkes Bay on the right were to lead the advance, supported by Taranaki right and Ruahine left. The leading companies were to leave the Apex at 4 a.m., giving fifteen minutes to cover the distance to the summit. The question of water rations and ammunition was discussed and, leaving Major Cunningham to go round and give the Company Commanders the neccessary orders, Lieut.-Col. Malone returned to Brigade Headquarters to endeavour to obtain a supply of water and ammunition before his battalion moved out. With soldierly instinct, he foresaw the next day's heavy fighting beneath a pitiless sun with water bottles empty and ammunition short. A party was immediately despatched to the beach to see what could be done. Col. Malone never felt the slightest doubt about his battalion taking the heights of Chunuk Bair, but he was anxious about his men's rations and ammunition supply. When he received the report that his Company Commanders had received their orders he realized nothing further could be done and turned in to his bivouac

THE WELLINGTON REGIMENT

under an oilsheet and slept soundly. At 3.30 a.m., he and his second in command proceeded to rouse the companies to ensure their moving out to time. Weary with 36 hours' incessant fighting and their night's heavy digging, the men were difficult to rouse and on the steep scrub covered hillsides it was a hard task in the dim moonlight to get companies out of their sheltered trenches and the battalion formed up.

Within a minute or two of 4 a.m., the leading companies in a solid phalanx, each company with two platoons in fours in line moved out along the narrow causeway or saddle leading from the Apex towards Chunuk Bair, whose ominous crest line was sharply defined in the faint light. The two supporting companies, Taranaki and Ruahine, followed close on the heels of West Coast and Hawkes Bay. Two companies of the 7th Gloucesters followed some distance behind the Wellington Regiment, having experienced difficulty in getting clear of the Chailak Dere. The battalion passed through the Auckland Regiment, where it lay in the old Turkish Trench reached on the previous day, and Col. Young gave a cheerful greeting to his old battalion as it passed over the trench in which he had his headquarters. The leading companies quickly assumed a fighting formation as they reached the open ground of the slopes leading up to Chunuk Bair, the leading platoons of each company forming up in two lines covering a frontage of 200 yards. This formation was reached without slackening the steady pace of the advance and the battalion, with grim determination, breasted the last rise, expecting every second to receive the full blast of rifle and machine-gun fire which had greeted the Auckland Battalion's advance the day before. Bayonets, however, fixed on the move before the crest was reached and, tired and weary though the men had been when they started from the Apex, instinctively, the battalion seemed to feel that at last the great chance had come and that Chunuk Bair was to be its supreme test. The men in a few strides had recovered their old jaunty spirit of the training days of Egypt and, led by their gallant

THE WELLINGTON REGIMENT

Colonel, they were in the right mood to tackle with cold steel any enemy that might stand to face them on the top. Incredible as it may seem, they braced themselves for a shock that never came. As they reached the crest, the leading lines of West Coast Company quickly over ran and captured a Turkish Piquet covering in a small trench overlooking the farm. Not another Turk was on the hill top and not a shot was fired at the attacking lines as they came over the top and moved forward down the eastern slope where they were halted. Col. Malone had most definite orders to take and hold the crest and, realizing that the precious crest was in his possession without a fight, he quickly ordered the two leading companies to dig a trench on the forward slope of the hill, while the two supporting companies were set to work on a support line in rear of the crest. West Coast and Hawkes Bay Companies placed four covering parties (two parties each) out in front of the digging lines. The two West Coast posts were in charge of Lieut. McKinnon and were located in old Turkish gunpits well down the forward slope. The Hawkes Bay Posts found similar positions in line with the front of West Coast.

By this time dawn had broken and visibility was increasing. A long sap was visible going down from the gunpits occupied by the covering parties and disappearing beyond. After Col. Malone had set the lines digging, Major Cunningham went round the forward posts and walked out some distance in front of them. Everything was perfectly peaceful and there was no sign of a Turk anywhere. Passing along the lines, it was quite evident that the digging on Chunuk Bair was no easier than it had been on the Apex and the same stoney conditions obtained. From the lines on the forward slope the narrows were plainly visible in the distance. Battalion Headquarters were established in the small straight trench which the Turks had occupied as an observation post on the seaward slope of Chunuk Bair overlooking the farm and near a very precipitous portion of the hillside. For quite an hour scarcely a shot was fired at the battalion and it was difficult to realize that the position had been gained without firing a shot. It was as uncanny as it was unexpected.

An explanation of how the Turkish position came to be deserted at the very hour chosen for the Wellington Battalion to attack it is suggested in Bean's Official History of Australia in the War Vol. II at page 669. The Turkish troops who had fought there so valiantly on the 7th, had, during the night or during the shelling, fled in panic or else had been withdrawn by mistake. There was at least an hour of comparative calm before the Turks were fully alive to the danger which threatened their line. This hour was pregnant with possibilities for the attacking force had communications with the Brigade and the Division been established and the success exploited. The very unexpectedness of the situation left Col. Malone very doubtful as to whether to risk disobeying the very clear and definite orders he had received to take and hold the crest at all costs and to push further forward with the idea of penetrating in to the enemies' rear lines, or to seize the precious period of apparent calm to get underground. After some hesitation, he chose the latter course. Had he made an isolated attack with his battalion with both flanks in the air, there was serious risk that he might be entirely cut off and overwhelmed. It would have been necessary for fresh troops to have been at hand at once to be pushed in behind him to ensure the gap being widened, and with the confusion of the previous day's fighting still unremedied, few battalions were in a condition to afford support to a rapid and unexpected advance. From the terrific Turkish attacks which ensued within an hour or so, it was quite evident that the Turks were in great strength in the vicinity and this fact renders all the more inexplicable that peculiar chance which enabled the Wellington Battalion to stumble in the dark into the only gap that had been left in the Turkish line.

No provision seems to have been made in the order for the advance to provide reliable communication with Brigade Headquarters. Later in the day, the Brigade Signal section, at great sacrifice, succeeded in getting a telephone wire from

THE WELLINGTON REGIMENT

Brigade Headquarters to Battalion Headquarters on Chunuk Bair, but, had wire been available, this valuable adjunct could have been installed at 4.15 a.m. and the Brigadier at once informed of the happenings on the heights. Had the Wellington Regiment reached the heights of Chunuk Bair twenty-four hours earlier, as was intended by the original operation order, with the Auckland Battalion then fresh and close behind it, and with Otago and Canterbury Battalions still full of fight, it is easy to see what a splendid opportunity the New Zealand Brigade would then have had of opening the way to the capture of the hill 971 and of assisting the forward movement of the Indian Brigade on its immediate left. But fate willed otherwise and, once more, Sir Ian Hamilton was out of luck. In the appalling country over which the attack took place it was only too easy for the advance to lose momentum. Again looking back to the fateful hours between 4 a.m. and 6 a.m. on the 8th August, when Chunuk Bair rested peacefully in our hands, a gap in the enemy's front was then open which offered a brilliant opportunity for a commander on the spot to seize. The Welsh pioneers, the Gloucester Regiment, and the Auckland Regiment were all handy; but the precious hours passed and the gap was finally and effectively closed, without any effort being made to exploit the success already gained. It was going on for 6 a.m. when the covering parties of the West Coast Company perceived Turks making their way along the sap leading out of the valley behind Chunuk Bair, and fire was very soon opened on these somewhat isolated posts. About the same time, more of the enemy appeared further along the ridge towards the old Anzac position and opened an enfilade fire on the digging lines.

The enemy attack gradually thickened and soon the advanced posts were subjected to a withering fire and, in addition, the Turks, creeping up in the dead ground, began to throw bombs. Most of the men in the posts were soon killed or wounded, with the exception of Lieutenant McKinnon and one or two men who, when all chance of holding out had passed, managed to escape back to the front line. The wounded men in the advanced posts were captured by the

Lieut.-Col. W. H. Cunningham D.S.O.

Corpl. L. W. Andrew, V.C.

A few hours after taking Rhododendron Spur.—Wellington, N.Z., Mounteds charging over the hill to reinforce New Zealand Infantry on Chunak Bair, Sunday, August 8th, 1915.

After the Landing.

Colonel Malone at Quinn's Post.

THE WELLINGTON REGIMENT

Turks and those who survived their wounds and the hardships of life in Turkey remained prisoners of war until they were released in 1919.

While the covering posts were fighting hard, the digging parties in the front line were forced to discard their spades and picks and pick up their rifles and defend the partly dug front line. Unfortunately this was not more than 1ft. 6in. to 2ft 6in. in depth. The stony ground had proved stubborn digging and the men were forced to defend this shallow trench as best they could against frontal and enfilade fire, realising how important it was to maintain possession of the forward slope with its view over the enemy's approaches and rear areas. With the onset of the Turks in force about 6.30 a.m. began one of the most intense infantry fights in the whole War. Clinging to their shallow trench until it was filled with dead and dying, the men of the Wellington Regiment fought like tigers to hold what they had gained. Fighting was not confined to the front line, for the supporting trench, which was only partly dug, also came under fire from the Turkish trenches on Battleship Hill. As soon as the front line was no longer tenable, the few unwounded survivors found their way back to the seaward slope among the supporting line. The attacking lines of the Turks, with the greatest bravery imaginable, surged towards the crest only to be met whenever they appeared with well directed volleys which took a heavy toll of their numbers and sent them reeling back behind the Crest again. In the intervals, men in any position they could find scraped hard with their entrenching tools to obtain a little shelter from the deadly and incessant rifle fire which enfiladed them from the direction of Battleship Hill. Casualties were numerous and ammunition began to get short. The pouches of the dead and wounded were carefully emptied and the ammunition saved. An attempt was made by the Battalion Machine-gun Officer to get the machine-guns into action, but the attempt was fruitless, the gun being disabled before it could be brought into action at all. As the morning wore on, the fighting became more stubborn. At least six times the Turks charged in the hope of carrying the Crest; but each time they were sent reeling back with deadly volleys from the defenders' rifles. Finding this method of attack could not succeed, the Turks tried bombing. Showers of egg bombs, fortunately with long fuses, were sent hurled over the hill crest among the defenders. Promptly and fearlessly were they picked up and hurled back to explode among the Turks.

Towards mid-day the Turkish attack had spent itself; but a fresh trial awaited the hard-pressed men of the Regiment on the exposed slopes of Chunuk Bair. A Turkish battery from the Anzac position started to shell the seaward slope with shrapnel. For at least two hours, salvoes perfectly timed burst over the slopes. One gun devoted its attention to the short trench in which Battalion Headquarters was located and in which at least three badly wounded officers, Major Cox, Lieut. Turnbull and the commanding officer of the Gloucester Regiment were sheltering. Shells burst just in front of the trench, the shrapnel bullets sweeping across it. The Gloucester Colonel raising himself during a temporary lull in the shelling to shift his cramped position, put his head above the trench and the next shell, bursting before he could get down, he got a ball through the cheek.

During this shelling, the Auckland Mounted Regiment made a gallant advance and reinforced the battalion, Major Schofield, who was in command, joined Col. Malone in the Headquarters trench.

Towards 5 p.m., the shelling seemed to have ceased and Lieutenant-Colonel Malone and Major Schofield stood up together in the trench with the idea of looking over the ground and deciding the dispositions of the troops to be maintained during the night and where the men of the Auckland Regiment might most profitably be employed. Just at this moment, the Turk fired his last salvo and the gallant Colonel fell with a ball through the head while Colonel Schofield received a ball through the lung. Throughout that long and arduous day, Lieut.-Col Malone had fought with his men and none knew better what a magnificent fight they had

THE WELLINGTON REGIMENT

put up. Armed only with an entrenching tool, he had, time after time, dashed in among the firing lines when the Turks threatened to break through, encouraging his men with his words and example. He was firmly resolved that the Regiment would rather perish than yield the hill.

As the day wore on, the rearward slopes of the hill were strewn with the dead, but the spirit of the survivors became more stubborn and unyielding. Their ranks thinned as the day waned and evening came with the little band of survivors still undaunted, still holding on, but hungry and thirsty and half-dead with the fatigue and the strain of the ordeal through which they had passed.

On the left, the Gloucester Battalion suffered during the day as heavily as the Wellington Regiment, losing all their officers and many of their senior N.C.O.'s, but still clung to the piece of crest they had seized in the early morning.

During the forenoon, the Brigade signal section had made several gallant attempts to establish telephonic communication between Brigade Headquarters at the Apex and Battalion Headquarters on Chunuk, and, finally, Lance-Corporal Bassett, displaying great bravery, successfully ran the gauntlet of machine-gun and rifle fire and got a line through intact. For his gallantry on this occasion, Lance-Corporal Bassett was awarded the Victoria Cross. The line, however, was difficult to maintain and was repeatedly cut by bullets, and, finally the attempt to keep it open had to be abandoned.

About 3 p.m., Lieutenant-Colonel Malone had despatched Captain E. S. Harston to Brigade Headquarters with a full report on the position of Chunuk Bair and with an urgent appeal for reinforcements. Captain Harston, a noted athlete, made short work of the deadly belt of bullet swept around between Chunuk Bair and the Apex and safely reached Brigade Headquarters, where he gave the Brigadier a full report of the happenings on Chunuk Bair. He was successful in returning to Battalion Headquarters within an hour and delivering the Brigadier's assurance that, immediately it was dusk, strong reinforcements would reach the Battalion. The realisation that our men had the summit of Chunuk Bair had spread through the Anzac Forces and had everywhere stimulated the troops.

Upon the death of Lieut.-Colonel Malone, the command of the Battalion devolved upon Major W. H. Cunningham and, Major Schofield being seriously wounded, the command of the Auckland Mounted Rifles devolved upon Captain Wood. Both these officers were in the Headquarters trench and, the firing having lulled considerably, they left the trench to reconnoitre the position and fix the dispositions to be maintained during the hours of darkness. Within a few minutes of leaving the trench and while standing together discussing the positions, both Major Cunningham and Captain Wood were seriously wounded by the same bullet. Captain Wood's right arm was badly shattered, and Major Cunningham returned to Battalion Headquarters and handed over command of the Battalion to Captain Harston who was acting as adjutant. By this time, it was growing dusk and a welcome reinforcement in the Otago Battalion commenced to arrive. The first company to reach the firing line was in charge of Major George Mitchell, and the rest of the battalion followed very closely.

As darkness settled on Chunuk Bair, numbers of seriously wounded men, who had been unable to move during daylight on account of the heavy fire, began to make their way down the hill to the dressing station. The stretcher-bearers came out from the Apex position and, working magnificently all night, were able to remove a great number of wounded too badly hit to walk. Before midnight, the remnants of the Wellington Regiment were relieved in the front line and returned to the Apex position.

Colonel Malone had been killed and also Captain L. S. McLernon, Commanding Hawkes Bay Company, Lieutenants T. M. P. Grace and T. A. Davidson, while scores of gallant men had been struck down.

THE WELLINGTON REGIMENT

Sir Ian Hamilton has written:—"I lay a very special stress on the deeds of Bauchop and Malone. These two heroes were killed whilst leading their men with absolute contempt of danger—Bauchop after having captured what was afterwards known as Bauchop's Hill, and Malone on the very summit of Chunuk Bair. Both Bauchop and Malone were soldiers of great mark and, above all, fearless leaders of men. Where so many, living longer, have achieved distinction, it is quite necessary that New Zealand should bear the names of these two gallant soldiers in tender remembrance."

During the night, the Turks massed behind Sari Bair. At dawn, the 6th Royal North Lancashires and 5th Wiltshires, now holding the ridge, were wiped out. Very shortly afterwards, the Turks delivered a tremendous counter-attack down the slopes of Chunuk Bair directed towards the British Battalions on the left of the Apex. On came the attacking waves. Canterbury had four machine-guns while Auckland were able to bring two guns into action. From Rhododendron Spur two Wellington machine-guns, the Maori gun and one Otago gun, firing over the heads of the guns on the Apex, commanded the whole of the approaches from Chunuk Bair. What a harvest of death for our machine-gunners! The Navy and Field Artillery picked up the range. Not a Turk could pass through such a zone of death. Wave after wave was mowed down. It was not long before the Turkish effort was spent. Later in the day, a number of Turks were seen to crawl back to their own lines.

During the afternoon, the New Zealand Infantry Brigade was relieved and English troops took over the Apex, with New Zealand machine-gunners behind them and behind them again the depleted New Zealand Battalions. A night of confusion followed. Next morning the New Zealanders were sent into the front line again with Auckland on the Apex with orders from Sir Ian Hamilton to "hold on for ever."

THE WELLINGTON REGIMENT

CHAPTER IX.

Rhododendron Spur—Cheshire Ridge.

INTO the welter of the 8th August, the 5th Reinforcements had been plunged. Not many of them survived.

The Regiment was but a shattered remnant now as it bivouacked on the side of Cheshire Ridge. Including the additions from the 5th Reinforcements, West Coast Company numbered only 51 instead of its full strength of 227. Other companies were in similar plight.

Water was very scarce and the daily ration was one quart. If we drank it, we could not wash; but we were not fussy about our personal appearance these days. Nearly everyone had grown a beard. There were no company cooks and everyone had to do his own cooking. At dusk, we would go into the partly formed trenches on Chesire Ridge and remain there until daylight. We had not only to be on the alert for an attack from the Turks but to widen and deepen the trench at the same time. The days in the trenches were hellish. The heat of the sun was terrific. Diarrhoea and dysentry were rampant. Flies were a torment. Splendid fellows of a few months ago were little more than scarecrows. We were but hanging on now. There were spells in the front line at Rhododendron Spur or at the Apex varied with days in reserve in Rhododendron Gully. It was all deadly monotonous. Everyone now had dysentery and was fast reaching the limit of physical endurance. They were indeed grim days.

There comes an end to all things. The long wished for spell had come at last. On the 14th September, the remnants of the New Zealand Infantry Brigade staggered down to Anzac Cove. The distance actually was probably not more than a mile; but, with full packs up, in our weakened condition it seemed a terribly long way to the beach. Barges were waiting there to take us out to the "Osmanich," which was boarded about midnight. No accommodation was provided for us on this vessel and we spent the night, which was very wet, lying on the iron decks with no shelter from the weather. On the following morning we sailed for Lemnos, and, on arrival there, went into Camp at Mudros West after another trying march, which may not have been half as long as it seemed. We probably cut off more than a mile by wading across an arm of the harbour. If we had not been able to take this short cut, few would have had the strength to reach the Camp site that night, as we could hardly drag ourselves along. There were many halts. After resting for a while, it was difficult for men to regain their feet and many fellows were too weak to do so and spent the night by the wayside.

CHAPTER X.
Lemnos.

AT Lemnos, no accommodation was ready for us and we had to bivouac out in the open. There was another Mediterranean downpour during the night and, as there was no shelter, it was pretty miserable. A few tents reached us next day and we were able to make ourselves more comfortable.

The first morning at Lemnos we were awakened by cocks crowing in the village some distance away. For a few moments one almost imagined one was back at home and that the past few months had been but a dream.

The battalion, which, normally, should have had a strength of 880 men, and with the five reinforcements it had received, should have tallied over 1000, had been reduced to less than 100 by the time it left the Peninsula. Companies had scarcely more than 20 men.

There was new bread, fresh meat and fresh eggs. For the first few days we did little more than eat and sleep. There was an ample supply of milk. What would have been given for it on the Peninsula? How many tins of bully beef would have bartered for one tin of milk? Grapes and tomatoes were plentiful and a few pence would buy a hatful of small but very sweet grapes. Very soon everyone began to feel better.

At the end of September, the 6th Reinforcements arrived. The old hands rather looked down upon them. One had to be a Main Body man in those days. It was all very different afterwards.

Life went on pleasantly enough through October and into November. During this time a number of sick and wounded rejoined and, with the reinforcements, the battalion reached about half strength.

Our faces were soon to be turned towards Anzac again. and on 8th November the New Zealand Infantry Brigade embarked once more for the Peninsula.

CHAPTER XI.

The Last Six Weeks on the Peninsula.

CONDITIONS on Gallipoli were now vastly different, and there was not the same hardships as before. The weather was very much cooler. There was no longer the unbearable heat of August. With the heat had gone the flies. No longer was every moment of the day a torment from flies. True, the lice were no less active than before and all spare time was devoted to the search for these vermin.

Proper dug-outs had by now been built and nearly all trench construction work had been completed, so that "resting" was not such hard work as before. All the main saps had been widened and protected from enemy observation and fire, and a road had been formed along the beach parallel to the old main sap which had been widened to five feet. In August, the main sap had been only three feet wide and, as it had to take all the traffic including the pack mules with supplies, progress through it was not easy. The dug-outs now afforded reasonable cover from shell fire. In the earlier days, dugouts had been only shallow excavations made with entrenching tools after the pattern of graves with oiled sheets stretched across the top to keep the sun out. There was now a greater sense of security, and, although equipment had to be kept on at all times, a certain amount of sleep could be had. To lighten the darkness of dug-outs there was improvised little lamps made out of tobacco tins. In the lids of the tins, holes would be made, through which pieces of rag ran down into a reservoir of reduced bacon fat. The light so produced was effective enough but the smoke was certainly a drawback, and lumps of light soot, almost as big as one's fist, would form and fall every few minutes.

Rifle fire, which before had been a feature, was now not nearly so intense. Gun fire, from our shore batteries and from warships, was still much the same as before and a number of shells were sent over each day. The Turks still shelled as before and with heavier guns; but there was now some protection from their shells. Both sides were content to sit still and watch each other and neither appeared willing to launch an attack. Casualties through wounds and sickness were not a fraction of those in the earlier days; but remainders of the August casualties were always present as in many parts of the newly formed trenches pieces of scrim concealed protruding bodies. Rations were more plentiful and varied and, as there was now plenty of water, we were never thirsty and always comparatively clean.

Tunnelling Operations were being carried on and listening posts constructed in the gully of No Man's Land beyond our wire entanglements. These listening posts were about six feet long by two feet wide and were reached by tunnels from our front line. In order to conceal them from the Turks in the daytime, a fresh branch of scrub was placed over them before daylight each morning.

Things went along quietly and comfortably for a week or two, and we thought we were to stay on over the winter without further fighting. About the middle of December, there was a rumour that another attack was to be made on Hill 971. As this hill had been strongly fortified during the past two months, the idea was not relished. A day or two later, however, there was another rumour, this time that the Peninsula was to be evacuated.

Shortly after our return to Anzac, Lord Kitchener had visited the Peninsula. We saw little of him, although some of our men down by the pier near Walker's Ridge caught a glimpse of him. Doubtless, the decision to evacuate the Peninsula was confirmed by Lord Kitchener at this visit.

Already there had been little snow and it was said that, in any event, our position would have become untenable when the January rains set in, as our trenches would have been washed away by the rush of water from the hills. Our position at the Apex was the farthest inland and, as we had about two miles to travel to the jetty at Walker's Ridge, we could easily be cut off at any point on the way, which for the most part ran parallel to the Turkish position. At some parts of the line there were only a few yards between the Turkish trenches and our own and our chances of getting away seemed pretty slim.

CHAPTER XII.

Evacuation of Gallipoli.

The Evacuation—Lemnos—Christmas Day, 1915—
Alexandria—Moascar—Suez Canal Defences.

THE rumours that the forces were to be withdrawn from the Peninsula which had been current for some time, were finally verified. On the 15th December, 1915, when General Godley issued his now famous Army Corps Order No. 21 to his subordinate commanders that orders had been received by him for the re-embarkation of the Army Corps and its transfer to Mudros.

The news reached the Regiment, of course, first through the Divisional Orders emanating from the Corps Order, and all officers and men were acquainted with the news.

The success that attended that great enterprise is well known. How 19,940 souls were evacuated from the confined area occupied by them in two days without the enemy having the faintest suspicion of the movement will ever be recorded as one of the best executed tactical movements of the whole War.

Every man from the Commander himself to the private soldier had, during those anxious hours, a grave responsibility, and every individual accomplished his task as befitted the men who held the line at Gallipoli.

The Wellington Battalion was at the Apex with Ruahine and Taranaki Companies in front line and Wellington-West Coast and Hawke's Bay Companies in the reserve trenches. In order to keep the information from the Turk, orders had been issued to keep the condition of affairs apparently normal.

THE WELLINGTON REGIMENT

On the 17th, the day preceding the first day of the retirement, all ammunition, bombs and trench stores not actually in the trenches were buried. Nothing was burned in case of attracting the Turks' attention. To the occupants of the Apex a huge fire of stores on the beach near the North Pier was visible. It began at 2 a.m. in the morning of the 18th and caused some concern lest it should alarm or inform the enemy of what was going on. At 8.50 p.m. of this day one officer and 44 other ranks left the battalion sector for the beach, where, at 11.30 p.m., they embarked on a lighter.

The next party to move was the Wellington-West Coast Company and the balance of Hawke's Bay Company, totalling three officers and 131 other ranks. They left the reserve trenches at 10.45 p.m. and embarked at midnight. On the second day of the evacuation the enemy registered our reserve trenches with some heavy artillery. It was, perhaps, the 8th Austrian Battery, of which information had been obtained from a deserter. The registering took the form of a very heavy bombardment, and the reserve trenches, which had only been vacated a few hours, were badly knocked about. That night the battalion completed its part of the evacuation. At 5.30 p.m., the first party of three officers and 92 other ranks left the Apex: at 9.15 p.m., the next party of three officers and 76 other ranks moved off, and the third and last party, consisting of eight officers and 59 other ranks, left at 2.10 a.m. on the 20th December. During the evacuation on the second day, men were detailed to walk rapidly along the trenches and fire rifles and throw bombs from different positions to mislead the enemy into believing that normal occupation of the trenches prevailed. The night of the 19th was beautiful—no wind to trouble the sea, and moonlight made the difficult and delicate task easier.

The evacuation was accomplished without casualty of any sort. It seemed that, whether from a high sense of duty or a great longing to be quit of the place, every man obeyed the special message that General Godley sent him on the 17th. The first two paragraphs of the message, written by General Godley himself and characteristic of the confidence he reposed in his Australasian troops, reads as follows:—

THE WELLINGTON REGIMENT

"1. The Army Corps Commander wishes all ranks of your Division to be now informed of the operations that are about to take place and a message conveyed to them from him to say that he deliberately takes them into his confidence, trusting to their discretion and high soldierly qualities to carry out a task, the success of which will largely depend on their individual efforts.

If every man makes up his mind that he will leave the trenches quietly when his turn comes and see that everybody else does the same, and that up to that time he will carry on as usual, there will be no difficulty of any kind and the Army Corps Commander relies on the good sense and proved trustworthiness of every man of the Corps to ensure that this is done."

The transports conveying the battalion proceeded at once to Mudros East and the battalion reassembled and camped at Lemnos.

The next day an advance party left Lemnos for Alexandria and on the 24th and 25th the rest of the battalion left by the "Simla" for Alexandria. Thanks to the Australian troops on board and to the ship's commissariat, Christmas was a day of cheer. For eight months the troops had been living on hard food with generally something a bit short of full ration. The food, if it could generally be described as wholesome, was uninviting. On board every man was treated to a feast for Christmas with Christmas pudding included. Spirits of troops move like mercury and already the troops, who for so long had become inured to a hard, cheerless life, showed in their animation a new outlook and fresh hopes.

For three days the troopship journeyed to Alexandria, and on arrival at port the troops were held on board another twenty-four hours before they were entrained for Moascar, near Cairo.

On arrival at Moascar, the battalion went into camps consisting of hutments. The battalion became a unit in the Canal defences, and it may be appropriate here to explain the nature

THE WELLINGTON REGIMENT

of the defence falling to the lot of the Army Corps. The defence of the Canal consisted of three lines to the East of the Suez Canal. These lines were known as the Front Line, the Intermediate Line and the Inner Line respectively. The Front Line consisted of a series of strong points sufficiently close to each other to cover each other's position with effective rifle fire. These points ran in a straight line about 11,000 yards East of the Canal. The line included all important points from which observed fire could be directed upon the Canal and would suffice to prevent interference by shell fire with the traffic. The Second or Intermediate Line was about 4,500 yards in the rear and approximately parallel to the Front Line. It was sufficiently in advance of the Canal to prevent effective enemy shelling, though from its position it surrendered many points whence the enemy could observe movement on the Canal. The Third, or Inner Line, ran along the Canal and consisted largely of the old defences which had already been used against the Turk by our troops before the Gallipoli campaign.

The lines were not continuous and were defended by garrisons varying in number from a battalion to a brigade. The garrisons were supplied with as many machine guns and as much artillery as possible so that each garrison could meet any enveloping attack from the enemy. While the primary object of the situation was passive defence, the garrisons were so situated as to enable other troops to advance between the points in attack on the enemy or in counter attack and to receive full assistance from the neighbouring defended points. Each garrison entrenched itself either by continuous line of trench sufficiently long to take all the troops of the garrison or in a series of shorter trenches with communicating saps to enable the whole garrison to move about under cover. This class of defence was formulated mainly on the assumption that the enemy, coming from a distance over the desert and having, accordingly, an attenuated line of communication and unable to carry much artillery or water, would have to carry out an attack, to be successful, covering only a few days.

THE WELLINGTON REGIMENT

The attack, never really expected, did not come while the New Zealand Division was in Egypt and the troops were able, therefore, to settle down to a system of training which, based on the experience of the fighting in France, proved of incalculable service later on when the troops took their place in the line in France and Belgium.

The Battalion rested in camp until the 1st January, 1916, when the whole of the brigade shifted camp to a point a half mile further west of the camp they were occupying at Moascar.

The different companies of the Wellington Regiment, as, indeed, of all the units of New Zealand troops which had been to Gallipoli, was decimated through casualties of all classes, and it was impossible without reinforcements to carry out any systematic training of much use. On the 8th January, 1916, however, seven officers and 266 other ranks, comprising the Wellington quota from the Seventh Reinforcements, were taken on the strength and the reorganisation of the battalion was at once set in hand. When the reinforcements had been allotted to their respective companies, it was then possible to start a programme of training.

THE WELLINGTON REGIMENT

CHAPTER XIII.

Formation of the New Zealand Division.

Birth of the Second Battalion—Further Training in Egypt.

BY February, 1916, it was reasonably certain that New Zealand would be able to organise a full Division, and, with reasonable casualties, be able to keep it at full strength. For reasons both practical and political, it was decided, therefore, to raise a Division.

The old battalion retained its individuality and became the 1st Battalion of the Wellington Regiment and one of the battalions of the first Brigade. The other battalions of that Brigade were the old battalions from Auckland, Canterbury and Otago. To form the 2nd Brigade certain officers and non-commissioned officers were drafted as a nucleus of the unit. Though none were willing to give up the associations made on the slopes of Gallipoli to help knock into shape a lot of new-comers, to the credit of the Commanding Officers, only officers and N.C.O.'s of ability were sent to the new unit. At that time, many officers as well as N.C.O.'s were away sick, and were returning at irregular intervals. On their return, until the 2nd Battalions were fully officered, these were drafted to them. During the strenuous days of training in Egypt there was a certain amount of acrimony between new soldiers and those of Gallipoli fame. While for the time it may have caused personal distress, yet it seemed to have the effect of instilling into both sections a spirit of enthusiasm,

THE WELLINGTON REGIMENT

bringing with it a determination to show that the newcomers were as good soldiers as the old hands, while the old hands took care to prevent the newcomers showing any superiority in drill and efficiency. With the passing days and under the violence of shell fire and sharing the same difficulties and privations with the opportunity of helping each other, in France this acrimony rapidly disappeared, and there existed only a friendly rivalry between fighting units, with never a whisper of bitterness or jealousy. To the Commanding Officers much credit is due for the complete understanding between the units, for they arranged parades together and the men frequently shared messes, sports meetings, and the idea of the Regimental spirit was inculcated into all ranks. Time proved that of all the Regiments in the Division for efficiency, whether discipline, or actual fighting, the Wellington Regiment was second to none.

One thing that helped to weld into one Regiment the two battalions was that both old and new had to learn a lot in their training that they had not heard of before. The new reinforcements had only the incomplete New Zealand training, while the old hands found that the fighting in France had brought about a new type of training. Officers and non-commissioned officers from the Guards Regiment, who had been rendered unfit for active service in France, were sent to train the troops in Egypt in the latest ways of circumventing the German and the training at the Officers' schools by one-eyed and one-armed soldiers of the "Old Contemptibles" laid a basis for the reputation that the New Zealand Division was afterwards to win in France. Undoubtedly there is no better soldier than the regular British soldier, and he is trained with a true appreciation of loyalty, and the need for systematic and modern training. It may be that, outwardly, the manner of the regular officer was at first misunderstood by the Colonial, but his worth was soon ascertained.

The dark nights of Egypt were used for the purpose of practising night marches and marching by the compass and stars. It was more often than not that the officer leading the unit would go a little astray in his directing, and the two

THE WELLINGTON REGIMENT

units destined for the same spot in the lonely desert would not meet. Officers were given as much technical instruction as possible; but the needs were changing so often in France and new devices were appearing every month or so that it was inevitable that the training in Egypt was found to need bringing up to date when the troops reached France. One thing it did, however, was to make every man who took part in the training as fit as it was possible to make him.

The hot days followed by the cold Egyptian night, and the camping on the sands of the desert took their toll of the men in dysentery and enteritis; but, apart from this, there was little sickness. The original steps taken to combat venereal disease were most effective, and the intelligence of the men in addition to their being well occupied, prevented their falling into the dangers that still beset them.

After the formation of the 2nd Infantry Brigade and on arrival of the Division in France the officers of the 1st and 2nd Battalions of the Wellington Regiment were as follows:

1st BATTALION.

Officer Commanding: Lieut.-Col. H. E. Hart, D.S.O.; Second in Command: Major C. F. D. Cook; Adjutant: Capt. A. B. McColl; Quartermaster: Lieut. J. T. Dallinger; Lewis Machine-gun Officer: Lieut. D. W. Curham; Transport Officer: Lieut. L. H. Bailey; Hon. Bandmaster: Hon. 2nd Lt. W. E. McLeod.

COMPANY COMMANDERS AND SECONDS IN COMMAND.

Wellington-West Coast: 1. Capt. W. F. Narbey; 2. Capt. H. S. Tremewan.
Hawkes Bay: 1. Capt. M. McDonnell; 2. Capt. R. F. Gambrill.
Taranaki: 1. Capt. C. H. Weston; 2. Capt. A. H. Carington.
Ruahine: 1. Major Fleming Ross; 2. Capt. J. S. Mackay.

THE WELLINGTON REGIMENT

1st BATTALION.

MAJOR: F. Ross.

CAPTAINS: C. H. Weston, W. F. Narbey, A. H. Carrington, A. S. T. Butler, J. S. Mackay, R. F. Gambrill, H. S. Tremewan, R. W. Wrightson, V. R. Bond.

SUBALTERNS: F. K. Turnbull, K. Munro, F. S. Varnham, A. B. Sievwright, C. E. Reid, G. W. Henderson, T. C. A. Hislop, A. S. Muir, L. H. Bailey, C. B. Lockyer, G. H. Fell, E. Morgan, A. H. Preston, G. G. Guthrie, C. A. Bicknell, A. S. Judd, M. S. Galloway, W. S. Hopkirk, R. Wood, G. L. Malone.

2nd BATTALION.

Officer Commanding: Lieut-Col. W. H. Cunningham; Second in Command: Major W. H. Fletcher; Adjutant: Capt. G. H. Hume; Quartermaster: Lieut. A. A. Browne; Lewis Machine-gun Officer: Lieut. F. C. Chaytor; Transport Officer: Lieut. S. P. Abbott.

COMPANY COMMANDERS AND SECOND IN COMMAND.

Wellington-West Coast: Major D. W. Talbot with Lieut. H. E. McKinnon 2nd in command.

Hawkes Bay: Capt. R. F. C. Scott with Capt. A. V. Webster 2nd in command.

Taranaki Coy.: Capt. M. Urquhart with Capt. F. A. Ruck 2nd in command.

Ruahine Coy.: Capt. G. W. Wardrop with Capt. A. V. Wayte 2nd in command.

SUBALTERNS: L. H. Jardine, W. H. Cannon, C. H. Joplin, J. N. Ranch, J. MacMorran, C. C. Gilbert, E. E. Somervell, G. S. Strack, C. C. Brindsley, B. H. Morison, H. J. D. Sheldon, R. E. W. Riddiford, C. A. L. Treadwell, H. R. Biss, A. T. White, R. H. Espiner, R. H. Quilliam, A. M. Thomson, A. C. Cowie, W. Pollock, F. Percy.

CHAPTER XIV.

Departure for France.

France—Estaires—Armentieres—First Taste of the Trenches—Intensive Shell Fire.

THE 1st Battalion left Moascar Camp on the 6th and 7th April. Hawke's Bay and Wellington-West Coast Companies, leaving camp on the 6th, proceeded by train to Alexandria and embarked on H.M. Troopship "Arcadian." The vessel left port at 6.30 p.m. on the 7th for Marseilles. The balance of the battalion, consisting of the Battalion Headquarters' details, and the Taranaki and Ruahine Companies, marched to Ismailia, entrained to Port Said, and there embarked on H.M. Troopship "Ingoma." The transport details, with horses and wagons, left on the 6th from Alexandria on H.M. Troopship "Eleele."

The 2nd Battalion left on the 8th, entrained for Alexandria and, on the following day, embarked on the two troopships "Knight of the Garter" and "Llandovery Castle," both of which left port on Monday, 10th April. No trouble from enemy submarines hampered the voyage to Marseilles. All precautions were taken against such an eventuality. The guns mounted on the vessels were manned continuously and the troops were instructed in boat and life-belt drill. The voyage across, owing to crowded conditions, made it well-nigh impossible to continue any serious training. The best that could be hoped for was to practise rifle drill and do a little physical training. On the 12th and 13th the troopships "Arcadian" and "Incoma" respectively reached Marseilles, while the "Eleele"

THE WELLINGTON REGIMENT

arrived on the 14th. The 1st Battalion thereupon entrained for the North of France. The troopships containing the 2nd Battalion reached Marseilles on the 18th April and the same day entrained for the British Sector in the North of France. After a short rest and somewhat scrappy training, much interfered with by reorganising units, Battalion orders were received to move into the front line sector and, on the 9th May, the 1st Battalion marched from its billets to Estaires. This was the first time our troops encountered the pavé roads of France and Belgium, and toll was taken from them by causing a good number of the men to fall out on the march. Perhaps the fact was partly to be accounted for by the great shortage of boots, supplies not by any means meeting the insistent demands of the quartermasters. Perhaps the fact might be explained, too, by both battalions possessing a large leaven of raw troops, recent reinforcements who, apart altogether from the question of *esprit de corps*, were too soft physically to stand a march which, even to hardened troops, was a big undertaking. The rounded stones of the pavé were torture to march on, and the only way satisfactorily to cope with them was to have boots sufficiently thick and comfortable to minimise the discomfort. On arrival at the billets, the troops quickly settled down in the places selected for them by the officers who had gone ahead in advance for that purpose. The next day the Commanding Officer and company commanders went up to the front line and inspected the sector which the battalions were about to take over.

The New Zealand Division was now to relieve the 17th Division in front of Armentieres. The relief was carried out according to plan. As the troops entered the area of the 17th Division, they came under that Divisional Commander's orders until the infantry relief was complete. In order to facilitate the relief the New Zealand Division took over all the telephone lines and instruments of the 17th Division and handed that Division its telephone lines and instruments. The New Zealand Division also took over the trench mortars, excepting the Stokes mortars.

THE WELLINGTON REGIMENT

The Division was distributed by the 1st Brigade taking over the right sector, the 2nd Brigade the left sector, while the Rifle Brigade were in divisional reserve. The 1st Brigade had two battalions in the front line and two in reserve, while the four battalions of the 2nd Brigade were in the front line.

To ensure that the relief would be effected without any hitch and so that (on the relief being complete) the troops should be ready for all emergencies, all the officers of the battalions reconnoitred the positions to be relieved, the intelligence officers and the snipers took over their positions two days before the Divisional relief.

On the 12th May, the 1st Battalion moved into the town of Armentieres preparatory to moving into the line the next day. That night they occupied billets in the town where they were quickly recognised as new troops by the large number of French civilians who still remained. Armentieres at that time had suffered very little from hostile gun-fire and was practically intact. The village of Houplines on the outskirts of the town was not so fortunate, and it was largely in ruins when our troops took over the Armentieres sector. In Armentieres there were shops of every description, and these restaurants —run entirely by civilians—found ready patronage from the troops. At Half-past Eleven Square (so-called because the clock on the Town Hall in the Square had been stopped by a shell at that hour), there was always a crowd of civilians to be found. Market Day was observed in the Square of the Notre Dame Church and, in many respects, Armentieres proceeded apparently unperturbed by the fact that it was sitting on the front line dividing friend and foe.

On the 13th May, the relief of the front line took place, the First Brigade taking over the line held by the 51st Infantry Brigade, 1st Wellington relieving the 7th Lincolnshires.

The relief was, of course, carried out in darkness. The battalion began to leave its billets at 8 p.m. and proceeded in companies with an interval of 50 yards between companies.

The relief was completed without incident at 11 p.m. The disposition of the battalion was that the sector was divided into two. The right, or No. 1 locality, also known as Pigot's

THE WELLINGTON REGIMENT

Farm, was held by Wellington-West Coast Company with one platoon, while the left sector (No. 2), called "The Mushroom," was held by Hawke's Bay Company, with two platoons. The balance of these companies comprised the company supports. Ruahine Company was in the right half of the subsidiary line, while the other half Taranaki Company occupied. Battalion headquarters was situated at Chapelle D'Armentieres. The quartermaster's store was at Armentieres, and the transport at the village of Pont de Nieppe, which was two and a-half miles from the town.

The 2nd Battalion reached the town at 4 p.m. on the 14th May, West Coast Company with Taranaki Company moving that night up to the line, the latter taking over the front line with the former in the support trenches. Battalion headquarters, with the remaining two companies, stayed the night in the town.

Next day the whole of the 2nd Battalion took over the portion of the line allotted to it, the relieved battalion being the 9th Duke of Wellington. Both Hawke's Bay Company and Ruahine Company took over front line trenches. The relief was carried out without incident or casualty and in fine weather.

The condition of the trenches made it imperative that they be built up and strengthened. They had been allowed to fall into a condition of disrepair that would never have passed muster by the G.O.C. Division. The work done naturally attracted the curiosity of the enemy, who endeavoured to satisfy his curiosity with shell fire without, fortunately, doing any harm to the new work. Our artillery had been registering on new targets and shelling any movements to an extent apparently out of all proportion to what the enemy had been experiencing for some time at least. On the 17th May he bombarded a locality about 500 yards from 2nd Battalion Headquarters, searching for one of the batteries. The battalion suffered its first casualties as a consequence, two of our men being wounded.

At this time there was a good deal of suspicion that spies were operating behind our lines. A good deal of the suspicion was due to the fact that civilians were living within a few yards of the trenches and the records show that the 2nd Battalion Headquarters' staff noticed pigeons rising about 7 p.m. from the rear of the Headquarters. Pigeons, however, were commonly found in the district during peace time and, no doubt, the novelty of the situation and the proximity of civilians gave rise to many rumours that had no facts to support them.

The troops quickly settled down, rumours became less frequent and the first efforts to obtain superiority in No Man's Land were taken in hand. The Artillery, too, began to assume a habit of shelling, which at first drew on them the concentrated shell fire of the Hun. It was only after many duels that the enemy realised that it paid him better to give up that superiority of shell fire he undoubtedly possessed, and his replies to our bombardments gradually dwindled in comparison.

It is appropriate here to mention how the troops were fed in the line in France. In this respect, it affords a happy contrast to Gallipoli. While, naturally, it was impossible to bring horses and transport up the Battalion Headquarters in the line during daylight, as soon as dusk fell, the quartermaster, who lived in Armentieres and had his store there, despatched the Regimental transport with supplies to the line.

Each quartermaster-sergeant, who lived at the store, also, came up with the stores and reported with them to the company commanders. The food stores were packed in sandbags, each bag containing eight men's rations. The company commanders gave their instructions to the quartermaster-sergeant each evening, and on account of the locality the troops were able to buy luxuries undreamt of on the bare hills of the Dardanelles Peninsula. The only stores not handled by the quartermaster-sergeants were the trench stores. These were relegated to the regimental sergeant-majors, who took them over, supplied them as required and handed them over to reliefs. The convenience of being able to bring stores in the transport within a few hundred yards of Headquarters reduced the arduous task of carrying by men to a minimum. It was characteristic of all commanding officers of the Wellington Regiment that transport and stores were compelled to do everything conceivable so that the troops in the line should be spared as far as possible.

One of the difficult tasks that fell to the 1st Wellington was holding and defending a sharp salient known as "The Mushroom," which jutted into No Man's Land and to within a very few yards of the enemy front line. When this sector was taken over, " The Mushroom " had not been much occupied and its defence rested largely on flank fire from machine-guns posted for the particular purpose. On the 15th May the enemy blew up a good deal of the already imperfect trench line in that salient and, throughout the night, played on the gaps made with his machine-guns. During the shelling, "The Mushroom" was cleared of troops, yet the enemy succeeded in killing one man and wounding five.

Two days later, the 1st Battalion carried out a relief between companies. The relief was held up for a while on account of gas alarms being sounded three times through the night. Gas was a weapon of war that the troops had little or no experience of at the time, and although much literature had been read by the officers and imparted to the troops, and gas drill had been taught and all ranks had been through a gas chamber before entering the trenches, yet it required experience of the real thing to make the troops realise what they had to do in the event of an attack. During the stay in the Armentieres sector there were many false alarms, which can be ascribed to inexperience rather than nerves.

It became manifest to the Germans that new troops of a particularly active kind were in front of them, and they took measures to prevent surprises. In front of the sector taken over by the Wellington Battalions the enemy had six balloons in the air for observation purposes. Our aircraft now began to display fresh activity over the sector and caused many a balloon to descend in haste.

The left flank of the 2nd Battalion, resting on the river bank, was exposed to the view of the enemy from the ruins of Frelingheim, opposite, and also from the other side of the river. The enemy took the opportunity this observation afforded them by shelling the line at the extreme left, trenches 87 and 88 receiving most attention. It was noticeable at that time that the enemy were using either very old shells or their manufacture was very defective. Our own Artillery at the same time were complaining of the poor quality of their ammunition.

In the first days of trench warfare in France, purely through inexperience, our snipers were no match for the enemy; but in a week or two they obtained the mastery over the wily German sniper and thenceforward our snipers could watch and snipe almost with impunity. The mastery was not obtained, however, easily, for the German sniper was a highly trained man with the very best equipment for the purpose. Our equipment at first was, on the contrary, most unsatisfactory: the telescopes were limited in number and the sights for the rifles as well as the Observation Posts were quite inadequate. It reflected the greatest credit on the officers in charge of these snipers for the manner in which they organised their sniping, and, gradually and intrepidly, asserted their superiority over the German.

On the 23rd May, the 2nd Battalion was relieved by the 4th Battalion of the Rifle Brigade. The relief was delayed through the enemy selecting that night for a bombardment of Armentieres. Lieut.-Colonel W. H. Cunningham had resumed command of the battalion. The 1st Battalion had already been relieved by 1st Canterbury and were in billets.

The two battalions, while out of the line, laid down a programme of training, which included the making of wire entanglements, sniping, signalling and bombing. Unfortunately, the programme was never in full operation as demands were made on the companies for large working parties for the trenches, and many guards had to be mounted over bridge-heads, cross-roads and dumps.

The demands for working parties were enormous, and batmen and other ranks such as bootmakers and incidental employees on Headquarters had to do their share in these parties. This was an innovation of which these comparatively privileged persons did not at all approve.

THE WELLINGTON REGIMENT

The whole of the Divisional front concentrated on improving the local defences and, with that end in view, wiring was pushed ahead. Patrols would go out and up to the enemy front line, and, behind these protective troops, the wiring would go on. At first a few enemy patrols were met with, and possession of No Man's Land was contested; but, very soon, the enemy was content to leave that strip of land in possession of our troops. Of course, now and then, when his front line was blown in or his wiring blown away, repairs would be effected; but, on the whole, the enemy refrained from trespassing on land, possession of which had been wrested from him.

On June 1st our troops had their first taste of intensive shell fire. The Germans shelled with all calibre of artillery the sector held by the 1st Battalion, partly concentrating on the front trenches and partly just in rear of Pont Ballot. Retaliation was forthcoming and, after an artillery duel, which had resulted in little damage to us, all was quiet. An incident worth recording was the escape from its anchor of one of our balloons. It was observing from near Pont De Nieppe. The wind was gently blowing over the line towards the enemy. As soon as the balloon broke away, it rapidly ascended, and then steadily drifted over towards No Man's Land. It was clearly lost to us and anxiety was felt for the two observers in the carriage of the balloon. They left it rather late to parachute down; but, as the balloon was passing over our lines, they jumped out and, from the ground, it was impossible to see if they would land on friendly or enemy soil. Luckily, they both landed on the right side. It was characteristic of the Hun's strange sense of sportsmanship that, as soon as the men were seen tossing in the air beneath their parachutes, they opened up seemingly every machine-gun in the area to try and riddle those helpless men. Both sides then opened on the balloon with their artillery, and the "Archies" could be heard popping away and bursting their shells all round the target. The shooting was ineffective: not one hit was recorded and the huge balloon slowly drifted over into enemy country, despite the determined efforts of our and the enemy artillery. The "Archies" were always looked on as almost futile and probably that incident laid the seed for that impression.

It seemed that the Germans were making what proved to be a spasmodic attempt to reassert themselves. The shelling increased. It was at this time that the British won the Battle of Jutland and for ever drove the German Fleet from the sea. Opposite the sector occupied by the 1st Battalion, the German troops hoisted a large board announcing the annihilation of our Fleet, giving figures and boats in detail to lend strength to the lie. The Australians had a battery nearby and shelled the notice. The enemy, in his attempt to assert himself, brought up a powerful high velocity gun, apparently a naval gun, and shelled Armentieres, choosing as a target the dome of Notre Dame Church. The shelling was very accurate, and many of the shells found their allotted billets. Those that missed continued on and hit a large brick building used as a hospital. Owing to the gallantry of the medical orderlies, the casualties were, happily, very small.

CHAPTER XV.

Patrols and Raids — Death of Capt. A. B. McColl — Gas Attacks—The Enemy Raids "The Mushroom" — The Australians Raid at Fleurbaix — We are Relieved at Armentieres.

NEITHER battalion took part in any active hostilities during the first fortnight of June, and it was not until the 19th that a partol of eight men under Lieutenant Sheldon, of the 2nd Battalion, carried out a reconnaissance opposite the breakwater for the purpose of ascertaining the strength of the enemy opposite and the manner in which the front line was held. The patrol party ascertained, on approaching the line, that there was a large working party of the enemy working on the wire. The patrol quietly withdrew. The information was sent back to the Artillery, and an intense bombardment was opened up on the enemy front line for a few minutes. The enemy wire was badly damaged, and it was noticeable that there was little retaliation from the enemy artillery and for a long time no attempt was made to repair the barbed wire.

On the night of the 16th June, the artillery in rear of the 2nd Battalion opened an intense bombardment on the enemy's position, concentrating largely on the waterworks. Guns of all calibre took part in the bombardment, which started about 11.15 p.m. Captain Alley had trained a special party to raid the enemy's trenches, bring back prisoners and get what information it could. After the bombardment had lifted the party left trench 88, Bay 3 found the wire uncut and cut it.

On the night of the 1st July, a highly successful raid was carried out by a raiding party, selected from the 1st Battalion,

THE WELLINGTON REGIMENT

under the command of Captain A. B. McColl. The party consisted of four officers and 77 other ranks, and the objective was a certain portion of the enemy's front line trenches. The night was dark and the weather was fine. The main raiding party was preceded by selected scouts, who moved out through Sally Port. Immediately it was dark enough, and, shortly before midnight, two of the scouts returned to lead out the remainder of the raiding party to a selected position in No Man's Land. As soon as the raiding party had taken up its position an artillery and medium trench mortar bombardment commenced, which lasted for twenty minutes. The artillery barrage then shifted, the medium trench mortar ceased, and an artillery barrage formed a semi-circular or box barrage around the area to be assaulted. The wire had been faithfully cut by the artillery, and it was necessary merely to cut away the loose wire. The party rushed forward and met with no opposition at all. All the enemy who had not been killed were found crouching in shelters under the parapet of the front line, and these were either sent back to our line as prisoners or killed if they refused to move. After staying eight minutes in the trenches, at a given signal, the whole party withdrew to our lines.

The enemy, meantime, bombarded No Man's Land heavily. Captain A. B. McColl returned with the party; but went back to help some streacher-bearers, who had got into difficulties in a ditch near our parapet. Having assisted them, he was severely wounded by machine-gun fire, as he was climbing over the parapet, and died before reaching a dressing station.

By the death of Captain A. B. McColl, we lost a very brave and gallant officer. He had been for some time Adjutant of the 1st Battalion, and, by his tact and genial disposition, had succeeded in maintaining an efficiency in the administration of the battalion not surpassed by any other. To use the language of Lieut.-Col. C. H. Weston, D.S.O., in his book entitled "Three Years with the New Zealanders," Captain McColl "was a great big handsome fellow. Although in years only a boy with a big man's heart, I fancy he loved the excitement of a fight. I had seen him a few minutes before they

THE WELLINGTON REGIMENT

went into No Man's Land, and as usual a joke bubbled out of him. Any of us that knew McColl will carry to the end the memory of a very gallant gentleman.''

The information gained by this raiding party was considerable. Definite information of the class of barbed wire erected in front, the manner in which it was erected and its effectiveness as an entanglement were ascertained. It was likewise ascertained that there were no dugouts under the parapet—there were merely shallow shelters.

The engineer who accompanied the raiders, on a large bomb store being found guarded by iron doors, blew the doors in and destroyed the store. A pumping station for keeping the trenches habitable was likewise destroyed. An officer who had been taken prisoner, and from whom it was hoped information would be gleaned, refused to cross No Man's Land and had, accordingly, to be shot. The time of the raid synchronised, apparently, with the change-over in the enemy lines, for the troops captured had their packs on their backs, and were due to move out. A number of valuable documents were found and much information obtained of the troops in the locality. It was noticed, on this occasion, that the use of steel helmets was not by any means universal with the Germans. None were found by the raiders—only spiked helmets and caps.

Lieutenant H. Espiner, of the 2nd Battalion, led a small party, followed shortly by Captain Alley and the main party, into No Man's Land. Before the party could penetrate the trenches, both Captain Alley and Lieutenant Espiner were seriously wounded and Lieutenant A. T. White, although wounded himself, led the whole party into the enemy trenches. Half of the party went to the right and the other half to the left. After staying in the enemy trenches for about an hour, the party returned to our lines, bringing back all the wounded and much booty.

The enemy retaliated with Minenwerfers, concentrating on trenches 86 and 87. Our trenches were practically levelled. Much information was gained by the party. The names of the regiments opposite were ascertained, and many of the prisoners gave valuable information to the Intelligence officers at Army Corps Headquarters.

The battalion suffered in casualties—1 officer killed, two wounded and 99 other ranks wounded.

The day following the 1st Battalion's raid, the 2nd Battalion carried out another raid. The party of four officers and 104 other ranks was under the command of Lieutenant Sheldon. The object was as usual to reduce the enemy's morale, capture prisoners and gain information. Unhappily, this raid was unsuccessful. During the day our artillery had been particularly active, having fired over 2,000 rounds into the sector. Possibly, this had the effect of warning the enemy to be ready, and it was with almost uncanny precision that they had blocked the trenches, and those members of the raiding party who succeeded in entering the trenches found them vacated. A large proportion of the raiding party, during our preliminary bombardment, had taken up positions in an old drain. The enemy immediately retaliated to our artillery fire and searched the drain with disastrous results. When the artillery lifted, our men advanced, but were immediately met with heavy machine-gun fire from the flanks. The party was compelled to use a gap in the wire only six feet wide, and, as soon as the front enemy trench was gained, the party was heavily bombed. It was necessary to withdraw, and this was rendered extremely difficult on account of the artillery and machine-gun fire. No useful information was gained and our casualties were one officer killed and two wounded, while 11 other ranks were killed and 34 wounded and three missing.

The result of these raids was that the requisites for a successful raid were considered to be (1) a careful selection of the point to be attacked coupled with a thorough reconnaissance both by map and on the ground of the enemy trenches and No Man's Land. (2) Selection of thoroughly reliable officers and men, with enough spare men as emergencies. (3) Adequate training of the party, so that each man knows his work as one of a team. (4) Complete co-operation with the artillery and trench mortars which should be sufficient in volume, and very carefully planned. The artillery should, apart from putting down a barrage, endeavour to locate the artillery opposite and the machine-gun posts, so as to reduce to a minimum the retaliation of the enemy.

By this time the situation had entirely changed. The activity in both sectors opposite our battalions was very different from that prevailing when the New Zealand troops first moved into trenches in France. In July there was almost continuous artillery activity on both sides, raids were of almost nightly occurrence and the enemy was plainly nervous. Our intense activity was part of a plan to keep the German divisions away from the Somme, where the great attack of July 1st was in full swing. On every available occasion the engineers brought up gas cylinders; but as the wind usually blew from the enemy trenches across to ours the cylinders would lie day after day in the front line unused. When, however, the wind was favourable then a gas attack would be made, all helping to upset the enemy opposite, and to keep as large a force as possible in the locality. The effect on our troops was that they were becoming worn and depleted. Nothing, however, was allowed to slacken the aggressive tactics which had been ordered and the New Zealand Division kept up a continuous series of attacks on the enemy front line, causing, as the information gleaned revealed, perturbation among the ranks of the enemy, as well as heavy casualties.

On the 8th July, the enemy made a retaliation against our raids and they selected the vulnerable "Mushroom," which was occupied then by a part of the 1st Battalion. After an intense bombardment about 10 p.m. a party of the enemy rushed out opposite the "Mushroom," but were bombed back. An hour later the enemy bombardment re-commenced, and a large party divided into two attacked "The Mushroom" from both flanks. The 1st Battalion had killed a good number in the garrison in "The Mushroom," and the rest were driven into the second line of trenches. Lieutenant Kibblewhite, N.Z.M.G. Corps, immediately organised a counter-attack; but, before we regained possession of "The Mushroom," the Germans succeeded in carrying away their dead and wounded, although, on account of the sharpness of the encounter, unable to devote any attention to getting information.

The 1st Battalion suffered heavily—two officers and 21 other ranks were killed, while three officers and 88 other ranks were wounded and three other ranks missing.

THE WELLINGTON REGIMENT

On the 14th July, the New Zealand Division was ordered to take over the front then held by the 8th Australian Artillery Brigade. This was preparatory to a large Australian attack in Fleurbaix sector. The New Zealand Division was ordered to be prepared to assist these operations by drawing the enemy artillery fire and by raiding his trenches. Accordingly, on the 16th July, the 2nd Battalion was relieved and moved into a subsidiary line extending from Buterne Farm to Irish Avenue. The battalion was then used until the end of the month for fatigue work. There were from 400 to 450 men working in the trenches, while every available man was sent to the Divisional baths at Pont de Nieppe.

On the 31st July, the Division resumed its original frontage from Pear Tree Farm to the River Lys.

The gallant but disastrous raid of the 8th Australian Brigade at Fleurbaix need not be recorded here.

On the 11th August, Lieutenant-Colonel W. H. Cunningham, who had been absent on sick leave, resumed command of the 2nd Battalion, and, on the same day, the battalion was proud to learn that Company Sergeant-Major William Edward Frost had been awarded the Distinguished Conduct Medal for his gallantry during the raid on the night of the 2nd July. To borrow the language of the Army Orders:

"In No Man's Land in front of trenches 87 and 88 during a raid by a party of the 2nd Wellington Regiment, on the nights of the 2nd and 3rd July, 1916, against the enemy's trenches, Company Sergeant-Major W. E. Frost, Ruahine Company, assisted Second-Lieut. R. E. V. Riddiford to cover the withdrawal of the raiders across No Man's Land to their own trenches. This withdrawal was ncessary owing to enfiladed fire from machine-guns and grenades thrown from enemy support lines. When the withdrawal to their own trenches had been completed, Company Sergeant-Major W. E. Frost twice returned to the company's lines through the enemy wire, and under heavy fire rescued and brought back two wounded men who were lying within a few yards of the enemy's parapet, and so prevented them from being taken prisoners."

THE WELLINGTON REGIMENT

The New Zealand Division was now being withdrawn from Armentieres sector and on the nights of the 15th, 16th, 17th and 18th August, the relief was carried out, the Division concentrating in the Blaringhem area. The 1st Battalion, which at the time was in the line, was relieved on the night of the 15th by the 4th Battalion Seaforth Highlanders, and the battalion took up allotted billets in Armentieres. The next day the battalion marched to Steenwerck and there entrained for Ebblinghem. The 2nd Battalion moved into Armentieres on the early morning of the 17th and next day marched to Steenwerck, there entrained for Ebblinghem, and, a few days later by marching and train, reached the village of Airaines, where the battalion began its training for the coming offensive in the Somme area.

The march of both battalions from the trenches revealed how the soft mud of the trenches, inactivity and the impossibility of active exercise, had undermined the strength of the troops.

The 2nd Battalion had the misfortnue to carry their packs on their backs, and the number of stragglers was large. That number would necessarily have been considerable even had provision been made for the men's packs to be carried by transport. It was, therefore, not surprising that many men failed to keep up with the column, and had to fall out and receive medical treatment. The ambulances were filled in a few hours by men willing enough to march but physically incapable of doing so.

The chiropodists attached to each battalion had been kept busy during the months in the line attending to the men's feet and coping with the incipient stages of trench feet. It was remarkable how successful these men became in treating their comrades.

The march along the hard pavé roads, in boots in many cases badly fitting or in bad repair, accentuated the position, and the chiropodists were kept busy for many days after the troops had reached their billets in dressing open sores on the men's feet.

CHAPTER XVI.

We Go Back to Train for the Somme--Fricourt and Airaines.

IN comfortable billets away from the harassing conditions of trench warfare, we rapidly recovered our good spirits.

A company in attack was practised as soon as the men were fit, and bayonet fighting and lectures on every phase of warfare formed part of the daily routine.

The reinforcements coming forward were soon absorbed.

While the 1st and 2nd Battalions were in Fricourt and Airaines respectively a good deal was done to foster the spirit of the Regiment. Church parades were arranged at which the battalions attended altogether, and, at such parades, battalions vied with each other as to their turn-out. In a few weeks an excellent regimental spirit prevailed in both battalions and small differences which had existed rapidly disappeared, so that we no longer looked upon ourselves simply as members of one or other of the two battalions, but as part of the Wellington Regiment.

The effect of the continuous trench warfare on the troops and the long route marching to Airaines and Fricourt was soon dissipated as all ranks found themselves living in comparatively congenial circumstances without the nerve-racking shell fire, without the muddy trenches, without the early morning stand-to and without the thousand and one other little details of life in the front line trenches.

The importance of getting every available man fit again was now paramount. Every effort was made to ensure a complete and rapid recovery to health of all ranks who had shown any signs of ill-health.

The rationing of the troops in Fricourt and Airaines was improved in every way possible. We voluntarily added to

THE WELLINGTON REGIMENT

the funds available contributions towards buying food outside the schedule of ordinary Army rations, with the result that green vegetables and delicacies not dreamt of since our arrival in France appeared daily on the menu. The effect was not only physical but psychological. Staleness gave way to cheerfulness and optimism, and reinforcements filling up the depleted ranks soon brought up the strength of the two battalions. For the first week or so it was found impossible to do much training; but at the end of that time both battalions spent the day-time in acquiring the latest knowledge of warfare and in making all ranks as efficient as possible.

We remained at Fricourt and Airaines until 2nd September, 1916. During that time route marches were frequent, and everything was done to produce soldiers of a maximum efficiency and in perfect health.

Morale improved wonderfully. Apart from the perfect discipline that prevailed in both battalions, enthusiasm caused everyone to do his respective work to the best of his ability.

CHAPTER XVII.

The March to the Somme—The Battle of the Somme —New Zealand Division's Share— Flers — Rain, Mud and Slush — Factory Corner — Goose Alley Gird Trench— Eaucourt l'Abbaye.

ON the 2nd September, 1916, the two battalions marched out of their billets for the Somme in great heart and in a state of efficiency never at any time exceeded during the campaign.

The 1st Battalion marched to Allery, a distance of about five miles, going into billets, and next day marched to Belloy, a distance of about twelve miles, passing en route through Airaines, Bourdon and Yseux. It spoke well for the condition of the men on this march that, notwithstanding many had been supplied with new boots, and that, on account of the necessity of keeping the roads clear, it was impossible to halt for lunch, yet very few men fell out of the march.

The next day the 1st Battalion rested and, on 7th September, marched through to Poulainville a distance of about ten miles, and then next day another fifteen miles to a bivouac near Dernancourt.

The 2nd Battalion left Airaines on the early morning of the 2nd September and marched to Cavillon. The next day that battalion marched to Breilly-sur-Somme. Here it was possible to hold a bathing parade, followed by a church parade. The next three days the battalion spent in the same village.

On the 7th September, the 2nd Battalion marched via Bertangles and Cadonette to Rainneville, and next day marched to a bivouac camp next to the 1st Battalion. From this camp the heavy firing of the guns could be heard most

THE WELLINGTON REGIMENT

distinctly and, at night time, the flares of the Very lights on the Somme front could be distinctly seen.

The 2nd Battalion was inspected by Major-General Godley on the morning of the 9th, while the 1st Battalion continued its march to Albert. The 1st Battalion, while in bivouac outside Albert was inspected by General Godley.

The 1st and 2nd Battalions held their last joint church parade prior to the Battle of the Somme on the 10th September, and in the afternoon the battalions independently marched on to Fricourt Wood. General Godley, who was present at the march past, congratulated the 1st Battalion on the magnificent appearance of its transport, remarking that there was no finer transport in the whole of the New Zealand Division.

On the 12th, the 2nd Battalion moved into Carlton and Check trenches. By the 13th the New Zealand Division had taken up its allotted ground preparatory to playing the great part it was destined to play in the Battle of the Somme.

We may here mention shortly the position of the line when we arrived at the Somme. The advance of July had carried the first enemy lines on a broad front, but the attack had failed between Gommecourt and Thiepval causing the anticipated breach in the enemy lines about eight miles short. The second attack of July 14th gave the Army Commander a yet narrower margin from Bazentin Le Petit to Longueval, and it was realised that, if the allied thrust were continued, a sharp and precarious salient might result. It will be remembered that to meet this Sir Douglas Haig broadened the breach by striking both to left and right of Pozières, and ground at Moquet Farm was taken and the outer flank of Guillemont and Ginchy. The result was that the British Front in this locality rested largely on high ground giving direct observation over the lower slopes of the valleys.

As a result of these successes the Germans prepared a strong line of defence and fortified the villages of Courcelette Martinpuich, Flers, Lesboeufs and Morval. Beyond this line of villages lay the fortified posts of Le Sars, Eaucourt L'Abbaye and Gueudecourt with the further line lying West of the Bapaume and Peronne Road.

THE WELLINGTON REGIMENT

Since the battle began in July, the Germans had, up to the second week in September, brought 61 divisions into action on the Somme. Men had been refitted and sent in again and, on the 14th September, the enemy was holding the line with 15 divisions.

Opposite the New Zealand Division, and, indeed, along the whole front about to be attacked a comprehensive bombardment now began stretching from Thiepval to Ginchy.

The 4th Army was to attack under the command of Sir Henry Rawlinson. On the left of the Main Front a Canadian Division had Courcelette as its objective, a Scottish Division had for its task to clear the remains of the old switch line and encircle Martinpuich. The Northumbrian and London Division—two Territorial Divisions—were to clear High Wood, while, immediately on their right, the New Zealand Division had Flers as its objective. Delville Wood lay on the right of the New Zealand Division and two divisions of the new English Army were ordered to take the ground East and North of Delville Wood in immediate line with the New Zealand Division. The Guards Division lay on the right of these divisions.

The New Zealand Division issued its operation orders on the 13th September for the attack that was to take place two days later. Two of the Divisions had been allotted four tanks. Already rumours had spread among the troops that a new engine of war was to be allotted to the Division. No one appreciated what this new machine was capable of, or how precisely it was meant to function, and it was inevitable that, in its first brush with the enemy, it should play a single-handed part until it was seen how it should fare and how best the troops could co-operate with it.

Our 2nd and 3rd Brigades were first to attack, while the 1st Brigade was to be in Divisional reserve. The 2nd Brigade was to attack and capture as its first objective what was called the Green line, while the 3rd Brigade was to go through and capture the remaining objectives which included the formation of a defensive flank facing North-west. The 2nd Brigade assembled with two battalions just forward of Worcester and

THE WELLINGTON REGIMENT

Tea Trenches, while the remaining two battalions occupied Savoy and Carlton Trenches. The 3rd Brigade, to which for the purpose of these operations 2nd Wellington was attached, occupied a certain part of Carlton Trench. Of the 1st Brigade two battalions remained in Mametz Wood and two at Fricourt Wood.

The ground over which the troops were to operate had been shelled first by our own guns in July and later by the enemy guns, so that with the addition of rain it was now a matter of great difficulty to move out into position prior to attack.

On the night of the 14th, all officers inspected the trenches to be occupied, and obtained as good an observation as possible of the locality over which we were to attack. Our own shell fire had become intense from the 12th September, and this was increased into a bombardment on the 15th prior to the advance.

The 1st Battalion on the 14th September was in Carlton Trench in Brigade reserve. The Canterbury Regiment in support of the 2nd Wellington Regiment was ordered to move up.

At 6.20 a.m. (zero hour) on the 15th September, the attack began. The artillery bombardment had been gradually growing more intense and now increased to a degree not comprehended before by our troops. The air seemed full of flying shells and bursting shrapnel, and it appeared some time before the Germans realised that the great attack, which had been foreshadowed, had actually begun. When they did realise this, they placed a barrage along the whole line attacked and along the Switch trench over which our men were advancing.

The 2nd Battalion moved forward from Carlton Trench. Wellington-West Coast Company moved to Dorset and Pear Trenches; Hawke's Bay to Worcester Trench; Taranaki Company to Seaforth Trench and Ruahine Company to Rifles Trench.

By 8.15 a.m., the Brigade had captured its second objective and the companies of the 1st Battalion moved for-

THE WELLINGTON REGIMENT

ward. That battalion had been ordered to be ready to assist the 3rd N.Z. Brigade when they moved forward.

On the afternoon of the 15th 1st Wellington moved forward to Check Trench and took up its position about 1,500 yards north of Montauban. Meantime the 2nd Battalion, at 2 o'clock, moved forward, Battalion Headquarters moving with the last company to the trench in front of Switch Trench, and which was subsequently known as Otago Trench.

Wellington-West Coast Company went through the village of Flers with the Rifle Brigade and occupied the trench in front of the village with Hawke's Bay Company on its left and Taranaki Company in support 100 yards behind. Ruahine Company occupied Flers Trench. Immediately this objective had been taken, all companies dug in. Battalion Headquarters took over a part of Otago Trench and occupied a huge shell hole a few yards in front of the trench, while the runners and others knelt in imperfectly-formed Otago Trench. At this time the shelling from the Germans increased into an intense bombardment. At the bottom of the huge shell hole occupied by Battalion Headquarters lay a huge unexploded shell. The view of the ground in front occupied by the Germans was clear and uninterrupted. At one stage of the bombardment, preparatory to what transpired to be an abortive counter-attack, a full battery of German artillery dashed down a sunken road which debouched at the edge of a small wood, unlimbered the guns and started shelling furiously. It was a brave and gallant action on the part of the German gunners.

Colonel Cunningham immediately tried to telephone to our heavy guns; but all the telephone lines had been broken, and the only way in which to send the information back was by runner. Accordingly, three runners were handed copies of the same note giving information of the battery and map references to where it was located. In about three-quarters of an hour, a battery of our heavy artillery concentrated on the spot, and our heavy shells fell amidst the battery, blowing men and guns to bits. The shelling became too intense, and Battalion Headquarters were moved to a small trench to the right of Switch Trench, called Ferret Trench. A few minutes later, on one of the runners returning, it was found that a German shell had exploded in the hole immediately before occupied by Headquarters, apparently exploding the "dud" lying at the bottom, with the result that the shell hole was now a small crater.

In the afternoon the Germans massed for their counter-attack. On the slopes and undulating country opposite, thousands of Germans could be seen marching, at about eight paces apart, along the front as far as could be seen and for a great depth, slowly advancing to the counter-attack. Our artillery was at once advised, and an intense bombardment of the advancing troops was begun, shrapnel bursting overhead with effective results and, to the amazement of all who watched the approaching attack, it, seemingly, disappeared into thin air. It was noticeable how much more accurate the bursts of our shrapnel were than those of the Germans. Our casualties would have been much heavier in the attack had not the German shrapnel burst too high in the air, and most of the troops experienced the rattle on their steel helmets of shrapnel bullets from a height too great to do any damage, while the heavy 5.9 shells, dropping almost perpendicularly, penetrated into the deep mud at a great distance before exploding; the result being that the explosions were circumscribed in effect and lateral bursts comparatively few.

The 1st Battalion moved up next morning to Flers, but experienced the greatest difficulty on account of the darkness and shell fire and the broken ground, for there had been no opportunity of previously reconnoitring the route.

At 6.30 a.m. the Battalion took up its position on a line from the N.W. end of Flers to Abbaye Road—Flers Trench—Cross Roads.

The 1st Battalion from this position carried out a further advance to improve the position of the two lines and the attack, which was exclusively that of the 1st Battalion, began at 6.30 a.m. Hawke's Bay Company was on the right flank, Ruahine Company on the left with Wellington-West Coast Company in support in Fort Trench and Taranaki Company in reserve in Flers Trench. The enemy counter-attacked with two companies against the Hawke's Bay Company; but was easily repulsed with rifle and machine-gun fire.

No. 1 Machine-gun Company, under Lieutenant Kibblewhite, and the tank, which was moving into position to help the advance of the troops on the Battalion's right, joined in and played an important part in repulsing the enemy. The 1st Battalion then attacked—the two leading companies moving in four waves with two waves from the Wellington-West Coast Company in support behind each of the leading companies. During the attack, the two waves behind Ruahine Company were withdrawn to supporting trench, while the two waves behind the Hawke's Bay Company joined up with that company. The objective was a certain part of Groove Alley, which turned out to be lightly held by the enemy and was taken without resistance.

Shortly after the trench had been taken our right flank was exposed to an attempted attack from the enemy which prevailed for a short time only, and the position was consolidated.

Lieutenant-Colonel Hart, in reporting on the position after its capture, said: "It is considered the enemy's advance just before our attack was an independent attack by them, and this probably accounts for the heavy barrage our men had to cross."

This made our casualties heavy, and we suffered also from machine-gun fire on both flanks.

The two waves of the Wellington-West Coast Company still in support of the Ruahine Company stopped at the support line, a trench running 250 yards behind the front line but ceasing before it reached Ligny Road.

A simultaneous attack on Gird Trench and Guedecourt was to have been made by the 123rd Brigade on our right. They failed to advance although the tank detailed to support this advance moved forward about 300 yards, where it was struck by a shell and abandoned.

The next day the 2nd Battalion was relieved, and moved back to Wood Lane and T Trench in rear of Switch Line.

There was intermittent shelling all the day, and the weather, which had been gradually growing worse, now set in very wet, making the conditions very unpleasant. It was almost impossible to move about without sinking up to one's knees in slush and mud. In spite of this, however, the fatigue parties detailed for bringing up hot food from the cookers at Green Dump, displayed wonderful persistence and succeeded in supplying warm soup to the famished troops.

On the 17th the Germans bombarded Flers heavily and threatened a counter-attack, but the threat did not materialise, except feeble local attacks against the right flank of the 1st Battalion, which were easily repulsed.

As soon as the bombardment ceased, the positions were consolidated and deep trenches dug, ensuring the holding of the ground captured.

To the credit of the battalion signallers, in spite of the fact that the telephone wires were repeatedly broken by shell fire, communication was almost continuously maintained from Battalion Headquarters to Brigade Headquarters until towards the evening of the 17th September, when a heavy bombardment irreparably destroyed the wire. A new wire was run out soon after midnight, and this wire was maintained while the battalion held the position.

The next day, in the afternoon, the 2nd Battalion moved into Flers. Battalion Headquarters took over a deep German dug-out at the junction of the cross roads of the village. Hawke's Bay Company moved out and took over the right sector; Ruahine Company the left, with Taranaki Company and Wellington-West Coast Company in support and reserve respectively.

An enemy strong point was causing a great deal of trouble and some casualties, and as soon as it was dark enough, an attack was made first by one officer and sixteen other ranks. This attack, however, failed on account of the great resistance of the enemy and the exposed ground over which the men had to move. The next day a second attack was again made which again failed. The Germans realised that this strong point was of considerable tactical value to them, and they manned the point in overwhelming force.

THE WELLINGTON REGIMENT

The next day, as already said, the 1st Battalion of the Rifle Brigade relieved 2nd Wellington, which moved back to Wood Lane Trench and Switch Trench.

On the night of the 18th, the 1st Battalion was relieved by the 2nd Battalion, the former moving back to Check Trench. The march was very trying, the track being a sea of mud, more than ankle deep in some places, and owing to this and the darkness, the move took a long time. Ruahine Company was shelled heavily while moving out, and had to disperse, with the result that the whole company was not collected until the following morning. The ground allotted was very muddy and had few waterproof bivouacs. The battalion had the misfortune to lose heavily in officers that day (16th). Major F. Ross, commanding Ruahine Company, 2nd Lieutenants W. Kirkley and S. O. Esam, both of Hawke's Bay Company, and 2nd Lieutenant L. W. Meuli, of Wellington-West Coast Company, being all killed in action. Captain H. S. Tremewan and Lieutenant R. H. Dodson died of wounds, while Major C. H. Weston and 2nd Lieutenants M. S. Galloway and A. R. McIsaac were wounded but stayed with their battalion. At this time the casualties of the 1st Battalion were 10 officers and 282 other ranks. The strength of the Battalion when it went into action on the 15th September was 25 officers and 784 other ranks.

The 2nd Battalion, having moved into Flers, set about improving the trenches and making them habitable. The work was, however, fraught with difficulties. The shelling, although intermittent, was very heavy at times. The enemy knew all the roads and routes that, of necessity, the battalion had to use. These he shelled, making communication between companies and Battalion Headquarters difficult. The weather played its part in making the lot of the troops difficult. Heavy rain with intense cold made work by day and night most difficult. To the great credit of the battalion transport, however, the men in the line on the night Flers was occupied by the Battalion were supplied with a hot meal. At that time, 2nd Lieutenant R. E. W. Riddiford commanded the battalion transport, and, in spite of the fact that the road had been shelled out of recognition, and was still being shelled, and notwithstanding the extreme difficult of bringing horses and transport through the muddy track at Delville Wood and Flers, as soon as darkness supervened, this gallant officer with the grit and determination, a sample of which he had given in Armentieres, led safely into the village and drew up at Battalion Headquarters the transport with the rations. Having unloaded he imperturbably led the transport back again.

There was no doubt that the officers had learnt their part well in the operations on the Somme. With great accuracy each learnt the position of the troops on the flanks. On one occasion this proved most useful. A runner from the left flank burst into Battalion Headquarters that his battalion was being heavily shelled and an enemy attack was expected momentarily and the bomb supply was exhausted. Colonel Cunningham immediately sent forward a carrying party and rushed 750 bombs to our comrades.

On the night of the 21st, the 1st Battalion of the Rifle Brigade relieved 2nd Wellington, which returned to Wood Lane and Switch Trench. The troops, although they had been heavily engaged for six days were, no doubt by their clear superiority over the enemy, in high spirits, and bore the difficulties with composure.

To assist in an attack by the whole of the 1st Brigade the battalion moved up on the 24th September to Flers Trench and Flers Support Trench as reserve for the brigade. The next morning the brigade attacked, having as its objective Factory Corner, North Road to Flers Trench. The attack was carried out with characteristic elan and the enemy was quickly overcome. All objectives were taken. As soon as these objectives were secured, 1st Otago took Goose Alley, extending to Abbaye Road. The situation now became somewhat obscure, and it reflected much credit upon Colonel Hart, commanding the 1st Battalion and his Company Commanders that they were able to appreciate the situation sufficiently accurately to enable them to realise that the Brigade Headquarters was not properly seized of the position when an attack was ordered. The movements of the 1st Battalion are interesting at this juncture. After the successful attack by

Lieut.-Col. C. H. Weston, D.S.O., V.D.

THE WELLINGTON REGIMENT

the whole Brigade on the 25th September, Taranaki Company moved up and to the left in support of an Otago Battalion taking up its position at the junction of Flers Support and Goose Alley. Here the enemy was within bombing distance, and casualties were suffered on both sides. It was here that our troops met for the first time the black-coloured egg bomb of the Germans. It had the advantage on account of its smallness of being able to be thrown a much greater distance than our troops could throw the Mills bomb. The egg bomb, however, never displaced the stick bomb as favourite in the eyes of the German, perhaps on account of the difficulty of manufacture or on the score of unreliability. During daylight, on the 26th September, with the exception of Taranaki Company, who were compelled to bomb a party of Germans out of a part of Flers Support Trench in order to establish a block there, the 1st Battalion was not called upon. At midnight the Battalion, in readiness to take part in a further Brigade advance, took up new positions in reserve for the Brigade. Taranaki Company moved to North Road; Wellington-West Coast Company occupied Link Trench, a short trench stretching from Ligny Road to Grove Alley; Hawke's Bay Company had one platoon in Fort Trench and the remainder in Grove Alley, near Abbaye Road, and Ruahine Company was formed up in Grove Alley, south of Abbaye Road to Flers Support. The Battalion Headquarters were on Abbaye Road. On the morning of 27th, Wellington-West Coast Company was selected by the enemy for heavy shelling and it suffered somewhat severely. In the afternoon, the Brigade made its attack, taking parts of Gird Trench and Gird Support Trench. All objectives were taken; but, on account of the Otago Battalion encountering much barbed wire and suffering casualties, it was not then known if the battalions were in touch. When these objectives were taken, Taranaki Company moved across and up to Factory Corner, Ruahine Company and Hawke's Bay Company moved to Goose Alley, and, in order to clear up the situation, moved to within 100 yards of the junction of Goose Alley and Gird Trench, when it was held up by the enemy. As soon as it was dark, 2nd Lieutenant M. S. Galloway took his platoon across the open and occupied Gird

THE WELLINGTON REGIMENT

Trench, east of Goose Alley. Thereupon, Hawke's Bay Company moved up to Goose Alley between Abbaye Road and Flers Support. The privilege of clearing up the obscurity of the position was given the 1st Battalion and it was for that purpose two companies of the 3rd Battalion of the Rifle Brigade and two sections of Light Trench Mortars gave assistance. A tank was also expected to put in an appearance before zero hour; but, if it ever started, it got lost in the mire of the battlefield.

The Operation Order issued in connection with the attack succinctly explained the duties of all concerned. It read as follows:—

1st Battalion.
Wellington Infantry Regt.
26th September, 1916.

The following positions will be captured by the Battalion:

  a. Gird Support Trenches from left of Auckland at M 26 b.93 to M 24 b.4.6.

  b. Gird Trench from left of Auckland at M 26 b.9.3 to M 24 b.2.4.

  c. Goose Alley from M 24 b.6.5 to M 24 c.8.6.

    W.W.C. Co. will capture, consolidate and garrison the objectives in B and C.

    A Company 4th Battn., N.Z.R.B. will capture, consolidate and garrison the objective in A.

    Each company will erect a block 60 yards west of the junction of Goose Alley with Gird Trenches and Gird Support.

    One Stokes Mortar and one section of Battalion bombers is allotted to each company.

    W.W.C. Co. will attack from Goose Alley and the company of the 4th Battn. N.Z.R.B. will attack from left of Auckland at M.26.b.9.3.

    The attacks will be simultaneous and will be made at 4 a.m., 27/9/16. The attack will be preceded by five minutes' intensive bombardment of Stokes Mortars commencing at 3.55 a.m.

THE WELLINGTON REGIMENT

A tank may be available, and, if so, it will precede the advance of A Company along Gird Support and there will not then be any bombardment of Stokes Mortars.

R. W. WRIGHTSON,
Captain and Adjutant.

As the tank did not arrive the parties moved off to their assembly points. Wellington-West Coast Company attacked and reached its objective, but the company from the Rifle Brigade came under a heavy barrage and the column was broken and that portion of the attack failed. The party could not be collected before daylight, and the ground covered was held. The situation was not improved and the Brigade ordered a fresh attack. Preparations were accordingly made for this, but, in the meantime, Colonel Hart, by making a personal reconnaissance, found that his companies were not connected up, there being about 100 yards distance between each, and they were about the same distance from their objectives. The objective lay in a hollow and neither the enemy nor our troops could hope to hold without first capturing the surrounding ridges. In the circumstances, Colonel Hart cancelled the projected attack on his own initiative, an action that was later approved of by Brigade Headquarters. The companies were ordered to extend towards each other and form a complete line. Trenches were dug to enable this to be done. Later the same night, the Brigade was relieved by the 2nd Brigade. The relief on account of the proximity of the enemy and the heavy intermittent shelling, was carried out by sections. The 1st Wellington Regiment returned to the comparative comfort of the bivouacs in Carlton Trench.

The operations in which the battalion had been taking part had been favoured by fine weather but the previous wet weather made it most difficult to move about on the shell-torn territory, and the stench of the dead will live in the memory of all who took part in those famous operations. For the five days in which the battalion had been engaged in the attack it suffered in casualties two officers and 96 other ranks. The 2nd Battalion took over the Gird Trench that had been captured by the 1st Brigade, making its headquarters at Factory Corner. The enemy realised that the Factory Corner would assuredly be made a headquarters of some sort, paid a great deal of attention to the brick structure, at the bottom of which was a cellar containing the Battalion Headquarters. The 2nd Battalion were not troubled in the Gird Trench, and every opportunity was seized for improving the defences and even making the trenches a little more habitable. The spirits of the battalion were wonderfully good. The artillery that had played a great part in heartening the attack were now partly from imperfect knowledge of the distance our troops had gone forward, bursting shrapnel short, to our great discomfort, though, fortunately, without injury. The fatigue parties carrying up the rations, performed their difficult tasks with great determination, and keeping the troops well fed and with a full supply of rum, helped materially to make the situation bearable. The last operation carried out by the battalion in the Somme was on the 1st and 2nd October. The battalion was relieved by the 1st Battalion of the Rifle Brigade to take part in a further advance to the left. Headquarters were taken up at Goose Alley, where part of the battalion also sought cover. The rest of the battalion was accommodated at Flers Support. At 3.15 p.m. on the 1st October the battalion attacked and captured Eaucourt l'Abbaye. The attack was carried out without much difficulty, though in the night the Germans made a half-hearted counter-attack which did not cause the battalion much trouble in repulsing. Throughout this operation the companies advanced so quickly that resistance was not strong, and a valuable addition to the tactical situation was the reward. In this operation under 2nd Lieutenant R. L. King, the battalion signalling section maintained an almost uninterrupted communication between company and Battalion Headquarters. The linesmen were intrepid to a degree and took great pride in the maintenance of the telephone lines.

The spell of fine weather broke again and cold and showery weather supplanted it to the intense discomfort of all. All positions were consolidated and, after nightfall of the 2nd

THE WELLINGTON REGIMENT

October, the Battalion turned its back on the Somme trenches, being relieved by the 1st Battalion of our Rifle Brigade. To assist, if necessary, in the attack on Eaucourt l'Abbaye, the 1st Battalion had moved up from Carlton Trench to Flers Trench and Flers Support. Though this was but a short distance and with no shell fire to cause delay, yet it took the companies from six to eight hours to move up. The ground was by now in an appalling condition—mud and slush to the knees, all tracks obliterated, the troops had to move round shell holes to reach their new position.

The Battalion was not called to play any active part in the attack on Eaucourt l'Abbaye, and on the night of the 3rd the 26th Royal Fusiliers relieved the Battalion. The relief was a part of the relief of the corps. The Battalion slowly made its way back to Pommiers Redoubt, worn, weary, but triumphant. The 2nd Battalion made its way back to Savoy Trench and thence to Fricourt and there gained from the inclemency of the winter the protection of tents.

On the 4th October the Army Corps Commander of the 15th Corps visited the lines of the 1st Battalion and thanked and congratulated them.

So ended the part played by the New Zealand Division in the famous Battle of the Somme of 1916. No division ever better earned the gratitude of its commander, or, indeed, of the nation, than did the New Zealand Division in that famous battle. Engaged continuously from the 15th September to the 3rd October, under the worst possible weather conditions, faced by a great mass of artillery and machine-guns, the division to a man fought with the steadiness of regular troops and with a spirit intrepid and indomitable. With one or two trifling exceptions where parties failed to gain their objectives, the division carried out the tasks allotted to it.

The battalions were faced by regular troops and by numbers far exceeding their own, yet with dauntless valour they drove the Germans back from their selected positions and dominated them in a manner that could not be gainsaid.

Of that division the two battalions representing the Wellington Regiment played their part nobly, and led by commanders of intelligence and bravery, by Company commanders and Platoon commanders in whom the men had implicit confidence, it was no wonder that the battalions showed themselves as equal to any others of the division and gained for themselves and for the Dominion they represented the admiration and gratitude of all.

To mention particular acts of bravery would be unfair to those who performed acts that were omitted to be mentioned. Those whose acts were mentioned would prefer, no doubt, that they should not be singled out from the many others who performed equally brave actions. So it were better, apart from those who were singled out by Divisional commanders as meriting particular praise, not to mention any particular officers or other ranks whose acts, brave as they were, were but the acts of most of the troops of our great Division.

Every member of the Division had a right to be proud of having had the opportunity of becoming a member of that great Division, to be proud of the fact that the Division was such a noble addition to the great Army that represented the British Empire, to be proud of the fact that it played no mean part in ultimately achieving for the betterment of the world the vanquishing of the guilty and of establishing right and justice throughout the world.

THE SOMME
Scale 1 - 40,000 Metres.

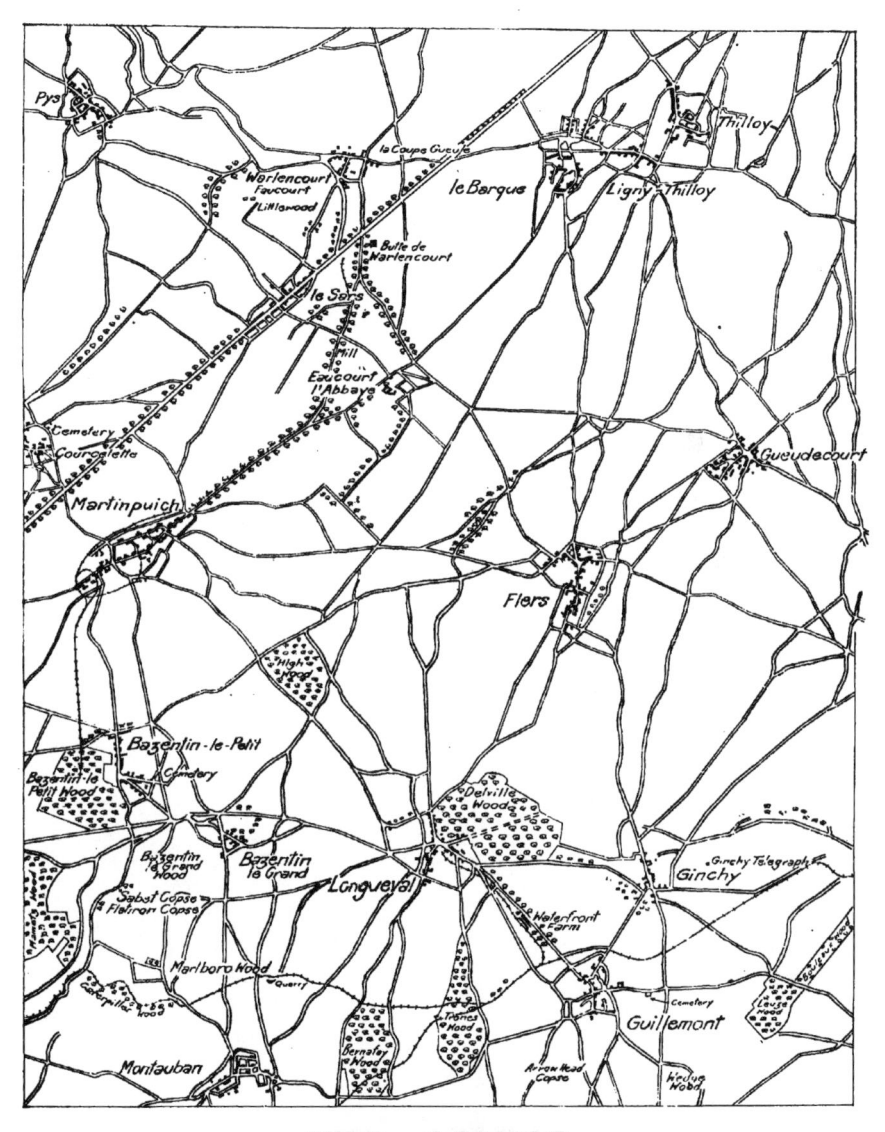

CHAPTER XVIII.

We Return to the North—Armentieres Again—A Quiet Time—Sailly-sur-Lys.

AFTER being relieved by the Royal Fusiliers, the 1st Battalion was strongly reinforced and marched to Albert, then entrained for Longpre and went into billets there. On the 10th October, the 1st Battalion said farewell to the 4th Army and entrained to Caestre in the 2nd Army area. From Caestre the battalion was taken by motor-lorry to Estaires. A few days later the battalion moved into the line again in the Armentieres sector, and relieved the 59th Battalion of the 15th Brigade of the Australian Forces, in what was known as Cordonnerie Sub-sector.

After spending two days in Fricourt resting, in which time every man was able to have a bath, the 2nd Battalion marched from Fricourt Camp to Edgehill and, having entrained there, detrained at Longpre at 11.15 p.m. and then marched eight kilometres to Erondelle. It was exasperating after leaving the train there for no apparent reason to march eight long kilometres by the side of the railway line and to see the train passing and re-passing. The battalion arrived at Erondelle exhausted. Next day the quartermaster's supplies were available and shortages were made up, and we were given leave to Abbeville, one of the old towns of France, full of interest, where restaurants and entertainments were in full swing to cheer the jaded.

After resting four days at Erondelle, the 2nd Battalion marched to Pont Remy and entrained there for Bailleul. Bailleul was not reached until 3 a.m. and the battalion then immediately marched straight on to Strazeele, a distance of eight kilometres. In the afternoon of the same day, the battalion proceeded by motor buses to Armentieres, taking over the position of Battalion in Brigade reserve in the old familiar left sector and occupying trenches 84 to 89 inclusive. Battalion Headquarters re-occupied Cambridge House, and the distribution of companies were three in the front line and one in support.

As soon as the two battalions took over the sectors of the front line, old hands led parties into No Man's Land for wiring and scouting. Nothing of interest occurred during the rest of the month of October. No raids were made either by our own troops or the enemy, and generally the line was quiet.

At the end of October Lieut.-Colonel W. H. Cunningham was awarded a Russian decoration for distinguished service in Gallipoli, Second-Lieut. R. Riddiford the M.C. for the gallant part he played in the raid carried out by part of the 2nd Battalion in Armentieres, and eight other ranks received the D.C.M. or Military Medal for gallantry. The Non-commissioned Officers and men were Sergeant L. R. Nicholas, Sergeant W. McKean, Corporal P. A. Gordon and Privates S. T. Dibble, E. Lymer, N. Orr, J. C. Harris and A. T. Ruane. These decorations were presented by the Army Commander of the 1st Battalion.

Sergeants R. C. Potter, D.C.M. for raid, A. D. Price, S. Gilshnan and C. B. Lepper and Corporal J. H. Hardy and Privates W. A. Gray, G. Adsett and J. Johnson were awarded decorations for acts of individual gallantry.

The month of November was without particular incident. Several attempts were made on the area occupied by the 2nd Battalion to loose gas upon the enemy. On only one occasion was this possible on account of the wind. Then, after a heavy bombardment by all the Artillery in the locality, gas was sent across. The usual S.O.S. flares were sent up by the enemy, but the artillery retaliation was very small. Indeed, during the whole of this month, it was obvious that the enemy was conserving his ammunition, and our artillery was not slow to take advantage of this.

THE WELLINGTON REGIMENT

In the early part of the month, the gas mask* which had done service ever since our troops arrived in France was supplanted by a more up-to-date and highly efficient gas mask known as the box respirator.† It took us a little time to get used to this new protection against gas; but in the end we much preferred it to the former because whereas the old P.H. helmet encased the head to the very ill content of the wearer, the new respirator merely protected the mouth and eyes and left the rest of the head uncovered.

On the 28th of November, the 2nd Battalion having been relieved by 2nd Otago, moved out from Armentieres to Sailly-Sur-Lys and took over billets there. Training was soon in full swing and we rapidly lost the careless and slovenly habits acquired on the battlefield and in the trenches.

The 1st Battalion remained much longer in the front line, and it was more difficult for it to organise training. About the middle of November a regimental school was established in Ruebiache.

It was inevitable on account of the enormous amount of work to be done in the trenches in repairing the parapets that were rapidly deteriorating as the cold and wet weather set in that all the N.C.O.'s were called on fairly frequently to take fatigue parties up into the line. It was always felt that our troops when in reserve were given too much work in the front line in the form of fatigue parties.

On the 30th November, a raid along the whole divisional front was carried out for the purpose of ascertaining the positions of the enemy's most advanced troops, and generally to report on the condition of the enemy's barbed wire in the rear of his front line. This raid was carried out in a singularly uneventful manner. It was ascertained that the front line trenches and dugouts were in a very bad state. The former were full of water, and the latter were impassable on account of the slush and mud. No prisoners were taken, and those few Germans who were met fled on sight.

On the 18th December, after the usual life in the trenches, the 1st Battalion was relieved by the 1st Otago, and went into brigade reserve, and three days later marched by

---
*P.H. Helmet.   †S.B.R. or small box respirator.

THE WELLINGTON REGIMENT

companies and took over billets from 2nd Wellington, who on being relieved took over the sector in the front line then occupied by the 1st Otago, and but recently vacated by 1st Wellington. Our 2nd Battalion was now very fit indeed.

When the 2nd Battalion marched into the line they were in a state of efficiency which had never been exceeded since the creation of the battalion twelve months before, and it is interesting to note the work the men were put to during their stay in Sailly-Sur-Lys.

Everything was done to improve the men physically and keep them mentally alert. The class of training was the most modern known, and the men entered into the spirit of the training, realising that by attention to this matter they would render themselves more efficient and more able when the time came to deal again with the enemy.

The following is a syllabus of the work set for all ranks of the 2nd Battalion from the 18th December to the 24th December.

2nd BATTALION WELLINGTON REGT. SYLLABUS OF TRAINING.

Monday, 18th December:
    8— 9   Kit inspection and inspection of billets.
    9—10   Physical exercises and bayonet fighting.
    10—11   Musketry, rapid loading, etc.
    11—12   Rifle exercises, saluting, squad drill.
  1.30— 2.30 Route march.
    9—12   All company bombers at Battalion Headqrs.
  1.30— 2.30 All company bombers at Battalion Headqrs.

Tuesday, 19th December:
    8— 9   Kit inspection and inspection of billets.
    9—10   Physical exercises and bayonet fighting.
    10—11   (b, c, d coys.) Musketry, rapid loading, etc.
    11—12   Rifle exercises, saluting, squad drill.
  1.30— 2.30 Route march.

"A" Company Bombing:
    9—10   1st platoon.
    10—11   2nd platoon.
    11—12   3rd platoon.
  1.30— 2.30 4th platoon.

THE WELLINGTON REGIMENT

Wednesday, 20th December:
- 8— 9   Kit inspection and inspection of billets.
- 9—10   Physical exercises and bayonet fighting.
- 10—11   (a, c, d coys.) Musketry, rapid loading, etc.
- 11—12   Rifle exercises, saluting, squad drill.
- 1.30— 2.30   Route march.

"B" Company Bombing:
- 9—10   1st platoon.
- 10—11   2nd platoon.
- 11—12   3rd platoon.
- 1.30— 2.30   4th platoon.

Thursday, 21st December:
- 8— 9   Kit inspection and inspection of billets.
- 9—10   Physical exercises and bayonet fighting.
- 10—11   (a, b, d coys.) Musketry, rapid loading, etc.
- 11—12   Rifle exercises, saluting, squad drill.
- 1.30— 2.30   Route march.

"C" Company Bombing:
- 9—10   1st platoon.
- 10—11   2nd platoon.
- 11—12   3rd platoon.
- 1.30— 2.30   4th platoon.

Friday, 22nd December:
- 8— 9   Kit inspection and inspection of billets.
- 9—10   Physical exercises and bayonet fighting.
- 10—11   (a, b, c coys.) Musketry, rapid loading, etc.
- 11—12   Rifle exercises, saluting, squad drill.
- 1.30— 2.30   Route march.

"D" Company Bombing:
- 9—10   1st platoon.
- 10—11   2nd platoon.
- 11—12   3rd platoon.
- 1.30— 2.30   4th platoon.

Saturday, 23 December:
- 8— 9   Kit inspection and inspection of billets.
- 9—10   Physical training and bayonet fighting.
- 10—11   Musketry, rapid loading, etc.
- 11—12   Rifle exercises, saluting, squad drill.
- 1.30— 2.30   Route march.

Sunday, 24th December:
        Church parade.
                LECTURES.
        Daily 11.30 a.m. to 12 (noon). All Officers.
                Monday—Commanding Officer.
                Tuesday—Medical Officer.
                Wednesday—Commanding Officer.
                Thursday—Bombing Officer.
                Friday—Lewis Gun Officer.
                Saturday—2nd in Command.

Company commanders will, during the week, train three wiring teams per company. Training to be under company arrangements, and teams to be trained during training hours.

Company commanders will pay special and personal attention during the week to the training and smartening up of their N.C.O.'s. Short classes should be held under company arrangements, and during drill hours every facility given to junior N.C.O.'s to handle their men.

During the daily route march, opportunity will be taken to do short tactical schemes in open fighting, so as to accustom all ranks to handling their commands.

                C. A. L. TREADWELL, *Lieut.-Adjutant.*

To the 1st Battalion leave was given liberally. The Band, in whom the battalion took an immense pride, and with much justification, played every day. Various forms of entertainment were got up, including sports competitions to maintain the spirit as high as possible. The winter of 1916-1917 was described by the local inhabitants as the coldest in memory, and we could see no reason to disagree with that opinion. Snow fell thick and lay on the ground in a way the New Zealanders were not accustomed to. The imperfect drainage system and the low-lying land presented a dismal and cheerless appearance. The intense cold caught many of us napping, and frost bite was at first common, but drastic measures were taken against it by daily inspection and massage of feet with oil.

On the 1st of the New Year the 2nd Battalion was relieved by the 2nd Otago Regiment and the battalion took over billets at Bac St. Maur.

CHAPTER XIX.

Fleurbaix.

January, 1917—Re-organisation of First and Second Brigades — Fleurbaix — 1st Battalion's Raid—Gas Alarm — An Enemy Raid — Second Auckland's Raid—Relief by 57th Division.

ON 1st January, 1917, the First and Second New Zealand Infantry Brigades were re-organised. Hitherto, as we know, the First Brigade had comprised the 1st Battalions of the Auckland, Wellington, Canterbury and Otago Regiments; and the Second Brigade had been made up of the 2nd Battalions of the same regiments. Henceforward, the First Brigade was to consist of the North Island regiments, i.e., 1st and 2nd Battalions of the Auckland Regiment and 1st and 2nd Battalions of the Wellington Regiment. The Second Brigade now comprised the South Island regiments, i.e., 1st and 2nd Battalions of the Canterbury Regiment, and 1st and 2nd Battalions of the Otago Regiment. The new arrangement while it broke old associations, had one beneficial result in that the two service battalions of each regiment being brigaded together would in future be in much closer touch. Second Wellington was now parted from its Brigade Commander (Brigadier-General W. G. Braithwaite), and came under the command of Brigadier-General C. H. S. Brown, Commander of the First Brigade.

New Year's Day, 1917, found our 1st Battalion in billets at Sailly-Sur-Lys. During the day, 1st Canterbury marched through on its way from Estaires, and we turned out to say good-bye to our old comrades of the 1st Brigade, our band playing Canterbury through the village. Second Wellington in the trenches, was relieved during the morning by 2nd Otago. The relief was completed by 1 p.m., and the 2nd Battalion then went into reserve billets at Bac St. Maur.

Lieut.-Col. W. H. Cunningham was now to receive his D.S.O. for services in the field during 1916, while Capt. H. E. McKinnon, Capt. L. H. Jardine and Lieut. S. G. Guthrie were each to receive the Military Cross.

Both battalions carried out training for a few days until the 8th January, when the 1st Battalion relieved the 4th Battalion of the Rifle Brigade in the line. On the same day, the 2nd Battalion relieved 2nd Battalion, Rifle Brigade, at Fleurbaix. Owing to lack of accommodation, 120 men of the 1st Battalion were left out of the line. The following day, these were returned to their companies, being replaced by 25 men from each company, under Second Lieuts. S. G. Guthrie, R. D. Boyle and G. H. Davey, selected to undergo special training.

The salient in that part of the line held by Ruahine Company (1st Battalion) having been patrolled only, and not held by the outgoing battalion after its bombardment on New Year's Day, the 1st Battalion took over the same arrangements. Later, the posts on the flanks were moved closer in, both to watch the salient and to cover the heads of Tin Barn Avenue and Abbot's Lane. It was here that Second Lieut. J. M. McQueen encountered an enemy patrol and, in an exchange of shots, was wounded. Battalion Headquarters were at Wye Farm; and the Regimental Medical Officer (Capt. Lee) and his staff in Jay Post. As this place was subjected to a good deal of shell fire, being too close up to the front line, the Regimental Aid Post was later moved back. Quartermaster stores and transport lines were in Rue Rataille. Transport, except isolated vehicles, could not come further than Elbow Farm before dark. The support company, owing to lack of accommodation, had to put nearly half its strength in Command Post in the subsidiary line. The enemy showed some liveliness with "pineapples" and minenwerfer, both by day and by night; but our artillery retaliation was effective.

THE WELLINGTON REGIMENT

Repairs to damage done to the trenches absorbed most of the working strength, although the left company (Taranaki) was able to do some wiring. The weather was cold, and snow lay on the ground from the 11th. Wire-cutting by our trench mortars provoked a certain amount of retaliation. Judging by the number of flares he sent up, and by his action in bombing his own wire at night, the enemy was very nervous.

On the morning of the 16th January, the 2nd Battalion, which had been supplying working parties for the front and support lines, relieved the 1st Battalion in the trenches, who then moved into the billets vacated by the 2nd Battalion at Fleurbaix. The 2nd Battalion remained in the trenches until the 24th January. The weather was frosty and fine. The front was quiet, although on the nights of the 20th and 21st, small hostile parties approached our posts only to be driven off by bombs and rifle fire. During the 2nd Battalion's occupancy of the trenches, the 1st Battalion's special party, in training behind the lines, sent up patrols each night to get familiar with the ground. On one of these patrols, a patrolman was hit by a bomb thrown by the 15th Royal Scots on our left, but, fortunately, he was not seriously wounded.

On the 24th January, the 1st Battalion again took over from the 2nd Battalion, who moved back to Fleurbaix, from there to supply the inevitable working parties—more than 300 men being supplied daily. The weather remained frosty and cold—well down below freezing point. Patrols from the special party were out; but could not go far, the snow making patrolling difficult. It was clear that, opposite the whole sector, the enemy held his front line lightly.

There was a certain amount of shelling and trench mortar activity during this period, especially on the 27th (Kaiser's birthday), when Jay Post was heavily shelled, and on the 28th, when, at 4 a.m. and again at 10 a.m., the enemy shelled the billets at Fleurbaix with "five nines," the 2nd Battalion fortunately, having only three wounded.

This was the time intended for the raid by the special party of the 1st Battalion which had been training since early in the month; but now the raid had to be postponed indefinitey and the special party returned to companies because the Second Brigade had taken over the sector on the left at short notice, involving a re-arrangement of artillery.

On the 28th, the 1st Battalion relieved 1st Auckland in the right battalion sector, having first been relieved by 2nd Auckland. This double relief was completed without a hitch. The new sector (right of Boutillerie Sector), was much quieter and in better order, although there was a little shelling and a few minenwerfers were sent over on the extreme left. It seemed that the enemy did not hold his front line here at all, being content to send a patrol up occasionally, although it was thought probable Clapham Junction was held. There was an absence of enemy flares and machine-gun fire on most nights, though little work could be done owing to the frozen ground. In spite of the snow, patrols went out nearly every night. On the night of the 30th January, a patrol under Lieut. A. S. Muir entered the enemy's trench at Turk Point and found it deserted and out of repair for fifty yards to the South.

On the 1st February, the 1st Battalion was relieved in trenches by the 2nd Battalion (Hawkes Bay Company of the 2nd Battalion did not go into the trenches on this occasion, having to remain in billets at Fleurbaix in isolation for mumps). Hardly had the 1st Battalion reached its billets in Fleurbaix, than its special party was called upon. Identification of the enemy opposite our sector was urgently needed, and the special party was to raid the enemy's trenches and secure prisoners for identification. On the 2nd February, the special party was assembled, material collected and the party organised. At 5.30 a.m. on the 3rd, the raid took place. Owing to the moonlight, the party was considerably reduced from the number first intended, in order to lessen the risk of casualties; but the raid was run on the lines practised, and the point of entry was the same. The sortie was simply to obtain identification and was entirely successful. Three prisoners were taken and the only casualties to the

THE WELLINGTON REGIMENT

raiding party were, Lieut. G. H. Davey, in charge of supporting party, slightly wounded, and one man wounded, after returning to our line. At the time of our raid, 2nd Auckland was holding the line.

Late that night, a gas alarm was given from the sector on the right, and,.shortly afterwards, gas shells came over, falling near the billets of Taranaki Company (1st Battalion) on the outskirts of Fleurbaix, happily without causing any casualties. Early the following morning, Taranaki Company's billets were again shelled with salvoes of three, composed of one high explosive and two gas shells. Many men ran down the road to shelter in the brewery cellar without putting on their S.B.R.'s*. As a result of this shelling, four men were evacuated early that morning, suffering from gas poisoning, and later in the day, twelve more. The first four included a billet sentry, at whose feet a gas shell had fallen, and those who ran to his help. Of these, three died within twenty-four hours. Four sergeants were amongst those evacuated.

On the 7th February, Croix Marechal was steadily shelled and Ruahine Company had one killed and two wounded, so that the 1st Battalion, in billets in Fleurbaix, had suffered more than the 2nd Battalion in the trenches, where a very quiet time had been experienced. On the 9th, the 1st Battalion relieved the 2nd Battalion, who returned to Fleurbaix. During the first few days in the line, a number of minenwerfer were fired into the 1st Battalion's sector by the enemy from positions at Bas Maisnil, and "rum jars" were sent over from the Maze on to the right of the sector—two Ruahine Company men being killed there. This culminated in a heavy bombardment of the 1st Battalion's left, and also of the battalion on its left. At about midnight on the 12th an enemy raiding party entered the latter battalion's line just left of Tin Barn Avenue; but was quickly driven out. Our artillery replied promptly to the S.O.S. The enemy also put gas minenwerfer near the junction of Convent Avenue and the support line, and several men became casualties. On the night of the 14th a Taranaki Company patrol entered Turk Point, but found

---
*Small box respirators, which everyone carried.

it deserted. The ground had been frozen hard till now with a heavy coating of snow, but, on the 11th, the weather became milder and a gradual thaw set in, and, a few days later, there was drizzling rain. The health of the men remained good during this cold weather, although there were two or three cases of trench feet. Every precaution had to be taken to prevent trench feet. Gumboots were issued, a daily change of dry socks was arranged, and everyone was required to massage his feet, each day, with whale oil.

On the 14th February, the 2nd Battalion relieved 1st Auckland in the left sub-sector of the Brigade sector, so that both our battalions were in the line when 2nd Auckland carried out a raid at 5.45 a.m. on the 21st. That battalion raided from the trenches held by our 2nd Battalion, who lent what assistance it could in the operation. The duck-walks of the front line along the length occupied by the raiders immediately prior to raiding, and the communication saps leading from it back to the support line were covered with straw, over which hessing fabric was nailed down. This had the effect of deadening the sound of the men moving up to position, and of the withdrawal of the front line garrison. All telephonic communications were overhauled and relaid, and emergency lines were laid at all vulnerable points. Stretchers and bearers were placed at the junction of the support line with City Post and Bay Avenue. These were to carry the wounded from the front line to the Regimental Aid Post. The Regimental Medical Officer (Capt. H. M. Goldstein) and his staff were placed at the disposal of the O.C. Raid and shared with the R.M.O., 2nd Auckland, the work of dressing and despatching the wounded to the Field Ambulance. During and after the raid, both our 1st and 2nd Battalions had to submit to the enemy's retaliation. Our 1st Battalion had three men killed and the 2nd Battalion one wounded, the enemy's fire being ill-directed on the 2nd Battalion's front.

The 57th Division was now to take over from the N.Z. Division. On the 21st, 1st Wellington was relieved by 2/5th King's Liverpool Rifles, and moved into billets in Sailly; while, on the 22nd February, our 2nd Battalion was relieved

THE WELLINGTON REGIMENT

by the 2/6th King's Liverpool Rifles, and moved to Estaires. On the 23rd February, the 1st Battalion marched from Sailly-sur-Lys, some eight miles to De Seule; while the 2nd Battalion proceeded from Estaires to Nieppe. On the following day both battalions rested.

CHAPTER XX.

Le Bizet.

Le Bizet—Pont De Nieppe—Le Touquet—Relief by Australians—Football at Nieppe—Bulford Camp—Working Parties.

ON the 25th February, the 1st Battalion marched to Le Bizet and took over billets in brigade support from 8th Border Regiment, while the 2nd Battalion relieved at Pont de Nieppe the 11th Cheshire Regiment in the line and the 8th Border Regiment in the subsidiary line. The village of Le Bizet was uninhabited by civilians, and the houses had been badly damaged by shell fire. It looked, and gave one the feeling of the "deserted village."

On the 1st March, the 1st Battalion relieved the 2nd Battalion in the line, the latter going into brigade reserve at Pont de Nieppe. The 1st Battalion had its headquarters at Surrey House. The trenches in this sector (Right sector—Le Touquet) were in bad shape, for the upper hundred yards of Long Avenue and portions of other trenches were under water. The whole of the parapet in the front line was very low, and in a bad state of repair: many of the dug-outs had fallen in: parados was non-existent in most places and, where it did exist, the trenches were much too narrow. Napoo Avenue and Watling Street were practically impassable. The support line in the left sector was uninhabitable, except for six dug-outs. There was no cook-house in the left company's sector, and the cooking was done at Widow House near Station Redoubt. Rations and supplies were brought by transport to Motor-car

THE WELLINGTON REGIMENT

Corner, and thence by a good tram-line to Battalion Headquarters and to Station Redoubt and Half-way House. There was an Engineer's dump alongside Battalion headquarters; but stores were very limited, and timber and rivetting material impossible to obtain. There was therefore much work to be done. The battalion in line heightened and strengthened the parapet, cleared drains and built up traverses and parados. Working-parties from the battalion in support opened up a drain under the duck-boards along the whole length of Long Avenue, also two other drains behind the support line, thus clearing the Avenue of water. When we took over the line, the enemy had a very marked superiority in sniping; but we soon gained ascendancy, killing at least three German snipers. A patrol of usually one officer and three men, went out from near the head of Barkenham Avenue every night. Our wire along the whole front was very poor, and that of the enemy generally very good. On the 3rd March, our light trench mortars fired 170 rounds from our left sector, and the enemy retaliated with 30 " pineapples." On the 8th March, both our medium and light trench mortars bombarded the enemy's line from the head of Long and Barkenham Avenues, the retaliation consisting of about twenty minenwerfers and a hundred "pineapples"; but, fortunately, no damage was done to us. Fine weather was now being experienced with a bright moon at night. It was very cold, and there was some snow.

On the 5th March, Lieutenant-Colonel H. Hart, D.S.O., was appointed temporarily to command 1st N.Z. Infantry Brigade, and Captain F. K. Turnbull, M.C., assumed command of the 1st Battalion, as Major C. F. D. Cook was on leave.

On the 9th March, the 2nd Battalion relieved the 1st Battalion in the line, the latter moving to Pont de Nieppe,. Wellington-West Coast Company of the 1st Battalion then being detached and marching to Ravelsburg to work on trenches, etc., at the new Divisional School there. The 2nd Battalion remained in the line until the 14th March, when it was relieved by the 43rd Battalion, 11th Brigade, A.I.F., and marched to Le Romarin. The 1st Battalion stayed at Pont de Nieppe until the 15th, but was greatly reduced in numbers by being called upon to supply two officers and about one hundred men for a brigade working party; two officers and seventy men for New Zealand Working Battalion; thirty men for the 3rd Canadian Tunnelling Company; and fifty men for a railway construction party (Proven Berques Line). On the 15th March, the 1st Battalion was relieved by the 42nd Battalion, A.I.F., and marched to billets in Nieppe. There, training was carried on daily, and in the afternoons inter-platoon Rugby matches and inter-company Soccer matches were played on very rough grounds. On the 18th March, the 1st Battalion marched about three miles to Bulford Camp and relieved the 10th Battalion, Royal Inniskilling Fusiliers. Both our battalions had now to garrison certain posts in G.H.Q. 2nd Line of Defence with picquets of one N.C.O. and six men each, relieved every twenty-four hours. Training was carried on as best the battalions could, for both were still obliged to supply a very large number of men for working parties. A great many men were employed by day on railway constructional work at Connaught Road, Romarin and Quarry Road Sidings, while, at night, parties were digging the subsidiary line on the left brigade front and wiring the same with double apron, while other night parties were digging a support line on the right brigade frontage. Towards the end of the month, the 1st Battalion was inspected at Bulford Camp by Brigadier-General C. H. J. Brown, D.S.O., Commanding First New Zealand Infantry Brigade.

The weather during March had been changeable with a fair amount of rain and occasional snow storms, and there was a certain amount of sickness.

CHAPTER XXI.

Ploegsteert.

First Time in Ploegsteert Wood—Red Lodge—Bunhill Row—Mud Lane—Prowse Point—St. Yves—The Douve Sector—Preliminary Work for Messines Offensive — Hutting Camp — Aldershot Camp — Neuve Eglise—Night Bombardments of Back Areas —Reprisals by our "Heavies"—We go back to train for Messines.

ON the 31st March, the 2nd Battalion went into Ploegsteert Wood, relieving 2nd Battalion, Rifle Brigade, in reserve there. The following day, the 1st Battalion relieved 4th Battalion, Rifle Brigade, in line in the Ploegsteert sector (St. Yves Hill), marching some four and a-half miles from Bulford Camp, via Connaught Road, Leinster Road, Romarin-Ploegsteert Road, meeting platoon guides at the Strand. Two platoons of the reserve company then proceeded to the Catacombs at Hyde Park Corner, the rest of the battalion entering the trenches via The Strand, Bunhill Row, Mud Lane Breastwork and Ontario Avenue.

The Rifle Brigade had done a great deal of work; but, in spite of that, the line was in a very bad state, and there was a great deal of work yet to be done; nor did a fall of snow make things easier. The companies had their cookhouses just behind Prowse Point, at St. Andrew's Drive, and at Mud Lane Breastwork respectively. Rations were brought up to Campac Dump by transport, thence by the Canadian Pacific Light Railway (mule drawn or hand pushed), to Mud Lane Breastwork, Prowse Point and St. Andrew's Drive. There

THE WELLINGTON REGIMENT

was an Engineers' Dump near Moated Farm; but stores were very limited. The whole of St. Yves Hill was a maze of old, destroyed or abandoned trenches and saps which made systematic work very difficult. Late one afternoon, and again the following evening, our heavy, medium and light trench mortars bombarded the enemy front line and supports doing considerable damage, the enemy replying with minenwerfer and canister bombs; but doing little damage. On the night of the 1st and again on the night of the 2nd, and morning of the 3rd April, snow fell, making it impossible to patrol to any extent.

The 2nd Battalion remained in reserve until 5th April. On the 2nd, the enemy had shelled its billets causing many casualties (1 killed, 17 wounded—two died of wounds). Captain L. H. Jardine, M.C., who had been commanding the 2nd Battalion for a week or so, now left for England to attend a Battalion Commander's course at Aldershot, and Major C. H. Weston from the 1st Battalion who had recently completed the same course assumed command of the 2nd Battalion (Lieut.-Col. Cunningham being at La Motte), with Captain H. E. McKinnon, M.C., second in command. On the 5th, 2nd Wellington replaced 2nd Canterbury in support in the Red Lodge area, and on the 6th, relieved 1st Canterbury in the line in La Douve sector opposite Messines, with 1st Auckland on its right and the 25th Division on its left. Although the trenches were exposed in many places, practically no sniping was done, although a few whizz bangs came over at odd times. The 2nd Battalion's headquarters were in McBride's Mansions, a comfortable row of dug-outs, and Auckland's were in Plus Douve Farm. Enemy artillery did considerable counter battery work and shooting at our rear lines.

The 1st Battalion was relieved in line, on the same day, by part of the 42nd Battalion, A.I.F., and moved into the left support area of the Red Lodge sector, only just vacated by the 2nd Battalion.

*The Douve sector faced, or rather was overlooked by, the remnants of the village of Messines, still clinging to the

---

[This account of the preliminary work for the Messines offensive is, by the kind permission of the author, taken from "Three Years with the New Zealanders," by Lieut.-Col. C. H. Weston, D.S.O.]

THE WELLINGTON REGIMENT

ridge to which it gave its name, and it was not long before we learned that in the coming offensive the task allotted to the New Zealand Division was to capture that village. The offensive was in the air. No longer were the same old trenches to be our everlasting home; they were now pieds-a-terre, and next winter we should camp in fresh ground, as we had hoped, far ahead of the present battle zone. For the moment there was work, more than enough, in making ready for the blows we were to deal the Hun.

Our right boundary was to be the river Douve, and our left beyond the Wulverghem-Messines road, both of which crossed No Man's Land at right angles to the two opposing lines of trenches. Across the Wulverghem-Messines road on our left, the trenches swung back almost at right angles, followed the road a little way, and then turned away sharply towards Wytschaete. On our left front the little river Steenbecque, there, in the middle of No Man's Land, ran through the road towards our right and bent back until it entered our line, ultimately emptying itself into the Douve. From the point where the Steenbecque struck it, to the Wulverghem-Messines road, our front line was not parallel to the German trenches, and it was therefore, decided to dig a new trench in No Man's Land which would give us a jumping-off place on the correct alignment. With a large body of assaulting troops it is of great importance that they do not have to change direction during an attack, and that they all have approximately the same distance to travel. The contemplated trench would run from where the Steenbecque entered our front line to a point on the Wulverghem-Messines road, about two hundred yards from our present line and would give an additional advantage in enabling us to overlook the bed of the Steenbecque river from its parapet. As it was, the ground sloped steeply down to the stream which divided us from the enemy and then still more steeply up to Messines, thus obscuring the river banks from our view.

It was no use disguising the fact that it was a ticklish business. The Engineers had to peg the site of the new trench at night, and, immediately after dark on the evening appointed, to tape it out. The working party of about four hundred men would then be marshalled on to the tapes and work commenced. The party would, of course, be protected by outposts, who would not be withdrawn until the work was completed. Of necessity the job had to be carried through in one night. The danger lay in discovery by the enemy while the work was in progress. No doubt his guns were laid on No Man's Land at night, and on a single signal from his sentries they would play terrible havoc with our men. The fact that the new trench in its curve beyond the Wulverghem-Messines road ran perilously close to the German line made discovery rather probable.

In the meantime, our patrols set to work to make No Man's Land our own, and to oust the enemy from a listening post he occupied on the road on our side of the Steenbecque. The post had been described as a heavily wired strong point on the maps in the possession of the Division, but on the evening of the 10th, a patrol from Hawkes Bay Company, 2nd Battalion, under Lieuts. Bollinger and Booklass, took possession before the Hun arrived. When he came, he did not stay long upon his going, but fled helter-skelter. From the careful reconnaissance they made, these two subalterns were able to supply the Division with correct information, and, thereafter, we occupied the post at night.

On the 11th April, Lieut. Keiller, an Engineer Officer, with Lieut. Molloy, 1st Otago, and 2nd Lieut. A. C. Wilson, 2nd Canterbury, pegged out the new trench. Unfortunately, just as work was completed Lieutenant Keiller was accidentally wounded by a bomb. On the following evening, Molloy checked the pegging, and on the night of the 13th, the work was done. The covering party, under Captain R. F. C. Scott, commanding Hawkes Bay Company, was found by that company and Wellington West Coast Company of the 2nd Battalion, the two detachments being officered by 2nd Lieuts. Booklass and McKenzie. Captain Scott reported them in their position at 9 p.m., and by

THE WELLINGTON REGIMENT

10.30 p.m., the four hundred men from 1st Battalion, Otago Regiment under Major J. Hargest, M.C., had commenced work. The work was completed at 2.30 a.m., and the party was clear of the battalion area on its way back to billets at 3 a.m. It was only then that the covering party was withdrawn. It was an anxious night, but, happily, the enemy remained oblivious to what was happening. Lieut. Col. Cunningham's arrangement of the covering party was considered excellent, and great credit was due to Major Hargest and his men. It is no easy matter to lead four hundred men in the dark out of a narrow trench to do a task in No Man's Land: to do it without noise and confusion was the result of excellent organization and discipline. The batteries supporting the sector stood by their guns while the work was in progress, and their commander took up his position in our front line to control them from there. The enemy's attitude to the new trench was mainly one of indifference, although he registered some of his guns on it next day, and shelled it lightly on the following night.

The entrance to the Douve Sector was by way of Plum Duff Sap, a narrow trench by the side of a road that ran down La Plus Douve Farm, and hard by the gate leading into the courtyard of the farmhouse was Ration Dump. On the 14th, there happened to be in the dump, about fifty "plum pudding" bombs, each weighing sixty pounds, and, a shell from a German battery striking them, caused a terrific explosion, killing five and wounding eleven men. A few days later, the German communique alleged that we had flown the Red Cross Flag over the dump, and, upon their suspicions being aroused by the number of men about, they had shelled it, with the result we have seen. Of course, no Red Cross Flag had been hoisted there, but there was a Dressing Station some three hundred yards away, which probably their observers had seen. However, after that, Ration Dump was an unhealthy spot, for it was shelled consistently and accurately. It was nevertheless, a busy place, as the first line transport unloaded the rations there at night and all reliefs were made by Plum Duff Sap.

THE WELLINGTON · REGIMENT

On the 15th April, the 2nd Battalion was relieved by the 1st Battalion, and established itself on Hill 63, with headquarters at Stafford Lodge, until April 24th. The lodge was a shack, probably built by Canadians, with trunks of saplings cut from the wood on the hillside. Tactically we were the supporting battalion of the brigade, the reserve battalion resting at Kortepyp Camp some two miles away. Up till now, the troops in the enemy trenches were a Saxon Division, but our intelligence learned from a German deserter that the 40th Division had relieved them. The Saxons have the reputation of being very passive opponents, their motto apparently, being " Live and Let Live ". It was surprising what little interference we met with in the work. Part of our sector lay spread out at the foot of Messines, and the new work was plainly visible to the German observers in the village. Yet the enemy made no effort to check it by his artillery. What a wonderful view there was from the place was not fully appreciated until we took it in June, and could look back over our own country.

An offensive, organised as was General Plumer's against the Messines and Wytschaete Ridge, entailed a great deal of preparatory work. Assembly and communication trenches had to be dug to protect the troops for the few hours prior to the assault, and battalion and brigade headquarters constructed.

The latter were underground affairs; some thirty feet down with several entrance shafts, and numerous box rooms opening off the tunnels. In later battles assembly trenches were dispensed with, and the men took their chance while they waited. Communications, also, were necessary. The signals in a modern battle form the most difficult problem. The surest method is by cable, buried in a narrow trench, from seven to nine feet deep, but the limit to this is our front line. Other means are telephone wire, simply run over the surface of the ground, wireless, flags, lamps, pigeons and runners. Different engagements, owing to the various circumstances, have proved the use of the several methods, but preparations are generally made for all of them. The most reliable of all proved to be the runner.

Providing the covering party on the night of the 13th did not close the 2nd Battalion's connection with the new trench by the Steenbecque, for on three nights it sent up working parties from Hill 63. Posts from the 1st Battalion protected the men on these occasions. On the night of the 17th, Captain H. E. McKinnon, M.C., commanding Wellington West Coast Company, with detachments from his own company (Lieut. G. P. Healy) and from Taranaki (Lieut. R. K. Nicol), dug a drain from the trench down into Steenbecque, and a continuation of the trench itself. Captain McKinnon's party had only one casualty. On the 18th, the 2nd Battalion found four officers and two hundred and ninety-five other ranks under Major C. H. Weston to make four communication saps from our old front line to the new one, and the work was done without a mishap. The following night, Captain R. F. C. Scott with four parties from Wellington West Coast (Lieut. McKenzie), Hawke's Bay (Lieut. Booklass), Taranaki (Lieut. Natusch) and Ruahine (Lieut. Taylor), totalling three hundred other ranks, carried the trench out further towards the Hun lines north of the Wulverghem-Messines road. That was the danger-point, and evidently the enemy saw either the covering party or some of our men, for he opened on them with rifle grenades, and rifle and machine-gun fire, killing two and wounding nine. It was bad enough, but fortunately he did not call up his artillery, and things quietened down. This digging was excellent training for a platoon or company. It was done by the companies. The officers had control of their own men, and made their own arrangements. The consequence was, officers, non-commissioned officers and men who would have to fight together were working together. It may seem strange, but that system had not always been followed. Previously, a battalion would be asked for several working parties, and, on the margin of men available being small, some of them had to be found from two or more companies, and placed, perhaps, under officers who were strangers to them. Moreover, on arriving at the job, the men would be handed over to the Engineers, who would take complete charge. Under the new system they would remain with their own officers, who were solely responsible for the work, but had one or two Sappers attached to them as expert advisers.

While the Infantry were digging, the Artillery and the trench mortar men (Plum Puddings and Stokes) were busying themselves in destroying the enemy trenches, strong points, machine-gun posts, and wire. There was to be a greater concentration of guns for Messines than ever before; the Somme and Arras would not stand comparison, and already the 60-pounders and heavies were pounding away at the German defences. "The Flying Pig," as the largest trench mortar was called, had not been installed, but its lesser brethren were doing great work; and, in spite of all, the retaliation from across the way was weak. The Miners, too, were steadily working, though of their plans we knew little. We rubbed shoulders with them in the narrow communication trenches, but there it ended.

And this scene of activity we thought we were leaving on the 29th April. The 2nd Battalion had relieved the 1st Battalion on the 24th, and were in turn relieved by the 2nd Battalion, of the Rifle Brigade, on the 26th, and marched back to Kortepyp Camp. The 1st Battalion was relieved in support by the 4th Battalion of the Rifle Brigade on the 27th, and moved to Romarin Camp, where it was billeted in huts. Two days were cheerfully spent in making ready for the anticipated trek to the training ground near St. Omer, and a start was to be made on the 29th. The battalions had had no real spell from trench life since Christmas, four long months, and how they would enjoy three weeks of Spring away from the sound of guns, where mud was unknown. But, as if to remind us that in the army our souls are not our own, late at night on the 28th, came a note from Brigade Headquarters cancelling the move, and next day at noon, we received orders to relieve the 13th Battalion, Cheshire Regiment, in the Wulverghem Sector to the left of the Douve Sector. In the afternoon, company commanders inspected the trenches, and the relief took place that night. It was a beautiful moonlight night, and the whole battalion was in by 4.30 a.m. Battalion headquarters were at St. Quentin Cabaret.

On the 30th April, the 1st Battalion moved from Romarin to the Waterloo Road near Neuve Eglise, battalion headquarters and two platoons of Ruahine Company being at Hutting Camp, Wellington-West Coast and Hawkes Bay Companies at Vauxhall Camp and the rest of the battalion at Hillside Camp, and, as no working parties were demanded from it for the next few days, the 1st Battalion had rather an easy time of it.

May 1917, was ushered in in delightful weather. The 2nd Battalion was still in the line, and, on the evening of the 1st May, Lieut. A. V. Young, a popular and efficient officer of Hawkes Bay Company, was shot dead by enemy machine-gun fire, while posting his platoon in support trenches at "Stand to." Our Stokes mortars were now registering from both their offensive and defensive positions, and they seemed to do considerable damage. The Germans, as was their wont, retaliated with minenwerfer and gun fire, which, fortunately, landed behind the front line, the 2nd Battalion having only one casualty. On the morning of the 3rd, the enemy shelled our right sector for several hours, intermittently and threw minenwerfer into the left sector. During the afternoon, the Stokes and medium trench mortars, assisted by the artillery, bombarded the enemy front line, while, on the divisional front, six hundred 60lb. bombs were fired at the enemy's trenches. The enemy again replied; but, fortunately, retaliation was moderate on the 2nd Battalion front, although, at 7 p.m. a small minenwerfer fell on a Ruahine post, killing two and wounding five.

Early on the morning of the 4th, during darkness, the 2nd Battalion was relieved by 1st Auckland, and marched to Aldershot Camp, about a mile south of Neuve Eglise, going into hutments there. Everyone was now able to have a bath, always a very real pleasure after a spell in the trenches. It was now definitely known that both battalions were, within a few days, to go out for Brigade training, and preparations were being made accordingly. There was, however, still no respite from digging; but most of it could be done in daylight, as the sector was not under enemy observation. On the morning of the 5th, Lieut. J. McMorran was wounded while in charge of a party burying cable on the Wulverghem-Messines Road, one of his party being killed and three others wounded.

The 1st Battalion remained in Hutting Camp from 30th April to the 8th May, the whole strength being employed during this period on working parties.

On the night of the 5th May, the enemy three times bombarded Neuve Eglise, Bulford Camp, and the transport lines along Connaught Road. As soon as the bombardment began, both battalions temporarily evacuated their camps, and all the transport animals of both battalions were shifted away in pairs nearer to Stenwerck, returning next morning. Though considerable casualties were sustained by other battalions both in men and horses, the Wellington battalions happily, sustained none. On the following night, similar action was twice taken by the enemy artillery. As a precautionary measure, as soon as the bombardment opened, companies moved into places of safety, and the transport horses were again shifted. Luckily, there were again no casualties with us. On the evening of the 7th May, at 8.45 p.m., every heavy gun on the 2nd Army front bombarded the enemy's rear lines for five minutes. The dose was repeated at 11 p.m. They were certainly a series of bad five minutes for the enemy. This was a reprisal for the enemy's attention to our back areas, and, as the enemy ventured to retaliate slightly, our "Heavies" repeated five minutes drum fire at 11 p.m. on the 8th.

Notwithstanding the unceasing work that was being done by working parties from both battalions, time was snatched on the 6th May for a football match between teams from the 1st and 2nd Battalions, the former winning handsomely.

On the 8th May, the 1st Battalion relieved 1st Auckland in the left brigade front of the Wulverghem sector with battalion headquarters at St. Quentin's Cabaret. The 4th

Red Lodge, Ploegsteert.

Dugouts in Ploegsteert Wood.

Our First Aid Post at Messines.

Winter at Hooge.

Birr Cross Roads.

THE WELLINGTON REGIMENT

Battalion, Rifle Brigade, was on the right and the Royal Irish Rifles on the left. On the 10th, the 1st Battalion was relieved by the 11th Battalion, Lancashire Fusiliers, and moved to the Waterloo Road, occupying the same camp as before. On the same day, the 2nd Battalion moved out of Aldershot Camp and marched to Petit Sec Bois, close to Vieux Berquin via Bailleul and Strazeele, marching past Lieut. General Sir A. J. Godley, Corps Commander, on the way. Lieut. Colonel R. Young had lent our 2nd Battalion the 1st Canterbury's band, the 2nd Battalion then having no band of its own, and its presence was a source of keen enjoyment. Next day the 1st Battalion marched to Grand Sec Bois, a distance of twelve miles, billeting there, in the village and adjoining farms.

The 1st Battalion remained at Grand Sec Bois, and the 2nd Battalion at Petit Sec Bois until the 19th May. For the most part, the weather during that time was delightful, and some excellent training was put in by both battalions.

While there the First Brigade held a horse show at Strazeele, and both battalions attended in force. The Regiment provided its share of competitors in all events, and took a share of prizes. In the two events for officers' chargers (owners up) Colonel Cunningham, Major Weston and several of the Company Commanders competed. The Colonel's black mare, Queenie, came third in her class (chargers ridden by officers of field rank) and Captain McKinnon's bay mare, Lucienne, was second in the other class. Driver Wilson, with his two splendid chestnuts, won the limbered wagon event. These beautiful animals, with many others, were killed early in August when an enemy aeroplane bombed the 2nd Battalion's transport near Kortepyp.

On the 17th, the transport moved ahead by road. The 19th May was a beautiful day, and both battalions marched to Bailleul and entrained there for St. Omer. On arrival at St. Omer we detrained and marched to billets. The 1st Battalion made Leuline its headquarters with Wellington-West Coast and Ruahine Companies at Etrehem, and Hawkes Bay and Taranaki Companies at Audenthun. The 2nd

Battalion marched to Tatingham, reaching there about 7.30 p.m., taking over fairly good billets and being quite compact, the whole battalion in the one village.

The following day was Sunday, and Padre Walls conducted the 2nd Battalion Church Parade, Brigadier General C. H. J. Brown, Commander First Brigade, attending. In the afternoon, Taranaki Company played Ruahine Company at Rugby.

Training was again in full swing, and, during the week, both battalions fired various practices on Commette Rifle Range. There was a little rain; but, on the whole, the weather was excellent.

During twelve days, very valuable brigade training was put in. Extensive manoeuvre grounds had been requisitioned from the peasants, and sites were chosen and trenches dug to imitate as closely as possible the Messines defences. The brigade was thus able to practise its own portion of the attack under somewhat realistic conditions. General Godley (Corps Commander), and General Russell (Commander N.Z. Division) came down to see the training and criticize the work, and both of them addressed the officers and non-commissioned officers of the brigade.

During May, more than the usual number of changes had taken place in the Regiment. Early in the month Captain R. W. Wrightson, Adjutant of the 1st Battalion, left to attend a three months' staff course, and Lieut. J. T. Dallinger (Quartermaster) thereupon became acting Adjutant, and Lieut. R. L. Thompson Acting-Quartermaster of the 1st Battalion. During the month also, Rev. Father Richards (1st Battalion) went back to the base, his place being taken, a few days later, by the Rev. P. J. O'Neil. In the 2nd Battalion, Lieut. Gilbert (Hawkes Bay Company) transferred early in the month to the Royal Flying Corps, and from Tatingham, Lieut. A. A. Browne (Quartermaster) also went away to join the R.F.C. while Lieut. R. K. Nicol left for duty with the light trench mortars.

By the end of May, the First Brigade training for Messines was completed, and both battalions were now fit for anything. The villagers had grown very fond of us,

THE WELLINGTON REGIMENT

and it was with genuine regret, and many expressions of *bon chance, bon sante*, that they parted with us on the 31st May, when we turned our faces Eastward again.*

During the stay, the officers of the 1st Battalion, entertained the officers of the 2nd Battalion at dinner, and it was indeed a merry party. Tatingham boasted a dining hall, and the two battalions between them produced a good share of crockery and spoons and forks. The 2nd Battalion officers sent their hosts home in the transport limbers, vehicles not designed for passenger traffic, and one of them, taking a corner rather sharply, turned over and shot the occupants on to the road. Several very dilapidated-looking officers were noticed when the 1st Battalion marched past the Brigadier two or three days later.

On the 31st May, the 1st Battalion marched to Bavinchove, a distance of about fourteen miles, and billeted there for the night, while the 2nd Battalion marched some fifteen miles to Zuytpene, near Cassell, via Arques. The following day, the 1st Battalion marched to billets in the Verte Rue area, a distance of about twelve miles. From Zutypeene, the 2nd Battalion marched to their former billets at Petit Sec Bois. On the second day's march, the officers and men who were not to go into action at Messines dropped out, and marched away to the Reinforcement Camp at Morbecque. On the 2nd June, both battalions marched some twelve miles to the concentration camp at De Seule, arriving there during the afternoon. Shelter trenches were dug in case the enemy should shell the camp, and alarm stations allotted to companies.

Early in June, Lieut. Colonel C. F. D. Cook, commanding the 1st Battalion, was to receive the D.S.O., while Captain R. W. Wrightson, Adjutant 1st Battalion, Captain F. H. E. Morgan and Lieut. H. Simmonds were awarded the Military Cross.

---

*Many months later, some of us had an opportunity of again visiting these villages where we trained for Messines. The villagers were delighted to see us. They enquired eagerly after those that were not with us, and on learning that some had been killed in action, were genuinely grieved, and wept bitterly.

THE WELLINGTON REGIMENT

CHAPTER XXII.

Formation of 4th Brigade.

The 4th Brigade — Formation of the 3rd Battalion of the Regiment—1st Wellington supplies New General — Brigadier-General H. E. Hart — Period of Training — 4th Brigade arrives in France — 3rd Wellington near Bailleul.

THE fourth New Zealand Infantry Brigade came into existence on the 15th March, 1917, and comprised the newly-formed 3rd Battalions of the Auckland, Wellington, Canterbury and Otago Regiments. The Wellington Regiment had the honour of providing the new General. Lieut.-Col. H. E. Hart, D.S.O., who had for long commanded was now promoted to be Temporary Brigadier-General, and was given the new brigade command. To fill his place, Major C. F. D. Cook, D.S.O., was promoted Lieutenant-Colonel to command the 1st Battalion. Major W. H. Fletcher, second in command of 2nd Wellington, was promoted Lieutenant-Colonel, taking command of the new 3rd Battalion of the Wellington Regiment in the Fourth Brigade. Major H. Holderness was now promoted second in command of the 1st Battalion; while Major C. H. Weston, up till now commanding Taranaki Company in the first Battalion, went to the 2nd Battalion as second in command and Major J. L. Short was appointed second in command of the new 3rd Battalion.

Towards the end of March, both battalions in the field sent over to England experienced officers and non-commis-

THE WELLINGTON REGIMENT

sioned officers and these, together with others then in England, recovered from wounds and sickness, formed the nucleus of the new 3rd Battalion. The 1st Battalion sent over Lieut. F. S. Varnham and Lieut. A. S. Muir, in addition to Lieut. Col. H. E. Hart, while Lieut. Col. W. H. Fletcher and Lieut. B. H. Morison went from the 2nd Battalion.

Training of the 3rd Battalion was carried out at Codford. Extensive training was carried out from 29th March 1917 to 29th May, 1917. His Majesty the King reviewed the brigade at Sling on the 1st May, 1917, senior officers being presented to the King after the review. The brigade marched from Codford to Sling for the review (20 miles) on 30th April, returning on the 2nd May, 1917. It was an inspiring spectacle.

On the 10th May, there was a further full dress inspection, this time by Field Marshall Viscount French, near Codford.

On leaving for France the officers of the 3rd Battalion were as follows:—

Lieut. Col. W. H. Fletcher, D.C.M. (Officer commanding); Major J. L. Short (Second in command); Lieut. A. S. Muir (Adjutant); Lieut. W. H. D. Coltman (Quartermaster); Lieut. S. M. Lang (Lewis Machine-gun officer); Capt. T. C. A. Hislop (Transport officer); Capt. I. E. Faris (Medical officer attached); Company Commanders; Wellington-West Coast Company, Capt. B. H. Morison (Capt. E. White, second in command); Hawkes Bay Company, Capt. F. S. Varnham (Capt. J. McRae, second in command); Taranaki Company, Capt. P. Oldham, (Capt. A. E. M. Jones, second in command); Ruahine Company, Capt. J. S. MacKay (Capt. F. L. Hartnell, second in command); Subalterns; Lieuts. W. B. Johnstone, W. H. Jones, P. J. O'Dowd, J. Brown, H. E. Crosse, R. Goldsman, O. Magnuson, J. Walker, H. H. Parkinson, L. L. King, H. Lawson, J. N. Bullard, C. E. Lee, A. W. Lafferty, R. H. Stables, R. M. Doughty, C. D. Stewart.

THE WELLINGTON REGIMENT

On the 28th May, the 3rd Battalion left Codford in two trains for Southampton, which was reached at 6.30 in the morning, and there the Fourth Brigade embarked for France. Of 3rd Wellington, Wellington-West Coast and Hawkes Bay Companies crossed the Channel in S.S. "Archangel" and Taranaki and Ruahine Companies in the S.S. "Australind."

The Channel crossing was without incident, and at four o'clock in the morning, Le Harve was reached. The 3rd Battalion then disembarked and marched to a Rest Camp.

The brigade was destined for Bailleul, to be utilized as Corps Reserves. Accordingly, at midday on the 30th May, the 3rd Battalion entrained for Bailleul arriving there at 12.30 p.m. next day. From here, a short march to a field alongside the Armentieres-Bailleul Road brought the battalion to where it was to bivouac for the next eleven days. The weather was perfect, and everyone was much impressed by the enormous amount of traffic on all roads, the numerous British aeroplanes coming and going from the Bailleul Aerodome, and the general activity that proclaimed the coming Messines offensive.

On the 2nd June, the 4th Brigade (including 3rd Wellington) was inspected by General Godley, Commanding II. Anzac Corps, and General Gough, commanding the First Army.

On the 3rd, Ruahine Company was detached and employed laying water pipes in preparation for the assault about to be made against the Messines-Wytschaete Ridge. Otherwise the Battalion was, until the 10th, employed on various fatigues and guards scattered throughout the II. Anzac area.

CHAPTER XXIII.

Battle of Messines.

Plans for the Attack—Preparations at De Seule—The March up — Gas—Hanbury Support—The Explosion of the Mines — Roar of the Guns — Blauwen Molen — Fanny's Farm — The 4th Australian Division pass through us — Digging In — Death of Brigadier General Brown—Casualties Holding On — Death of Capt. R. F. C. Scott — Relief by the Australians—Bulford Camp.

UNDER General Godley's command in II. Anzac Corps at the beginning of June, were the Third and Fourth Australian Divisions, the 25th Division and the New Zealand Divisions. For the capture of the Messines-Wystschaete Ridge, the attack of the II. Anzac Corps was divided into two phases. There was first to be the attack and capture of what was called the black line. This was to be carried out by divisions disposed side by side, The Third Australian Division on the right from St. Yves to the River Douve: in the centre, the New Zealand Division on a front of some 1500 yards from the Douve to just North of the Wulverghem-Messines Road: on the left, the 25th Division on a narrower sector at the Wulverghem-Wytschaete road. For the first phase, the Fourth Australian Division was to be in reserve.

After the black line had been captured, the second phase attack was to be carried out by the Third and Fourth Australian Divisions, the troops of the latter division passing through the New Zealand and 25th Divisions.

The tasks of the New Zealand Division were to capture the village of Messines, establish itself on the black line, and consolidate that line strongly as a reserve line of occupation and to establish a series of strong posts to serve, primarily, as jumping-off places for the Fourth Australian Division, on that division going forward to capture the final objective, the Green line and, afterwards, as supporting points to the Fourth Australian Division, when that Division had established itself on the Green line. Tanks were detailed to co-operate; but all plans were based on the assumption that no co-operation from them would be forthcoming.

On the New Zealand Division's front, the attack was to be led by the Rifle Brigade on the right, and the Second Brigade on the left. The task of those brigades was to assault and capture certain defined objectives and to dig in there. They were allotted nearly two hours to do that, and, when they had accomplished it, the First Brigade was to pass through the leading brigades and capture the Black line and establish posts in front of it. The object of this was to hold Messines securely, and allow the Fourth Australian Division to push through to the final objective. First Auckland was to be on the right of the First Brigade front, and its task included the establishment of one post in front of the Black line. First Wellington was to be on the left with objectives limited to the Black line itself. Two companies of 2nd Auckland were to go through First Wellington and establish four posts in front of the Black line. Second Wellington and the other two companies of 2nd Auckland were to be in brigade reserve.

Until the night of the 6th June, 1st Wellington lay at De Seule. During the afternoon of the 3rd, 2nd Wellington had relieved 2nd Otago at Red Lodge, and passed a very disturbed and uncomfortable night there. The active bombardment of the enemy positions had commenced. And he retaliated with lethal and lachrimatory gas shells, necessitating all in

THE WELLINGTON REGIMENT

the 2nd Battalion passing part of the night in their respirators.

How hot was the following day when battalion and company commanders reconnoitred the assembly trenches! On the 4th, the enemy shelled the Red Lodge Area, killing two, and wounding four men of the 2nd Battalion.

Early in the morning of the 5th, the 2nd Battalion was relieved by the 3rd Battalion of the Rifle Brigade and marched back to the concentration camp at De Seule. Although the battalion moved in half platoons with 100 yards distance between, it nevertheless, suffered fourteen wounded by shell fire. At De Seule, it was another scorching day. The 6th June was a busy day in the Concentration Camp, at De Seule, fitting out with all things that goes to make up fighting kit. In the evening, Padre Walls had a short open-air service, and, after that all had coffee, cakes and cigarettes at the expense of the Salvation Army, while the officers of the 2nd Battalion met in the largest hut in the camp and toasted the King and the Regiment.

Shortly after 9.30 o'clock on the night of the 6th, the 1st Battalion marched out from De Seule en route to the assembly trenches. The 2nd Battalion followed at 10.30 p.m.

The parade states were:—

1st BATTALION: 22 officers (including Chaplain and R.M.O.) and 795 other ranks.

HEADQUARTERS: Lieut. Col. C. F. D. Cook, D.S.O. (in command), (R.M.O.) Capt. Cameron, Lieuts. J. T. Dallinger (Adjutant), D. W. Curham (Lewis Gun Officer) and G. H. Roach (Signalling Officer), and about 35 other ranks.

WELLINGTON-WEST-COAST: Capt. J. R. Cade, Lieuts. G. H. Davey, A. R. Blennerhassett and H. C. Patchett and about 190 other ranks.

HAWKES BAY COMPANY: Lieut. S. G. Guthrie, M.C., Lieuts. P. S. George, S. King, F. Howard* and about 190 other ranks.

*Killed in action at Messines.

THE WELLINGTON REGIMENT

TARANAKI COMPANY: Capt. W. F. Narbey, Lieuts. G. H. Fell,* R. Wood, M.M., F. W. Medcalf, and about 190 other ranks.

RUAHINE COMPANY: Capt. H. Oram, Lieuts. F. E. Asby, L. M. Dixon, C. W. Jones, and about 190 other ranks.

In addition, one officer (Lieut. A. R. McIsaac) and 21 other ranks acted as a brigade carrying party. At Dump 2nd I.C., Q.M. and Transport Officer.

2nd BATTALION: 22 Officers (including Chaplain and R.M.O.) and 726 other ranks.

HEADQUARTERS: Major C. H. Weston (in command), Captain H. M. Goldstein (R.M.O.), Lieuts. C. A. L. Treadwell (Adjutant), T. L. R. King (Signalling Officer), J. K. E. Jackson (Intelligence Officer), and 47 other ranks.

WELLINGTON-WEST-COAST COMPANY: Capt. H. E. McKinnon, Lieuts. A. G. Melles, A. T. Duncan, and G. A. Robbie, and 177 other ranks.

HAWKES BAY COMPANY: Capt. R. F. C. Scott,† Lieuts. G. W. Bollinger,† S. A. Murrell and W. G. Gibbs, and 165 other ranks.

TARANAKI COMPANY: Capt. D. S. Columb, Lieuts. A. T. White, N. F. Little and C. Natusch, and 164 other ranks.

RUAHINE COMPANY: Capt. M. Urquhart, Lieuts. F. Bolton, H. T. M. Fathers, and Taylor, and 173 other ranks.

In addition, Lieut. W. Pollock and 20 other ranks formed a brigade carring party, and Padre Walls proceeded to Khandahar Advanced Dressing Station for the time being, while his burial party remained at the Q.M. Stores, awaiting an opportunity to go forward.

---

*Killed in action at Messines.
†Died of wounds received in action at Messines.

THE WELLINGTON REGIMENT

The march was a tedious one. The enemy knew from the course of events that our advance would now not be long delayed, and shelled the tracks with gas shells. Fortunately, he employed no mustard gas (we were to have our first experience of mustard gas a few weeks later), and few lachrymatory shells, and we were able to dispense with the eye-pieces of our respirators and rely on the mouth-pieces alone. The gas shells burst on both sides of our moving columns, and in front and in rear. As gas shells explode with but little force, we were in no great danger of being struck by flying fragments but how we came not to receive direct hits from the gas shells themselves will ever be a matter of wonder.

The 1st Battalion found Hanbury Support no sanctuary, for that sap was shelled with high explosive and gas shells, here mostly lachrymatory, and some casualties were sustained. Both battalions were in position by the time appointed, and some men were able to snatch a few minutes' sleep.

Zero hour was at ten minutes past three in the morning. At that very moment, there was a muffled roar, that seemed to die down and then increase and die down again. Then there was a shake that rocked the very earth. Between the last roar of the mines exploding and the opening of the guns was no perceptible interval. The guns belched forth their concentrated fury. Never had the heavens looked so awe-inspiring as they did that morning.

The honour of capturing Messines itself was given to the New Zealand Division. The attack on the divisional front was led by the Rifle Brigade on the right, and the Second Brigade on the left. In spite of strong opposition, they met with complete success.

Meantime, three-quarters of an hour after Zero, 1st Wellington left the assembly trenches at Hanbury support, and moved forward in readiness to take part in the assault upon the final objectives of the New Zealand Division. While at Hanbury Support, the 1st Battalion had received a good deal of shelling, and, although our casualties had not been heavy, we had already lost several men and two officers—Lieut. G. H. Fell and 2/Lieut. F. Howard, killed. Companies moved in small columns over the open, and then picked their way up the hill to Messines, skirting the village and not going through it. To ensure being in position before the barrage began to move forward again, we had to keep close upon the heels of the leading brigade and, indeed, in one instance on the left, such was the anxiety not to miss the barrage, that our men arrived at one objective even before the troops detailed to assault it.

At 5.20 a.m., two hours and ten minutes after Zero, the First Brigade under Brigadier-Gen. C. H. J. Brown, D.S.O., had attacked and captured the Black line (the New Zealand Division's final objective) beyond the village of Messines. First Auckland was on the right, and 1st Wellington on the left. Ruahine Company (Capt. H. Oram) was on the right of our 1st Battalion's attack, Taranaki Company (Capt. W. F. Narbey) in the centre and Hawkes Bay Company (Lieut. S. G. Guthrie) on the left. Wellington-West Coast Company (Capt. J. R. Cade) had detailed two platoons, under 2/Lieut. A. R. Blennerhasset, to capture Blauwen Molen and the sap leading to it. The remainder of that company was in battalion reserve.

Each platoon in the battalion reached its objective and completed its task, a testimony to the leadership of platoon commanders and to the knowledge of all ranks of their tasks. The men of the Wellington-West Coast Company rushed Blauwen Molen with great determination and captured three machine-guns and twenty-seven prisoners with but very little loss. Here, Corpl. J. Fernandez and his men displayed marked gallantry, and Pte. R. Alexander captured a machine-gun and its entire crew single handed.

Ruahine on the right did not meet with much opposition; but they too captured two machine-guns and twenty-five prisoners. Sergt. Roy Corkill led the platoon on the right of the battalion sector with skill and determination, reorganising and maintaining direction under difficult conditions. Upon reaching its objective, Sergeant Corkill was struck in the eye

THE WELLINGTON REGIMENT

by a sniper's bullet; but refused to leave his post, until his platoon had made touch with Auckland on the right, and consolidation was well advanced, when he collapsed from pain and exhaustion.

Taranaki, in the centre, had the sharpest fighting, cleaning up what had been an enemy battalion headquarters. The platoon on the left, in particular, met with strong opposition from enemy riflemen in shell holes; but, under Lieut. R. Wood's gallant leadership, they fought with magnificent courage. In a charge led by Wood, in which they captured a machine-gun and twenty prisoners, the platoon sustained heavy losses. Although Wood himself was wounded, he, Sergt. M. Beck and Lance-Corpl. C. W. Hansen, led the survivors—twelve in number—and attacked the enemy with such resolution that they killed over fifty and drove the rest away. For their gallantry on this occasion, Lieut. R. Wood was awarded the Military Cross, and Sergeant Beck, and Lance-Corporal Hansen the Military Medal.

The rest of Taranaki Company had Fanny's Farm and Oculist Trench to clear and did so with great dash and determination. Their total prisoners amounted to one hundred and thirty-five, and, as our men had an opportunity to use their rifles, they also killed a large number of the enemy.

Hawkes Bay Company on the left, also had opposition, and that company captured two machine-guns and forty prisoners. There were many acts of courage by the men of Hawkes Bay; but one notable feat of fearless gallantry was on the part of Private J. A. Lee.* He tackled, single-handed, a machine-gun near the Wytschaete Road, and captured the four gunners. Later, when Taranaki Company was checked by an enemy post, Lee, with two of his comrades, worked round behind the enemy and rushed the post, capturing two machine-guns and forty men, and so enabled our advance to proceed.

The final objective was reached at 5.20 a.m. and all set to work to dig themselves in. The assistance rendered throughout by the Stokes mortars must not be overlooked.

---

*Now a member of Parliament.

THE WELLINGTON REGIMENT

Near the Wytschaete Road, they drove out a machine-gun from a concrete emplacement, while they silenced another for us near Fanny's Farm.

Our 1st Battalion captured in all, seven machine-guns and close on two hundred prisoners, including five officers. The Germans probably showed more stout resistance on 1st Wellington's front than elsewhere, although the enemy's morale generally was high.

The barrage again moved forward, and one platoon from 1st Auckland on the right, and two companies from 2nd Auckland on the left, moved a short distance forward and established five strong points in front of our trench line. These were to be the jumping-off points for the 4th Australian Division later in the day.

What of second Battalion in reserve.? It had emerged from the new subsidiary line fifty-five minutes after zero, when the dawn was still grey, and by companies in single file made for Hanbury Support, but recently vacated by our 1st Battalion. A few seconds wait to make sure every one was there, and then up on to the road along which ran Plum Duff Sap, we turned to the right down the Artillery track by the River Douve, then to the left and across country on the parapets of trenches to our new position. A heavy smoke fog lay a few feet above the ground, and the unmistakeable odour of lethal gas was everywhere. It was no use attempting to shout orders: the roar of artillery and machine-guns overwhelmed all other sounds: one could not even distinguish the explosion of our own shells from the shells of the enemy's barrage now falling close to us.

To the 2nd Battalion moving forward, there was ample evidence that our storming troops, while waiting their turn to advance, had not escaped altogether, for in one trench, lay the bodies of five men killed by a single shell, and close by an abandoned tank. A little further on lay several of our 1st Battalion dead.

The 1st Battalion had lost no time in digging in. There is no greater incentive to digging than hostile machine-guns. The line consolidated was the correct one according to plan, save that, on the right of Taranaki Company, the barrage had halted too soon, and our men had there to dig in a little short of the proper line. On our left, the 25th Division went some three hundred yards beyond us before starting to dig in, resulting in a gap at this point. We were in touch with them though, through two Vickers guns on our immediate left, and we were also in touch with them along October Reserve.

At one o'clock in the afternoon, the 4th Australian Division, leapfrogging the New Zealand Division, continued the advance and captured the Oostaverne Line (the final objective). Along the frontage of three Army Corps the same success was achieved. The whole operation was carried through, as it was planned with the utmost precision, and having regard to the magnitude of the enterprise, the casualties were remarkably few.

As soon as the enemy realised he had lost the ridge, he began to shell the whole area, particularly at about three o'clock in the afternoon when the Australians were to be seen moving up. The result was an ever increasing casualty list. At Messines, the losses were not so great in the course of the advance itself; but in the holding on, the crouching down in shallow ditches, and submitting hour after hour to the concentrated hate belched forth from the enemy's guns. The nature of the ground prevented us from digging very narrow or deep trenches, for water was soon reached and the sides of the trenches would slip in. Ruahine Company, on the right of the 1st Battalion, particularly were in a very exposed position, and were severely punished by enemy shell-fire.

Shortly after 1.30 o'clock in the afternoon, the enemy made his first real attempt at a counter attack; but our protective artillery barrage was prompt and effective. At about 8 o'clock in the evening, a report came back to us that the Australians on our right were being pushed out of Green Chain Line. Our barrage clapped down again and the enemy made no progress. Later, when things quietened down, the night was spent in improving and extending our trench line.

Meantime little untoward had happened to the 2nd Battalion in reserve, save that, during the afternoon, Lieut. S. A. Murrell had been wounded while reconnoitring the ground near Messines.

Early on the morning of the 8th June, the posts established in front of our 1st Battalion by 2nd Auckland were reconnoitred by Major C. H. Weston, Capts. R. F. C. Scott, and M. Urquhart of the 2nd Battalion, and, later in the day, these posts were relieved by the 2nd Battalion, two posts on the right being taken off by two platoons from Hawkes Bay Company, with a third platoon in support, while two platoons from Ruahine Company took over two posts on the left with another platoon in support. Enemy shelling was heavy during the afternoon and, as the positions were fully exposed to view, being on the forward slope of Messines Ridge, the relief was not easy to carry out. Hawkes Bay Company was able to rush forward its Lewis Gun sections by daylight; but, during that operation, Lieut. G. W. Bollinger was severely wounded, and subsequently died. Second Battalion headquarters were established at about 11 a.m. at Blauwen Molen, east of the village. It had been a German Artillery headquarters with an elaborate telephone exchange, and, close by, were underground dug-outs absolutely full of dead. (Blauwen Molen had fallen to Wellington-West Coast Company of the 1st Battalion early in the day). About 3 o'clock in the afternoon, orders were received for the rest of the 2nd Battalion to relieve the 1st Battalion, and the relief was made during the evening, although not finally completed till midnight. Just before the relief was complete the enemy commenced a heavy bombardment and seemed to be on the point of counter-attacking. All troops stood to, and our artillery clapped down a thunderous barrage. The enemy counter-attack, however, did not pass the Australians in front of us and, luckily, the German barrage succeeded generally in missing our trenches.

Lieut.-Col. F. K. Turnbull, D.S.O., M.C.

Sergt. J. G. Grant, V.C.

On the way to Passchendaele.

Aeroplane photograph of Kron Prinz Farm showing effect of shellfire shortly before our attack.

THE WELLINGTON REGIMENT

Liaison between the Australians in front and ourselves was poor, and, at that time, the situation was obscure, so far as regards the occupation of the Green Line (the Australians' objective), and the intermediate strong points. Accordingly, after the 2nd Battalion had taken over, Lieut. A. G. Melles took charge of two strong reconnoitring patrols and brought back information of the utmost importance regarding the occupation of the ground in front, which completely cleared up the position. Lieut. Melles's task was a difficult one, accentuated, as it was, by intermittent heavy enemy shell-fire; but he displayed cool bravery and fine dash and the success of the enterprise entitled him to the greatest credit. For his conduct that night he shortly afterwards received the Military Cross.

On being relieved by the 2nd Battalion, 1st Wellington moved back some distance and took over from 2nd Canterbury, for the Second and Third Brigades were then being withdrawn.

It was early in the morning of the 8th, that Brigadier General C. H. J. Brown was killed. General Russell had been up to see him at the First Brigade's advanced headquarters at Moulin de l'Hospice, and was on the point of saying good-bye on the road, when shrapnel burst overhead, killing General Brown instantly and wounding General Russell's A.D.C. General Brown's career from August 1914, had been one of unbroken success. He was a most capable leader, of rare tact, and his death was a sad blow to the while Division, but particularly to the First Brigade.

Beautiful weather continued the following day, for, it must be remembered, it was midsummer. The 2nd Battalion made itself as comfortable as possible in the newly dug trenches. Padre Walls brought up his burial party, and in spite of the constant shell-fire, carried on during the whole day, few of our dead being left unburied.

During the afternoon of the 9th, the 2nd Battalion lost one of their company commanders in Capt. R. F. C. Scott, commanding Hawkes Bay Company. Thoroughly tired out, he was asleep in the bottom of a trench, and was struck by a piece of shell. He never regained consciousness, and died before he reached the casualty clearing station. He was a gallant leader, and for long afterwards, Hawkes Bay Company, who called him "the Black Prince" and liked and respected him tremendously, were very sad at his death, and at that of dear old Bollinger.

Late that night, both our 1st and 2nd Battalions were relieved by the 14th Battalion, 4th Brigade, 4th Australian Division. From various causes, the relief was very much delayed, and, so far as the 1st Battalion was concerned, was not complete until nearly 4 a.m. Companies then made their way down to Bulford Camp, and both battalions went into reserve there. Shortly after one of the platoons of Ruahine Company (2nd Battalion) started on its way out, a big shell burst in its midst and killed and wounded several. All that could be done was to dress the wounded and lift them to a place of comparative safety, near by, and leave them there. The four company stretcher-bearers who were with company headquarters in front, did not hear of this till they had reached Bulford Camp five miles away; but, without hesitation, they turned back, faced Hades again, and carried the wounded out. The Australians had promised to see that our wounded were looked after, and, no doubt, would have done so; but the Ruahine stretcher-bearers thought it their duty to get their own mates into safety before they themselves rested in Bulford Camp.

Among many acts of marked courage and devotion to duty was a notable one on the part of Lance-Corporal Robert Poots, 2nd Battalion chiropodist. During the day of the 8th June, under particularly heavy shell fire, Poots, by unflagging energy, rendered most valuable assistance to his battalion at the Regimental Aid Post at Boyle's Farm. Again on the night of the 9th June, during the relief, six men were wounded at the cross roads near Blauwen Molen. At this time the enemy was shelling our position heavily with particular attention to the locality where these men lay. In spite of this, and with a complete disregard of his own safety, Corporal Poots went out to dress the wounds of

THE WELLINGTON REGIMENT

these men. On arriving there he found the fire too intense to attend to them where they lay, so he removed each of these men to a place of safety, and dressed the wounds.

Lieut. A. R. McIssac had worked with untiring energy and determination for three days when in charge of the 1st Battalion's carrying party, whose duty it was to keep that battalion supplied with material from the brigade dump. It was necessary for the party to make each trip under very heavy shell-fire, and it was largely due to McIssac's fine personal example that the supply was maintained.

Unfortunately, a Regiment cannot take part in an engagement like the Battle of Messines without casualties, as the following table shows:—

1st WELLINGTON.

	Killed	Missing.	Wounded.
Officers	2	—	11
Other Ranks	71	8	326

2nd WELLINGTON.

	Killed	Missing.	Wounded.
Officers	2	—	3
Other Ranks	13	7	124

N.B. This list covers a period of five days only, from the 6th to the 10th June (inclusive).

CHAPTER XXIV.

Rest after Battle.

Brune Gaye — Rue de Sac — Inspection by and congratulations from General Godley—3rd Battalion's Baptism of Trench Warfare—Lieut. T. L. Ward Crosses the Lys and Reconnoitres Frelinghein.

ON the 11th June, the 2nd Battalion moved from Bulford Camp, to billets at Gravier—Brune Gaye and, on the 12th, the 1st Battalion marched to the Rue de Sac area, the battalions remaining in these billets until the 18th June.

On the morning of the 13th June, the First Brigade was inspected by the Corps Commander (Lieut.-General Sir A. J. Godley), who congratulated it on its performance at the Battle of Messines. On the 17th, a combined Church Parade of both battalions was held at which General Russell was present, Padre Walls taking the service.

On the 10th June, the 3rd Battalion had re-assembled and moved to billets in Pont de Nieppe. At 4 p.m. on the 11th, Hawkes Bay Company of the 3rd Battalion was ordered to report to the Commanding Officer of the 36th Battalion of the 9th Australian Infantry Brigade, which battalion had suffered heavy casualties in the recent fighting. The night before, a company of this battalion had attacked and taken some high ground, 700 yards ahead of the front line at La Potterie Farm, and Hawkes Bay Company was instructed to relieve the former company, which

THE WELLINGTON REGIMENT

was very weak in strength—consolidate the advanced post, and hold it against counter-attack. In moving overland to the position, Hawkes Bay Company had one man killed and three wounded by shell-fire. The Germans shelled the post heavily the next afternoon and evening, wounding seven more men. Fortunately, the enemy fire was directed at their old trenches about fifty yards in rear, otherwise we would have suffered more casualties. Hawkes Bay was relieved at 10.30 p.m. on the 12th by 4th Company, 1st Otago, and marched back to Pont Nieppe arriving there at 3. a.m. on the 13th.

On the 14th June, the 3rd Battalion was to receive its real baptism of trench warfare, for, at 10 o'clock that night it relieved 3rd Auckland in line in Le Touquet Sector. Nor was the start an auspicious one, for the enemy had not yet recovered from the loss of Messines, and was shelling the sector continuously, with the result that the 3rd Battalion had several casualties, one of them being the Commanding Officer (Lieut.-Col. W. H. Fletcher) who was severely wounded. Major J. L. Short now assumed command. The battalion remained in the line eight days, and, during that period, was active in patrolling, the indications being that the enemy was falling back to the east side of the river Lys. On one occasion, the battalion pushed standing patrols forwards three-quarters of a mile from the front line, no opposition being met.

During this, the 3rd Battalion's first experience in the trenches, Lieut. T. L. Ward was responsible for a very gallant exploit. About 1.30 o'clock in the afternoon of the 15th, Lieut. T. L. Ward, a Sergeant and Private G. Brown, crossed the Lys by a damaged enemy pontoon. Leaving the Sergeant to guard the river, Ward and Brown went along the road into Frelinghien, then in the hands of the enemy. A reconnaissance was made but the village seemed deserted, the Huns, no doubt, taking their midday siesta. Turning through an archway into a factory, however, they came upon a cellar with three Bavarians lying there asleep. These, they took prisoners and came back with them to our lines unchallenged. The Bavarians quite saw the joke, Frelinghein, they said, was held in strength, and the bridge guarded, and a machine-gun detachment whose sentries must have been asleep. The same night, Lieut. Ward led a patrol along the river bank and brought back a valuable report upon the state of the bridges. The extreme fearlessness and initiative displayed by Lieut. Ward during both these operations were responsible for much valuable information being obtained. An attempt to cross the Lys, the following evening found the enemy keenly alert along the river.

CHAPTER XXV.

Trench Warfare after Messines.

Hill 63 — Mustard Gas—Exploits of 2nd Battalion's Patrols—Activity in the Air—Observation Balloons —The "Archies" — Midsummer Days — The Duke of Connaught at Bailleul—3rd Battalion at Nieppe

THE New Zealand Division was now taking over the front on the right of the 4th Australian Division from Post Office Corner to the Warnave River, and, indeed, some of the New Zealand Brigades were already in the line. Within a few days, the First Brigade was to relieve the Second Brigade in the trenches.

At dusk on the 18th June, after a hot day with a heavy thunder-storm, the 2nd Battalion relieved 1st Canterbury in the front line immediately opposite La Basse Ville, with Wellington-West Coast Company in the posts, and front line (an old German trench near Au Chausseur Cabaret), Taranaki Company in support, Hawkes Bay and Ruahine Companies in reserve, the former in Bunhill Row, and the latter in the Catacombs, Captain W. H. McLean now assuming command of Hawkes Bay Company in place of Capt. R. F. C. Scott, who had died of wounds at Messines.

On the same day, the 1st Battalion relieved 1st Otago in brigade reserve at Hill 63, with Battalion headquarters first at Limavady Lodge and, after being shelled out of that, at Fort Garry. The 1st Battalion remained at Hill 63 until the 23rd, nearly the whole strength of the battalion being employed on working parties. Every night Hill 63, was heavily shelled with gas and H.E. and some casualties were sustained.

At this time, the enemy had not quite recovered from the disorganisation resulting from the Messines-Wytschaete battle. Artillery action on both sides was fairly violent, although most of our heavy guns were now being withdrawn.

The 2nd Battalion in the line was fairly active, Wellington-West Coast Company sending out several patrols, one under Lieut. A. G. Melles, exploiting part of La Basse Ville. Another, consisting of Sergeant Fisher and Private Goddard from No. 3 Post, coming upon a German machine-gun, called upon its crew to surrender, and shot two. The enemy gun at once opened fire, forcing our two men to withdraw. Goddard managed to get back to his post in safety; but, unfortunately, Sergt. Fisher did not return, and it was ascertained from one of the German prisoners taken by us a few nights later that he had been wounded and was a prisoner.

Here also, Lieut. H. Simmonds, M.C., 2nd Battalion Intelligence Officer, had a most trying experience. Early one morning, he and Corporal Taylor came right on to a German machine-gun post. Corporal Taylor shot one of the crew; but, the Germans opening fire, Lieut. Simmonds and he were obliged to disperse. Taylor worked his way down the hedges back to our lines; but Simmonds was obliged to take refuge in a shell hole, where he had to remain for twelve hours. So close was he to the Germans, that he could hear them talking and digging all day. After dark, Simmonds ran the gauntlet of the Germans rifle fire. It was a very exhausted Intelligence Officer that returned to our lines; but the battalion was very relieved to have him back.

Hawkes Bay and Ruahine Companies in reserve supplied the working parties, digging a considerable portion of the travel trench for the new front line.

After a few days, artillery fire noticeably decreased on both sides. The 2nd Battalion now received orders to carry out certain patrolling operations in co-operation with 1st Auckland, supported by Artillery barrage. For this purpose, on the night of the 21st June, Wellington-West Coast Company provided two platoons, No. 3 under Lieut. A. G. Melles on the right, and No. 1 platoon under Lieut. P. D. Healy on the left while First Auckland provided a third platoon. The object was to clear the ground to the immediate front of all enemy posts. Night operations such as this, undertaken with but the scantiest preparation, are extremely difficult and apt to miscarry. Our No. 1 platoon and the Auckland platoon were, unfortunately, delayed and unable to take any real part in the operation. It was, therefore, left to our No. 3 platoon under Lieut. A. G. Melles to carry out their job by themselves.

The main and only street of La Basse Ville ran parallel to and between the railway line and the River Lys. Melles divided his four sections into two parties, and with one crossed the railway at a spot near the Messines Road, which strikes the main street at right angles at the southern end of the village. The sugar refinery, at that time merely a skeleton of twisted girders and broken iron, was situated on the river Lys side of the junction of the Messines Road and the main street. Melles led his men into the street at this point and they fought their way northwards along it. Bomb, bayonet and rifle were used, in hand to hand fighting. We were to learn afterwards from prisoners, that there was a considerable German garrison in the cellars of the buildings of La Basse Ville, and great must have been their surprise as they struggled out into the darkness of the night, to find a daring enemy in possession of the village.

It was a great fight, and to hear it recounted afterwards was to bring back to memory the stories of the way in which British sailors in days gone by, boarded enemy ships and swept their decks with pistol and cutlass. The explosion of the bombs of both sides, the British Mills' bomb being distinguished by its metallic ping, could not drown the noise of the sweating, fighting men, the groans of the wounded, and the screams of those in their death agony. Our men were out-numbered; but indomitable. They cleared the street, and drove the Huns out of the end of the village behind a tall hedge which ran at right angles down to the river. Here, Melles was joined by his other two sections, which had crossed the railway line higher up, and had struck the Tissage* at the top end of the village. As they found it impossible to enter this building from its northern side, they worked round it to its southern side, and, after killing a few Germans there, joined Lieut. Melles, whose party was engaged bombing the enemy sheltering behind the hedge.

Melles very wisely chose this opportunity to withdraw his party. His casualties were already severe, and no good purpose could be served by staying longer. He, accordingly, got his party together, and moved down the street. There again they met some of the enemy, who had probably come up out of the cellars in the meantime. Some of these were killed by our men, others taken prisoner. No further opposition being encountered, Melles' platoon withdrew across the railway line and returned to our lines. Our casualties were, one killed, one wounded and missing, and sixteen wounded, out of a total of forty-two. The missing man had been so badly wounded that he could not be shifted and our men had had to leave him. He fell into the hands of the enemy and had to have one of his legs amputated in a German Hospital. Not many months afterwards, he was repatriated to England.

For his daring leadership, Lieut. Melles received a bar to his M.C. (the first bar to be awarded in the division). It was only a few weeks before at Messines, that he had won his M.C. Corporal J. D. Fraser and Private Ernest Henderson were awarded the Military Medal for their gallantry, and well each of them deserved it. Good work was also done by Lieut. R. K. Nicol, with two guns of the First Light Trench Mortar Battery, who bombarded certain machine-gun emplacements. The task of getting his guns into posi-

*A large spinning factory.

THE WELLINGTON REGIMENT

tion, and getting up ammunition was a difficult one, but was well carried out.

Our left platoon got disorganised on its way up to the point of assembly, two sections losing their way, and was, therefore, unable to take any real part in the operation. The commander of this platoon, 2/Lieut. P. D. Healy, was so badly wounded in the foot, that a few days later, he had to have his foot amputated.

In view of the failure on the left, a similar operation was undertaken the following night, again in conjunction with 1st Auckland. On this occasion, it was confined to clearing the ground between our posts, and the Armentieres-Warneton railway line, our men on the right having only to patrol towards La Basse Ville. A very effective barrage was put down by our artillery, and, under its protection, three platoons from Taranaki Company (then holding the front line) under Lieuts. A. T. White, C. T. Natusch and N. F. Little, did the work. The garrisons of several enemy posts were destroyed, and identification obtained, after which our men withdrew to our own lines. In the meantime, Ruahine Company had come up from the Catacombs, and occupied our front posts, so that Taranaki Company were then able to go right back to the Catacombs. Our casualties were, two killed, one missing, and twenty-five wounded, mostly slight. For his courage and leadership that night, Lieut. N. F. Little was shortly afterwards to receive his M.C., and for other acts of gallantry during these operations, Military Medals were awarded to the following:—
Sergeant L. J. Rennie, Pte. J. A. Coombes, Pte. M. Nielson, Pte. T. Bullick, Pte. G. A. Ward, Pte. F. Wright, Pte. S. J. Venning.

On the evening of 23rd June, the 1st Battalion relieved the 2nd Battalion in the line and the 2nd Battalion moved back to bivouacs and dug-outs on the wooded slope of Hill 63. It had been noticed the enemy was now disposed to shell every night Hyde Park Corner and Mud Lane, through which we had to pass. For that reason, the relief was commenced early, and while it was yet light. That turned

THE WELLINGTON REGIMENT

out to be fortunate, because, later that night, the enemy opened a heavy bombardment with H.E. and gas shells on Hill 63, and on all roads in the vicinity; yet the relief was made with hardly a casualty.

Before Messines, the Germans' guns seemed unable to range on the Southern Slope of Hill 63, and, troops being comparatively safe, as many as four battalions used to bivouac there, some feeling particularly happy and altogether safe under the shelter of a sheet of corrugated iron, not proof against even an army biscuit. After Messines, losses on the Hill began to mount up and it was not long before the numbers there were reduced.

The 1st Battalion in line made the same dispositions as before, and concentrated its efforts on consolidating and improving the positions held, the 2nd Battalion sending up working parties to dig trenches during darkness, returning at daybreak. The 2nd Battalion's first two nights on the Hill were the essence of discomfort. For nearly two weeks, the enemy had been using his new mustard gas, and he now bombarded the Hill with H.E. and gas shells—(mostly lachrymatory, but some phosgene and some mustard). There was nothing to do but to endure it, and we would all seek such shelter as was available if possible, in the trenches towards the top of the hill, and there spend the night, weeping copious tears into our respirators from inflamed and streaming eyes.

There was now considerable activity in the air, and, looking up and down the line from Hill 63, it was no uncommon thing to see close on a hundred aeroplanes in the sky at the same time. Early morning or in the evening was the time. Many an aerial duel did we watch and many a plane did we see come hurtling to earth. Here in the early mornings, we could sometimes see a squadron of German aeroplanes with yellow bodies. These "yellow bellies" were understood to be in Richthofen's Travelling Circus. One of the most famous of German airmen was Baron Richthofen. His squadron never remained in any particular sector; but whenever an attack was made at any part of the line, his squadron would appear.

From Hill 63 also, during the daytime, we would watch many attacks against our observation balloons by enemy aeroplanes. Often these attacks would be fruitless; because, as soon as the enemy plane appeared, our "Archies"* would put up round the balloon in jeopardy, a protective barrage, which, as a rule, the German aircraft would not venture to penetrate. Sometimes, however, the enemy would meet with success—for instance, one hot midsummer day, when large billowy clouds were blowing over from the enemy lines, a German aeroplane suddenly emerged from one of these clouds, within a short distance of one of our balloons and, before our "Archies" had spotted him, the enemy airman had fired his rocket into the balloon, and down it came in flames, our observers only just escaping in their parachutes. Encouraged by this victory, the enemy plane returned by the same artifice again and again, and, within an hour, had brought down in flames before our very eyes, no less than four of our huge observation balloons.

In midsummer, the days can be as hot in Belgium as in New Zealand. In June, the wood on Hill 63, was wearing a thick green cloak, so different from its chilly nakedness of April. It seemed sacrilege that shells should tear its beautiful limbs to pieces. Even to us, it brought a feeling of sadness; but what angry bitterness must have welled up in the heart of its owner, and the owner of the chateau, for there was hardly a fragment of the chateau left. It is true the Lodge was there, and on the Maori Pioneer Battalion moving out, our 2nd Battalion made Red Lodge its headquarters.

The 1st Battalion in line found the enemy again crossing and establishing posts on our side of the railway line. From the building in La Basse Ville, there came a good deal of sniping and machine-gun fire; but, this was largely stopped by a bombardment of the buildings on the 26th

---

*" Archies "—anti-aircraft guns.

June, combined with our own organised sniping. On the same day, two officers of the 2nd Battalion Rifle Brigade (the battalion on our right), went up to the Sugar Refinery in daylight, and were fired on at close range, one being wounded. Subsequent attempts at rescue were unsuccessful, and added to the casualties. 1st Wellington was working in conjunction with the Second "Dinks"; but, owing to warning not reaching our standing patrol in front of No. 2 post in time, this patrol came into conflict with a party of rescuers after dark, with the result that one of the rescue party was wounded, and two of our men killed, and one severely wounded by the explosion of a bomb.

Work was now the motto of the whole division, and all ranks fell to digging, in furtherance of an ambitious programme of improving the sector. However, our spell of work was short, as the 4th Australian Division was shortly to come over from the Messines sector and relieve us and we were to move out once more to billets.

While yet on Hill 63, the 2nd Battalion was able to be represented at the Parade of representatives of the II. Anzac Corps before H.R.H. The Duke of Connaught. Major C. H. Weston attended on behalf of the 2nd Battalion, and with him went Sergeant Ward (Ruahine), Segeant C. Gore (Hawkes Bay), Private Watt (Taranaki), and Private Coombes (Wellington-West Coast), while Capt. F. S. Varnham, Lieuts. C. G. Stewart and E. Edwards and six N.C.O.'s represented the 3rd Battalion. The Parade was held in the square at Bailleul, and was intended as a compliment to the Corps for the capture of Messines. Many trophies of victory were parked before the Town Hall, and British troops lined the four sides of the ancient square. General Plumer (Commander of the Second Army) was there; but he seemed to wish General Godley, the Corps Commander, to be the chief figure before His Royal Highness, and contented himself with pottering about the parade ground looking at the men and the captured guns.

On the 28th June, the 2nd Battalion left Hill 63, and marched back to De Seule, occupying the same ground as on arriving back from Tatinghem, before Messines. The day was spent in resting and bathing. In the evening, there was heavy thunder and a rain storm.

On the following night, the 1st Battalion was relieved, the 15th Brigade A.I.F. taking over front, support and subsiduary lines from both 2nd Auckland and 1st Wellington. By relieving the rear companies in daylight, and getting the front line company forward by sections before dark, the relief was made smoothly, and quickly, and was complete before 11.30 p.m. The bombardment of Hill 63, Hyde Park Corner, and Prowse Point being heavier than usual that night, the 1st Battalion was fortunate in sustaining no casualties during its relief, or on its march back to De Seule.

June had been a gruelling month for 1st Wellington. From the 24th to 30th alone, it had had six killed and ninety one wounded, while the total casualties for the whole month were,—

Officers—Killed 2, Wounded 11.
Other ranks—Killed 78, Wounded 426, Missing 8.
Total 575.

That of course, included the battle casualties at Messines.

On the night of the 22nd June, our 3rd Battalion had been relieved in the trenches by 3rd Otago. Already, the sector had noticeably quietened down, and the enemy artillery activity was daily growing less. No casualties were sustained during the relief, and the 3rd Battalion went back into rest billets in Nieppe, there to remain for the rest of that month, and during the first week of July. The only noteworthy happening during that time, was the inspection of the rations by the Q.M.G. Second Army, and the Q.M.G. U.S.A. Army.

CHAPTER XXVI.

A Well Deserved Spell.

Le Verrier — St. Marie Capelle — Cassell — Sports at Doulieu— Hawke's Bay (2nd Battalion) go Back Early to Train for La Basseville—Kortepyp Camp —Back to the Trenches—3rd Battalion at Brune Gaye—A Brush with Enemy Patrols in Le Touquet Sector.

ON the 30th June, the 1st Battalion marched to billets in Le Verrier Area, and there it remained until the 19th July. Platoon and company training was carried out, and, on two different days, all companies carried out two courses of musketry on a 25 yards range. During this period of training also, the 1st Battalion was inspected by Major General Russell.

On the 29th, an advance party from the 2nd Battalion had marched to Steenwerck, and entrained for Hazebrouck. On arrival there, it marched to St. Marie Capelle, about four miles from Hazebrouck. The 2nd Battalion itself followed in the afternoon by the same route, arriving at its new billets at 9.30 p.m., after a pleasant day's journey.

The 2nd Battalion was indeed in luck's way. St. Marie Capelle was a pretty village at the foot of the hill on which the town of Cassel was built. Across a valley was the wooded Mont des Racollets, and further Eastward, Mont des Cats, with its summit crowned by an ancient monastery. What a wonderful view there was from Cassel. At night, there could be seen the opposing trench lines marked by

Major McKinnon at one of the Cookers.

Face p. 184.

A Group of 1st Battalion Officers.

Pill Box at Korek.

Menin Road.

the gun flashes, while by day, if the air were particularly clear, it was said the cliffs of Dover might be seen. How far away, we seemed to be from the din and strife of battle. Why, only upon a particularly heavy bombardment, could we hear the guns at all, and then only their dull boom. Little did we think as we lay at St. Marie Capelle, in July 1917, that, before the war should be won, the enemy would penetrate even into its peaceful serenity, and lay waste its fields and bombard the aerodrome, not half a mile from these billets of ours.

Nor was Cassel without its compensations. Never had one seen so many red tabs before. All were of the staff. They ranged from white haired Generals, down to dapper young Staff Lieutenants. Why, we had hardly been at St. Marie Capelle a day, before His Majesty the King himself was at Cassell! There were shops: there were tramcars: there was La Belle Sauvage Inn—alas, for officers only.

During this period of rest and training, divisional swimming sports were held, one of the 2nd Battalion's representatives, Pte. E. W. Cobledick (Hawkes Bay Company) winning the second prize in the 100 yards race. On the following day, a Divisional Gymkhana was held at Doulieu. Pte. E. W. Cobledick won the 880 yards race and the three miles cross country steeplechase, while Wellington-West Coast Company's (2nd Battalion) Tug-of-war team pulled into the final; but were then beaten by a very heavy Maori team from the Pioneer Battalion.

Towards the end of its stay at St. Marie Capelle, the 2nd Battalion held a platoon tournament, to which it invited the Mayor and all the villagers. The invitation was circulated by a notice in the church porch, and the whole village came. We gave them coffee and cakes, and all seemed thoroughly to enjoy themselves.

Lieut.-Col. Cunningham had assumed temporary command of the First Brigade on the 4th July, when Brigadier-General Melvill went on leave to England, and, upon the latter's return, his own leave became due, so that Major Weston remained in command of 2nd Battalion.

THE WELLINGTON REGIMENT

Shortly before the 2nd Battalion moved back to the line, on the 12th July, the Hawkes Bay Company (Capt. W. H. McLean) was sent forward by motor lorries to Kortepyp Camp to train for a special operation that involved the capture of the village of La Basse Ville. The rest of the 2nd Battalion did not leave St. Marie Chapelle until the 18th July, when they moved to Kortepyp Camp in two trips of twenty motor lorries. By that time Hawkes Bay Company was already in hard training for its "stunt."

During the evening of the following day, the 2nd Battalion moved into the trenches opposite La Basse Ville, relieving parts of 51st and 52nd Battalions of the 4th Australian Division, with battalion headquarters at St Yves Post Office. Hawkes Bay remained at Kortepyp to continue its special training.

On the same day, the 1st Battalion (now under the command of Major H. Holderness, Lieut.-Col. Cook being on leave), marched to Hill 63, and relieved 1st Auckland in brigade reserve, being camped in the dugouts and tunnels round Red Lodge, and from there supplying large working parties daily. Hill 63 was subjected to periodical shelling by the enemy, and a few casualties occurred almost daily, either at Red Lodge or on the working parties. At night, the area was bombarded with gas shells to the great discomfort of working parties passing through Ploegsteert Wood and round Hyde Park Corner.

On the 8th July, the 3rd Battalion had moved from Nieppe to Brune Gaye, and for the next week, was called upon to supply working parties for the New Zealand Engineers. On the 16th July, it took over the front line trenches in the Le Touquet Sector from 3rd Auckland, and, that night, Taranaki Company's advanced posts had a brush with a German patrol, eleven strong. One wounded German was taken prisoner, while we had two wounded. On the following night, Sergeant Pennefather and his patrol (Hawkes Bay Company), saw some Germans proceeding along the river Lys in a boat: whereupon they threw six bombs, and fired their rifles into the boat, causing it to

THE WELLINGTON REGIMENT

capsize. There is little else to chronicle during this spell in the trenches, save much artillery activity on both sides.

On the 24th, our 3rd Battalion was relieved by 3rd Otago, and moved to billets in brigade reserve at Oosthove Ferme and Pontceau where a large number of reinforcements joined up. Here the battalion remained until the 1st August, some companies being employed on working parties under the New Zealand Engineers, while others carried on with training.

CHAPTER XXVII.

La Basse Ville.

Hawke's Bay (2nd Battalion) Capture La Basse Ville; but are Driven Out—The 2nd Battalion Captures La Basse Ville and Holds It—Andrew Wins the Victoria Cross—Lieut. Nicol's Gallantry.

[*Practically the whole of this chapter has, with the kind permission of the Author, been taken from "Three Years with the New Zealanders," by Lieut.-Col. C. H. Weston, D.S.O.*]

THE 2nd Battalion stormed and captured La Basse Ville on two occasions. On the 27th July, Hawkes Bay Company had little difficulty in taking the village, but the Germans, a few hours afterwards, counter-attacked in comparatively great strength, and drove out the posts left by us as a garrison. On the 31st July, Wellington-West Coast Company, with two platoons of Taranaki Company, again seized the place, and this time all the attackers remained and held it against the counter-attacks that followed. This operation was made conjointly with Ruahine Company, clearing the hedge row system on our left between our posts and the railway line.

The week preceding the attack by Hawke's Bay Company was one of busy preparation. The Company trained hard at Kortepyp Camp, and every evening its officers and N.C.O.'s in turn, went up and patrolled the area between No. 1 post and the Railway Line, and sometimes across the line towards the village. Two patrols were out on the night of the 21st, and one of them, under Sergeant

L. W. Butler, encountered a Hun Post on their side of the Railway and had a brush with it. Two nights later, an enemy patrol came into our country and hiding in a ruined cottage in front of No. 2 Post, surprised our patrol on its return journey. In the fight that followed, 2nd Lieut. B. Brookes was wounded and Sergeant L. Murnane killed. It was understood that the 2nd Battalion was to tackle the job of clearing the hedgerows also, and preparations were made for that as well. We afterwards learned, from the prisoners captured on the 27th, that the garrison numbered about 200, and that, curiously enough, the middle of the village formed the boundary of two sectors; a company from one sector holding the Sugar Refinery, and another company from an adjoining sector occupying the buildings at the northern end. The latter sector included the hedgerows, which were garrisoned by still another company; and the hedgerows formed the front line. So the Germans could not be said to hold the line lightly.

Since Lieut. Melles' exploit of the 21st June, the enemy had been busily wiring the land between the railway and the village. This our patrols and the aerial photographs told us. It was left to Ruahine Company to discover on the night of the 21st July, what wiring he had been doing in the hedgerows. We knew there was a machine-gun post behind the hedge, in a corner of the field opposite No. 3 Post, and at midnight a detachment of the First Light Trench Mortar Battery, under Lieut. R. K. Nicol, fired sixty Stokes bombs into the position, and at ten minutes past twelve, the 15th Howitzer Battery N.Z.F.A., placed three salvos at a point about 200 yards behind. The machine-gun was evidently hit by the Stokes, because it was not brought into action by the enemy. The Stokes gun is liable to fire so rapidly that eight bombs are in the air together, and the effect of sixty bombs exploding in a very short space of time can be imagined. Directly Lieut. Nicol ceased fire, Lieut. G. A. Robbie led forward his fourteen men and struck the hedge about 150 yards from the corner. They found it heavily wired, and exchanged bombs with some Germans on the other side; apparently with some effect, for groans were heard. Here, unhappily, Lieut. Robbie was mortally wounded by a bullet from a rifle fired through the hedge. Lance-Corporal N. G. Harding, the senior N.C.O. present, led the party along the hedge in a north-westerly direction towards the corner where the machine-gun was. He could hear an officer or N.C.O. endeavouring to rally the garrison on the other side, but a few more bombs being thrown at them, they made off. Wire was met with all along the hedge. The object of the party had been attained, and Harding, sending a man back to No. 3 Post for a stretcher, withdrew, carrying Lieut. Robbie with him. The latter, however, died before they reached the post. We buried this gallant officer next day at the Military Cemetery at Prowse Point, 3,000 yards south of Messines, on the northern edge of Ploegsteert Wood.

The 2nd Battalion thought it necessary, as part of the preparation for the attack, to occupy the railway line before the village, and also to establish a new post on the eastern corner of the field in which No. 3 Post was situated. The latter was not done until the second attack on the 31st July, but, three more groups of sentries were placed on the railway. If the Hun had forestalled us there, perhaps his posts would have escaped our artillery barrage, and might have caused a check to the advance before our men had got into their stride.

For assembly trenches we dug a new sap along the Messines-La Basse Ville Road, which we named Cabaret Road, and opened up an old trench (Unnamed Sap) that ran from No. 1 Post to the railway. We dared not take either of these two trenches as far as the railway for fear of raising suspicions of a projected attack, and so dug them only half way. Unchained Avenue was a German communication trench leading from the Au Chasseur Cabaret to the railway and passing to the north of No. 1 Post, and this we opened right up to the line. No 1 Post was enlarged to hold another platoon, and a communication trench, which we called La Truoie Sap, was dug to provide a shorter route from the Power Buzzer Dugout to No. 1 Post and to the village, via Cabaret Road or Unchained Avenue. All these saps would serve the further purpose of communication with the village after its capture, and, indeed, the telephone wire to the place where company headquarters was to be situated during the action, was laid down Unchained Avenue two nights before.

Dumps also had to be made. Stokes bombs were needed in front of No. 2 Post to feed the guns that were to bombard the Estaminet, a two-story detached building at the northern end of the village. We suspected the existence of a machine-gun in the second story of the Estaminet, and our suspicions proved correct. A larger general dump was made in La Truie Farm buildings on the Cabaret Road, containing S.S.A., rations, water, flares, etc., for the use of the future garrison of the village.

The 2nd Battalion's preparations were all completed by the night of the 25th, when Hawkes Bay Company came up from Kortepyp and relieved Taranaki Company on the right of the front line including No. 1 Post. The whole company thus had twenty-four hours in which to view the approaches to the village and to study, through the glasses, the portion of it allotted to them in the attack. Unfortunately, the Hun put down one of his favourite artillery barrages on the right of the line next morning, and Hawkes Bay Company lost four killed and eleven wounded.

At 1.30 on the morning of the 27th, Hawkes Bay Company (3 officers and 136 other ranks) was in position waiting for zero hour. Lieut. J. S. Hanna, with No. 7 platoon, was on the right in Cabaret Road ready to seize the Sugar Refinery. Sergeant C. N. Devery, with No. 8 platoon, in the centre in Unnamed Sap to attack the heart of the village, and Lieut. W. G. Gibbs, with No. 6 platoon, on the left, lay in Unchained Avenue, his objective being the Tissage. Captain W. H. McLean held No. 5 platoon in reserve, and made his headquarters in a trench parallel to the railway running from Unchained Avenue to the Cabaret Road. At 2 a.m. our barrage came down, like a thunderclap, and

THE WELLINGTON REGIMENT

under its cover the three platoons stormed the village. Lieut. Hanna's party had but little difficulty in taking the Sugar Refinery, probably owing to the fact that its garrison of forty Bavarians, so we learned from a prisoner, was concentrated in a large cellar underneath the building. Into this cellar incendiary bomb were thrown, causing an explosion of ammunition and not one of its garrison emerged. Sergeant Devery's platoon cleared the centre part of the hamlet, and met with considerable opposition, that was overcome with severe loss to the enemy, thirty bodies being counted in the street alone, apart from any killed in the buildings. To capture the Tissage, Lieut. Gibbs had to fight hard, but nothing could stop the men, and they swept the place clear of its defenders, of whom a number where killed by our Lewis guns, as they fled towards Warneton. Cellars and dugouts were bombed. Ten bodies lay near the Tissage. Four posts of seven men each were left behind, two on the banks of the Lys and two facing towards Warneton, and the remainder of the company withdrew from the village as ordered, to avoid casualties from shell-fire. It was considered most unlikely, that the enemy would counter-attack during the day, and it was intended to reinforce the posts at dusk to meet any stroke in the night.

So far the affair had been a wonderful success, and our losses were insignificant. But, in a very short time, the position was reversed. Fifty minutes after zero the German gunners put down a box barrage along the railway that completely cut off the village from the rest of the company, and drove Captain W. H. McLean and his reserves out of the position they had taken up. Two small counter-attacks were beaten off by the two northern posts, to be followed, however, by one from the same direction in the strength of about 250 rifles, and later identified as a whole support battalion of the 6th Division. No appeal for artillery help came from the posts by means of the very pistols that they carried, and the Germans, by sheer weight of numbers, overwhelmed them. They attacked and drove back to the railway, the left of the two northern posts, and then con-

MESSINES AND **LA BASS VILLE**
Scale 1 – 20,000 Metres.

THE WELLINGTON REGIMENT

centrated on Sergeant Devery's posts, one the right of the northern end, and the other on the river bank. Some of the attackers climbed on to the roofs of the houses in the main street and kept up a galling fire on our men, who retaliated as best as they could: but the latter's chief efforts were directed to stemming the main tide of the attack. These two posts fought to the bitter end, one man, besides Devery, surviving. Lieut. Hanna made an effort to assist Devery, and he and his men went some distance down the main street, and only when they saw the posts had gone and the numbers were against them did they withdraw across the railway to face a further advance upon No. 1 Post, if such were attempted. Communications went a short time after the Hun barrage came down, and the first news of the events in the village was brought to Captain McLean by one of Devery's wounded. McLean promptly led two platoons forward, and a platoon of Ruahine Company followed him, but by the time he reached the railway the enemy was in full occupation, and he wisely decided to accept the position and withdraw. Time was given to the enemy to remove his, and also we hoped our, wounded, and the heavies were then turned on to the ill-fated village. Our losses were four killed, fourteen missing and thirty-one wounded, and, in the circumstances, can only be regarded as extraordinarily light.

Had it been a raid our success would have been complete; but it was our intention to hold the village. Plainly, the enemy's strength had been under estimated. It was a pity that our four posts had not been concentrated at the Warneton end of the village, for it was really only from there that the enemy could have delivered a counter-attack. Be that as it may, the performance was an extremely gallant one. Hawkes Bay Company had worked magnificiently and the work of that company reflected the greatest credit on Capt. W. H. McLean. McLean was shortly afterwards to receive the M.C., and Sergeant Devery and Pte. M. Vestey the D.C.M., while for their share in the operation the Military Medal was awarded to Corpl. R. P. Northe, Pte. A.

E. Still, Pte. T. Chirnside, Pte. A. A. Rossiter, Pte. D. H. Larsen and Pte. H. Blakemore, the last named a very gallant stretcher-bearer.

A few days later, the 2nd Battalion received the following letter from General Godley, the Commander of II. Anzac Corps;—

"The Corps Commander has read this report with much interest and thinks that the action reflects great credit on Capt. McLean and all ranks of his company. It also proves the value and thoroughness of their previous training."

Ruahine Company relieved Hawkes Bay Company in the afternoon of the 27th, and the latter withdrew to Kortepyp Camp to bind up its wounds. Next night, the rest of the 2nd Battalion moved back, its place being taken by the 1st Battalion. While the relief was proceeding, the S.O.S. went up from our front and from the 1st Auckland on our left, and our guns started in, "Hell for leather." It was an anxious time, as the system of small posts is a standing invitation to a determined enemy to mop one or two of them up in a raid. The German raiders made a valiant effort to reach the Auckland posts, and were successful in driving one advanced post back temporarily with flammenwerfer. Against the Wellington front, little determination was shown and the enemy was driven off.

The enemy was not to be left in enjoyment of his success. A few hours later, Major C. H. Weston was summoned to Brigade Headquarters and at a conference there, General Melvill notified that, as part of a big advance in the Ypres Salient, the 1st Brigade would make another attempt to take and hold La Basse Ville, capture the hedgerow system as far as the railway, and, on the left of that, raid the enemy posts and advance our line. On the left of the 1st Brigade, the Australians were to carry out a similar operation. 1st Auckland would make the raid, 2nd Auckland establish the new line of posts, and 2nd Wellington was to seize the village and hedgerows, and would thereby be the extreme right battalion of the "big push" in the salient.

THE WELLINGTON REGIMENT

The 31st July, was the day appointed. There were but twenty-four hours clear for preparation. Wellington-West Coast Company (Captain H. E. McKinnon, M.C.), with two platoons from Taranaki Company was given the job of seizing the village, and Ruahine Company (Capt. M. Urquhart) —less one platoon—the hedgerows, and, at the Brigadier's suggestion, nine volunteers from Hawke's Bay Company, who were through the first attack, were attached to Captain McKinnon to act as guides. There was a good deal to be done and arranged. Unfortunately, our Artillery barrage just missed the hedgerows, and with nothing else being done, the German garrison, with their machine-guns, would face undisturbed our advance in that quarter. Lieut. R. K. Nicol, however, came to the rescue with his Stokes mortars. He provided four guns, and a dump of 200 shells was established for him. A Vickers gun from the 1st Machine-Gun Company and three Lewis guns from 1st Wellington, would fire into the Germans until the 200 shells had been exhausted. Thereupon, Captain Urquhart's men would advance. Nicol, according to the plan, would then take up his guns and make for La Basse Ville, picking up a party of men waiting for him at La Truie Farm with more bombs, and help in the defence of the village against counter-attacks. Captain Urquhart sent up his remaining platoon on the night of the 30th, to dig a post in which he could make his headquarters and keep his reserve platoon near the eastern corner of the field. As can be imagined, this facilitated his task immensely. When his two assaulting platoons left their assembly points, he simply moved forward with his reserve platoon to a trench dug beforehand, and attached his telephone to a wire already laid. The communications with the village constituted a difficult problem. The enemy's box barrage had repeatedly destroyed the wire on the 27th, and the signallers now reconnoitred a route by way of some disused trenches south of the Sugar Refinery, but that was abandoned and a more direct route taken. Lamps, pigeons, telephone and runners were all to be used. In the action the lamps proved a

THE WELLINGTON REGIMENT

failure, owing to the smoke from the exploding shells shrouding the light, and the wires, although repaired several times, did not hold. The runner, as often has been the case, was the surest messenger. The dump at La Truie Farm had been set on fire by the enemy gunners on the 27th, and had burned merrily for hours, so that had to be refilled.

The afternoon of the 30th, gave the two company commanders time to have a conference with their section leaders and men, and discuss final details. Zero hour was 3.50 a.m., and the 8 officers and 328 other ranks, apart from Headquarters and medical personnel, marched out of Kortepyp Camp at 11.15 p.m. This allowed three hours for the march, one hour to collect the impedimenta of war at Prowse Point and for unforseen delays, and half an hour for rest in the assembly positions before zero. Lieut. W. Pollock had gone ahead to have the bombs and flares ready for the companies as they passed through. The cooks went with him and took up their quarters at Prowse Point. Headquarters had moved up earlier, and had established themselves in the Power Buzzer Dugout by 10.55 p.m. In the early hours of the following morning, the platoons of Wellington-West Coast and Taranaki Companies could be heard moving through Ploegsteert wood and along the slippery duck-walks of St. Yves Avenue and Ultimo Avenue (for it had commenced to rain early in the day) and out to their assembly points at La Truie Sap and Cabaret Road. All were in position by 3 a.m.

The operation turned out a distinct success, although won at the cost of hard fighting. The casualties out of the 8 officers and 328 other ranks, were officers 1 (2nd Lieut. G. Kinvig) killed, and 4 wounded, and other ranks 36 killed and 93 wounded. As usual, many of the casualties were incurred from Artillery fire after the objectives had been gained.

The Ruahine Company had a difficult task. However, Captain Urquhart's scheme of attack was sound, and he displayed great acumen in making alterations of plan necessitated by the changing conditions as the battle in his quarter swayed to and fro, and further he was assisted by Wellington-West Coast Company on his flank at a critical moment. Lieut. H. R. Biss, with No. 15 Platoon, was to clear the railway near the top end of the village and establish posts. His leading section under Corporal W. Bargh, while advancing towards the line, met with heavy fire from a machine-gun planted in the fence along the railway, and, suffering severe casualties, was hung up, in shell-holes. Lieut. Biss himself went forward, leaving his Sergeant, W. Borlase, to bring on the remainder of the platoon, and got into touch with Corporal Bargh. It is a costly operation charging a machine-gun across the open, and, no doubt Lieut. Biss would have been obliged to stalk it, had not a few men from Wellington-West Coast Company, including Corporal L. W. Andrew, worked along the railway. Seeing them, the Germans wavered, and Lieut. Biss, with all his platoon, for Sergt. Borlase had come up, rushed the position and captured two guns. Biss was wounded, but carried on until the post was on the way to consolidation, In the meantime, on his left, Sergt. S. C. Foot led a party from No 13 platoon (2nd Lieut. C. S. Brown) along a hedge and, in spite of continuous machine-gun fire from the railway and from his left flank, established a post. Thus, along the railway we had gained success.

On the other hand, Lieut. C. S. Brown's centre party was almost wiped out in a frontal attack against the hedge where poor Robbie had met his death on the 21st July, Brown himself being wounded. His left party made excellent progress, almost reaching the road by an advance along the Northern hedge; but they too were reduced to three from the rifle and machine-gun fire of the Huns lurking behind their wire. However, the enemy's flank had been turned from the railway, and soon Sergeant Foot noticed they were beginning to trickle back towards Warneton. He immediately sent the best shot he had (Private Stumbles) right round to their northern flank, and both he and Stumbles kept up a rapid fire. Several Germans dropped, and the remainder, totalling twenty-four, held up their hands. Four of them were sent to carry out a wounded Auckland officer, and the remainder escorted to Battalion Headquarters. Before they departed, Sergeant Foot extracted the information that they were part of a Prussian Company garrisoning the hedgerows. They had only taken over the line an hour or two before our attack commenced. Foot then pushed on and established another post in a commanding position. In a concrete dugout he found the Prussian Company Commander's batman, a mere boy, who volunteered the information that the officer had hastily retreated, directly our barrage had opened.

Meanwhile, Captain McKinnon's men had taken the village with a rush, half an hour's work with bomb, rifle and bayonet being sufficient to clear it. This time, the more difficult fighting was encountered in the shell-holes between the railway and the top end of the village, in the buildings there, and in the hedges and ditches nearer the river. Many Germans were killed in these defences, and those that broke and fled were shot as they ran along the river bank or in the open towards Warneton.

Two sections from Wellington-West Coast Company under L.-Cpl. Andrew, were detailed expressly for the destruction of the occupants of the estaminet on the Warneton Road, which had been so troublesome to Sergt. Devery and his men on the 27th. As they moved forward, they found a machine-gun post on the railway line to the north, holding up Ruahine Company. They moved across to this gun, killed several Germans and captured the gun, and so enabled Ruahine Company to continue its advance. They then turned upon their special mission. The machine-gun in the estaminet fired continuously. Andrews and his men moved round to one side, and crouching and crawling their way through a patch of thistles, they crept within striking distance of their prey. They flung a shower of bombs, waited, and then rushed, some of the Germans were killed; others fled towards the river. The gun was ours. While some of his men carried back the captured gun,

Andrews himself and Pte. L. R. Ritchie went further afield, in pursuit of the enemy until, some three hundred yards along the road, they came to the Inder Rooster Cabaret, where some Germans were hiding. Besides the Inn our men found a machine-gun post in an open trench. They at once rushed the post, and then turned their attention to the cellars and dugouts which they thoroughly bombed. For his leadership and gallantry that day, Andrew was awarded the Victoria Cross, the first in the Regiment.

This time, the 2nd Battalion was well prepared for counter-attacks. At 5 a.m., the enemy counter-attacked in force, from the direction of Warneton between the river and the road. He was observed at the Inden Rooster and was caught in our S.O.S. barrage. Those that got through our barrage were shot by our Lewis guns and rifles before they could reach our trench.

During the day, La Basse Ville was subjected to an exceptionally severe bombardment. One would hardly believe its defenders could live through it. All McKinnon's officers were killed or wounded (Lieut. J. G. Kinvig had been killed early in the attack), and that brave fellow, Nicol promptly handed over his Stokes guns to his Sergeant and took charge of the front line. Shortly afterwards, at about 3.15 p.m., a party of about fifty of the enemy collected under cover of the river bank and attacked the right flank. Nicol, at the moment, was near the centre of the line, and, taking a few men with him hurried down to the spot. His party grew to ten as he went, and with a shout they left the trench and fell on the enemy with the bayonet. It was estimated that twenty were bayonetted: the remainder fled. It was firmly believed that Lieut. R. K. Nicol's exceptional bravery during the whole of that day, would be marked by the award of the V.C., but, he was rewarded with Military Cross and never was one more gallantly earned. The enemy was not even now prepared to accept defeat, for, at about 7.30 p.m., he was observed by our observation posts, massing near Inden Rooster. The S.O.S. was at once sent up. The enemy came forward in a very determined manner through our barrage to within about 100 yards of our line, when they were dealt with by our Lewis guns and rifle fire.

While these counter-attacks were in progress, the enemy clapped down a heavy barrage on our original front line trenches and posts held by the 1st Battalion, and during these bombardments, Taranaki Company (1st Battalion) in the posts were subjected to very heavy shell fire and sustained several casualties, Lieut. W. T. Doughty in charge of No. 2 Post being killed and 2/Lieut. S. M. Hobbs in charge of No. 3 Post wounded. During the day, in response to an application for reinforcements, Lieut. E. Malone in No. 1 Post sent up ten men of Taranaki Company, under Sergt. Wasley, to 2nd Wellington in La Basse Ville.

On the night of the 31st July, the 1st Battalion relieved the 2nd Battalion in La Basse Ville. It was raining steadily now, and probably no troops ever handed over their responsibilities more cheerfully than the 2nd Battalion did that night. A piping hot meal had been provided for them at Prowse Point, and warm blankets and a comfortable camp awaited them at Kortepyp. Happily, Capt. H. M. Goldstein was again able to evacuate all the wounded before withdrawing from his improvised dressing station, not far from Au Chasseur Cabaret.

During the day of 1st August, no further counter-attacks were made by the enemy against 1st Wellington and that night our 1st Battalion was relieved by 2nd Otago, and moved back to billets in Nieppe. It was not very inspiring for 2nd Otago, for nearly two days of steady rain had reduced the trenches to a quagmire and all work and movement were attended with the greatest difficulty.

While the 1st Battalion was in the forward posts, one who showed extraordinary valour was Pte. Daniel Murphy.*
On three occasions, he passed through very heavy shell-fire to bring up stretcher-bearers. The last time, though buried by a shell burst, he completed his errand and, failing to obtain bearers, returned to the shelled area and carried out a badly wounded comrade on his back. During the same period, half the post being destroyed by shell-fire, and all

---
*D. Murphy subsequently died at Te Puke.

rations with it, Murphy volunteered to go back and bring up food. Finally, when the post was relieved after a terrible ordeal, he remained behind to look after the wounded until stretcher-bearers could be sent up.

During the day we buried Lieut. J. G. Kinvig at Prowse Point Cemetery, the Rev. Mr. Dobson reading the service. Never more would Gordon Kinvig, that sterling athlete, take his place on Wellington football or cricket fields. La Basse Ville claimed many athletes. Here Wellington-West Coast Company lost Sergt. C. Sciascia, M.M., a well known Horowhenua Maori footballer, and a gallant soldier, while, a few days later, that doyen of Maori footballers, Lieut. A. P. Kaipara (Pioneers), was killed in the same locality.

For their services at La Basse Ville, Capt. H. E. McKinnon received a bar to his Military Cross, while Capt. M. Urquhart and Capt. H. M. Goldstein (R.M.O.) were awarded the Military Cross. Company Sergeant Major W. McKean, whose gallant conduct throughout, had been invaluable to Ruahine Company, received the Distinguished Conduct Medal as also did Sergt. S. C. Foot of the same company; and whose gallantry we have already noted; and Pte. J. E. Ryan (Wellington-West Coast Company), a very brave runner who had never spared himself throughout the operation, and had shown the most utter disregard of the intense enemy shelling. Sergt. P. A. Gordon was to receive a bar to his Military Medal for the skill with which he had organised communications and for his own personal bravery and devotion to duty. Corpl. W. H. Jacques was awarded the Military Medal for untiring energy and determination as a stretcher-bearer, while others to be recommended for awards for notable acts of gallantry were:—Corpl. W. Bargh, Sergt. W. W. Borlase, Sergt. A. N. Tod, Pte. A. N. Coombes, Corpl. Alex McCully, Lance-Corpl. O. H. Johnson, Pte. A. J. Steadman, Pte. R. J. Ure, Lance-Corpl. W. C. Hannan, Corpl. E. A. Tuke, Pte. G. H. C. Hart, Pte. A. E. Johnson, Corpl. W. B. Overden, Pte. N. Knight.

CHAPTER XXVIII.

3rd Battalion at Pontceau—Pennefather Swims the Lys—2nd Battalion's Transport near Kortepyp Destroyed by Bombs—Inspection of 2nd Battalion by General Godley and General Russell—Boxing Tournament at Nieppe—First Australian Division on the March—St. Yves.

MEANTIME, how had the 3rd Battalion been faring? On the 29th July, Hawkes Bay and Taranaki Companies of the 3rd Battalion had been heavily shelled in billets, the former at Ooschove Ferme and the latter at Pontceau (doubtless a backwash from La Basse Ville) and had had to move into new billets at Pont de Nieppe. On the 1st August, the 3rd Battalion relieved 3rd Otago in the trenches, and remained in line until the 9th, pushing on with wiring in No-Man's-Land, and between the front and support lines. A fairly quiet time was experienced, although on the 7th and 8th, the enemy put over some gas from which the battalion had several casualties. On the 9th, we were relieved by 3rd Otago, and moved into Pontceau. A few days later, battalion headquarters were shelled, and some anti-aircraft gunners nearby suffered some casualties, our men doing good work in rescuing some of them in their dugout. Here at Pontceau, General Godley inspected the battalion.

The enemy was now making life unpleasant for everyone by his shelling of back areas, with high explosive and gas, and the 3rd Battalion had its full share of the almost nightly gas bombardment, and sustained some casualties. It was now deemed advisable to close the baths at Pont De Nieppe.

THE WELLINGTON REGIMENT

On the 17th August, the 3rd Battalion again relieved 3rd Otago in the La Touquet sector, and on the 19th, Lieutenant Colonel C. H. Weston took over the command of that Battalion. It was from here that the first man from the 3rd Battalion was sent on leave from France.

Here, a very daring piece of work was performed by Sergeant S. S. Pennefather of Hawkes Bay Company. One afternoon, in broad daylight, he swam the river Lys, which divided us from the enemy, and reconnoitred the enemy ground. While there, he discovered a raft on the enemy side of the river, which he secured, and with the aid of some of the enemy's telephone wire, turned it into a ferry. After dark, he ferried three men across with him and attacked an enemy post. A stubborn fight ensued, during which Sergeant Pennefather was shot through the right wrist. The enemy post, however, was captured, and three of the enemy killed, our patrol returning to our own lines. The three who crossed with Sergt. Pennefather were 2/Lieut. K. Strack* (who joined the party at the last minute to be in the adventure unknown to his company-commander), Corpl. Jary and Pte. Brown. For this exploit, congratulations were received a few days later from General Godley. Sergeant Pennefather was recommended for, and shortly afterwards received, the D.C.M. for his gallantry, and richly he deserved it, for his fine leadership on this occasion greatly inspired all ranks in the 3rd Battalion.

On the 25th August, 3rd Otago relieved the 3rd Battalion, who moved into Pont de Nieppe. All civilians now had been evacuated from Pont de Nieppe and other townships and villages in the vicinity. What a power of shifting these civilians took! How they clung to their homes! The war had been raging at their very doors since 1915. Their fields had been ploughed by German shells, yet it was only now they could be prevailed upon to forsake these battered homes of theirs.

The 3rd Battalion remained at Pont De Neippe until the 31st August, when it was relieved there by the 2nd

---
*This gallant officer was later killed at Gravenstafel.

Battalion, Scottish Rifles, and moved, in the afternoon, to Stuff Camp on the outskirts of Pont de Nïeppe.

The 1st Battalion had lain at Nieppe in billets till 17th August, carrying on with training and supplying night working parties.

The 2nd Battalion, after remaining at Kortepyp Camp for a day to rest, had moved back to De Seule, which camp, owing to the wet and boisterous weather, was very dirty and slushy. They were to remain there only a day or so and then moved back to Bulford Camp. When word was received that Major C. H. Weston had been promoted to the rank of Lieutenant Colonel and to command the 3rd Battalion, to celebrate that event, an impromptu dinner had been held in the headquarters' mess. While at Bulford Camp the Battalion was inspected by Brigadier-General Melvill, D.S.O., who congratulated it on what he described (referring to La Basse Ville), as the most successful minor enterprise the New Zealand Division had ever undertaken. The General also spoke personally to several N.C.O.'s and men who had distinguished themselves. We were to learn with great regret that day, that Brigadier-General, F. E. Johnston C.B., had been shot by a German sniper, while going round the trenches.

While at Bulford Camp too, Captain M. Urquhart and the officers of that company, entertained Ruahine Company at a dinner in the Y.M.C.A. tent.

At about four o'clock one morning, a squadron of enemy aeroplanes passed over the camp and dropped several bombs near it, without doing any damage. Worse was to follow, for a few days later, at about 2 o'clock in the morning, of the 11th August, bombs were dropped on the transport lines of the 2nd Battalion, and the First Machine-Gun Company, whose animals were together near Kortepyp. The effect was disastrous. Thirty-three horses and mules of the 2nd Battalion were either killed or had to be shot. Four other animals were wounded, including Colonel Cunningham's charger which was wounded in the chest. In addition, the 1st Machine-Gun Company lost over fifty animals. Fortunately, only one of our men was injured, Driver Holms, on picquet duty, being wounded in the back. The spread of the exploding bombs was very low, and the animals that were killed, mostly had their legs cut off. After the noise of the explosion, there was only the long drawn-out groan from the unfortunate animals, and then the rattle of their chains and dull thuds as they fell. Among the horses lost, were the 2rd Battalion's two chestnut draught horses of which it was so justly proud. The scene was a distressing one, and it was some days before the chaos was cleared up.

On the 12th, at Bulford Camp after Church Parade, the 2nd Battalion was inspected by Lieutenant-General Godley, accompanied by Major-General Sir A. H. Russell, and Brigadier-General Melvill, General Godley stopping to say a few words to several men. After the inspection, the battalion formed a hollow square, and General Godley referred in high praise to its work at La Basse Ville and added that we had now won the reputation that there was no better battalion in the British Army in the field. The inspection over, the battalion marched past and, afterwards, General Godley spoke to several officers individually to congratulate them on their own share in the operations.

Training was going on as usual, and digging parties were going up every night to the trenches. Many a narrow escape did these digging parties have from aeroplane bombs, for enemy aircraft were now particularly hostile in this direction.

While at Bulford Camp also, the officers of the 2nd Battalion gave a dinner. Brigadier-General H. E. Hart, Major N. W. B. Thoms and Lieut.-Cols. Murray and Hardic Neil were present, as also were Lieut.-Col. C. F. D. Cook (1st Battalion) and Major Short (3rd Battalion). The evening was a pleasant one. Lieut. J. K. E. Jackson made one of his inimitable speeches. While here, too, Brigade boxing competitions were held at Nieppe, and the whole battalion marched down to them. The 2nd Battalion entered in only five classes and succeeded in winning four. Lieut. J. K. E.

Jackson had put in a lot of time training our men, and he himself led off by winning the heavy-weight, after first accepting a lot of punishment with his usual nonchalence.

Another event of importance while at Bulford Camp was the marching past our camp, one hot and dusty day, of a great many battalions of the 1st Australian Division, who were staging forward to the Salient preparatory to their attack on and capture of Polygon Wood. They had just come from a period of rest and training. How splendidly fit they looked. But many of them now lie buried in Polygon Wood.

On the 17th August, the 2nd Battalion's spell at Bulford Camp was to come to an end, for on that day, Ruahine, Taranaki, and West Coast Companies marched by platoons to Regina Camp replacing 1st Otago there, while Hawkes Bay Company moved to the Catacombs. The same night, our 1st Battalion relieved 2nd Canterbury in the line with headquarters at St. Yves Post Office, the relief being carried out without incident. First Wellington remained in line until the night of the 21st August. During that time the front line companies improved and added to the wire and traversed and improved the front line posts, and carried out patrolling operations. The support companies employed all available men in carrying trench boards to the posts. Hawkes Bay Company of the 2nd Battalion, living at the Catacombs, provided a carrying party nightly to carry up wiring material and trench boards to the front line posts. On the night of the 21st August, our 1st Battalion was relieved by 1st Auckland. The relief was complete by midnight, and the battalion moved out to Romarin Camp. About 12.20 a.m. the enemy opened a heavy bombardment on the back area with high explosive and gas shells. A favourable wind carried the gas down as far as Romarin Camp. Wellington-West Coast Company had to stay at Prowse Point till the shelling was over, and arrived in camp later on, having had to march most of the way in respirators. Before midnight the same night, 2nd Wellington relieved 2nd Auckland in the front line and posts on the right of La Basse Ville with battalion headquarters at Lewisham Lodge. This sector was comparatively quiet, although we had to ask for artillery retaliation from time to time to check the enemy's penchant for shelling our front line with "pineapples" from Wickardt Farm. The weather was gloriously fine, and a great deal of work was done in improving the front line and communication saps.

CHAPTER XXIX.

Training for Passchendaele.

We go back to Train for Passchendaele—Hondeghem — Caestre —Wizernes—Billets at Selles, - Lottinghem and Henneveux — A Trip to Ambleteuse— Brigade Training at Harlettes—Inspection by Sir Douglas Haig and Mr. Winston Churchill — The March up into the Ypres Salient.

ON the 25th August, the 1st Battalion had moved by motor lorries to Hondeghem in the Caestre Area.
Battalion headquarters, Wellington-West Coast and Taranaki Companies were in billets near Hondeghem, while Ruahine and Hawkes Bay Companies, in tents near Terdeghem, were kept busily emloyed in erecting sand bag walls round the tents. Each Company filled and laid 12,000 sand bags. Hawkes Bay rejoined the battalion in billets on the 27th, and Ruahine rejoined while on the march to Caestre.

On the 26th, the 2nd Battalion had been relieved in the line by the 1st Sherwood Foresters. The relief was commenced at 6 p.m. and was complete by midnight. The weather, which had been excellent during our spell in the line, unfortunately, now broke, and the relief was made during a heavy thunderstorm, the 2nd Battalion marching back by companies to Romarin in torrential rain. It was indeed, bad luck for the Sherwood Foresters to receive a thorough soaking just as they took over from us.

On the 27th, the 2nd Battalion left Romarin for Hondeghem in two convoys of motor lorries, one leaving, during the morning, from Romarin and the other, during the afternoon, from Pont d'Achelles. The convoys stopped at Hazebrouck, and it was not a far cry from there to the 2nd Battalion's billets.

On the 29th, the 1st and 2nd Battalions marched to Caestre railway station and entrained there for Wizernes. The 1st Batalion detrained there, and proceeded thence by motor busses to Selles. That battalion had made an early start, leaving billets at 5.45 o'clock in the morning, and reached their destination at 2 o'clock in the afternoon. The 2nd Battalion did not leave Hazebrouck till 2.30 o'clock in the afternoon, and had a long wait at Caestre before entraining. On our arrival at Wizernes late that night, the Y.M.C.A. provided a cup of hot tea and biscuits which were greatly appreciated. The 2nd Battalion then proceeded to Lottinghem by motor busses, arriving there after midnight. The 1st and 2nd Battalions now settled down in billets which were not altogether satisfactory for the billets themselves were poor and companies widely dispersed.

Up to this point the Fourth Brigade had not really been a part of the New Zealand Division, being an extra Brigade, and utilized as corps troops. In September, the Rifle Brigade was temporarily detached from the New Zealand Division and proceeded north to dig; thereupon the Fourth Brigade took their place, and for the first time became a unit of the Division, and directly under the command of Major-General Russell.

The 3rd Battalion was not to wait long before it also went back into the training area, for, on the 2nd September, it marched from Pont de Nieppe to Steenwerck, and there entrained for Wizernes. Arriving at Wizernes early in the afternoon, the 3rd Battalion marched some nine miles, and was then taken on to Henneveux by motor lorries, its transport reaching there in good order the following day, having marched the whole distance, being three days on the road.

It was clear that we were shortly to be called upon for a further attack, for had we not been travelling de luxe, per motor buses?—to our minds a certain sign of our shortly being sent "over the top" again.

The weather, which had been wet and changeable during our move, was soon to take up again, and however disappointing billets may be, they are far superior to trenches, and far superior to hutments in reserve, nightly made hellish by gas. As a matter of fact, in billets the 3rd Battalion was in clover. Headquarters occupied a chateau in the village of Henneveux, and the companies were in nearby farm houses, except for Wellington-West Coast Company in tents. The chateau was a delightful change after the Flemish farm-yards. Its gardens and lawns, though neglected, possessed some borders gay with scarlet begonias, and the band (converted gardeners temporarily) soon remedied all neglect. With the lawn cut, its edges trimmed, and the paths weeded and raked, the place looked charming.

Training by companies and battalions was soon in full swing. On the 6th September, the 1st Battalion at Selles, and the Second Battalion at Lottinghem, were inspected by the G.O.C. Division, Major-General Russell.

A few days later, Sir Thomas MacKenzie, then High Commissioner for New Zealand in London, visited the 2nd Battalion headquarters and chatted with officers and those non-commissioned officers and men who had earned distinction at La Basse Ville.

While at Selles, the 1st Battalion had a pleasant break, going by motor lorry to Ambleteuse on the sea coast for a day's sea bathing, returning in the evening.

Brigade training was now entered upon, the battalions marching several times to Harlettes, where attacks were practised under the eye of Brigadier-General Melvill, and frequently Major-General Russell.

During this period of training, a memorable review was held of the 1st, 2nd and 4th Brigades of the New Zealand Division by Field Marshall Sir Douglas Haig, on the 14th. In beautiful weather, it was indeed an inspiring sight as battalion after battalion took up its station in the large

THE WELLINGTON REGIMENT

field. Sir Douglas Haig was accompanied by the Right Hon. Winston Churchill (then Secretary of State for War). Both were, of course, mounted; but Mr. Churchill seemed rather incongruous in his tweed suit amidst the wealth of khaki. All three Wellington battalions were on parade. The Division was first inspected in line of battalion in close column of companies, Sir Douglas Haig speaking a word or two to battalion commanders. The inspection over, we marched past the Commander-in-Chief in columns of platoons, the whole Division making a most excellent showing.

On the following Sunday (the 16th), the opportunity was taken to have a joint Church Parade of the three battalions of the regiment at Selles. General Russell paid the regiment the compliment of being present. Afterwards, the men all lunched together in the open, and the officers at the headquarters of 1st Wellington. In the afternoon, a football match was played between 1st and 2nd Wellington, 1st Battalion winning, thanks largely to Billie Wilson, always a great scorer for the 1st Battalion in these matches.

We knew now we were destined for the Ypres Salient. The march was commenced on the 25th September. On that day, the 1st Battalion marched to the Wardrecque area, and billeted at Heuringhem. The 2nd Battalion marched to Le Sablon, and the 3rd Battalion from Henneveux to Seninghem, a distance of about 12 miles. The distance marched by the 1st and 2nd Battalions was about 25 miles and the march was a most exhausting one. The day was hot, and the men marched in full marching order (i.e. full pack up), and for the greater part of the distance upon cobbled roads. These all combined to test severely our endurance, because, during the whole month's training, we had been marching to and from the manoeuvre grounds in fighting kit, and on roads that were not cobbled.

On the following day, the 1st Battalion marched from Heuringhem, some twelve miles to Wallon Cappel, and billetted in farms there. The 2nd Battalion marched about eight miles to Staple, while the 3rd Battalion marched from

THE WELLINGTON REGIMENT

Seninghem to Arques, a distance of nine miles, and went into billets there. How beautiful the countryside now looked! These delightful wooded valleys, with the leaves of the trees now taking on their autumn tints.

On the 27th September, the march was continued, the 1st Battalion marching to No. 2 Area Watou, a distance of twelve miles, and going into tents at Mill Camp. The 2nd Battalion marched to Pear Tree Camp, four miles west of Poperinghe. The march began at 6.30 a.m. and was completed at 3.30 p.m.; but a long halt had been rendered necessary at Steenvoorde to enable other troops to pass ahead. The 3rd Battalion marched from Arques to Eccke, a distance of eighteen miles, and was severely tried by the march.

The next two days were spent in resting after the march and in final preparations for the coming operations. Those being held in reserve were now withdrawn from their battalions and left for the Reinforcement Camp at Morbecque. The Battalion and company commanders went forward by motor lorry to reconnoitre the line being taken over, and the country over which the attack was to be made.

CHAPTER XXX.

Gravenstafel.

Gravenstafel and Abraham Heights — Plans for the Attack—Vlamertinghe— Goldfish Chateau—Wieltje —Kansas House—Korek and Boetleer—Kron Prinz Farm—Waterloo — Relief by West Riding Regiment—Back again at Goldfish Chateau—Poperinghe.

FOR the attack on the 4th October, the II. Anzac Corps' final objective ran from near the intersection of the Ypres-Roulers railway along the eastern slopes of the Gravenstafel Spur to Kron Prinz Farm. The 3rd Australian Division, with whom the New Zealand Division had for long been associated, was to attack on the right and the New Zealand Division on the left, with a brigade from each of the 49th and 66th Divisions in Corps reserve. The New Zealand Division's frontage was about two thousand yards, and the enemy's defences were to be penetrated to a depth of about one thousand yards and no more, in pursuance of the policy of strictly limited objectives which then obtained. The first objective was to be called the Red Line, and was to be just short of Gravenstafel village. The final objective was to be beyond Gravenstafel down towards the Stroombeek valley, and was to be known as the Blue Line, behind which there was to be a support line known as the Blue Dotted Line.

The First and Fourth Brigades of the New Zealand Division were to attack side by side, the latter being on the right. On our 4th Brigade's right was the 3rd Australian Division, and on the left of our 1st Brigade, the 48th

THE WELLINGTON REGIMENT

British Division of another Army Corps. The 4th Brigade's frontage was about eight hundred yards, its task being considered likely to be the more difficult one, including as it did, the village of Gravenstafel and Abraham Heights. The system of leapfrogging was to be adopted and, when 3rd Auckland and 3rd Otago had reached the first objective (the Red Line), 3rd Canterbury and 3rd Wellington were to pass through them on to the final objective, the Blue Line, 3rd Wellington going through 3rd Otago. The latter's area embraced Wimbledon dugouts and Van Meulen Farm, while 3rd Wellington included Gravenstafel village, Berlin Pill Boxes, and Waterloo Farm.

As for the First Brigade, it was to advance on a 1200 yards frontage with 1st Wellington on the right and 1st Auckland on the left. They were to take the Red Line, and then 2nd Auckland was to pass through 1st Wellington, while 2nd Wellington went through 1st Auckland on to the final objective.

The 2nd Battalion was the first to move up into the line, for, on the 30th September, that battalion was taken by buses to Vlamertinghe, and from there marched to a position in the old German support line, with battalion headquarters at Cal Farm. On the 1st October, both 1st and 3rd Battalions marched to Goldfish Chateau and bivouaced in the fields there, the men digging holes in the ground in which to sleep, so that, unless by direct hit, aeroplane bombs would be unlikely to injure them. Owing to the great amount of traffic on the dusty road, the march was much delayed, and very tedious. What a handsome residence Goldfish Chateau must once have been!

On the following day, final details for the attack were completed. That evening, the 1st Battalion relieved 2nd Canterbury in the front line system of posts of the right brigade sub-sector with headquarters at Kansas House. On the way up Capt. R. W. Wrightson and Lieut. G. H. Roach (Adjutant and Signalling Officer respectively) were wounded by shell fire near Wieltje Dugout. The same evening, half the companies and all the officers of the 3rd Battalion marched up, via No. 5 track, to the old British Front Line, where they were joined, the following day, by the remainder of that battalion.

On the 3rd, in fine weather, detailed reconnaissances of forward areas were made by battalion and company commanders, and, as far as possible, by platoon and section commanders in daylight. Routes of approach to assembly positions were allotted and extra crossings over the Hanebeek Stream arranged for, and all details made for assembly and the preliminary move forward.

During the evening of the 3rd October, the companies of the 3rd Battalion, one by one, left the old trench and moved up to the point of assembly at Pommern Redoubt. The men lay in shell holes there, and made themselves as comfortable as possible for the night.

Shortly after midnight, our 2nd Battalion also began to assemble, Taranaki Company (Major Hamilton) and Ruahine Company (Capt. H. F. Boscawen) moved via St. Julien Road and assembled east of the Hanebeek, while the other two companies moved along the road past Spree Farm and assembled in rear of Schuler Galleries. All were in position by 4 o'clock a.m., with 2nd Battalion headquarters at Schuler Farm.

Zero hour was fixed for 6 o'clock in the morning. About midnight the weather had broken and light rain started to fall. It was a wet, bleak morning with a cold wind blowing from the Hun lines, and pitch dark, as we mustered for the attack.

Meantime, the 1st Battalion, already in the front line so as to be in the first wave of the assault, was making preparations, and, by 5 o'clock, that battalion was formed up ready, with Wellington-West Coast Company on the right and Taranaki (Capt. J. Keir) on the left across the Hanebeek. With Wellington-West Coast were six sections of Ruahine Company attached as moppers-up The rest of Ruahine Company was in support immediately behind Wellington-West Coast Company and Hawkes Bay was in reserve behind Ruahine Company. At about 5.20 a.m. the enemy artillery opened a heavy fire on our forward areas and barraged the Hanebeek along the western slope of Hill 32; but we were lucky to escape with comparatively few casualties, although, among others from the 1st Battalion now wounded was Capt. Stratford.

At 6 o'clock, zero hour, our artillery barrage came down and the attack commenced. The whole of the 1st Battalion at once moved to the attack, following as closely as possible behind the barrage. There was no difficulty in keeping up with the barrage in spite of mud and, though the Hanebeek was very boggy, it did not present any serious obstacle. Owing to 1st Auckland drifting off to the left, when the first two companies of the 1st Battalion, Wellington -West Coast and Taranaki, arrived on their objective, they were the only troops on the whole brigade frontage. The right company of 1st Auckland, which should have passed through Boetleer, took Albatross Farm and there were no Auckland troops between that spot and Korek. Wellington-West Coast Company established itself with about two platoons in front of Korek, and Taranaki Company (Capt. J. Keir), which had drifted to the left to keep in touch with 1st Auckland, came up on the front which had been allotted to Auckland. Owing to this loss of direction, there was a considerable amount of ground uncovered and the support company (Ruahine) pushed itself into the gap and mopped up the ground between Taranaki and Wellington-West Coast. Some very stiff fighting was experienced whilst mopping up, particularly in the neighbourhood of Boetleer, and machine-gun fire from two dugouts on the crest of the ridge just in front of the village of Korek greatly annoyed Wellington-West Coast Company in its advance. Third Otago also was affected by these machine-guns, and it was necessary to silence them. Accordingly, parties from Wellington-West Coast Company under Sergt. F. E. Chappel, together with a party from 3rd Otago, rushed forward, venturing right into our own protective barrage, and threw bombs into the entrances of the pill boxes. One of these pill boxes was fairly large, and must have been of some importance. Sergeant A. Paterson entered to find some thirty Germans dead or dying from the havoc our bombs had wrought. There seemed to be an inner recess in which was a German Major with some men. As soon as Sergeant Paterson entered, the German officer set fire to a mass of papers with some incendiary material. In a moment, the whole place was in flames, Sergeant Paterson came out; but the Germans were all incinerated. This dug-out burned for hours afterwards.

Rapid progress was impossible. Fire from the German machine-guns was too heavy to permit that. Against one of these guns, whilst his men were engaging it with rifle grenades, Sergeant K. A. Goldingham worked round to a flank and rushed the gun single-handed, killing the crew of four. When his company was checked by another machine-gun, Private D. Jones dashed forward alone under heavy shell-fire and single-handed killed the whole gun crew and such other Germans as came in his way, in all twelve men.

Another section of our men were held up by a machine-gun which could not be located. Private T. Geange, a Lewis Gunner, whose gun had early been put out of action, at last located it, and armed only with his revolver, rushed forward against the post. Geange's courage induced another man to follow his lead. Both were wounded (the second man dying later); but their gallantry diverted the enemy machine-gun and afforded the other men in the section the opportunity to push forward and capture the enemy gun, killing the crew.

By similar acts of individual gallantry and by the grim determination of all ranks, allied with skilful leadership of officers and non-commissioned officers, 1st Wellington pushed on to the Red Line, capturing the whole brigade frontage on schedule time.

The two leading companies at once began to dig in, and, later in the morning, a company from 1st Auckland moved over on to the First Brigade front and took over some two hundred yards of trench which had already been dug by Taranaki Company. As the work proceeded, it became evident that the two companies in front could not possibly complete the work of consolidation, and the support company was pushed in to help with the digging.

Captain J. Keir led Taranaki Company with great ability in the attack. When 1st Auckland had lost direction during the advance, he had filled the serious gap in the line so occasioned in a most skilful manner and saved a dangerous situation. Now, after reaching the objective, Capt. Keir moved about under heavy shell-fire along the whole front of the battalion, organising the consolidation and setting a magnificient example. 2nd Lieut. L. M. Dixon had taken command of Ruahine Company when Captain Straford had been wounded at the opening of the attack. Whilst moving forward in support, Dixon led a small party of men into a gap in the line, where an enemy machine-gun and riflemen were causing heavy losses, killed the gun crew and captured the gun. On his own initiative, he filled a dangerous gap in the line and made good the position. Lieutenant E. L. Malone too led his platoon with great determination, and organised and took part in the mopping up of concrete dugouts under heavy shell and machine-gun fire.

While 1st Wellington was so advancing, similarly gallant work was being performed by the other battalions on their allotted parts of the Red Line.

Two hours were allotted for the capture of the Red Line. While the Red Line was being captured, the other battalions of the First and Fourth Brigades were moving forward and assembling in rear of the Red Line for the attack on the Blue Line. Hardly had our barrage opened in the first phase of the advance, than down had come the enemy barrage. The battalions now moving in columns abreast, each in single file, separated by about one hundred yards, would indeed have been lucky if they had altogether escaped casualties.

The 2nd Battalion had gone no distance before an enemy shell landed among Ruahine Company's headquarters and killed Capt. H. T. Boscawen, commanding that Company, and his two runners. A few minutes later, Lieut.-Col. C. H. Weston, commanding the 3rd Battalion, was struck by a piece of shell and very seriously wounded, and, as had been arranged, Capt. F. S. Varnham (Hawkes Bay Company) at once took over command of that battalion, leaving Lieut. E. Morgan in command of Hawkes Bay. To the battalions now moving forward, it was noticeable that the enemy had organised a double line of shell hole defences about three hundred yards apart. Each shell hole contained from two to four dead Germans. The enemy losses must have been very severe. We were to learn afterwards that the enemy had himself been massing for an attack, and our barrage must have wrought havoc amongst his assembled troops.

Owing to the configuration of the ground, it was difficult to maintain direction, and it became necessary to use the compass. Advancing to the capture of the Blue Line with our 2nd Battalion, Taranaki Company (Major Hamilton) swung off well to the left of its prescribed objective although not nearly so much as 1st Auckland had done. That, however, was soon remedied, and it was not long before 2nd Wellington had captured the whole of the Blue Line allotted to it. Stout resistance was met with from a short line of trench near Kronz Prinz Farm; but this was captured, under the very gallant leadership of Sergeant S. C. Foot of Ruahine Company, who had only a few weeks before received his D.C.M. for gallantry at La Basse Ville.

Our men worked their way up to the German position, and then rushed in with the bayonet. Here we took seven machine-guns and thirty-nine prisoners and left the enemy trench full of German dead.

Great Gallantry was shown during the advance by Sergt. M. Ward of Ruahine Company. At the very outset, as we have noted, Captain H. T. Boscawen, commanding Ruahine Company, had been killed, while not long afterwards all the other officers of that company became casualties. Thereupon, Sergeant Ward took command of that company and led it forward with great courage and determination. He was shortly afterwards to receive his D.C.M. for his work that day, as also was Sergeant C. E. Menzies, Ruahine Company's Lewis Gun Sergeant. Menzies had been wounded early in the advance; but stuck to his job. After the objectives had been reached, he frequently visited the posts of his guns under heavy machine-gun fire and encouraged his gunners, and himself kept in action one of the guns after its crew had been knocked out.

Captain G. H. Hume displayed excellent leadership in directing Hawkes Bay Company through a heavy barrage and reorganising them without a casualty, and showed great courage and judgment throughout, while Lieut. J. K. E. Jackson at all times displayed all his accustomed coolness and good humour.

It turned out that Kron Prinz Farm had been an enemy battalion headquarters, and the plans and papers captured there were to yield much valuable information. It was near here that Lieut. D. A. Harle fell mortally wounded.

Immediately the Blue Line had been taken, consolidation was pushed on until all troops were well under cover. The 2nd Battalion now established its headquarters in a shell hole and small trench in Boetleer. Communication by visual was quickly established, and by 10.20 a.m. telephone communication was made with companies from battalion headquarters and was maintained almost uninterruptedly throughout the operation, a striking tribute to the work of Lieutenant T. L. R. King and his signallers.

In the assault upon the Blue Line, the 2nd Battalion had been on the left of the entire Corps front. On 2nd Wellington's right was 2nd Auckland, and on Auckland's right was 3rd Wellington.

With 3rd Canterbury on its right and 2nd Auckland on its left, 3rd Wellington pressed down the eastern face towards the Rayebeek.

At one point on the left of Berlin, the advance was held up for some twenty minutes; but, under cover of the Stokes mortars, the place was rushed. Just on the right of Van Meulen, in front of the Red Line, Ruahine Company was held up by three machine-guns firing from two pill boxes. Lieut. F. C. Cornwall rallied his men and, dividing them into two parties, worked round both flanks, and bombed the

THE WELLINGTON REGIMENT

enemy out from the back capturing twenty-five prisoners. Though wounded, Cornwall, continued on till the final objective was reached. Hawkes Bay Company already had had Lieut. K. J. Strack killed and some twenty others killed or wounded. A little later, Lieut. J. S. Marsden of the trench mortars was killed on his way back to battalion headquarters to report the position of his guns. Shortly after 9 o'clock, Wellington-West Coast Company and Taranaki Company had reached the Blue Line and were digging in with all speed. Both companies made Waterloo House their headquarters. They had both suffered heavy casualties: Lieut. H. O. F. Marden had been killed, while Captain A. E. M. Jones,* commanding Taranaki Company, and Lieut. Little had been wounded, and all Sergeants with the exception of one had been either killed or wounded. With Wellington-West Coast, Lieut. O. Magnusson had been killed and Lieut. H. H. Parkinson wounded. Ruahine Company (Capt. A. J. Williams) too had had many casualties. Wellington-West Coast Company captured a case of German map orders, etc., with which, during the afternoon, Capt. B. H. Morison sent Pte. Worthington back to battalion headquarters. Worthington had done good work during the day carrying messages under heavy shell-fire. He had also captured three prisoners and a machine-gun. Sergt. E. K. Blundell set a splendid example of courage and initiative throughout the operations. When his platoon commander was wounded, he took command of the platoon and led it to a successful attack on a machine-gun.

Capt. F. S. Varnham, both in command of the 3rd Battalion and of his own Company had shown conspicuous gallantry throughout. Later in the day, Major S. Mackay came up from reserve and took command of that battalion.

Shortly after mid-day, our 1st Battalion received a message giving warning of a counter-attack. Thereupon, Hawkes Bay Company, which had, up till now, been in reserve, was moved up to about 300 yards in rear of the gap which existed in the line between Taranaki

---
*Capt. A. E. M. Jones died of wounds, 11/10/1917.

and Ruahine Companies. On the left of this gap immediately after the first objective had been taken, Lieut. Flanagan (No. 1 Machine-Gun Company) had established himself with two Vickers guns. No sooner had Hawkes Bay Company arrived there than it was ordered to go up to the Red Line and push into the gap in the line, which it did accordingly and at once began to dig in there.

At 5 o'clock in the afternoon, 2nd Wellington were ordered to push forward three posts to conform with a proposed attack and capture of Alder Farm by troops from the brigade on its immediate left. The 2nd Battalion carried out its task; but, owing to the advance upon Adler Farm not being made, was subjected to an intense machine-gun and rifle fire from Adler Farm, so that it was found necessary after the new posts had been established to withdraw to the original line.

Up till about 3 o'clock in the afternoon, the weather had been moderately fine; but heavy rain had then set in and the battlefield quickly became a quagmire, making the work of carrying parties and stretcher-bearers extremely heavy. Nevertheless, our wounded were taken out as soon as could possibly be done, the stretcher-bearers working continuously and with the greatest bravery.

Just before dark, the enemy was seen massing about 500 yards in front of the 3rd Battalion; but through the prompt action of Captain B. H. Morison in sending up the S.O.S., our artillery barrage quickly dispersed them before they could launch an attack.

During the night of the 4th, rain was intermittent, and the weather bleak and cold. The following day, the captured positions were consolidated, and the rest of our wounded got in, and the dead buried. During the day, divisions on both flanks called for artillery assistance, but no counter-attack developed against the New Zealand Division's newly captured positions. Later in the day, orders were received that the three Wellington Battalions were to be relieved by the 5th, 6th and 7th battalions of the West Riding Regiment.

THE WELLINGTON REGIMENT

The relief was complete shortly after midnight, and all three battalions then moved back to bivouacs near Goldfish Chateau. On the 6th, the 3rd Battalion marched to Vlamertinghe and proceeded from there by motor buses to Eecke, while the 2nd Battalion, late in the day, marched to another camp, which it reached at 11 p.m. There was no rest for the weary (and how weary are men after battle) for enemy aeroplanes bombed neighbouring camps during the night, some of the bombs dropping within seventy-five yards of the 2nd Battalion's camp. The following day, that Battalion moved to another camp near Poperinghe.

On the 7th, the 1st Battalion marched to the Brandhoek Area and camped in tents, near Poperinghe Railway Station, remaining there till the 15th. The weather was now very wet and all camps in a state of liquid mud. Things were very unpleasant, and it was quite impossible to keep dry.

The 1st and 2nd Battalions were to spend another day resting and re-organising and were then called upon to supply large working parties to bury cable in the forward area.

CHAPTER XXXI.

Belle Vue—12th October—3rd Battalion Move Forward to Spree Farm—Worst Farm—Kron Prinz Farm.

ALL battalions were now strongly reinforced. The 3rd Battalion remained at Eecke until the 11th. The Fourth Brigade was to be in Divisional Reserve for the attack of the 2nd and 3rd Brigades on the 12th October. Early on the morning of the 11th, therefore, the 3rd Battalion marched three miles to Godswaersvelde and entrained there. Detraining at Ypres, it marched to Y. Camp, one mile south of St. Jean, and there bivouaced for the night, which turned out very wet and cold.

On the 12th October, the 2nd and 3rd Brigades of the N.Z. Division attacked at 5.25 a.m. It was the Division's one failure on a large scale. It suffices to say that nothing which courage and self-sacrifice could accomplish was left undone by those brigades.

At 5.30 a.m., the 3rd Battalion had moved forward by companies in single file and taken over bivouacs in the old British and German front lines, remaining in readiness there to move forward at half-an-hour's notice. At noon, it moved forward again some two miles to the vicinity of Spree Farm, with headquarters in Capricorn Keep. There it remained that and the whole of the following day in miserably wet and cold weather, and until late in the afternoon of the 14th, when it moved forward to Worst Farm line with headquarters at Kansas House.

During the next few days, the 3rd Battalion was employed burying dead, and salvaging arms, equipment, etc. Rations were brought up to Kansas House by pack mules, only with the very greatest difficulty, on account of the heavy shell fire and the deep mud.

Face p. 224.

Kansas Farm

Hooge

On the 17th, the 3rd Battalion made preparations to take over the line from 3rd Otago. The relief was completed by half-past ten that night, 3rd Battalion Wellington's headquarters being at Kron Prinz Farm. The weather was now fine; but the nights cold. Enemy activity was slight, and artillery fire spasmodic. Enemy aeroplanes, however, were very active, flying very low, and firing into our trenches at dawn and dusk.

CHAPTER XXXII.

After Belle Vue—Holding the Line—Gravenstafel—Waterloo Road—Otto Farm—Relief by the Canadians.

OWING to the non-success of the attack made by the 2nd and 3rd Brigades on Belle Vue Spur on the 12th October, it was decided that the 1st Brigade should now take over and hold the line until the relief of the II. Anzac Corps by the Canadians was complete. Accordingly, on the 15th, 1st and 2nd Wellington both marched to Goldfish Chateau, and bivouaced there overnight.

Next day, the 1st Battalion moved up, relieving 1st Otago in support at Pommern Castle, where it remained until the 19th. The area was heavily shelled on several occasions, Lieuts. E. L. Malone and A. J. Nimmo being amongst those wounded. On the 16th, the 2nd Battalion moved forward via Salvation Corner and No. 5 Track to the old German Support Line, North of Wieltje—Spree Farm Road, with headquarters at Call Farm.

On the following day, the 2nd Battalion moved forward to a line from Banks Farm to Pommern Castle. On the 19th October, 1st Wellington took over the front line from 3rd Canterbury in the right sub-sector of the Divisional front, with battalion headquarters at Waterloo Farm, while 2nd Wellington moved forward and relieved 3rd Auckland in support to 1st Wellington. The 2nd Battalion's line was now approximately Korek-Gravenstafel-Abraham Heights with battalion headquarters at Otto Farm.

On the night of the 20th, the 3rd Battalion was relieved by 1st Auckland, and moved back to near Spree Farm—a very tedious and tiring journey owing to the mud.

On the 21st October, the 3rd Battalion was relieved late in the afternoon by the 1st Battalion Canadian Mounted

THE WELLINGTON REGIMENT

Rifles. The relief was carried out under heavy shell fire; but, fortunately, the casualties were light. On being relieved, the 3rd Battalion moved back to a camp near St. Jean cross roads. Here we were able to get baths, and were issued with extra winter clothing.

The 1st Battalion in the front line faced Belle Vue Spur, with the 2nd Battalion behind it in support. The position was in full view of the enemy and movement was kept down to a minimum to avoid drawing fire. The whole area was continuously shelled and the men suffered great discomfort from cold and wet, though, fortunately not much more rain fell. There was an almost complete lack of machine-gun and rifle fire, and very few flares were seen. Rations were packed to a point just short of Gravenstafel cross-roads, and the 2nd Battalion did its cooking at Abraham Heights. Patrolling was actively carried out by the 1st Battalion, particularly to ascertain the damage done to the enemy wire, and to reconnoitre the crossings of the Ravebeke.

One afternoon, one of our long range guns made an attempt to demolish the pill-boxes on the crest of Belle Vue Spur, and a remarkably accurate shoot it was too. After the first shot, the pill-box was quickly vacated, and Germans could be seen scurrying across the sky-line. Then, when one of our shells hit the concrete blockhouse fair and square, the ranks of Tuscany could scarce forbear to cheer. A little later, a figure could be seen slowly wending its way down the spur towards us, and a poor shell-shocked German walked right into Auckland's lines.

Early in the evening of the 23rd October, both 1st and 2nd Battalions were relieved by the Canadians, the 1st Battalion by the 43rd Battalion Canadian Infantry, while the 58th Battalion Canadian Infantry took over from the 2nd Battalion. The relief of the 1st Battalion went through very quickly and was completed by 8 p.m.; but, just before it was completed, the whole of Company Headquarters of Taranaki Company (1st Battalion), were either killed or wounded. The Canadians had actually taken over and Taranaki headquarters were about to leave when a huge shell burst right in the shell

THE WELLINGTON REGIMENT

hole which had been serving as headquarters. Capt. J. Keir and Lt. S. Paul were killed outright, also the sergt.-major and two of our runners, while two Canadian officers and four of their men were killed. It was indeed bad luck. Capt. Keir did not live to know that he had been awarded the Military Cross he had so well earned a few days before.

On relief the 1st Battalion moved back into support, with headquarters at Pommern Castle, and remained there until the following day, when it was relieved by the 50th Battalion Canadian Infantry and then moved back to a camp near St. Jean. Here Lieut. Clark and several others were wounded by aeroplane bombs.

The 2nd Battalion, on being relieved at Gravenstafel, had moved right back to a camp between Dead End and Salvation Corner, a hot meal, and a very welcome one indeed, and a ration of rum being supplied at Cal. Trench. Second Battalion headquarters were near St. Jean. The camp near Salvation Corner comprised some huts and a number of bell tents and as many as twenty men occupied one tent. Here we lay for the day and night of the 24th, many having a good look round Ypres itself, or rather what was left of it, taking advantage of an opportunity which had not hitherto presented itself.

CHAPTER XXXIII.

We Go Back for a Rest — Senninghem and Affrinques — Bayinghem — Bouvelinghem — Henneveux.

ON the following day, both 1st and 2nd Battalions moved right back to a rest area. Heavy rain had fallen overnight; but the day was fine with a cold wind. An early start was made, reveille being at 4 a.m. A hot breakfast was provided and both battalions moved off to entrain. The 1st Battalion entrained near the Asylum, Ypres, and proceeded to Wizernes, finally marching to billets at Seninghem and Affrinques, with headquarters at Seninghem. There had been a long wait for the train at Ypres, with the result that billets were not reached until after dark. Considering their condition, the men stood the march at the end of the journey very well.

The 2nd Battalion marched to Dickebusch to entrain, passing Ypres station at 6.15 a.m. At Dickebusch, we entrained in an empty supply train and moved off at a quarter-past nine, detraining opposite our billetting area at Bayinghem at half-past three in the afternoon, had then barely a quarter of a mile's march to billets.

The 3rd Battalion had already moved back to the rest area, for, after being relieved near Spree Farm by the Canadians on the 21st October, it had, the following day, marched from St. Jean some seven miles to Dickebusch and entrained there for Nielles. A start had been made that morning from St. Jean at 6 o'clock, and Nielles was not reached till 4 o'clock in the afternoon. However, at Nielles a very welcome cup of tea was supplied by the Y.M.C.A., which fortified us for another seven mile march to our billets at Bouvelinghem, where we arrived at half-past nine that night very tired and footsore.

THE WELLINGTON REGIMENT

All three battalions now rested and re-organised. There was a good deal of sickness; but no serious illness. The " B " teams returned from Morbecque, and a large number of reinforcements came up from the base.

While at Bayinghem, Ruahine Company (2nd Battalion), had a company dinner, which proved a great success. Capt. M. Urquhart, who had for some time commanded that company, was shortly to return to New Zealand on duty and was to take leave of his company at Escouilles a few days later.

On Sunday the 4th November about three kilometres from Bouvelinghem, the three battalions had a combined Church Parade.

On the 8th, the 4th Brigade paraded at Bouvelinghem and the Commander, Brig.-General Hart, D.S.O., presented ribands to those N.C.O.'s and men who had been awarded medals for gallantry in the recent fighting.

The 1st Battalion remained at Seninghem until the 9th November, when it marched to Henneveux, going into rather crowded billets there. There was now a sort of general post, for, on the same day, the 2nd Battalion moved to Alinethun area and took over from the 2nd Battalion of the Rifle Brigade, billetting as follows: Wellington-West Coast Company and Ruahine Company at Escouilles, Hawkes Bay Company at Serques, Taranaki Company at Le Plouy. Training was gone on with as before, although interfered with a good deal by unsettled weather. There was a good deal of football too.

On the 13th, a parade was held at Henneveux, where Brigadier-General Melvill, Commander of the 1st Brigade, presented ribands to those N.C.O.'s and men of the First Brigade who had recently been awarded medals for gallantry.

On the 14th, the 1st Battalion marched back to their old billets in Seninghem and Affrinques, while the 2nd Battalion marched back to Bayinghem, the billets there having been vacated by the Rifle Brigade, staging forward. Unfortunately, the motor transport which was being provided for this move, let us down badly, with the result that neither battalion had blankets that night, and a very cold night it was too, to our very ill content.

CHAPTER XXXIV.

Back to the Salient—Polygon Wood—Butte de Polygon—Micmac Camp—In the Line—Heavy Shelling—2nd Battalion starts Burying Cable—Canal Bank—Belgian Chateau.

IT was clear we were soon to turn our faces eastward. Billetting parties were sent forward and the heavy transport started the long trek back to Ypres by road. The 3rd Battalion was the first to move. On the 12th November, an early start was made, the 3rd Battalion marching out from Bouvelinghem at 6 o'clock in the morning and proceeding to Wizernes, a distance of fourteen miles. There it entrained during the afternoon and arrived at Hopoutre at about 7 o'clock at night, then marching some ten miles to "A" Camp, Chateau Segard area. On the following day, the 3rd Battalion moved up to Zillebeke Bund, and relieved 8th Battalion Leicester Regiment in brigade reserve. Owing to limited accommodation, companies were taken in 100 strong, the remainder being left in the brigade details camp. On the afternoon of the next day, the 3rd Battalion relieved 7th Battalion Leicester Regiment in Butte de Polygon sector.

Nor were our other battalions to be long in following, for, on the 15th November, both 1st and 2nd Battalions in full marching order marched to Wizernes to entrain there for Hopoutre. The cookers had gone on ahead and a hot meal was provided at Wizernes. Both battalions entrained at 3 p.m. and hot tea and biscuits were provided for everyone by the Y.M.C.A. We reached Hopoutre at about 7.30 p.m., and were met there by our billetting parties. At Hopoutre siding, the Y.M.C.A. was again ready with hot cocoa and biscuits, which were greatly appreciated. We then formed up in a small field close by and moved off for Micmac Camp, a distance of some seven miles, which, marching in the dark, took us some three hours to reach, and there settled down in tents.

The 3rd Battalion had been having a fairly quiet time in the line. The weather was fine, and the battalion was busily employed improving its sector. On the night of the 18th November, however, an enemy party, numbering about ten, rushed one of Ruahine Company's advanced Lewis gun posts consisting of five men. Four of our men were wounded, and our gun captured, while one German was killed. At mid-day on the 21st, the Butte area was shelled with mustard gas and Capt. F. S. Varnham, Lieut. Walker, and Lieut. E. Edwards and a number of others were slightly affected and had to be sent to hospital the following day. That night, the 3rd Battalion was relieved by 3rd Otago and moved back to Tillebeke Bund. On the night of the 25th, the 3rd Battalion relieved the 7th Battalion West Riding Regiment in Dead Mule Dugouts, there to remain for the next few days, employed, during the mornings, carrying R.E. material and ammunition to the front line dump, and, in the afternoons, on salvage. Here we were under constant shell-fire both by day and by night, yet our casualties were comparatively slight. On the morning of the 30th November, the 3rd Battalion was relieved by the 3rd Battalion Rifle Brigade, and moved out to Howe Camp, via Ypres Moat baths.

Meantime, the 1st and 2nd Battalions were both at Micmac Camp. The 1st Battalion remained there until the 26th, when it relieved the 2nd Battalion and part of the 3rd Battalion Rifle Brigade, in the line near Polygon De Zonnebeek, and came under the command of the 4th Brigade Commander. The battalion marched to Ouderdom, and proceeded from there by light railway to Birr Cross Roads, where it waited several hours. The cookers were brought up to this point and a meal was had. The relief was then made under cover of darkness, the battalion moving by the Menin Road to Clapham Junction, and thence by track into the trenches, not, however, without incurring some casualties. The 1st Battalion's spell in line was not to be a particularly happy one, for, during the period from 27th to 30th November, a programme of intensive bombardment of the enemy's positions was carried out twice daily by our artillery with particular attention to Polderhoek Chateau, and the enemy did not neglect to retaliate. On the 28th, and again on the 30th November, our artillery put down an intensive bombardment in the form of a barrage on the Chateau and neighbourhood for more than an hour, and on the 30th, shortly after seven o'clock in the morning, an intensive bombardment was put down on the enemy positions in front of the 1st Battalion's left company. During this latter bombardment, the left company was withdrawn, returning to the front line at its conclusion. The enemy retaliation was very heavy. For hours at a time, the enemy subjected our trenches to an intense bombardment. Practically the whole of the line on our left front was blown in and some casualties sustained. The conditions were very difficult indeed, as our line on the left consisted of an untraversed continuous trench and on the right we had only small unconnected posts. Luckily, only a little rain fell. Rations were, as a rule, brought by limber to Clapham Junction and thence carried; but, on some nights, owing to shell-fire, the rations could not be brought by limber further than Hooge. No cooking was possible, and consequently, cold meat was brought up and cold tea in petrol tins. Ration carrying was now very heavy work. Here, during four days, while merely holding the line, the 1st Battalion had ten killed, three officers and thirty-two men wounded, and one missing. Such was the toll of shellfire.

The 2nd Battalion remained at Micmac Camp for over a week. From Micmac Camp, Lieutenant T. L. R. King, M.C., left us on transfer to the Divisional Signallers. A very efficient officer, he had been signal officer to the battalion since June, 1916, and had become very popular.

The 1st Battalion had temporarily gone under the command of the 4th Brigade; but the rest of the First Brigade now became Corps troops for work, and 2nd Wellington was allotted the task of burying cable. Every morning the 2nd Battalion would supply a party of 10 officers and not less than 400 men. The party would leave camp before 6 o'clock in the morning, march to Ouderdom, and go up from there on the light railway to Birr Cross Roads. There the party would start work under the direction of the Corps Signals officer. The work consisted of digging a trench six feet deep, laying a cable in it, and filling up the trench again. Enemy shelling frequently necessitated the temporary withdrawal of parties from dangerous places. Work was usually finished by one o'clock, and we were back in camp as a rule by 4 p.m. When we first took up the work, the cables were being laid near Hooge, but gradually the work took us further afield. It was then clear that Micmac Camp was too far away from the work, for it was taking us three hours to reach the job, and three hours to get back to camp, while hardly more than three hours' actual digging was done. Accordingly, on the 26th, all those engaged on the work moved to the Canal Bank, where they were accommodated in dug-outs, cellars and shelters. The rest of the battalion (battalion headquarters, school, and details) moved to Hoograaf, going into huts there. Captain W. H. McLean, M.C., was placed in command of the Canal Bank party. Cable burying proceeded apace, although more than once work had to be abandoned on account of the enemy's heavy and continuous shelling. The billets of the Canal Bank working party received some attention from the enemy guns. The working party was not to remain there for long, however, for, on the 29th, it moved to the vicinity of Belgian Chateau, going into huts and tents there.

CHAPTER XXXV.

Polderhoek Chateau — Preparation for the Second Brigade's Attack—Hoograaf—Work with Canadian Tunnellers—Walker Camp—Reutel Sector —Christmas 1917—Belgian Chateau—Manawatu Camp.

ON the night of the 1st December, the Rifle Brigade relieved the Fourth Brigade in the line, and 1st Wellington, remaining in the line for the time being, came under the orders of the G.O.C. Rifle Brigade. In preparation for the attack on Polderhoek Chateau by the Second Brigade, the line of the left front company was thinned out at daylight on the 3rd December, reducing the garrison there by twenty-five per cent. At noon on the 3rd December, the Second Brigade attacked Polderhoek Chateau and grounds, the Lewis guns, machine-guns, and trench mortar batteries attached to the Rifle Brigade (to which 1st Wellington was temporarily attached) co-operating. There being a lack of satisfactory information that night as to the result of the attack, a patrol of three of our men, under Lance-Corporal E. A. Billing, was sent across the Reutelbeek. This patrol reconnoitred the position held by the Second Brigade and returned, reporting that 1st Otago held posts facing the Chateau and forty yards west of it. On the same night, a patrol, under Lance-Corporal H. M. Black, reconnoitred the front near Juniper Cottage, and reported on same for a defensive line. The 4th December, passed quietly and that night, a working party from 1st Battalion of the Rifle Brigade, covered by a party from the same battalion, dug a communication trench from the front line and established a Lewis gun post. Early on the following morning, this post was taken over by Wellington-West Coast Company of 1st Wellington. The 5th was uneventful and, that night, 1st Wellington was relieved by 2nd Battalion Rifle Brigade. The relief was completed without casualties by 9 p.m., and companies moved back independently to Birr Cross Roads, where buses were waiting to take the battalion to the II. Anzac Reserve Camp at Hoograaf, where it went into rest.

A day or two later, a party of seventy-five was detached for employment with the 1st Canadian Tunnelling Company at La Clytte. A number of the 1st Battalion's Lewis gunners from Ruahine and Hawkes Bay Companies were also detached for anti-aircraft work with the 1st Machine-Gun Company, while a model platoon was now formed for instructional purposes. A few days later, the parties attached to 1st and 3rd Canadian Tunnelling Companies were each made up to a strength of four officers and two hundred other ranks. In addition, thirty men were attached to 1st Auckland, engaged on work at Belgian Chateau. 1st Battalion headquarters and the remnants from companies remained in camp at Hoograaf Cabaret.

During the period from 26th November to the 5th December, the casualties sustained by the 1st Battalion were: Four officers wounded, Lieut. (Temporary Captain) M. S. Galloway, M.C., Lieut. A. R. Blennerhassett, Lieut. A. Smith (shell-shock), Lieut. L. J. Maule (shell-shock), and other ranks, one missing, sixteen killed, fifty-nine wounded.

A few days before Xmas, Lieut.-Col. C. F. D. Cook, D.S.O., arrived back from leave and resumed command of the 1st Battalion.

December with our 3rd Battalion passed rather uneventfully. On the 1st December, the 3rd Battalion had been relieved in the support area by 3rd Battalion Rifle Brigade, the relief being carried out in daylight with no casualties. The 3rd Battalion then proceeded to Howe Camp hutments, and, after a few days there, moved back to Walker Camp. From there, the usual working parties were sup-

THE WELLINGTON REGIMENT

plied, mainly employed on salvage work in the Hooge area. It was now that Captain A. S. Muir, who had been adjutant of the battalion, left for Division and 2nd Lieut. E. G. Stewart became acting adjutant. The weather was now very cold and a good deal of snow fell, to be followed by rain. Conditions were rather unpleasant, nor were they improved by the enemy shelling Walker Camp and its vicinity. The 3rd Battalion had received a good many reinforcements, and was not for long to remain out of the trenches. On the 15th December, it entrained on the light railway at Dickebusch Siding for Hellfire Corner, and from there, proceeded to the line, relieving 2nd Otago and going into the Reutel Sector for the first time, battalion having three casualties during the relief. Owing to the severeness of the weather, the difficulty of the overland routes and the bad state of the sector taken over generally, our men during this period had a trying time. Nor did we escape casualties for eight were killed, and twenty-five wounded, while sick evacuations were heavy. Luckily, the 3rd Battalion was to remain only a week in the trenches, and, on the 22nd December, it was relieved by 2nd Otago and proceeded to Manawatu Camp, Lieut. E. G. Cousins being slightly wounded on the way out. From Manawatu Camp, for the next few days, we supplied working parties for the reserve line and Hooge area. On Christmas Day, however, we rested. No working parties were required. The weather was miserable with snow and rain. Christmas parcels were distributed and a special Christmas dinner of plum pudding and turkey was provided.

On the 27th, the 3rd Battalion relieved 2nd Otago in the line in the Reutal Sector. The weather was now freezing, but the trenches had been a good deal improved and we were able to make ourselves more comfortable than last time. Shelling by the enemy was but intermittent, and our casualties were not serious, although we had one man killed and eight wounded. Our observation of the enemy was keen, and we obtained good sniping results.

THE WELLINGTON REGIMENT

For the whole of December, the 2nd Battalion's headquarters and school were at Hoograaf, with the majority of the battalion with the working party at Belgian Chateau. Early in the month, the weather was fine and frosty, and everyone began to swing into cable burying with a will. The work was now along the Ypres-Zonnebeke Railway, and near Chateau Wood, and 400 or 500 yards were completed every day. The 2nd Battalion had been singularly free from casualties. The work was being done only a mile or so from the front line, and many shells came over. We had all quite made up our minds that cable burying was a "cushy" job and would "do us for the duration" when we received a severe set back. On the 14th December, the battalion supplied the usual party of four hundred. In the first place, the trains which took us to the work were two hours late in starting. Then at Stirling Castle, the engine of one train was derailed, necessitating a long march to the task. We, therefore, arrived at the work very much later than usual. Two companies including Ruahine, had actually started work while the other two companies were just filing on to their tasks, when the enemy sent over one or two shells. The first fell dangerously close, to be followed immediately by another of heavy calibre which, bursting amongst the men of Ruahine Company, caused no less than thirty-three casualties (ten killed, six missing, and seventeen wounded). It was hard to believe that one chance shell could do such damage. It was a great blow to everyone. We had been so fortunate up till now while on this work, that we had begun to think the work hardly dangerous at all, and yet now, more than ten* were killed before our very eyes, some of them blown to fragments. However, it was war, and what was one to expect. The work was pushed on with vigour until Christmas Day. Unfortunately, the weather broke and a good deal of snow fell during the afternoon and evening; but Christmas Day was made as pleasant as possible under war conditions. A good Christmas dinner was provided at

---

*It turned out afterwards that of the six reported missing several were killed.

Belgian Chateau. Arrangements were made for the transport to have dinner in the transport lines, and those attending the Brigade school to have theirs at Bertheu. Battalion details, including the band, went to Belgian Chateau for the day, returning by lorry to Hoograaf in the evening. Everyone appreciated the festive meal. During the afternoon, the band played a number of selections. In the evening the officers of the 2nd Battalion had a very jolly dinner, and among those present was our old comrade, Major L. H. Jardine, M.C., who had recently arrived back from England to join the Rifle Brigade.

Christmas Day over, work was again the order of the day, and the working party was out bright and early on Boxing Day and for many days to follow. The 2nd Battalion was to remain on cable burying and other incidental work, such as draining and repairing Westhoek road and repairing the road near Hooge Crater, until the middle of January. During December, there had been a good many changes in the officers of the 2nd Battalion. Captain C. A. L. Treadwell, who had been adjutant since May 1916, a long period—and had been mentioned in despatches for distinguished services in the field was given a rest, and was detailed for duty with and left to join the Reserve Battalion at Sling. There he remained only a short time, being placed in charge of a new legal department at headquarters in London. Lieut. A. T. White, M.C., was also detailed for a four months' tour of duty at Sling. Lieutenant W. Pollock, Assistant Adjutant, now went to First Brigade headquarters for instruction in Staff duties. Lieutenant H. Simmonds, M.C., took over duties as acting adjutant, while 2nd/Lieut. C. G. Robinson became Intelligence officer. In the middle of January, Lieut.-Col. W. H. Cunningham, D.S.O., also proceeded to Sling to take command of the Reserve Battalion there, and Major W. H. McLean, M.C., assumed command of the 2nd Battalion temporarily.

CHAPTER XXXVI.

New Year 1918—Reutel Sector—Manawatu Camp—Enemy Aeroplanes—Walker Camp—Otago Camp—Breaking up of the 4th Brigade—3rd Wellington Ceases to Exist—Bavinhove—Staple.

NEW Year's Day 1918, found the 3rd Battalion still in the line in the Reutel Sector. There was intermittent shelling during the day, and Lieut. A. T. Duncan was wounded. On the 2nd, we were relieved by the 3rd Battalion Rifle Brigade and procceded to Manawatu Camp. On the journey out, our front and support line companies met with fairly heavy shelling, and five were wounded. The battalion was at once called upon for working parties. Very early one morning, enemy aeroplanes flew over our camp, one bomb being dropped on one of the huts, but, fortunately, it was a "dud." Verily is it better to be born lucky than rich! Whether as a result of our early morning visitor or not, the enemy shelled the camp at short intervals all day, ceasing at 7 p.m., only to open out again at 11 p.m. for an hour. By great good fortune, we had no casualties; nor did we have any a few days later, when the vicinity of the camp was shelled for fifteen minutes with gas shells. On the 8th January, it was snowing hard, and the 3rd Battalion was conveyed back to Walker Camp on the light railway, taking over from 1st Otago.

Some of the days were now very cold with frequent snow showers. From Walker Camp, the same old working parties were provided, although from this camp we used to go up to our work, which lay in the Hooge area, on the light railways. While at Walker Camp, some attended a lecture

Abandoned Tank at Gommecourt.

In the Front Line at Gommecourt.
Lieuts. B. Brooks, A. J. Trevena, E. G. Cousins, A. G. Melles, C. E. Lee.

THE WELLINGTON REGIMENT

by Major General Wood, U.S.A. Army, on "America at War."

As for our 1st Battalion, the New Year found Battalion headquarters still at Hoograaf, with the majority of the battalion detached on various working parties in the vicinity. That state of affairs continued until the 17th January, when battalion headquarters marched to Walker Camp, and the Battalion relieved the 3rd Battalion there in Divisional Reserve. All working parties detached from the battalion now rejoined and the battalion was reorganised. Early in the month, Major H. Holderness had left the Battalion to attend the Senior Officers' course at Aldershot, and Major W. F. Narbey was appointed temporarily second in command. On the 20th, the 1st Battalion marched to Manawatu Camp and there took over from 1st Canterbury and formed part of the brigade in support. Owing to lack of accommodation in Manawatu Camp, surplus personnel were camped at Scottish Lines. During its stay at Manawatu Camp, the 1st Battalion supplied working parties daily and we had one killed and seven wounded.

About this time, Lieut.-Col C. H. Weston was awarded the D.S.O. for his gallantry and skill at La Basse Ville and Gravenstafel while, shortly afterwards, Capt. A. T. White, Capt. B. H. Morison and Lieut. H. Dallinger were to receive the Military Cross for their services in the field during 1917.

The 2nd Battalion's spell of cable burying came to an end on the 17th January, and on that day we left Belgian Chateau, which had been our home for many weeks, and moved to Howe Camp where Battalion Headquarters joined us the following day. A few days later, we moved to Otago Camp, and from there, one working party wired a reserve line, another party built a cookhouse in Cambridge Road, another built dugouts at Westhoek, while others were engaged in draining Cambridge Road, in salvage work in the vicinity of Glencorse Wood, and in carrying parties from Westhoek to the support line.

Otago Camp was on the outskirts of Ypres, and it was a sad sight to look back at that ruined city from our lines. From near our camp, observation balloons used to be sent up, and the enemy was often prompted to shoot at them. Usually the shells would be very wide of the mark; but, on one occasion, he managed to cut the rope tethering one of the balloons to the ground. Our balloon immediately ascended, and it was not long before its occupants jumped out and slowly parachuted to the ground near our lines. The no-longer captive balloon ascended higher and higher in the sky, and, as soon as the parachutes were clear, our "Archies" and the enemy's also opened fire upon it. It was good practice for them, but seemingly, little harm was done to the balloon, and the last we saw of our huge "sausage" was a mere speck high in the sky, rapidly proceeding towards Germany.

From Otago Camp, the 2nd Battalion moved into the line, taking over from 2nd Otago in the Reutel Sector. Trench warfare was quite a novelty, and for those who had joined up with the 2nd Battalion since Gravenstafel, it was their first experience of the trenches.

On the night of the 26th January, the 1st Battalion relieved 1st Canterbury in the front line trenches, Judge Sub-sector, Reutel Sector, moving up along the Pioneer-Helles-Glengorse tracks via Chateau Wood and Crucifix Dump. The relief was completed by 9 o'clock p.m. with only one man slightly wounded. On the first two nights of our occupancy of the front line, active patrolling was carried out; but, on the following nights, a bright moon made this duty difficult. The 1st Battalion remained in the line until the 1st February, its casualties being one killed and eleven wounded. It was about this time that Major R. D. Hardie, D.S.O., now Divisional Machine-Gun Officer, was severely wounded near Wattle Dump.

On the 18th January, after having been relieved by the 1st Battalion at Walker Camp, the 3rd Battalion headquarters had moved to Hoograaf. The Fourth Brigade was now to be Corps Troops for work. Wellington-West Coast,

THE WELLINGTON REGIMENT

Hawkes Bay and Ruahine Companies of the 3rd Battalion moved to Busseboom for work with the 3rd Canadian Tunnellers, while Taranaki Company moved to Dranoutre for work with the 1st Australian Tunnellers, while six Lewis gun teams went to various anti-aircraft posts. At Busseboom and Dranoutre, the men were in splendid quarters. The work they were engaged on was mostly tunnelling, the building of shelters in support and reserve lines. The 3rd Battalion remained on such work until the 7th February, on which date the 4th Brigade ceased to exist.

Ever since the Division's October losses at Belle Vue Spur, the maintenance of four brigades of infantry in the field had been a matter of concern and, early in the New Year, it was considered no longer feasible. The Fourth Brigade, therefore, ceased to exist on the 7th February and with it, of course, the 3rd Battalion of the Wellington Regiment went out of existence. Our 3rd Battalion had been eight months in France. It had borne a full share of the burden and always acquitted itself with credit. Those associated with it will always look back upon that battalion with pride and satisfaction as, indeed, they have every right to do. Such of the personnel of the former 4th Brigade as was not immediately absorbed into the Division, was now employed under the name of the New Zealand Entrenching Group, commanded by Lieut.-Col. G. Mitchell, D.S.O.

On the night of the 1st February, the 1st Battalion was relieved by 1st Battalion Rifle Brigade, in the Judge Sub-sector, and marched back to Manawatu Camp, the relief being carried out without casualties. On the 3rd February, Lieut.-Col. C. F. D. Cook, D.S.O., left to take charge of the First Brigade School at Scottish Lines, and Major W. F. Narbey assumed temporary command of the battalion, only to fall sick a few days later, and to hand over to Captain H. Oram. During daylight on the 8th February, 1st Wellington relieved the 2/6th Lancashire Fusiliers in support in the Judge Noord sub-sector. From the 8th to the 13th February, companies were employed on work in the forward area, salving, improving accommodation, etc. This period passed quietly, and there were only two casualties. On the 14th February, we were relieved in the Judge Noord sub-sector by 2nd Battalion Rifle Brigade, and moved back to Dickebusch by light railway from Birr Cross Roads. From Dickebusch during the following week, we supplied daily strong working parties for work with our own Engineers. On the 23rd February, we marched to Manawatu Camp, and became Corps troops for work on the Corps Line, and, after a few days there, we moved to Forrestor Camp, and from there went on with the same work as before. On the 8th March, the 1st Battalion was relieved by 3rd Battalion, Rifle Brigade, and marched to Halifax Camp. On the following day the battalion proceeded by motor buses from Halifax Camp to Bavinchove, and went into billets there.

The 2nd Battalion, having gone into the line on the 26th January, remained in the Reutel Sector until 1st February. The weather was fine but very misty. On the 1st February, we were relieved by the 4th Battalion Rifle Brigade, temporarily commanded by Major L. H. Jardine, M.C., so well known in 2nd Wellington a year before. From Otago Camp, numerous working parties were supplied, digging a trench in support line at Cameron Covert, building dugouts at Westhoek, and draining Cambridge Road. After a week so employed, we again moved back into the line in the same sector. Things were now very much quieter than during our previous spell in this sector. A fighting patrol of one officer and twelve other ranks searched Celtic Wood, but found no sign of the enemy; but, a few nights later, one of our patrols dispersed an enemy patrol, four of whom were taken prisoner by the battalion on our left. One day, when the enemy artillery was a little more active than usual, Captain F. D. Gaffaney was wounded. On the 14th, after a quiet day, we were relieved by 4th Battalion Rifle Brigade, late in the afternoon. We marched out as far as Birr Cross Roads, and there entrained on the light railway for Walker Camp, Dickebusch. At Walker Camp, the Battalion was in divisional reserve, and as the weather was fine, and the battalion not called upon for working parties, we were able to put in a few days recreational training. It was not long, however, before working parties were in full swing again. On the 21st February, Major F. K. Turnbull, M.C., rejoined from hospital, and assumed command of the battalion, taking over from Major H. E. McKinnon, M.C., who had been in command since his return from leave at the end of January. On the 23rd February, the 2nd Battalion was attached to the 49th Division as Corps troops for work, and moved to Vancouver and Winnipeg Camps, and next day, Sunday, a combined Church Parade with 1st Auckland was held in Vancouver Camp, at which Lieut. General Sir A. J. Godley was present. A working party, nearly four hundred strong, was now supplied daily for the task of building strong points in the Corps line. This work lasted a fortnight with little to relieve the monotony, except a very enjoyable concert one evening by a party from 2nd Canadian C.C.S. On the 10th March, the 2nd Battalion moved to billets in Staple.

The 1st Battalion in billets at Bavinchove, and the 2nd Battalion at Staple now spent their time in reorganising and training, both battalions receiving a good many reinforcements. The weather was delightful, and it was not long before we were all in high spirits. A good deal of football was played. The 1st Battalion played both 1st Auckland and 2nd Auckland, and won both games; while the 2nd Battalion held inter-company football matches, which aroused the keenest rivalry, and also played 1st Auckland who narrowly beat them. A football match was also played between teams of officers from each battalion. This was followed in the evening by a dinner given by the 1st Battalion, at which Brigadier-General Melvill (First Brigade Commander) was present. At Staple also, a combined Church Service was held for both Wellington Battalions.

While at Staple, a very sad accident occurred in Hawkes Bay Company of the 2nd Battalion, resulting in the death of Corporal H. C. Pattison and Private A. A. Rossiter, M.M. That Company was practising musketry one evening in gas helmets, loading with dummy cartridges and aiming, when by some mischance a live cartridge was loaded into one of the rifles and fired. Pattison and Rossiter were in a squad on the other side of the field, and were both struck by the bullet, one being killed out-right and the other expiring very shortly afterwards. Both Pattison and Rossiter were splendid fellows, and very popular, and their death in this unfortunate way was a sad blow to the whole battalion.

CHAPTER XXXVII.

The Germans Break Through on the British Front in the South—We Go Down to the Somme—Filling the Gap—Mailly Maillet—Colincamps—Some Hard Fighting.

EVER since December, the British Command had been aware that a mighty thrust by the German Armies would not be long delayed. The difficulty was to know where that thrust would be made. By the end of February, however, there were unmistakeable signs that the enemy's initial attempt would be made against the British Front in the south. It therefore became necessary to withdraw many divisions from the northern Armies and place them at the disposal of the Fifth and Third Armies in the southern sector of the British Front. The New Zealand Division was one of the divisions so held in reserve to be thrown in wherever necessary.

On the 14th March, a warning order had been issued throughout the Division providing for rapid movement in case of emergency. On the 21st March, when the Germans were found to be attacking in such strength on the Somme, the New Zealand Division was ordered to be ready to entrain for the south at short notice. On the 22nd, the Division was under orders to transfer to the Third Army and to start entraining on the afternoon of the 24th. Both 1st and 2nd Wellington entrained at Cassel on the morning of the 25th March. At Ailly-sur-Somme, both battalions detrained. The 1st Battalion bivouaced for the night there, and awaited motor lorries. The 2nd Battalion marched to Pont Camon, bivouacing there at 3 o'clock the following morning. A few hours' rest there, and at 9 a.m.

on the 26th, the 2nd Battalion was on the march again. Hedauville was reached at 5 p.m., and the battalion billetted there for the night. By 7.30 a.m. on the 26th, only four motor lorries had materialised for the 1st Battalion, and the Commanding Officer (Major W. F. Narbey) with one Wellington-West Coast Company platoon, five Lewis gun sections and some details, ninety in all, went forward and reported to Divisional Headquarters at Hedauville. The remainder of the 1st Battalion, including Ruahine Company, which had detrained at Amiens, was later conveyed by lorries to Pont Noyelles and then marched to Hedauville, arriving there at about 8.30 p.m. The night was spent in bivouac, ready to move forward at a moment's notice.

Other elements of the New Zealand Division had reached Hedauville early in the day, and had been thrown into the ever-widening gap between the V and IV Corps. The situation was one of the greatest anxiety and danger. At all costs the enemy's advance had to be arrested. The 1st Battalion of the Rifle Brigade was the first to go into action, moving forward at 6 o'clock in the morning of the 26th March, to be followed later by the two Canterbury Battalions and a machine-gun company.

During the afternoon, 1st and 2nd Auckland, 2nd Battalion Rifle Brigade, and a machine-gun company had arrived, and, at 5.30 p.m., this force went into action under the command of General Melvill, advancing north and south of the Serre Road.

On the night of the 26th, a serious gap in the line between the New Zealand and the 4th Australian Divisions near Hebuterne was reported to the New Zealand Division. It was vital to fill this gap without delay. By this time, further troops had arrived at Hedauville, viz, 3rd Battalion Rifle Brigade, 2nd Wellington, 2nd Otago, 1st Wellington and 1st Otago. 2nd Wellington was the only Battalion thrown into the action which had not the assistance of transport by motor bus from the detraining point. The more rested troops, comprising the 3rd Battalion Rifle Brigade,

Support Line near Colincamps.

Face p. 248.

Dinner at Solesmes.

Left to Right—Standing: Capt. H. M. Goldstein, Medical Officer; 2nd Lt. R. L. King, Signal Officer; 2nd Lt. F. C. Chaytor, Lewis Gun Officer; 2nd Lieut. A. A. Browne, Quartermaster; Lt. H. Simmonds, Intelligence Officer. Seated: Major W. H. Fletcher, 2nd in Command; Lt.-Col. W. H. Cunningham, Commanding; Lt. C. A. L. Treadwell, Adjutant.

Our Field Kitchens near Grevillers.

2nd Wellington and 2nd Otago were at once formed into a composite force under Lieut.-Col. A. E. Stewart and ordered to extend the line northwards up the Hebuterne Road. 1st Wellington and 1st Otago were to remain in divisional reserve for the time being.

At 1 a.m. on the 27th, Col. Stewart's force left Hedauville and marched through Mailly Maillet reaching Colincamps at 4 a.m. Here 2nd Otago was thrown out as a screen to protect the advance of 2nd Wellington and the 3rd Battalion Rifle Brigade. The two latter battalions rested a little in the shelter of the buildings, and then at daybreak moved forward, covered by advance and flank guards, with 2nd Wellington on the right and 3rd Battalion Rifle Brigade on .the left, towards Hebuterne. 2nd Wellington advanced with Taranaki Company on the right, Ruahine Company on the left, Wellington-West Coast Company in support and Hawkes Bay Company in reserve. On the left, the 3rd Rifles met with but little resistance. On the right, 2nd Wellington ran right into enemy machine-guns firing from near La Signy Farm. During the operation, Wellington-West Coast Company (Capt. A. G. Melles, M.C.) attacked an enemy post, killing 14 and capturing 1 officer and 52 other ranks, Lieut. J. T. Thomas doing great work, and showing a fine personal example. Enemy machine-guns forbade further progress, and 2nd Wellington was obliged to dig in 400 yards short of its objective, the Hebuterne Road. Touch was, however, established with the battalions on both flanks and the gap in the line filled.

The enemy made numerous attacks against the New Zealand line during the day (27th) and, striking against its position about 7 o'clock in the evening, on a front of 1500 yards mid-way between the refinery and Hebuterne, 2nd Wellington was forced to give ground. Hawkes Bay Company (Captain G. H. Hume, M.C.) which had lain in reserve all day, was now called upon to counter-attack. That company advanced shortly before 9 p.m.; but, hardly had it gone any distance at all, than it ran into a large party of the enemy armed with machine-guns. Hawkes Bay fought well, killing about sixty of the enemy and capturing five machine-guns; but that company's own casualties were heavy, and it was unable to re-establish 2nd Wellington's line. In this counter-attack, three officers of Hawkes Bay Company, viz., Lieuts. J. K. E. Jackson, D. H. Donaldson and E. C. Clifton were wounded, while earlier in the day, Lieut. D. L. Robertson (Wellington-West Coast Company) had been killed. Altogether 2nd Wellington that day had the following casualties; 4 officers, 69 other ranks. Lieut. Jackson died of wounds the following day to the great grief of the whole Regiment. Poor old Stonewall! Starting as a private in the Main Body, he had had a long innings. It was a queer thing. Some went into action supremely confident, only to be struck down before they had gone five yards; others had a presentment that death was near. For months, yea years, Jackson had flirted with death: he had laughed at shells: scoffed at bullets. Yet in the train going down to the Somme, the gay and debonair "Jacko" was quiet and thoughtful. He made no secret of it; he felt he would be killed. And so it was to be. We shall not hear his merry sallies again: nor see him play cricket or football: nor watch him box; nor cheer him on in a cross country race. Still he will never grow old in our memory.

Late in the afternoon of the 27th, 1st Wellington marched two miles to Mailly Maillet, going into Brigade Reserve in billets there, relieving 2nd Battalion Rifle Brigade.

Early in the morning of the 28th, 2nd Wellington was relieved by 4th Battalion Rifle Brigade and moved back into Divisional Reserve near Courcelles. After dark that evening, 1st Wellington relieved 1st Auckland in the line. There was spasmodic shelling over the whole front; otherwise, next day was quiet. A curious thing happened here. While the ration limbers were being unloaded at the Sugar Refinery they were shelled, and one of them, loaded with rations and bombs, bolted along the road leading to Colincamps via Euston, which was held by the enemy. It was not stopped until it reached Colincamps, from where it was brought back to 1st Wellington's headquarters.

At 2 o'clock in the afternoon of the 30th (Easter Sunday), 1st Wellington co-operated with 2nd Auckland on its left in an attack on certain high ground with a view to improving the position north of the Serre Road.

Taranaki Company stood fast, Wellington-West Coast Company in the centre, and Ruahine Company on the left, advanced their line with complete success from One Tree Hill on the right to the southernmost point of the hedge on the high ground just above the Serre Road. Sergeant R. Hatton led a party three times against an enemy post before capturing it. On the left flank, Lieut. F. E. Ashby's platoon was faced by a position held by a force of forty or fifty Germans and six machine-guns. Ashby organised bombing attacks and then led his men with splendid dash in final rush which captured the machine-guns and twenty-five prisoners. Our whole attack was successful. Seventy-four prisoners and twenty-two machine-guns were captured, while our casualties were, two officers wounded, twenty others ranks killed, fifty-five wounded, and three missing. During the consolidation of the captured position, the enemy was seen twice concentrating for a counter-attack; but each time his parties were broken up by our artillery fire. Once the enemy tried to bring a machine-gun into action; but Sergeant M. Macaskill, at once, rushed the gun and put it out of action, killing all the team, and by his prompt and courageous action preventing many casualties.

In the centre, 2nd Auckland was equally successful, and four platoons from 2nd Wellington were placed at the disposal of that battalion for carrying purposes and as a battalion reserve.

On the left, however, the 4th Battalion of the Rifle Brigade met determined opposition and, only after hard fighting all day, did the enemy fall back under cover of darkness.

THE WELLINGTON REGIMENT

With our 1st Battalion the night passed quietly. The weather turned very wet; but, although the going was heavy, all wounded were clear by 3 a.m.

Major F. K. Turnbull, M.C., now took temporary command of the 2nd Battalion, vice Lieut.-Col. J. L. Short, who left for England on duty, and, on the 31st March, that battalion moved into the line at La Signy Farm, relieving 2nd Auckland.

THE WELLINGTON REGIMENT

CHAPTER XXXVIII.

The Trenches at La Signy Farm — A Dump Blows Up — We Relieve the Australians — Hebuterne — A Patrol from the 2nd Battalion is Captured — Death of Col. Cook in England — A Minor Operation Astride the Road to Puisieux-du-Mont — A Gallant Corporal — Sailly-au-Bois — Rossignol Farm — Brushes with Enemy Patrols — Horse Show at Vauchelles — 1st Battalion Wins a Guard Mounting Competition.

ON the 2nd April, the 1st Battalion was relieved by 1st Auckland in the line, moving on relief into billets in Mailly-Maillet. Two days later the 1st Battalion moved from Mailly-Maillet and became part of Divisional Reserve, bivouacing in the open. We were now able to bathe and rest, and no training of any kind was attempted. The health of all ranks was good and the spirit splendid. Here, unfortunately, Hawkes Bay Company had one man killed and four wounded through an enemy gun shelling the back area. While in Divisional Reserve, Major H. Holderness returned from England and assumed command of the battalion, taking over from Major W. F. Narbey.

Second Wellington remained in line in front of La Signy Farm until the 5th April. The enemy was quiet, our machine-gun fire keeping him well under, except in back areas where a good deal of movement could be seen. Owing to recent rain, the trenches had become very muddy and difficult to walk through, and the front line companies had plenty to do in cleaning up the trenches, while other companies were engaged in digging a new support line. Daylight patrols, reconnoitring in front of La Signy Farm, found a trench there unoccupied which we proceeded to occupy by posts. On the 5th, the 2nd Battalion was relieved in the front line by the 4th Battalion Rifle Brigade, and thereupon took up a position in the Divisional Reserve Line. Before completion of relief, the enemy attacked in the mist under cover of a very heavy barrage; but was completely repulsed with heavy losses. Our casualties were light, but in consequence of this attack two platoons of Ruahine Company and Battalion Headquarters were not relieved till the following morning.

Lieut.-Col. W. H. Cunningham, D.S.O., now returned to the 2nd Battalion from England and took command. A large number of officers and men joined up from the Entrenching Group and from the Base, including Captain J. MacMorran, who went back to Hawkes Bay Company, and Lieutenant S. A. Murrell, who was appointed assistant adjutant and bombing officer.

On the 9th April, 1st Wellington relieved 3rd Battalion Rifle Brigade, in the line, while 2nd Wellington relieved 2nd Battalion Rifle Brigade in support. At this time, the enemy was very inactive and our casualties were but slight. On the 14th, the 1st Battalion was relieved by 1st Auckland, and went into the brigade reserve line west of Colincamps. On the same day, 2nd Wellington relieved 2nd Auckland in the front line in La Signy Farm sector. The weather was still very foggy and misty. Several daylight patrols from the 2nd Battalion worked down saps towards La Signy Farm, and had bombing encounters with the enemy, inflicting casualties. One morning, about a battalion of the enemy were seen some 3000 yards away moving in our direction; but no attack developed and nothing untoward followed. Again, early one morning, the enemy shelled the front line, several shells falling in our trenches, and in the afternoon an enemy shell landed on a large dump of Stokes Mortar bombs, causing a tremendous explosion. One platoon of Ruahine Company had several wounded and others were badly shaken. Shortly afterwards, a big enemy dump was blown up, and burnt fiercely for nearly an hour. Our 6 inch Howitzers fired for over an hour on La Signy Farm buildings, registering about ten direct hits, and completely blocking up the doorway of the big cellar. For the rest of the day, our guns contented themselves with firing short rapid bursts on enemy positions. On the 17th, 2nd Wellington was relieved in the front line by 1st Otago and then marched to a canvas camp. During the relief, Capt. R. L. Evatt was badly wounded. On the same day, 1st Wellington was relieved by 2nd Otago in Brigade Reserve, and now became part of Divisional Reserve for the following week. There was little of incident. The weather was cold and showery with a little snow. The usual working parties were being supplied, and baths could now be had at Bertrancourt.

On the 24th April, our 1st Battalion relieved the 13th Battalion, A.I.F., in Brigade Reserve north of Sailley-au-Bois, while the 2nd Battalion relieved the 15th Battalion, A.I.F., in the front line south of Hebuterne, making the same dispositions as the Australians. At this time, the 15th Battalion, A.I.F., was commanded by Lieut.-Col. McSharry, D.S.O., M.C., an old friend of the Wellington Regiment in the days of Quinn's Post, Gallipoli. The trenches were left in excellent order by the Australians and the relief went through smoothly, although limbers with Lewis guns were held up in Sailly by traffic control police and this delayed the relief. We lent two of our limbers to the Australians to take out their Lewis guns, their own transport having left the previous day for their new billeting area.

Next day, the enemy was quiet except for an occasional shelling. On the other hand, our artillery was particularly active with harassing fire. The 2nd Battalion headquarters' mess had a small dinner to celebrate the third anniversary of the Gallipoli landing, and a pleasant evening was spent in the capacious dugout. Only two members of the mess had been at the landing, Colonel W. H. Cunningham and Major F. K. Turnbull. The following day, the weather was misty and one of our 2nd Battalion patrols consisting of five men led by Lieut. J. T. Thomas, M.C. (1) met with disaster. The patrol reported at a listening post near the front line at 3.30 a.m.; but was not seen nor heard from afterwards. Bombing and rifle fire were heard some distance away at 4 a.m., and it was conjectured that, having lost its way in the mist, the whole patrol was either killed or captured. The 2nd Battalion sent out search parties as soon as the patrol was reported missing but no trace of it could be found. Lieut. Thomas was an excellent officer and was greatly missed. Unhappily, S.S.M. J. D. G. H. Durand (2) of the A.S.C., attached to the 2nd Battalion for experience before going for a commission, had gone with the party at his own express wish. It was indeed bad luck, for he was a Main Body man.

During the next few days, both battalions did a good deal of work improving their positions. On the 30th, 1st Wellington relieved 1st Auckland in the front line at Hebuterne, while the same night 2nd Wellington was relieved in the front line by 2nd Auckland and moved back into Brigade Reserve at Sailly-au-Bois.

The whole Regiment was now to receive a grievous blow by the death of Lieut.-Col. C. F. D. Cook, D.S.O., the Commanding Officer of the 1st Battalion.

The death of Lieut.-Col. C. F. D. Cook in England at the beginning of May, removed one of the Regiment's most revered commanders. Charles Frederick Denman Cook had had a distinguished career, both at work and at games. At the University he had won a Senior University Scholarship in Latin and Greek, and had secured first class honours in classics for his M.A. degree. At games, in addition to being a very able cricketer and footballer he had, for several years, represented Canterbury College at athletics, his specialty being the high jump, for which he long held the University record. His all-round excellence was such that he was chosen as the first candidate from Canterbury College for the Rhodes Scholarship. That

---

(1) Lieut. J. T. Thomas became a prisoner of war.
(2) S. S. M. Durand was killed.

THE WELLINGTON REGIMENT

Cook should be one of the very first to offer his services to his country on the declaration of war was, therefore, in keeping with the man. The outbreak of war found him an officer in the Territorial Forces and, joining the Main Body as a Captain, he was posted to Hawkes Bay Company. During the Gallipoli campaign, Cook served as Staff Captain to the New Zealand Infantry Brigade and, for his services in that capacity, never ostentatious but unvariably efficient, he was mentioned in despatches. On the formation of the 2nd Battalion of the Regiment early in 1916, Cook became second in command of the 1st Battalion, and served with that Battalion on the Somme of 1916. On Col. Hart's appointment to the command of the new 4th Brigade in April 1917, Cook was appointed to the command of the 1st Battalion, an appointment he held right up to the time of his death. In April 1917, he had been again mentioned in despatches and, early in June, he was awarded the Distinguished Service Order. In March 1918, very much against his will, Col. Cook was sent across to England for a rest. He was very run down; but it seemed to be nothing more than war weariness. At Brockenhurst, however, disease gripped him and he passed away at Netley near Southampton on the 2nd May. Alas! Like so many more, he was not to see the triumph of our Arms, to which object he had so faithfully and unsparingly devoted himself. The memory of his fine character, quiet, dignified and manly, will not soon be effaced.

On the night of the 4th May, with a view to the improvement of our position in front of Hebuterne, a minor operation was carried out astride the road to Puisieux-Au-Mont by 1st Wellington in conjunction with 1/5th Manchester Regiment. Our 1st Battalion's attack was entrusted to Taranaki Company. At the same time, in order to distract the attention of the enemy artillery, two feints were made, one at La Signy Farm and the other at Rossignol Wood. Taranaki Company advanced at 8.52. Within a few minutes, Minny Trench was captured, unoccupied except for two men who were taken prisoner. Advancing from Minny Trench, a portion of Fusilier Trench was captured, while some of our men advanced up Warrior Sap. Some thirty yards in advance of Minny Trench, our men were held up by two enemy machine-guns firing from a sunken road and sustained heavy casualties. The two sections in Fusilier Trench moved along to the left, meeting an enemy bombing post, and coming under the fire of two machine-guns in Fusilier Trench. The majority of our men reached the final objective and altogether ten prisoners were taken. Owing to lack of co-operation between the assaulting troops, drawn as they were from two divisions, and to the intensity of enemy machine-gun fire, the enterprise was not wholly successful. Arrived at their objective, our men found themselves subjected to enfilade machine-gun fire, and to showers of bombs from bombing posts that they were not able to drive out. After losing five men killed, and eighteen wounded, two of whom died, the position was considered untenable, and we evacuated Fusilier Trench and came back to Minny Trench and there established touch with the 1/5th Manchesters on the left. We had, at all events, substantially advanced our positions and shortened our line. A narration of this minor operation would not be complete without recording the devotion to duty of Corporal A. Bradley of Taranaki Company. As our men were nearing their objective, Bradley had one of his feet blown off by a bomb. Suffering intensely, as he must have been, this gallant N.C.O. continued to urge his men forward and refused all offers of assistance. Crawling back to our lines unaided, he came upon two Germans attempting to return to their lines, and shot them both.

On the following night, the 1st Battalion was relieved in the line by 2nd Otago, and then went into reserve at Rossignol Farm.

Meantime, 2nd Wellington at Sailly-au-Bois was supplying the Engineers with working parties daily for work on strong points. On the 6th, the 2nd Battalion relieved 2nd Canterbury in what was called the Purple Line, a trench system running in rear of Mailly-Maillet, Colincamps and Hebuterne, while 1st Otago took over the vacated position as counter-attacking battalion.

The next few days slipped quietly by. The 1st Battalion in huts at Rossignol Farm was still resting, while the work of the 2nd Battalion's parties was not onerous. The weather was fine and large numbers were able to go to the baths daily, while one afternoon a good many officers attended a lecture on tanks at Bus-les-Artois. It was not long, however, before we found ourselves in the line again, for, on the 12th May, the 2nd Battalion moved once more into La Signy Farm sector, relieving 3rd Battalion Rifle Brigade. On the same night, 1st Wellington relieved 1st Battalion Rifle Brigade in the support line. Here our 1st Battalion remained in support for six days and had only one man wounded. The 2nd Battalion too, in the front line, found the enemy quiet enough, but, as ever, the New Zealand Division was not content to let sleeping dogs lie. On the 13th, a fighting patrol of one N.C.O. and eighteen men from the 2nd Battalion attempted to get into an enemy post north of La Signy Farm buildings; but was driven off by machine-gun fire and bombs. One of our men was missing and two wounded. The following day, a valuable reconnaissance of La Signy Farm ruins was made by Lance-Corporal R. Smith (2nd Battalion), who crawled out through the enemy posts after dark and located enemy machine-gun posts. The 15th was the day 1st Auckland Battalion carried out a successful raid on the enemy positions. Things were normal again the following day, except that several heavy minenwerfers were fired on our front line, and our own artillery was active against enemy positions. On the night of the 18th May, 1st Wellington relieved 1st Auckland in the front line, while 2nd Auckland relieved our 2nd Battalion, who thereupon moved back from the front line into support. The 1st Battalion remained in the front line for six days. The weather was fine, warm and sunny: the enemy inactive and our casualties slight. On the night of the 21st May, a

THE WELLINGTON REGIMENT

patrol from the 1st Battalion encountered a strong enemy party in No Man's Land, and, although one prisoner was brought back to our lines, we lost Lieut. C. J. McHardie,* Sergeant R. Freeman* and Private A. R. G. Kenny (wounded and missing). On the night of the 24th May, the 1st Battalion was relieved in the front line by 2nd Otago, and marched to Rossignol Farm. On the same night, the 2nd Battalion was relieved in the support line by 1st Otago and marched back to tents in the Bois au Warmimont. The weather had broken and hot cocoa, biscuits and cigarettes supplied on arrival in camp by the Y.M.C.A. were much appreciated after the long march in the rain.

On the 28th May, both battalions marched to the First Brigade Horse Show held near Vauchelles. Here, the 1st Battalions won one first prize with its horses, and six other prizes, while the 2nd Battalion's horses won nine ribbons, including three first prizes. Here, also, the 1st Battalion won the Silver Challenge Cup for Guard Mounting, presented by Brigadier-General C. W. Melvill, with 88 points, 2nd Wellington being second with 78 points.

---

*Afterwards found to be killed.

THE WELLINGTON REGIMENT

CHAPTER XXXIX.

Midsummer in the Trenches — Relieved by the Manchester Regiment — A Welcome Spell — A Combined Church Parade at Henu — Vauchelles — Divisional Sports — Old Friends Foregather — Divisional Band Concert and Boxing Tournament — Hon. W. F. Massey and Sir Joseph Ward attend Church Parade.

THE 1st June was spent by both battalions in making preparations to go into the line again and, that night, the 2nd Battalion relieved 1st Battalion of the Rifle Brigade in the front line in the Hebuterne sector. (Major F. K. Turnbull, M.C., was now commanding the 2nd Battalion, vice Lieut.-Col. W. H. Cunningham, D.S.O., Acting-Brigadier, temporarily in command of the First Brigade.) The same night, 1st Wellington moved into the support line, relieving 4th Battalion of the Rifle Brigade. While in the line here, two officers from the 74th Division, a division lately arrived from Palestine, joined up with the 2nd Battalion for four days to obtain an insight into conditions of trench warfare.

Midsummer now, and fine sunny days. The trenches were very good, in some places, bordered with trees and hedges, which gave a very welcome shade to the garrison. We were not to remain long in the line, for, on the night of the 6th June, 1st Wellington was relieved in the support line by 6th Manchester Regiment, and marched back into reserve. By midnight of the same night, the 2nd Battalion had been relieved in the front line by 7th Manchester Regiment, and marched back to the canvas camp in Bois de Warnimont.

On the 11th, the 1st Battalion, in reserve in the purple line, was relieved by the 2nd Battalion, and moved back to the Bois de Warnimont. Major H. Holderness was now promoted Lieut.-Col. and to command the 1st Battalion, vice Lieut.-Col. C. F. D. Cook, D.S.O. (died in sickness).

On the 14th June, both battalions marched to a tented camp in the Henu area to carry on with training. While at Henu, many had the opportunity of being present at the enjoyable entertainments provided by " The Kiwis" (New Zealand Divisional Concert Party). On the 21st, we were on the move again, this time to Vauchelles, both battalions marching to a hutment camp there and practising manoeuvres on the way. The following Sunday (the 23rd) advantage was taken of the two battalions of the Regiment being camped along side each other to hold a combined Church Parade in the morning after which both battalions marched to the Divisional Sports. Here 1st Wellington represented the First Brigade and won the Divisional Guard Mounting Competition. It was a very enjoyable day, and a grand opportunity for old friends throughout the division to foregather.

On the following evening, the officers of the 2nd Battalion entertained the officers of the 1st Battalion at dinner. There were present also Brigadier-General Melvill, Major W. I. K. Jennings, Lieut.-Col. D. N. W. Murray, Major A. S. Muir (now D.A.Q.M.G.) and Capt. R. Riddiford. Many toasts were honoured and many excellent speeches made; but, alas! none by "Stonewall Jackson" this time. There were eighty present, which indicates how strongly both battalions were officered at this time, as, indeed, they had been ever since the breaking up of the Fourth Brigade.

Towards the end of June, both battalions attended the Divisional Band Concert and Finals of a Boxing Tournament. The 2nd Battalion's band secured third prize (second place for music), while the 1st Battalion's band obtained fifth place. Considering the 2nd Battalion's band was at that time the youngest in the Division, great credit was due to all concerned, but, particularly, to the bandmaster,

Mr. Osborne, for his good work in preparing for the contest.

On the 29th June, a start was made at 6.30 a.m. on a brigade tactical exercise, which occupied until 2 o'clock in the afternoon, and was carried out to the entire satisfaction of General Melvill. On the following day (Sunday) a combined Brigade Church Parade was held on the 2nd Battalion's parade ground. This was attended by the Prime Minister of New Zealand, the Right Hon. W. F. Massey, the Minister for Finance, Sir Joseph Ward, and party. Brigadier-General G. N. Johnston, then acting G.O.C. New Zealand Division, was also present. Afterwards, in the afternoon, the 1st and 2nd Battalions competed in a sports tournament, the honours of the day being with the 2nd Battalion.

Towards the end of June, Capt. W. H. McLean, M.C., returned to the 2nd Battalion from Aldershot. Early in the month, Capt. J. N. Ranch of the 2nd Battalion and Lieut. H. E. Crosse formerly of the 3rd Battalion had been awarded the Military Cross for services in the field.

THE WELLINGTON REGIMENT

CHAPTER XL.

Rossignol Wood—Gommecourt—Couin Wood—Working Parties — The Enemy Withdraws — A Substantial Advance of Our Line—The Americans—A Platoon from the 2nd Battalion Attends Army Memorial Service at Ranchicourt.

THIS pleasant interlude was shortly to come to an end, for, on the 1st July, the 1st Battalion relieved part of the King's Own Regiment and part of the 1st Royal Munster Fusiliers, in the line at Rossignol Wood, while the 2nd Battalion embussed at Vauchelles and proceeded to Souastre, thence marching via Fonquevillers to Gommecourt, becoming battalion in reserve to the left Brigade of the Division.

Large numbers of men of both battalions, as, indeed, of the whole division, were at this time suffering from Spanish influenza, a fore-runner of the malady which was shortly to sweep England, and, in a more virulent form, New Zealand itself. The numbers were soon so great that a Divisional Isolation Camp had to be formed. In 2nd Wellington alone during the first week in July, over one hundred men were afflicted.

On 9th July, at about 11 o'clock in the morning, Lieuts. W. G. Salmond and L. W. H. Grace and Pte. C. J. Dallard of the 1st Battalion were exploring Rossignol Wood, when they were attacked with bombs from the enemy in one of the pill boxes among the trees. Both officers were severely wounded and Dallard slightly. Dallard carried Grace some sixty yards back to safety and then returned to rescue Salmond who was lying within fifteen yards of the enemy post. He was greeted by a further shower of bombs, and was himself again wounded in three places. When he got close to him, he could see that Salmond was already dead. Dallard* then retraced his steps to Grace, and, notwithstanding his own wounds, carried him to within thirty yards of our own lines, when a party went over the parapet and brought in both Grace and Dallard.

On the night of the 9th July, the 1st Battalion was relieved by 2nd Canterbury, and, on relief, marched by qcmpanies to a tested camp in Couin Wood, where it remained for more than a week.

There was little of incident with the 2nd Battalion, engaged as it was on working parties under direction of the Engineers, although there was some jubilation on that battalion receiving an allotment of English leave, the first for some months.

Early in July, on our left, a gas attack was delivered on Bucquoy, from gas projectors—a considerable cloud resulting. On the 9th July, the 2nd Battalion was relieved by 2nd Otago, and proceeded to Sailly-au-Bois, and helped to garrison Chateau de la Haie Switch. There was work in plenty now. Numbers were employed on a new shaft at the Catacombs; others were working at deep dug-outs in each company sector: others again were moving the transport lines at Couin. The baths at Coïgneux were taken full advantage of.

On the night of the 17th July, the 1st Battalion relieved 3rd Battalion Rifle Brigade in support while 2nd Wellington relieved the 1st Battalion of the same brigade in the front line. The latter relief was complete at midnight with but few casualties, considering the fact that the advanced trenches had only just been captured by the Rifle Brigade from the enemy. The following day, Ruahine Company (2nd Battalion) pushed out patrols in daytime and successfully established advanced posts at night in Jean Bart Sap, while one evening a few days later, two platoons of Wellington-West Coast Company and two platoons of

---

*Private C. J. Dallard was awarded the D.C.M., for his gallant conduct. He died at Taihape on 2/9/21.

Ruahine Company moved forward from Jean and Ford trenches and, after bombing several German posts, occupied the line Jean Bart—Home Avenue. As was only to be expected, enemy machine-gun fire and artillery were active against the new line shortly after consolidation was completed.

At 2 o'clock in the afternoon of the 20th July, word was received that the enemy was evacuating Rossignol Wood. At 4 p.m., a telephone message was received from the Brigadier that the Second Brigade on the left had penetrated through Rossignol Wood, and that 1st Auckland was moving forward in touch with the Second Brigade and was making progress in Duck Ally and Swan Ally. It was thought that the enemy might be moving back on the whole brigade front, and 2nd Wellington was ordered to push forward patrols and endeavour to occupy an advanced line.

By 6 p.m., our patrols were pushing forward down Guesclin Trench, Jean Bart, Brisouk and Knox Saps, and, two hours later, our posts were established on the line ordered. Several enemy posts were encountered in Chasseurs' Hedge; but the Germans ran on the approach of our patrols, without offering resistance. One light machine-gun was captured. We, ourselves, had no casualties.

The following day was quiet. The night was spent in improving and deepening the saps leading into our new positions. Patrols worked forward of Chasseurs Hedge, and penetrated down Nairn Street and Caber Trench, which were found to be unoccupied. On the afternoon of the 22nd, information was received that patrols from 1st Auckland on our left had penetrated some distance down Nameless trench and found it clear to the enemy. Second Wellington was now ordered to connect its line in Chasseurs' Hedge with Nameless trench by posts making touch with 1st Auckland in Nameless and Nameless support trenches.

THE WELLINGTON REGIMENT

As soon as it was dusk, this operation was effected by the left company without casualties—three fresh posts being established. The next days were spent in improving communications to our new line, and in pushing out patrols in front by night and day.

On the night of the 25th July, the 2nd Battalion was relieved in the line by 2nd Auckland, and moved back to Sailly. The average advance made by the 2nd Battalion at that time was 500 yards, on a front of about 1000 yards. It was a taste of that open warfare everyone had been looking forward to for so long. Everyone showed a keen interest in the work, while several N.C.O.'s and men showed exceptional courage and resource in patrolling. It was unfortunate that no satisfactory support was forthcoming from the battalion of the division on our immediate right, for, had they conformed with our advance, there was every reason to believe that, in the earlier stages of the operation, La Signy Farm and Red Cottage Spur could have been had for the asking.

During this period in the front line, nine American officers were attached to the 2nd Battalion for forty-eight hours, for the purpose of gaining an insight into conditions of trench warfare in our sector. Two were attached to each company and one to battalion headquarters. These were followed a few days later, by eleven American officers and fifteen N.C.O.s and, on the 25th July, when the 1st Battalion relieved 1st Auckland in the front line trenches, four platoons from A Battalion, 318th U.S.A. Regiment, were attached to it and accompanied it into the line. One American platoon was attached to each of our companies, while one platoon from each of our four companies formed a composite fifth company in the battalion.

First Wellington remained in the line until the night of the 2nd August, when it was relieved by 2nd Canterbury and marched to Rossignol Farm, where it remained for eight days carrying on with training. Meantime, the 2nd Battalion had been engaged in trench construction and drainage in the Hebuterne Sector and on road repairs at

THE WELLINGTON REGIMENT

Sailly-au-Bois; but, on the 2nd August, that Battalion had been relieved by 1st Otago, and had moved back into divisional reserve under canvas at Couin, once a camp in the woods now, more or less, a mud hole.

At the memorial service held at First Army Headquarters, Ranchicourt, on the 4th August, 1918, 2nd Wellington had the honour of providing the platoon to represent the New Zealand Division. The officer selected to command the platoon was Lieut. T. L. Ward, M.C. The platoon had put in some few days training at the brigade's details camp at Marieux, and then left for Ranchicourt by motor lorries. On arrival there, the party was billetted in Houdain. The parade was held on the Sunday morning in the Chateau grounds. The scene was an impressive one. There must have been between four and five thousand men on parade, including detachments from the French, American and Portugese Armies, and the Canadian, Australian and New Zealand Forces.

There was also a contingent of nursing sisters. The Army Commander, General-Sir Henry Horne, delivered an address and this followed by a commemoration service. At the conclusion of the service, the Army Commander called for three cheers for His Majesty the King, and those were given lustily by the assembled troops. The Army Commander then reviewed the troops. Coming to our platoon, General Horne stopped and shook hands with Lieut. Ward and expressed his pleasure at the New Zealand Division being represented, and complimented the platoon on its turn-out and bearing. The ceremony concluded with a "March Past," the Army Commander taking the salute. From the smile he bestowed upon it as it went by, our platoon must have acquitted itself well in General Horne's eyes. Lieut. Ward was entertained to lunch and dinner by the Camp Commandant, and, on his invitation, the platoon remained at Houdain until Monday morning. On Sunday afternoon, General Horne sent for Lieut. Ward. The General was in a small room surrounded by maps, and had evidently been at work. He shook hands and talked to

Lieut. Ward for a few minutes, putting him quite at his ease, and again expressed his pleasure at a New Zealand platoon being there, complimenting it on its excellent showing. He asked particularly if the men had been pleased to come, and made solicitous enquiries as to their comfort and entertainments. The platoon left Houdain on the Monday morning, and arrived back with the battalion at Couin in the afternoon. Before leaving, General Horne sent Lieut. Ward a letter for delivery to Major General Russell. The letter read as follows:—

"Headquarters,
I. Army,
Aug. 4th 1918.

"My Dear Russell,

"This is to thank you for sending the platoon of Wellington Regiment to represent New Zealand at our anniversary service to-day—and very worthily they did so. They looked splendid. Very fine body of men and very smart in every way. I think we were all much impressed by their appearance and training. We had troops on parade of Canada, Australia and South Africa as well as France, Portugal and United States, and I am delighted that you were able to complete the picture. I hope that Ward and N.C.O.'s and men have been well looked after and have enjoyed their visit to I. Army.

"Again thanking you and with all good wishes for good future and hoping that we may come together again some day.

Believe me,
Yours sincerely,
(Sgd.) H. S. HORNE."

CHAPTER XLI.

We Fraternise with the 18th Royal Irish—A Cricket Match — Gommecourt — Fish Alley — A Further Enemy Withdrawal.

AT the beginning of August, the 2nd Battalion ascertained that in billets at St. Leger was the 2nd Battalion, 18th Royal Irish Regiment, to which the 7th Wellington-West Coast Regiment in New Zealand was allied. The 2nd Battalion, 18th Royal Irish, served in New Zealand during the Maori War, and for long had had its headquarters at Wanganui. Col. Cunningham at once rode down and called, and arrangements were made for exchanging visits and, if possible, getting some photographs. The Royal Irish invited three officers from our Wellington-West Company to lunch with them the following day, and Col. Cunningham and Capt. J. R. Cade were able to accept this cordial invitation.

Early in the afternoon of the 4th August, Wellington-West Coast Company headed by the battalion band marched into St. Leger. They received a great reception from their Irish comrades. A most enjoyable afternoon was spent by all ranks, who left their hosts realizing that they had experienced real Irish hospitality, and that the 18th Royal Irish had upheld their traditions. Their transport was freely requisitioned to return their guests to their billets, and several senior officers were nothing loth to avail themselves of so humble a conveyance as the battalion mess-cart. Taking place as it did on the fourth anniversary of the outbreak of war, the meeting of the 18th Royal Irish and 7th Wellington-West Coast, will long be remembered.

It was then suggested that either a football or cricket match should be played between the two Regiments, and, a few days later, when writing to thank Lieut.-Col. M. C. C. Harrison, M.C., for the hospitality bestowed upon us by his battalion, we offered to play a football match. Col. Harrison replied that, as most of his footballers were on leave or at courses, he feared a Rugby match would be rather a farce; but suggested that we should send over a cricket team. In a day or two, a cricket team from both our 1st and 2nd Battalions, journeyed to Achieux in motor lorries to play the Royal Irish. Unfortunately, the latter were then under orders to leave Achieux; but our team played a scratch match and, later, the Royal Irish were able to get a team together and a one innings game was won by them by ten runs. They gave us tea, and a very hearty send off.

On the 9th August, the 2nd Battalion, now in a new camp which it had made for itself at Couin, was inspected by General Russell who expressed his pleasure at its turn-out. From here, three officers with long service with the 2nd Battalion left for England on a tour of duty at Sling Camp. They were, Capt. J. N. Rauch, M.C., Lieut. J. H. Catchpole, M.C., and Capt. H. Simmonds, M.C., the last of whom, for some time past, had been adjutant of the battalion. A few days later, Capt. J. T. Dallinger came over from Sling to take over the duties of adjutant to the 2nd Battalion.

Both battalions were now for the line again, and, on the following afternoon, 1st Wellington relieved 2nd Battalion Rifle Brigade in the reserve line at Gommecourt, while, after dark, our 2nd Battalion relieved the 1st Battalion of the same brigade in the front line. The weather was fine and we were not long in settling down. 2nd Wellington found an enemy machine-gun troublesome in Fish Alley, and Wellington-West Coast Company planned to knock out the post on the following day. During the day a prisoner was taken by that company and good information extracted from him. Ruahine Company, feeling particularly hostile, stole a march and made an attempt during the afternoon on the unwelcome machine-gun, and failed, much to the disgust of Wellington-

West Company, for it spoiled that Company's plans. The next day or two were quiet, except for minnenwerfer; to which our artillery rendered prompt and effective retaliation.

On the 14th, 1st Otago, on the right, reported that the enemy was retiring and that they were pushing forward patrols. Second Wellington immediately pushed out patrols; but, as the enemy retired as we came up, our patrols were unable to get in touch with him. We pushed on our line in conjunction with 1st Otago, on our right, and 1st Auckland on our left and, by shortly after mid-day had made substantial progress, and established a new line from Box Wood to Fork Wood. Here, fine work was done by a bombing party under Lieut. R. V. Hollis, in driving three enemy machine-gun posts before it, and so facilitating the task of the battalion. During this operation, eight prisoners were taken by Wellington-West Coast Company, and valuable information was obtained from them to the effect that the enemy was retiring by forty-eight hour stages to Achiet-le-Petit line. Later in the day, patrols were pushed well out, and came in touch with the enemy at several points.

On the following day, there were signs of a further evacuation of the enemy towards Achiet-le-Petit. The village of Puisieux-au-Mont was shelled by the enemy, and 1st Otago on our right pushed well round its southern flank. From noon till midnight, the enemy heavily shelled the front trenches on the hill held by Taranaki and Hawkes Bay Companies, Katipo trench held by Taranaki Company being levelled in places. Our casualties were slight in proportion to the severity of the gun fire. During the night, our patrols again pushed out and formed observation posts. On the following day, there was again very heavy shelling of our front line trenches and 2nd Lieut. L. D. O'Sullivan,* while working with a patrol in the outpost line was severely wounded. Our outpost line was maintained and the enemy was reported east of Puisieux-au-Mont. Towards evening,

*Lieut. O'Sullivan died of wounds on 24th August.

THE WELLINGTON REGIMENT

1st Auckland on our left, in conjunction with the English Brigade on their left, advanced their line to the front of Bucquoy to conform with the general line, and several prisoners were taken. Our artillery was now moving up, and occupying forward positions.

On the next night, 1st Wellington relieved both 1st Auckland and 2nd Wellington, and became the front line battalion of the New Zealand Division, while 2nd Wellington took over 2nd Auckland's position in brigade reserve. Our 1st Battalion was not to remain long in that position, for, on the following night, it was relieved by 2nd Battalion of the Rifle Brigade, and then in turn relieved 1st Battalion Rifle Brigade in the outpost line of resistance in what was called the Green line.

CHAPTER XLII.

Loupart Wood — Grevillers — Biefvillers—A Check at Thilloy—The Envelopment of Bapaume.

AT 11 a.m. on the 21st August, both 1st and 2nd Battalions were ordered to mobolize, and the 1st Battalion assembled accordingly, two companies in Biez Switch, one company in Cod trench, and one in Fish Alley, while the 2nd Battalion assembled in or near Grayline trench and Gommecourt trench. Both battalions remained in readiness that day, and the whole of the following day. During the morning of the 22nd, the enemy counter-attacked against the division, but he was easily beaten off and some three hundred prisoners taken. Again that night, there was a further counter-attack and the S.O.S. went up along the whole front. No information seemed to be available as to the position.

During the afternoon of the 23rd August, the First Brigade was ordered to move in the direction of Achiet-le-Petit, to start immediately and be on the road between Rossignol Wood and Bucquoy within an hour. A start was made at once, 1st Wellington and 2nd Auckland leading with 2nd Wellington following and 1st Auckland bringing up the rear. Halting near Achiet-le-Petit, the companies bivouaced in trenches round about. Late that night, in 2nd Wellington Battalion Headquarters, battalion commanders met General Melvill, who then explained the situation and unfolded the plans for the attack at dawn next morning. The brigade orders, given verbally by the Brigadier, were:—The brigade will attack and capture Loupart Wood and Grevillers—1st Wellington on the right to take Loupart Wood; 2nd Auckland on the left, to take the objectives from Grevillers inclusive to the railway on the edge of Biefvillers: 2nd Wellington in support to cover the junction of the leading battalions and 1st Auckland to be in brigade reserve. A road running direct from Achiet-le-Petit to Grevillers marked the boundary for the advance between 1st Wellington and 2nd Auckland. It was then after midnight, and, as zero was fixed for 5 o'clock in the morning, and we had to move more than three thousand yards to the point of assembly, there was little time to be lost.

Both battalions were in positions by 4 o'clock a.m. There was a fresh breeze blowing and the sky was overcast. First, there was to be no barrage; then, later, word came through that a barrage would be put down at 5 a.m. By that time, companies were moving. However, there was no barrage finally, and so, at 5 a.m., the operation started without it, in the grey light of the morning. First Wellington, with Taranaki Company on the left, Wellington-West Coast on the right, Hawkes Bay in support and Ruahine Company in reserve, supported by the Wellington Machine-Gun Company and two tanks, attacked Loupart Wood.

It rained heavily for a few minutes, and visibility was bad. That, however, was fortunate for it enabled us to cover a considerable distance of open ground and beyond his first screen of machine-guns before the enemy knew we were upon him. When day broke, the mist cleared. First Wellington encountered strong resistance on the right from machine-guns and rifle fire, and for a time, companies were held up. Sergeant H. H. Thomason and Corporal J. R. Blake each led a section of bombers against a machine-gun post, killing the crew and capturing the gun. Sergeant W. Murray, with the aid of a runner, captured a machine-gun and crew of five. It was not long before the reserve company (Ruahine) had to be sent forward. Then two extra tanks lent their aid. Lieut. G. A. A. Barton in command of Wellington-West Coast Company pushed on with great vigour and determination, and cleared the section in front of his company, capturing a machine-gun and 26 prisoners, and leading his men with conspicuous gallantry and energy. It was not easy, however, to make progress against well concealed machine-guns with no artillery barrage.

Wellington-West Coast (2nd Battalion) early became involved at Grevillers, filling in between 1st Wellington and 2nd Auckland. Here, excellent work was done by two platoons under Lieut. R. V. Hollis in clearing the southern part of Grevillers where several machine-guns and three eight inch Howitzers were captured. Hawkes Bay Company (2nd Battalion) on the right assisted 1st Wellington to clear Loupart Wood where enemy machine-gun nests were proving very troublesome. Ruahine Company, supporting the Auckland left, crossed the railway to the north and associated itself with 2nd Auckland and the tanks and later with the 2nd Brigade in clearing up the area west of Biefvillers just north of the railway, and in capturing Biefvillers itself. By noon, the enemy's resistance had been overcome, Grevillers and Loupart Wood captured, and 1st Wellington and 2nd Auckland firmly established in posts, on the edge of the wood with a company in support in the open ground behind it.

Early in the morning, Lieut.-Col. S. S. Allen, commanding 2nd Auckland had been wounded in the mouth, and compelled to go out, while, later in the day, Major W. F. Narby was wounded also and Captain F. S. Varnham, M.C., took command of First Wellington.

About ten o'clock in the morning, the 2nd Brigade pushed out to the north of Grevillers, clearing up Biefvillers and the trench system to the north of it. Towards evening 2nd Wellington received orders to co-operate with the 63rd Division in a further advance which was being undertaken immediately. This operation was cancelled by a later message, not, however, before Taranaki Company had gone forward and substantially completed its task.

At 5 o'clock the following morning (the 25th), the 63rd Division on the right of 2nd Wellington and the 2nd Brigade on the left attacked, with 2nd Wellington patrols co-operating. The 63rd Division met with very hot machine fire from Thilloy, and our patrols, endeavouring to push forward, received a very warm reception from strongly posted enemy machine-guns. The 63rd Division made no progress, nor did our patrols. The 2nd Brigade on our left was more successful; but it was a very long time, owing to the intense machine-gun fire, before any information filtered back from companies. The rest of the day passed fairly quietly.

On the morning of the 25th, 1st Wellington had gone back into reserve where it remained until the evening of 27th. Major F. K. Turnbull, M.C., was now transferred from 2nd Battalion and appointed to command the 1st Battalion with the temporary rank of Lieut.-Col.

At dusk on the 25th, Ruahine Company (2nd Battalion), who had remained in Biefvillers, moved up and relieved a portion of the 2nd Brigade in the front line, while battalion headquarters were now shifted to the Shrine. The night was very dark and wet, and runners had great difficulty in getting through to company headquarters, to none of which there were wires. While making a personal reconnaissance of the outpost line, Lieut. R. V. Hollis encountered four of the enemy who had filtered through the line. He attacked them single handed, killing two with his revolver, and closing with the other two. One he knocked down with his fist, whereupon the other fled. Hollis collected a couple of his men and at once returned to the fray; but found the ground clear of all except the dead Germans.

An attack was to be launched the following morning, by the 63rd Division and the New Zealand Division with artillery support, with the object of enveloping Bapaume by passing beyond it on each flank and establishing a line Reincourtles-Beugnâtre. 2nd Wellington was ordered to co-operate in this attack by pushing out strong patrols, and following up closely any enemy retirement resulting from the attack.

In general conformity with the 63rd Division's movement, 2nd Wellington made an attempt to get forward in broad daylight on the morning of the 26th August. We were met by a murderous machine-gun fire, and, though patrols made slight progress at various points, and a company of 1st

Auckland moved up to help us, no material gain was made. The 63rd Division met similar machine-gun fire from Thilloy, and was held up there. Here, that fine officer, Lieut. C. E. Lee, 2nd Battalion Intelligence Officer, was killed early in the attack. He had gone forward to reconnoitre, and was killed outright by a machine-gun bullet. Captain A. T. White, going forward to ascertain the position of his company, also received a nasty wound in the head. The day passed without further progress being made.

It had been demonstrated, beyond all doubt, that the pocket was strongly held by the enemy, and that it was idle to tackle a very strong machine-gun nest in broad daylight. About mid-day, 1st Auckland were ordered to prepare to undertake the task that had been allotted to 2nd Wellington; but this was cancelled later, and no further attempts were made that day. Before midnight, 1st Auckland relieved 2nd Wellington, who, thereupon, moved back into support with three companies at Grevillers. Unfortunately, Lieut. N. MacLachlan was killed by shell fire while the relief was in progress.

Late in the afternoon of the 27th, 1st Wellington received orders to take over part of the front line before darkness if possible, and at six o'clock in the evening, that battalion moved from the reserve area and relieved 1st Canterbury in the line, two companies (Taranaki and Hawkes Bay) in the front line facing Bapaume, Ruahine Company in support in Avesnes, and Wellington-West Coast Company in second support responsible for the defence of Biefvillers. On the following day, two sections of the New Zealand Machine-Gun Battalion were attached to 1st Wellington. The position was strengthened and reconnoitring patrols sent out at night.

The 2nd Battalion remained in its location until the evening of the 28th August. No operations took place, and the men who were very tired, had a fairly good rest in quite comfortable quarters. On the evening of the 28th, 2nd Wellington was relieved by 2nd Auckland in support and then

THE WELLINGTON REGIMENT

moved to a position north of Achiet-le-Petit-Grevillers Road, where our men prepared new bivouacs for themselves.

During the afternoon of the 28th August, 1st Wellington received orders to hold themselves in readiness to make an assault on Bapaume the following day, and, preparations were made accordingly, but, at five o'clock in the morning of the 29th August, patrols reported that the enemy was evacuating Bapaume. 1st Auckland on the right, confirmed the retirement of the enemy on its front. At 7 o'clock, orders were given to follow up and get in touch with the enemy. The leading company of our 1st Battalion at once pushed forward patrols and followed them up in strength. Taranaki Company worked round the south of the town, keeping in touch with Auckland. Hawkes Bay Company worked forward to the northern and eastern edge of the town, and, at 9.30 a.m., when our artillery was finally called off from the bombardment of the town, strong patrols from Ruahine Company pushed through Bapaume, keeping in touch with Taranaki Company on the right and 3rd Battalion Rifle Brigade, on the left. Hawkes Bay Company then followed up through the town and Wellington-West Coast Company, as a reserve company, worked round to the south. In the meantime, orders were received for the New Zealand Division to advance due east. This necessitated a change of direction to the left; but still substantial progress was made with hardly any casualties. By 4 o'clock in the afternoon, the 1st Brigade had reached a point over a mile down the Peronne Road. Shortly after 6 o'clock, the New Zealand Division held securely the German trench system south and south-west of Bapaume to the Peronne Road and thence to the sugar factory on the Cambrai Road, whence the line continued to the north-east. The flank divisions had made equal satisfactory progress, and the positions at Ligny Thilloy and Thilloy, so sternly defended only a few days before, had now been yielded without opposition.

During this operation, there had been attached to 1st Wellington, a troop of the Royal Scots Greys under Lieut. Olliver, a section of the 1st Battery, N.Z.F.A., under Lieut.

THE WELLINGTON REGIMENT

Page, two sections of Wellington Company, New Zealand Machine-Gun Battalion, under Lieut. Forsyth, and a section of the First Light Trench Mortar Battery, all of whom rendered valuable co-operation.

At mid-day of the 29th, the 2nd Battalion had moved forward some distance with battalion headquarters in Grevillers. Late in the afternoon, however, it was ascertained that the 2nd Battalion would not be moving further that night and everyone settled down to get as much sleep as possible.

The advance was temporarily discontinued; but arrangements were already in train to press on along with the rest of the Army at daybreak on the following day.

THE WELLINGTON REGIMENT

CHAPTER XLIII.

Bancourt — Fremicourt — Stiff Opposition — Enemy Counter-attacks — Some Ground is Given—But is Re-captured in Hard Fighting — Sergeant J. G. Grant Wins the V.C.

THE tasks of the IV. Corps on the 30th August, were assigned as follows: The 42nd Division, on the right, was to seize Riencourt, the New Zealand Division, in the centre, Bancourt and Fremicourt, and 5th Division, on the left, Beugny. The Rifle Brigade was to attack Fremicourt, and the First Brigade was to attack Bancourt and secure the high ground on the east of it, connecting up with the 42nd Division on the right and the Rifle Brigade on the left. The task of capturing Bancourt was allotted to 2nd Auckland, and 1st Wellington was to co-operate with and, if necessary, support 2nd Auckland, and, on the capture of both Bancourt and Fermicourt, push forward to certain high ground (afterwards generally known to us as Bancourt Ridge) and gain touch with the battalions on the flanks. 2nd Wellington was to be in brigade reserve.

First Wellington's operation orders were issued at 2 a.m. but, on account of the darkness and the shell torn area to be crossed by the runners, they did not reach companies till nearly 3 a.m. As the companies assembled for the attack, they were subjected to a rather severe bombardment and sustained a number of casualties.

At 5 a.m., the attack was commenced, 1st Wellington keeping in touch with the Rifle Brigade, who advanced on Fremicourt under a barrage. Shortly before the hour fixed for the attack, the 42nd Division had notified 2nd Auckland it would not be ready to attack till later, and, in accordance with orders, 2nd Auckland had postponed its start. The operation became thus a rather difficult one for 1st Wellington; but, fortunately, the resistance in Bancourt was dealt with by two tanks handled by their commanders with great skill and courage, and, at first, our 1st Battalion was able to make progress towards the crest beyond the village. Moving up the slope, one of its platoons was held up by a machine-gun. Private G. J. Scothern at once rushed forward with his Lewis gun and engaged the enemy, and so enabled the rest of platoon to rush the gun and continue the advance. From the right, however, the enemy turned a great many machine-guns upon our ranks, in the face of which it became impossible for our 1st Battalion to continue the advance, and there was nothing for it but to dig in and establish a line on a small spur short of its objective. Here, Scothern was again active with his Lewis gun. He crept forward and, handling his gun with courage, was able to keep the enemy fire down until his platoon had dug in. Then his gun was put out of action; but, undismayed, as soon as it was dark, Scothern secured a German gun, and was not long in bringing it into action. Another Lewis gunner in Private T. M. E. Richmond showed conspicuous devotion to duty. Twice all his mates were rendered casualties, but Richmond stuck to his gun and remained alone in an isolated and dangerous position on the second occasion for no less than twelve hours. He showed splendid courage and initiative in handling his gun, and by maintaining his position, which was of great importance, was the means of maintaining the line intact.

The 42nd Division had moved shortly before 6 a.m. and 2nd Auckland with them. It was then broad daylight with no protecting mist, and the enemy was, of course fully alive to the attack. The 42nd Division was checked by withering fire from further down the Peronne Road, and was unable to take Reincourt. This check made it impossible for the moment for Auckland's right flank to reach its objective, but it was able to establish a foothold well up the ridge. The left company of 2nd Auckland made good progress, and by 8 a.m. had cleared Bancourt and gained touch with 1st Wellington.

THE WELLINGTON REGIMENT

On the north, the Rifle Brigade had had no walk over; but after overcoming staunch opposition, had taken Fremicourt. After the capture of Fremicourt, Hawkes Bay Company (1st Battalion) on the left, had been able to gain its objective, but its right flank had had to swing back to conform with 2nd Auckland's line.

Before 2nd Auckland had had time to dig in, the German snipers and machine-gunners returned to the huts on the Haplincourt Road, and from there and from Riencourt, still in the hands of the enemy, a very heavy fire was poured into 2nd Auckland. From a sunken road in front, mortars were hurled at 2nd Auckland's position, while anti-tank guns from the direction of Villers-au-Flos raked the exposed forward slopes. 2nd Auckland's position became untenable, and it was forced to withdraw behind the crest. When this withdrawal became known, orders were issued immediately for the re-establishment of the line and, to that end, Hawkes Bay Company of 2nd Wellington was sent forward. However, the project was abandoned, the position being considered satisfactory for the time being.

During the day, 1st Wellington's line, on the slope and subject to enemy observation was swept by machine-gun fire as well as receiving more than an ample share of shelling. There were also several half-hearted counter-attacks. During the night, companies continued the consolidation of their positions, and patrols were sent out. Taranaki was now on the right, Wellington-West Coast in the centre, Hawkes Bay on the left, with Ruahine in support. The troop of the Royal Scots Greys, the section from 1st Battery N.Z.F.A., the two sections of machine-gunners, and the section from the Trench Mortars again co-operated with our 1st Battalion.

After dark, the 42nd Division made a further attack upon Riencourt, and finally captured that village.

At half past four the following morning, the enemy counter-attacked accompanied by tanks and under protection of a heavy bombardment. Our 1st Battalion's line as well as that of the battalions on both flanks, was pushed back two or three hundred yards; but by ten o'clock in the morning the line was re-established and, indeed, slightly improved. Fighting continued during the day with but little change in the position. What a hard day it was for the 1st Battalion, for the day's casualties testify, viz.:—2 officers killed, 5 wounded: 47 other ranks killed, 161 wounded, 11 missing. Capt. J. MacMorran, then, commanding Hawkes Bay Company in the 1st Battalion, but well known in both battalions, had been killed in the fighting at Bancourt.

About mid-day, about two hundred and fifty reinforcements had been received by the 1st Battalion, and these were at once organised into a reserve company.

Although none of the enemy infantry penetrated as far as its position, the 2nd Battalion in support in the suburbs of Bapaume did not escape its share of shell fire during the counter-attacks. Several shells knocked down portions of the walls immediately above battalion headquarters' cellars. There were a good many gas shells and one, falling in the cellar occupied by battalion details, badly gassed nine men.

Before midnight, warning orders were received by both battalions for an attack under an artillery barrage at dawn the following morning.

This operation of the 1st September, was necessary in order to retake the portion of the crest lost on the 30th, and also, now that the 42nd Division had taken Reincourt and protected the right flank, to extend our footing on the high ground and so secure wider observation. It was considered that the crest line was held too strongly by the enemy to be taken without artillery co-operation, and, accordingly, an artillery barrage was arranged for. The attack was to be delivered by the 42nd Division on the right, and the New Zealand Division on the left, with the 5th Division on our left, co-operating. The Rifle Brigade and the 1st Brigade were to be the New Zealand Brigades in action, and the attack was fixed for 4.55 a.m.

In accordance with these plans, at zero, the Rifle Brigade moved forward through the outpost line. They met little real resistance, and, 5.30 a.m., they had reached their

THE WELLINGTON REGIMENT

objective and, indeed, their centre had passed beyond it, and had taken prisoner some seventy of the 23rd (Saxon) Division. The 5th Division had not been able to advance at the time appointed; but, later in the morning, that division pushed forward as far as possible, and, in the evening, under cover of darkness, advanced its line to conform with the Rifle Brigade's.

At the same time as the Rifle Brigade had advanced on the left, the 1st Brigade attacked on the right; with 2nd Auckland on the right and 1st Wellington on the left of the 1st Brigade's front. 2nd Wellington was assigned the role of being in close support to the leading battalions. 1st Wellington advanced with Taranaki Company on the right, Wellington-West Coast Company in the centre, and Ruahine on the left. Hawkes Bay Company was in reserve with orders to be ready to move at any time. The artillery barrage moved forward by leaps of a hundred yards every three minutes, until the line from a certain light railway to Delsaux Farm was reached, and, behind this barrage the First Brigade followed closely. That brigade was not to reach its objective in the same easy way as the Rifle Brigade had on the left. On the contrary, some staunch resistance from German machine-guns was met with. On reaching the crest, Taranaki Company (1st Battalion) found that a line of five enemy machine-gun posts offered a serious obstacle to further advance. Sergeant John Gilroy Grant was the commander of a platoon of Taranaki Company. Throughout the two previous day's hard fighting, Sergeant Grant had displayed coolness, determination, and valour of the highest order. Now, under his leadership, Grant's platoon rushed forward under point blank fire. When some twenty yards from the guns, Grant, closely followed by Lance-Corporal C. T. Hill (1), dashed ahead of his platoon and made for the centre post. How the German bullets missed them will ever remain a mystery; but Grant reached the gun and jumped down into the post, demoralising the German Gunners. His platoon

---

(1) Lance-Corporal C. T. Hill was awarded the D.C.M.

THE WELLINGTON REGIMENT

was not slow to follow him, and Grant now rushing to the left cleared two more posts, while his men quickly disposed of the others. For this gallant enterprise, Grant was shortly afterwards to receive the Victoria Cross, the first one awarded in the 1st Battalion and the second in the Regiment (1).

That night, 1st Wellington were relieved by 2nd Otago, the 2nd Brigade taking over the line.

---

(1) Corporal Leslie Wilton Andrew had gained the first V.C. in the Regiment at La Basse Ville.

CHAPTER XLIV.

Haplincourt — Bertincourt — Havrincourt Wood — Villers-au-Flos.

PRESSURE on the enemy was to be continued relentlessly. So far as the IV. Corps was concerned, on the right, the 42nd Division was to capture Villers-Au-Flos: on the left, the 5th Division was to seize Delsaux Farm and the high ground east of Beugny. The New Zealand Division in the centre, was to drive the enemy off the broad crest overlooking Haplincourt.

In accordance with these plans, the attack was launched shortly after 5 o'clock on the morning of the 2nd September, and, by nightfall, after a day of hard fighting, the Second Brigade had established itself in advance of the objective assigned to the New Zealand Division; the 42nd Division had early captured Villers-au-Flos and the 5th Division had taken Delsaux Farm, but had been checked in front of Beugny.

On the following day, the advance was continued. Haplincourt was at once taken. The 42nd Division early reached Bavastre, and pushed on through Haplincourt Wood. Beugny, yesterday so formidable, now fell without opposition to the 5th Division. In the centre of the advance, the New Zealand Division made rapid progress. By 9.30 a.m., the Second Brigade had reached the western edges of Velu Wood, and the outskirts of Bertincourt, and by mid-day, Bertincourt itself was in our hands. General Russell now moved his headquarters forward to Fremicourt.

In view of the enemy's retirement, the III. Army issued order for the advance to be continued the following day.

During the night, the enemy fell back from Ruyaulcourt and, on the morning of the 4th, the Second Brigade pushed patrols through it and established posts on its outskirts. As soon as it was daylight, British observation balloons went up very close behind the front line.

At 7 o'clock in the morning, the advance was resumed. On the New Zealand Division's front, the Second Brigade again pushed forward, clearing Ruyaulcourt of every vestige of the enemy, capturing Pauper trench, and moving forward to high ground, from which could be seen Havrincourt Wood.

During the afternoon, the advance on the left reached within six hundred yards of the Wood; but, on the right, the 42nd Division was checked in front of Neuville-Bourgonval. In the evening, the 42nd Division renewed its efforts against that village and succeeded in capturing the northern half of it, although the southern portion still remained in the hands of the enemy, and it was not until late the following afternoon that the whole of Neuville-Bourgonval was in possession of the 42nd Division. By 7 o'clock on the night of 5th, the line was established all along the sunken road some six hundred yards from Havrincourt Wood.

The IV. Corps on the right, was now also over the Canal du Nord, and VI. Corps on the left, had reached its western bank near Hermies. The enemy was still to be harried by our advanced guards with the object of driving in his rearguards and outposts, and ascertaining his dispositions. With a view to the early resumption of the offensive on a big scale, troops were now to be rested as much as possible, resources conserved, and communications improved. As many divisions as possible were to be withdrawn into reserve for rest and training.

In accordance with this policy, on the night of the 5th September, the IV. Corps front, hitherto held by three divisions, was reconstituted so as to be held by two divisions only, viz:—the 37th Division and the New Zealand Division. This increase of frontage made it necessary for the Second Brigade to put three battalions in the front line, with one in support. 2nd Wellington was now moved forward to the Beugny line

THE WELLINGTON REGIMENT

and placed at the disposal of General Young, commanding the Second Brigade, as a counter-attack battalion.

On the 6th September, the Second Brigade continued the advance, meeting with but little opposition. At Metz, there was some resistance; but, by late in the afternoon, 1st Otago had taken that village. By 10 o'clock that night, the Second Brigade had advanced two miles, and penetrated a considerable distance into Havrincourt Wood. At daylight, on the 7th, the Second Brigade regained touch with the 37th Division, and pushing forward, found itself confronted with the Trescault Ridge. The enemy had now been driven back to within three miles of his notorious Hindenburg line.

On the night of the 7th, in pitch darkness, the Rifle Brigade took over the line from the Second Brigade, who now withdrew to positions in support.

The first effort against Trescault Ridge and the other high ground was made on the 9th September, when the V. Corps on the right, attacked with the Rifle Brigade protecting the V. Corps' left flank. Hard fighting waged throughout the day. The stubborness of the enemy and the strength of his counter-attacks made it clear that he intended to maintain a deep outpost zone in front of his main line of resistance. Plans had, however, been already completed for a resumption of the advance on a grand scale. As a preliminary to an attempt to break the Hindenburg line, the III. Army was to capture the enemy's outposts including Trescault Ridge. The main attack was fixed for 12th September, and the New Zealand Division's task was to storm Trescault Ridge along with the 37th Division.

Meantime, how had the Regiment been faring? Since the 1st September, 1st Wellington had been having a comparatively easy time. On the 6th, the First Brigade had become divisional reserve, and 1st Wellington had moved to positions north of the Bancourt-Haplincourt Road, while the 2nd Battalion had moved to Villers-au-Flos. Both battalions remained in these positions until the 11th. Some training was done in fine weather, and a good deal of time was devoted to salvaging and clearing up the area.

THE WELLINGTON REGIMENT

On the First Brigade becoming the Brigade in support on the 11th, 1st Wellington moved forward and took over from 1st Otago in Bertincourt, and the area forward of that village, while 2nd Wellington moved to Neuville-Bourgonval.

CHAPTER XLV.

Trescault Ridge—Chip Lane and Snap Trench—Soot Avenue and Smut Trench—The Jaegers Fight Stubbornly—2nd Battalion Repels an Attack on Donrayen Trench—Relieved by the 5th Division—Back to Haplincourt Wood.

THE task of storming Trescault Ridge on the 12th September, was allotted to the Rifle Brigade, in co-operation with the 37th Division on the left. Following a heavy barrage laid down by our guns, the Rifle Brigade pressed forward, and after a fiercely contested day, succeeded in reaching Snap Reserve, Snap Trench and African Trench, positions somewhat short of the final objectives.

At the close of the day's fighting, the 1st Battalion of the Rifle Brigade was relieved in the front line by 1st Wellington, while our 2nd Battalion relieved the 4th Battalion of the same brigade. This move was commenced as soon as it was dark, and was completed by two o'clock the following morning, with 1st Wellington's headquarters established at Battery Post, and 2nd Wellington's in the Quarry. The weather was wet and wintry: there was considerable shelling and much confusion in the front line, where bombing was still going on. Nevertheless, the actual relief was effected without casualties, although Major G. H. Hume, M.C., and Lieut. C. R. Menzies, D.C.M., had been wounded while on reconnaissance work earlier in the day.

Before dawn on the 13th, Wellington-West Coast Company of the 1st Battalion had pushed forward along Chip Lane, and joined up with 2nd Wellington at the junction of Chip Lane and Snap Trench. At noon, by pushing forward patrols, Wellington-West Coast Company had established posts along Soot Avenue and Snap Trench, although considerable machine-gun fire was experienced from the high ground. During the morning, a patrol from Ruahine Company worked down Smut Trench and reported all clear. After the Field Artillery and Stokes Mortars had bombarded several machine-gun positions, Wellington-West Coast and Ruahine Companies (1st Battalion), during the afternoon, in conjunction with the 15th Company, 1st Auckland, on the right, simultaneously sent strong parties to work down forward saps to establish a line along Snap Trench. Wellington-West Coast Company were successful in establishing a post at the junction of Snap and Midland Trenches; but, by some mistake, the post in Smut Trench had been vacated and a platoon of Ruahine Company working down this trench was surrounded and lost heavily, having no less than thirteen men missing. Forward of Dead Man's Corner, Ruahine Company and 1st Auckland were at first successful in their enterprise, Ruahine Company taking eight prisoners; but the enemy, who belonged to a Jaeger division, proving stubborn fighters, launched a series of counter-attacks, and, after three hours' fighting, we were forced back to our former line.

During this fighting there were numerous acts of bravery. One of outstanding gallantry was that of Lance Corporal L. Greenbank. He first led his section against an enemy machine-gun post. Having captured that gun himself, he pushed on, in spite of heavy casualties in his section, with two others, and, coming upon a strong enemy position, set upon the Germans with bombs, and finally gained his objective.

Lieut. R. L. Okey* was in command of a platoon, which had captured a certain portion of Snap Trench. For forty-eight hours his platoon was in constant conflict with the enemy, who occupied a part of the same system of trenches. They were repeatedly bombed and continuously under fire

---

* A fortnight later, viz.: on 30th September, 1918, Roy Okey was killed. He had long service with the Regiment and originally had been batman to Col. Malone.

THE WELLINGTON REGIMENT

from enemy machine-guns and snipers. By skilful handling of his men, he was able to extend his front quite two hundred yards, and although, while consolidating his position, he was driven out, he immediately counter-attacked and re-occupied the posts and then for thirty hours successfully resisted all attacks.

Shortly after 6 o'clock that evening, under cover of a heavy barrage, a storming party of about fifty of the enemy endeavoured to enter the 2nd Battalion's line. A forward post in Donrayen Trench put up the S.O.S., and opened on the enemy with rifles and Lewis guns. The enemy made three separate attempts to enter our position; but was beaten off by our fire and caught in our barrage when he retired. The 2nd Battalion's line remained intact.

About 10 o'clock that night, a hostile aeroplane which was returning after bombing our back area was brought down by our aircraft near 1st Battalion headquarters and the pilot captured.

At daybreak on the 14th, the enemy again counter-attacked the 1st Battalion's forward posts (Wellington-West Coast Company), this time with flammenwerfer; but was driven off. Except for machine-gun fire and periodical bursts of shell fire, the day was fairly quiet. Before midnight, both our battalions were relieved in the front line by battalions of the 5th Division, and moved to billets for the night at Haplincourt. During the following morning, we marched from Haplincourt Wood to rejoin the division which was now in reserve, taking up positions in the vicinity of Biefvillers. Before leaving the line, there had rejoined the 2nd Battalion, a number of officers, nearly all of whom had had long service with that battalion, either as officers or N.C.O.'s, viz., Captain D. S. Columb, Lieut. H. D. Banks, Lieut. C. A. LeLievre, 2nd Lieut. C. N. Devery, D.C.M., 2nd Lieut. W. Carruthers, M.M., 2nd Lieut. A Hindlesmith, 2nd Lieut. W B. Cooke, 2nd Lieut. H. Pettit. Captain D. S. Columb now assumed command of Taranaki Company, while Lieut. D. Cowan, returning from leave, took over Hawkes Bay Company.

THE WELLINGTON REGIMENT

Immediately before the relief, Lieut. W. G. Gibbs was wounded, and was later to die of wounds. A gallant officer, Gibbs had had a full share of fighting, but, like so many more who had fought at Messines, La Basse Ville and Paschendaele, he was not to see victory achieved.

Both battalions now settled down for a spell. That their bivouacs were capable of a good deal of improvement was only too plain when, during a very heavy thunderstorm, every bivouac leaked and some were swamped out. An enemy aeroplane was here brought down near the 1st Battalion's camp, and the whole New Zealand Division seemed to stand to and cheer.

CHAPTER XLVI.

A Spell at Biefvillers—Americans at Baseball —Football—Awaiting Orders.

DURING this spell of rest and training, the 1st Battalion played the 2nd Battalion at Rugby football. On the same day, an exhibition game of baseball was played by teams of Americans from the 301st Tank Battalion. The game was watched by a large number of interested spectators from the Regiment. Our 1st and 2nd Battalions each entertained one team to tea, and several American officers also stayed to dinner at one or other of the officers' messes. A few days later the Wellington Regiment beat the Auckland Regiment at Rugby. Here, also, one evening, the 2nd Battalion played a Soccer match against the R.G.A., and were beaten by 2 goals to nil, while next day, we beat them at Rugby. However, it was not all football, for a good deal of musketry and other training was done. General Russell inspected the 1st and 2nd Battalions separately, and on different days. To each battalion he addressed a few words, highly commending each for its excellent turn out and for the good work done in the recent fighting. During this period, both battalions were at two hours' notice to go forward to the Bertincourt area to act as Corps Reserve in the event of attack.

While at Biefvillers, both battalions received a number of reinforcements, and 2nd Lieut. J. Makin,* W. S. Brown, M.M., S. S. Pennefather, D.C.M., B. S. Hastedt, so well known in the 1st Battalion, now returning from England with Commissions, were posted to the 2nd Battalion. The award now came through of the D.C.M. to Corporal H. P. Gilbert, and of

---
*Lieut. J. Makin was killed in action on 30/9/18.

the Military Cross to 2nd Lieut. R. V. Hollis, to be followed only a few days later by a bar, for that officer's gallantry already noted. Now also, Lieut. W. R. Burge was to receive the M.C., and the late Lieut. C. E. Lee's bravery was not to go unrewarded, for an award of the M.C. was now made to him also, although too late for him to hear of it.

On the 26th September, both battalions carried out a route march, the 1st Battalion headed by the band, marching through Grevillers to Five Cross Roads and back. That, however, was the end of this pleasant spell, for, from 5 a.m. on the 27th, both battalions had to be ready to move at an hour's notice to the Neuville sector. Accordingly, preparations were made for the move, and, late in the day, orders were received that both battalions would move at 4.30 a.m. the following morning by motor lorries, starting from Monument Wood on the Bapaume-Arras Road.

Major F. K. Turnbull, M.C., was now to receive the D.S.O. During many days hard fighting he had been in command of the 1st Battalion and had handled it with great ability, repelling several determined counter-attacks. During the whole time, his unfailing cheerfulness and example of personal courage had greatly encouraged his officers and men.

On the 18th September, on a seventeen miles front south of Gouzecourt, the IV. and III. Armies had undertaken operations, successful over practically the whole front. The two armies had captured nearly 12,000 prisoners and 100 guns. The smashing of the Hindenburg line was now imminent.

THE WELLINGTON REGIMENT

CHAPTER XLVII.

Welsh Ridge—Bonavis Ridge—La Vacquerie Valley —Lateau Wood—The Enemy is Demoralised.

THE general battle had been resumed on the 27th September, by the II. and IV. Armies, and, by the afternoon of the 28th, the IV. Corps had reached Gouzeaucourt and Couillet Valley. Patrols of the 42nd Division on the left, had advanced towards Welsh Ridge, and, although opposition had been met with, it was expected that, before darkness, Welsh Ridge would be carried and possibly Bonavis Ridge as well. Those expectations, however, were not realised, and the New Zealand Division was now to be thrown into the battle.

A start was made by both Wellington battalions bright and early on the 28th, reveille being at 2.30 a.m. Both battalions arrived in the Neuville sector about 7.30 a.m., the 1st Battalion occupying trenches on the Ypres-Neuville Road, with a fighting strength of 20 officers and 512 other ranks, after the "B" teams had been withdrawn. We remained there till 5 o'clock in the afternoon, when a move was made by road through Neuville-Metz-Trescault to the Hindenburg Line, which was reached some three hours later. On the march, Lieut. W. Perry, who had by now become quite one of the old identities with the 1st Battalion, was wounded. Although the wound was thought but slight at the time, it was to cost him his right arm.

The information was that the enemy still held Welsh Ridge, and the First Brigade (2nd Wellington and 1st Auckland leading) was ordered to attack that Ridge and on to Bonavis Ridge, and then push on to the St. Quentin Canal, with the Second Brigade on its right. If the attack was successful, 1st Wellington, with 2nd Auckland on its left, was to follow through across the canal. Zero was fixed for 4.30 o'clock the following morning.

It was fine and misty on the 29th, when the First Brigade's share in the attack was launched by 2nd Wellington on the right, and 1st Auckland on the left. The operation was carried out with splendid dash by all ranks. Shortly after 5 o'clock, our men were down in La Vacquerie Valley and pushing up the slopes of Bonavis Ridge. One of 2nd Wellington's companies being held up by machine-gun fire at close range, Lieut. D. G. B. Morison crawled along a sap and threw bombs into the enemy post, and so enabled his platoon to advance above ground and capture the enemy gun and crew, although he himself was wounded.

Early in the advance, on his platoon commander being wounded, Corporal W. E. Cooksley took command of his platoon, and, in the course of the attack his men captured machine-guns and forty prisoners. Later on, Cooksley again led a platoon to the final objective and formed a defensive flank, which protected a wide gap. Leading a section, Corporal J. H. Griffiths attacked ten of the enemy, who were working four field guns over open sights, being mainly responsible for the capture of both men and guns.

By six o'clock, the leading companies of the First Brigade were beyond the northern edge of Lateau Wood and over the Cambrai Road, and in those advanced trenches on the forward slopes which the British had captured and held for ten days in November 1917.

Taranaki and Hawkes Bay Companies of the 1st Battalion had followed up the 2nd Battalion and, later, the rest of the 1st Battalion moved forward to Welsh Ridge. There they were fired on by concealed machine-guns from the left; but these were soon dealt with by our men and the Aucklanders. Before 7 o'clock in the morning, the 1st Battalion had established its headquarters in La Vacquerie Valley.

THE WELLINGTON REGIMENT

The First Brigade front was now re-organised for, owing to the darkness and unexpected swiftness of the advance, battalions were a good deal intermingled and disorganised. The two original assaulting battalions (1st Auckland and 2nd Wellington) assumed responsibility for the front line and pushed out strong patrols to the St. Quentin Canal. Later in the morning, Hawkes Bay and Taranaki Companies of the 1st Battalion were sent forward to fill up a gap between the two front line battalions and remained there until relieved during the evening. By noon on the 29th September, the whole of our gains were well consolidated.

After the objective had been reached, it was discovered that a party of nine of our men had pushed forward and was practically surrounded by the enemy. On his own initiative, Corporal T. R. Crocker worked his way forward and reached the party of which he took command, and, on his way back, mopped up such of the enemy as came in his way, capturing four, killing three, and inflicting heavy casualties on the rest.

It had been a day of wonderful success for the First Brigade. Our fellows practically over-ran the enemy to a depth of four thousand yards. 2nd Wellington alone captured 285 prisoners, 20 field-guns and 29 machine-guns while its casualties were only 43. Two officers in Lieuts. J. R. Taylor and D. G. B. Morison had been wounded, and Lieut. W. Carruthers, who had returned to the battalion with his commission only a fortnight before, had been killed.

Bonavis Ridge had been the limit of the British advance in the Battle of Cambrai in November 1917, and the First Brigade was now occupying the trenches which had then been dug by the 12th Division. In front of us now lay a new world, beautiful green fields as yet unscathed by war.

Our patrols pushing down towards the St. Quentin Canal were able to see what dire straits the enemy was in. His transport was moving rapidly hither and thither. Gun teams were being galloped up to guns; guns were being rapidly limbered up and removed. Our machine-gunners did not lack for targets, and horses and men were scattered by their fire. However, later in the day, small parties of German Infantry moved back to the banks of the canal, and enemy guns began to shell the ridge.

CHAPTER XLVIII.

An Attempt to Cross the St. Quentin Canal Fails—A Further Attempt is Successful—Crevecour—2nd Battalion Holds on Tenaciously — Ruahine Company Saves the Day.

ON the 29th, the Fourth Army had struck in the south, and had met with remarkable success. The Third Army was to deliver further blows. On the IV. Corps' sector, the Fifth Division was to complete the capture of the Hindenburg line south-east of La Vacquerie. Early in the morning of the 30th September, the New Zealand Division was to secure, if possible, the eastern bank of the canal between Vaucelles and Crevecour and secure the bridgeheads.

Shortly before midnight on the 29th, 1st Wellington received orders to attack across the canal to Esnes, early the following morning, in conjunction with 2nd Auckland on the left. The attack was to be made at 5.45 a.m. under a barrage hurriedly arranged for. Second Wellington was not to move until Lesdain and Crevecour had been captured; but was then to follow up and form a protective flank in case the Second Brigade should fail to cross at Vaucelles.

Shortly after midnight, orders were issued verbally to company commanders of the 1st Battalion. It was a horribly wet night and Battalion Headquarters moved to a forward position at 4 a.m. and the services of a party of Engineers were secured to assist in the repair of the bridges over the canal. Hawkes Bay now pushed forward, the intention being that that company should secure the bridgeheads and Wellington-West Coast on the right and Ruahine

Company on the left follow through across the canal. First Wellington, apparently, thought its attack was to be made at 5 a.m. No barrage came down on its front and, as daylight was approaching, Hawkes Bay, believing the operations called off, withdrew from the exposed forward slope. Communication was now established with 2nd Auckland, who had decided to attack without a barrage, and, at 6 a.m., with Ruahine Company leading, followed by Taranaki and Hawkes Bay, the 1st Battalion advanced towards the canal with the Engineer party following up. In the meantime, when the barrage had come down on the right at 5 a.m., Wellington-West Coast Company had pushed on down to the right and captured a line of trenches, inflicting heavy casualties on the enemy and capturing eight prisoners. As we now moved forward, it was found that the Second Brigade was not across on the eastern side of the canal as expected, and we were subjected to fire from both machine-guns and field-guns on the high ground across the canal on the right. We now bore too much to the right and lost touch with 2nd Auckland. The village of Les Rues des Vignes was reached; but the enemy maintained his hold on the bridgeheads by fire from machine-guns. Accordingly, a line was established along the edge of the village and we regained touch with 2nd Auckland. During the hours of darkness, our patrols worked down to the bridgeheads and secured them with posts.

Shortly before midnight on the 30th September, our 2nd Battalion had been relieved by 2nd Canterbury and, during the early hours of the following morning, the 1st Battalion was relieved by 2nd Auckland and 2nd Canterbury without casualties, and moved back to the area which had been occupied by 1st Auckland, our 1st Battalion now going into brigade reserve. Two platoons of Ruahine Company (1st Battalion), which were in an exposed position on the banks of the canal, were not then relieved but remained in position until dark, because the relieving battalions were holding in smaller strength than we had held, and also because of the danger of getting out in daylight.

THE WELLINGTON REGIMENT

The importance of at once securing a foothold on the far bank of the canal could not be over-estimated. Accordingly, plans were at once made for a renewal of the attack on the following day (1st October) by 2nd Wellington and 1st Auckland. It was now thought the attack might be delivered with more chance of success from the north rather than by frontal assault, and preparations were made accordingly. The First Brigade would cross under cover of darkness to the north bank on the western reach and assemble there in the VI. Corps' sector to strike south-eastwards at Crevecour. On the left, 1st Auckland would capture the high ground overlooking Crevecour valley from the north and seize the road running north from the Old Mill of Lesdain.

Before midnight, 2nd Wellington and 1st Auckland moved to their assembly positions, crossing by a wooden bridge. A little rain fell but towards morning ceased. The battalions were in position by 5.15 a.m., 2nd Wellington on the right and 1st Auckland on the left. At 6 a.m., our artillery barrage came down, to be answered immediately by the enemy guns shelling the line of the canal. By 8 a.m., 2nd Wellington had taken Crevecour and some 150 prisoners. Just before reaching the final objective, 2nd Lieut. H. Pettit had noticed a party of the enemy moving along a sunken road, and, holding them up at the point of his revolver, albeit an empty one, captured no less than thirty-five Germans. As soon as our men were seen in the village, the enemy, with enfilade machine-gun and shell fire, caused heavy casualties. 1st Auckland had pressed on to their final objectives in the face of stern resistance, and were in touch with 2nd Wellington. 1st Auckland's left, however, was very much exposed, and it was not long before a heavy counter-attack from Seranvillers and the north developed against 1st Auckland and 2nd Wellington's left company (Ruahine). 1st Auckland was forced to give ground; but Ruahine Company held on stubbornly, despite the loss of fifty per cent. in casualties. Two platoons of the reserve company (Wellington-West Coast) were sent for-

THE WELLINGTON REGIMENT

ward to help Ruahine Company. For some time the whole area to a considerable depth was subjected to extremely heavy shell fire and the position was most critical. The splendid stand by Ruahine Company commanded by Temp. Captain W. R. Burge, M.C., there is little doubt, saved the whole First Brigade front that day. Burge himself was severely wounded and greatly shaken by a shell burst close to him; but stuck to his company until the danger was past, and his example was such that Ruahine Company refused to give a yard of ground.

Lieut. W. B. Cooke (who had been awarded the Military Medal and bar with Medical Corps before receiving his commission in the Regiment) showed conspicuous gallantry that day. He hung on with his platoon on a flank in a most exposed position. It was a most critical time; but Cooke, in disregard of his own safety, moved about and encouraged his men to stick it out.

Lieut. G. F. Pott's platoon had maintained its position when isolated by the counter-attack, and, later, when his company commander became a casualty, Pott himself took command of the company and handled it with skill at a critical time.

Corporal S. T. Dibble of the battalion signallers here showed great devotion to duty. On the 29th, one of his party had been killed and Dibble and another wounded; but, nevertheless, Dibble established early communication with the attacking companies. On the 1st October, three more of his section became casualties; but Dibble kept his other men working, and, even after he himself had been wounded a second time, carried on for twenty-four hours.

During the operation, Lieut. A. J. Williams* was killed and Lieuts. J. E. R. Benton and C. N. Devery, D.C.M., wounded. The day's casualties in the 2nd Battalion were 4 officers and 142 other ranks, while 1st Auckland had suffered even more severely.

---

*Williams as a D.O. with 1st Canterbury had been the first member of the N.Z.E.F. to be wounded in January, 1915, on the Suez Canal.

THE WELLINGTON REGIMENT

During the morning, our 1st Battalion, in brigade reserve, had sent Wellington-West Coast Company (Captain J. R. Cade) forward to reinforce 1st Auckland. Later, the other three companies were moved forward under brigade orders and held in readiness to move across the canal to reinforce the forward battalions. The other companies, however, were not called upon, but, after dark, Wellington-West Coast Company took over the front line from the remnants of the 1st Auckland Battalion, Capt. J. R. Cade showing untiring energy during these operations, inspiring all by his determination.

Throughout the following day, the whole area occupied by the 2nd Battalion was heavily shelled. Wellington-West Coast Company from reserve now relieved the sadly depleted Ruahine Company in the front line. The same positions were maintained all that day, and the following day. The First Brigade was then to become brigade in reserve and, after dark on the 3rd October, 2nd Wellington was relieved in the front line by the 1st Battalion of the Rifle Brigade. Just before the relief commenced, the enemy heavily bombarded our front lines; but no infantry action followed. Earlier in the evening, 1st Wellington in reserve had been relieved by the 2nd Battalion of the Rifle Brigade, and had moved back to trenches at Welsh Ridge. There was now a general cleaning up, full advantage being taken of the divisional baths at Marcoing.

During the operations near Crevecour, Lieut. G. H. Robinson (Brigade Intelligence Officer) daily went round the front line, visiting all posts and locating enemy points of resistance and otherwise displaying gallantry and skill of a high order.

Both Wellington battalions were to remain in reserve until the 9th October. On the 1st October, the Second Brigade had taken over a new brigade front south of Les Rues des Vignes, but had not succeeded in crossing the canal. It is true that early in the morning of the 4th, a total silence of his guns had indicated a retirement on the part of the enemy; but, on the fog clearing, it almost seemed as if he had, on the contrary, strengthened his defence, and was even contemplating a counter-attack against Crevecour.

Although the Third and Fourth Armies were now at a standstill the Fourth Army had, on the 3rd October, completed its task of breaching the Hindenburg Line opposite its front, and so turned the enemy defences on La Tierriere plateau.

On the morning of the 5th October, there were unmistakable signs of an enemy withdrawal on our front, for was he not now shelling Vaucelles and the eastern bank of the canal? Patrols from the Second Brigade at once pushed across the canal, penetrating a considerable distance without resistance. The Third (Rifle) Brigade co-operating with the Second Brigade, it was not long before substantial progress had been made towards the Beaurevoir-Masnieres line, an advance which greatly facilitated the Engineers' task of bridging the Scheldt Canal and River.

The Battle of Cambrai and Hindenburg Line closed on the 5th October. There was still bitter resistance in the envelopment of Cambrai; but the whole Hindenburg defence system was in the hands of the British. The struggle in entrenched positions was at an end, and the menace to the enemy's railways and lines of communication became immediate. Except for the Beaurevoir-Masnieres line and some other less complete defences, no artificial obstacle barred the way to Maubeuge. In Flanders, Ploegsteert Wood, Messines and Polygon Wood were once more in the hands of the British.

CHAPTER XLIX.

Further Enemy Withdrawal—We Capture Briastre—Joy of Inhabitants — Across the Selle — Ruahine Company (1st Battalion) Suffers Severely—Enemy Fires Villages—Hard Fighting at Belle Vue Station —River Crossing at Briastre Secured — Good Billets at Fontaine-au-Pire — A Visit from the Prince of Wales.

THERE now remained to develop and exploit the successes won all along the line by co-ordinated action on the part of the British, French and American troops, with every possibility of turning the enemy's retreat into a rout. This combined attack was fixed for the 8th October. It is true the whole purpose of the attack was not to be at once realised; but the result was to make the enemy's position increasingly desperate.

The IV. Corps was to attack on its front with the 37th Division on the left. The New Zealanders' task on the 8th, was allotted to the 2nd and 3rd Brigades. Formidable resistance was expected and complete preparations were made for the attack. As it turned out, neither infantry nor machine-guns put up a stubborn resistance, and the New Zealanders were everywhere successful, taking shoals of prisoners and reaching their final objectives with inconsiderable casualties and then pushing forward to exploit their successes. Preparations were at once made to continue the advance the following day.

On the 9th October, as the 2nd and 3rd Brigades again advanced, it became apparent the enemy had stolen away in the darkness, leaving no rearguards to contest progress.

By 9 o'clock in the morning, both brigades had reached their final objectives, the 2nd Brigade, Le Cateau-Cambrai Railway, and the Rifle Brigade, with the Guards Division on its left, the railway south of Cattenieres.

Since the 3rd October, the First Brigade had been in reserve. During this period, a number of reinforcements, both officers and other ranks, had been taken on strength by both Wellington battalions.

Early on the morning of the 9th, the 1st and 2nd Wellington battalions were under orders to be ready to move at half an hour's notice. At mid-day both battalions commenced the march forward. There was over an hour's halt near the canal for dinner. We were soon on the march again, moving with one hundred yards distance between companies, passing through Crevecour and north of Esnes. Late in the afternoon, we halted again and bivouaced for the night on bare country.

Major H. E. McKinnon, M.C., was now in command of the 2nd Battalion, for Colonel Cunningham had been sick for a week or two, and, before moving on the 8th had gone back to the "B" teams, on the orders of the Brigadier, for a few days' rest.

The First Brigade now lay in support to the Second Brigade and all battalions of the First Brigade were under orders to move at an hour's notice to exploit the Second Brigade's successes.

Before noon on the 10th October, battalion Commanders were summoned to brigade headquarters, returning with orders to move at once. Both battalions moved in artillery formation to an area east of Beauvois, where the men had tea and the officers reconnoitred the country in front from some high ground. The First Brigade was now to take over from the Second Brigade the divisional front with 2nd Auckland on the left, 1st Wellington on the right, 2nd Wellington in left support and 1st Auckland in right support. It was not an ordinary relief, for 1st Wellington was to pass through 1st Otago and capture Viesly and, if possible, push through Briastre and secure the bridgeheads on

THE WELLINGTON REGIMENT

the river Selle. Orders were issued orally to company commanders at 5.15 p.m. Half an hour later, as 1st Wellington was moving forward, information was received that 1st Otago had already taken Viesly, and 1st Wellington was, therefore, to push through Briastre, cross the river, and secure the railway line on the east side of the river. The 1st Battalion advanced with Ruahine Company on the right, Hawkes Bay on the left, and Taranaki Company in support. Wellington-West Coast Company was held in reserve with battalion headquarters at La Guisette Farm. At 9 p.m., forward battalion headquarters were established at Viesly, and the reserve company moved forward. By 11 p.m., our leading companies had moved through the Otago lines and pushed forward their patrols. About 1 o'clock the following morning the river was reached. It was found that no enemy was west of the river on our front; but the bridges were down. Our patrols worked through Briastre and, shortly before dawn, the 1st Battalion's two leading companies crossed the river by a bridge erected by the Royal Engineers about 900 yards south of our allotted frontage. 2nd Lieut. S. S. Pennefather, D.C.M., commanded the two platoons first across the river. Hawkes Bay Company now worked up the east bank of the river to the factory on the outskirts of Briastre, and Ruahine Company followed, both companies endeavouring to shake out and cover the allotted fronts before moving forward against the railway line. When dawn broke, however, our men were seen by the enemy, who opened fire upon them with machine-guns from the railway line and the road just west of it. Hawkes Bay Company was able to get under cover, Lieut. Pennefather (Ruahine Company) showing courage and skill in holding his men together; but Ruahine Company, on an exposed slope suffered heavy casualties. Both companies re-organised and established a line, gaining touch on the right with the 37th Division, who had four platoons only across the river. Second Auckland on the left, had been unable to cross the river, and Taranaki Company was disposed through Briastre to fill in the gap, Wellington-

THE WELLINGTON REGIMENT

West Coast Company pushing up to cover the western edge of Briastre.

At the factory, Hawkes Bay Company erected across the river, an improvised footbridge, which enabled communication to be maintained and wounded to be evacuated.

Meantime, before daybreak 2nd Wellington had moved forward from Beauvois and established battalion headquarters at Aulicourt Farm. There it lay awaiting orders while 2nd Auckland pushed forward. As he retired, the enemy was destroying everything he could, and fires were now burning in villages on all sides. At 8 o'clock in the morning, the 2nd Battalion moved its headquarters forward to Herpigny Farm, and the First Brigade established its headquarters at Aulicourt Farm.

During the hours of daylight, the 1st Battalion found it impossible to push forward further on account of the strength in which the road and railway line were held by the enemy, and the difficulty of crossing the river. The day was fairly quiet, and arrangements were made with the battalion on the right to occupy the original frontages during the hours of darkness. It was found that about one hundred and seventy French civilians were in the town of Briastre, and with what joy did they greet our men! Some of 1st Wellington have since blushingly admitted to embraces by matrons and maidens—many not too clean from enforced hiding in cellars.

Early in the afternoon, the 1st Battalion established its forward battalion headquarters in Briastre, which at 5 p.m. was shelled heavily by the enemy for half an hour. In front of Hawkes Bay and Ruahine Companies, several of our men lay wounded within a hundred yards of the enemy's advanced positions. Those companies were not long in organising rescue parties and, during the day, men went out time after time, in face of machine-gun fire at close range, to bring in their wounded mates. Notably gallant work was performed by Corporal H. B. Smith, Privates R. Campbell, M.M., and G. H. Buchanan. Lieut. Pennefather himself went out no less than eleven times, and though repeatedly fired on, succeeded in clearing the whole of his company's front of wounded.

Some of the 1st Battalion, under the instructions of Lieut. A. W. Thomas of the Engineers, succeeded, during the day, in making a bridge of trees and rails, and across this, after darkness, the casualties sustained early in the day by Hawkes Bay and Ruahine Companies were evacuated. During the night, Ruahine Company was relieved by a company of the 8th Somerset Light Infantry, and moved back to support Hawkes Bay, which had moved up to the left and established itself on a road along the east bank of the river running from the factory.

At noon that day, a battalion of the 42nd Division had arrived and taken over the billets of the 2nd Battalion, who had then moved to chalk pit. Here, late that night, a mess cart drove over a bank on to the bivouac occupied by the Padre and the doctor, and Padre Walls* had the bad luck to have both legs broken.

At dawn the following morning, the 37th Division on our right was to make an attack against certain high ground, 1st Wellington's orders being to co-operate by protecting the left flank of the 37th Division by forming a flank from Belle Vue, where a liaison post was to be established back to the river on the left of our frontage.

Accordingly, at 5 o'clock on the morning of the 12th October, the attack by the 37th Division commenced under a heavy barrage. The two platoons of Taranaki Company under 2nd Lieut. G. McSaveney attacked simultaneously and reached Belle Vue; but were driven off with loss. Unexpected enemy strength was encountered at Bell Vue Station, and from the buildings on the Solesmes Road; and no touch could be gained with the Division on our right, which had gained its objectives on its right; but failed to reach Bell Vue.

A strong section from Hawkes Bay Company, which had followed up the Taranaki attack on the right to deal

---

*Chaplain Captain Charles Walls was later awarded the Military Cross for distinguished service in France and Flanders.

with certain buildings and to protect the right flank, joined up with a section of the 37th Division, and established a post on the Briastre Road, while another section from the same company pushed out to the left and established another post just short of the Road. Eleven prisoners were taken; but the Belle Vue Station and the copse on the Solesmes Road remained in enemy hands.

In reply to this attack, Briastre was subjected to heavy shelling throughout the morning, while Viesly was shelled with heavy guns at frequent intervals. It was soon apparent, that against this unexpected resistance a far stronger barrage was needed, and, shortly before noon, all available guns were turned upon the German positions. Notwithstanding this, enemy machine-guns were as active as ever.

The 37th Division had by now captured the high ground on the south; but we were in no position to protect its flank. During the afternoon, under an intense barrage, the enemy attacked the forward and exposed troops of the 37th Division, and recovered the high ground and forced that division back to the railway. After severe fighting, the Taranaki force from 1st Wellington, had to be withdrawn back to its original position.

The enemy was not long to hold the ground recovered. Our guns poured a concentrated fire on the Bell Vue Station and the enemy positions on the road and railway. First Wellington's attacking force was strengthened, and, at 6 p.m., Taranaki Company on the right and Hawkes Bay Company on the left attacked under a heavy barrage provided by artillery and machine-guns. In spite of the bombardment by our artillery, the Jaegers fought with extraordinary stubbornness. Taranaki Company captured Belle Vue, and gained touch on our right with the 37th Division, who had pushed forward a battalion to connect up with us. Hawkes Bay's advance was impeded by an enemy machine-gun; but rifle grenades were rained into the post and four Germans, jumping out of their pit, ran for their lines. Lance-Corporal B. Quentin, commanding a party on Taranaki's left, who had held his ground against the fire from this machine-gun, allowed none of the Germans to escape his vigilant Lewis Gun. Hawkes Bay Company then pressed on and cleared the copse and captured the buildings on the main road, which had held up Taranaki early in the day, and swung back to the left, down the ridge to our previous left flank post. A machine gun near one of the buildings hung on tenaciously; but this was dealt with by a special party from Wellington-West Coast Company, two platoons of which had been moved forward to the river when the attack commenced. By 8.30 p.m., our positions had been consolidated, and the river crossing at Briastre secured.

During the two days' fighting at Briastre, there were numerous noteworthy acts of gallantry but, as usual, many must go unrecorded. His company commander (Capt. T. C. A. Hislop) being early wounded on the 11th, Lieut. T. H. Crawford took charge of Hawkes Bay Company, and by resolute leading pushed across the river and established and maintained a position near the objective under heavy artillery and machine-gun fire, and throughout displayed marked gallantry and skill. During the attack on the 12th, Sergt. W. J. Lewis, M.M., led his platoon very ably and repelled an attack from the rear, when the enemy worked in behind from a flank. Lieut. W. K. Fowler had been in charge of the left flank platoon of his company in the attack on Belle Vue. Our barrage came down on a part of his platoon, necessitating immediate reorganisation. Then when starting to follow the barrage, Fowler was shot through the right arm by machine-gun fire; but he continued on with his platoon to the objective, staying there until he obtained a clear idea of the position, then reporting back with valuable information. Private W. Sheriff had been indefatigable early in the day in helping to carry wounded back through heavy shell fire, and, later in the attack, he again went out and, whilst carrying in a wounded man, a shell burst killing the other stretcher bearer. Sheriff, thereupon, carried the wounded man on his back to an advanced dressing station.

Some idea of the efficiency of the artillery bombardments and barrages that accompanied the attacks of Taranaki and Hawkes Bay Companies on the railway may be gauged from the fact that, when, a fortnight later the 1st Battalion was allotted an area including the railway line at Belle Vue to clear of dead, in the first hundred yards along the line going north from the level crossing of Belle Vue, our men found thirty-eight dead Germans. All these were on the railway itself, and did not include those found in the posts in front and behind the railway.

The 1st Battalion's casualties for the day were 28 killed, 76 wounded, and 11 missing. During the morning attack, we had taken eleven prisoners, while in the evening another ten prisoners were taken and one machine-gun.

The New Zealand Division was now to be relieved by the 47th Division. At midnight, 1st Wellington was relieved by the 8th Battalion, Lancashire Fusiliers, and marched back in cold drizzly rain to Fontaine-au-Pire. Second Wellington, who had been held in reserve with 1st Auckland, was relieved late in the day by the 7th Battalion, Lancashire Fusiliers, and marched to billets and huts in Longsart.

The 1st Battalion now settled down comfortably in the best billets that battalion had had since its arrival in France. It occupied practically the whole of both sides of the Rue de Saules, and, although not damaged to any extent by shell fire, a great many houses had been left in a filthy state by the retreating enemy. Accumulations of filth and latrine refuse were features at almost every building and examples of wanton destruction, and such as beds and chairs ripped open, glass and crockery smashed, and furniture chopped about, were common. On the other hand, there were houses which had not been despoiled, appearing as if the inhabitants had just vacated them. The village had been cleared of inhabitants. Nothing was done until the following day, when the cleaning of billets was tackled in earnest. "B" teams and reinforcements now rejoined their respective battalions and platoons were re-organised.

Colonel Cunningham now returned from the Rest Camp, and re-assumed command of the 2nd Battalion, while Captain W. F. Currie, R.M.O., returning from hospital took over his

THE WELLINGTON REGIMENT

duties again from Capt. W. C. Reid who returned to his Field Ambulance. Captain Haskins (R.M.O.) now left the 1st Battalion to join the 2nd Field Ambulance. The Rev. G. T. Brown now joined the 2nd Battalion, replacing Padre Walls, while Lieut. A. N. Tod came back to his old battalion for duty as signalling officer.

On the 14th October, H.R.H. The Prince of Wales paid a visit to the New Zealand Division, and early in the afternoon both battalions lined the road and cheered lustily as the Prince and General Russell rode slowly by. It was quite an informal inspection, and the Prince frequently stopped and spoke a few words to Battalion Commanders.

The following week was devoted to training. Many men were able to go to the baths, either at Fontaine-au-Pire, or at Esnes. Battalion tailors and bootmakers had a busy time repairing the damage of a few days in action.

On the evening of the 17th October, at 1st Battalion Headquarters' Mess in Fontaine, a re-union was held of all those who had left New Zealand with the Main Body and were now officers in the Wellington Regiment. A splendid spread was provided, and it was a thoroughly happy function. Some of those present were:—Brig.-Genl. H. E. Hart, C.M.G., D.S.O., Brig-Genl. R. Young, C.M.G., D.S.O., Lieut. Col. W. H. Cunningham, D.S.O., Lieut. Col. L. H. Jardine, D.S.O., M.C., Lieut. Col. F. K. Turnbull, D.S.O.,M.C., Major H. E. McKinnon, M.C., Capt. B. H. Morison, M.C., and Capt. J. T. Dallinger, M.C. The Commander of the First Brigade, Brig.-Genl. C. W. Melvill, C.M.G., D.S.O., was also present.

CHAPTER L.

Enemy on the Run — Billets in Solesmes — Colonel Cunningham Leaves 2nd Battalion—Preparing for the Capture of Le Quesnoy.

ON the 20th October, the Second and Fourth Armies continued the advance. The New Zealand Division was held in reserve and, although all battalions were ordered to be ready to move at two hours' notice, the Division was not called upon. As a result of the operations that day, the line was advanced between 3000 and 4000 yards on the IV. Corps' front; but only after stubborn fighting.

On the 22nd October, 2nd Wellington marched in full marching order in steady rain to Fontaine, where 1st Wellington and the rest of the First Brigade had been for more than a week.

On the 23rd, the advance was resumed on a wide front. In the IV. Corps, the 5th and 42nd Divisions were the leading divisions in the morning's advance. Before mid-day, our Second Brigade passed through the 42nd Division, the Rifle Brigade being in divisional support at Solesmes, and the First Brigade in reserve at Fontaine. At the same time, the 37th Division passed through the 5th Division on the right. The enemy was now on the run and all objectives were taken with comparatively few casualties. There was not the stubborn fighting that had marked the action of the 20th, and by nightfall, 1st Canterbury patrols had seized Beaudignies, and, later, that night, pushed up Le Quesnoy Road and established a post five hundred yards beyond Beaudignies. Before midnight, 2nd Otago had occupied fifteen hundred yards of the Salesches-Beaudignies Road, meeting little opposition. Our Second Brigade had advanced altogether four and

THE WELLINGTON REGIMENT

a half miles, going beyond its objectives and securing the Ecaillon crossings.

Still the enemy was to be given no respite, and the Second Brigade, ordered to continue the advance, had, before dawn on the 24th, reached the sunken road running from Ghissignies past the eastern edge of Beaudignies. For the rest of the day the battalions of the Second Brigade were engaged in exploiting their successes. By nightfall, the Second Brigade line ran from the Ruesnes road on the left, to the north-eastern extremity of the De Beart Wood on Le Quesnoy road and then through the trees, with outposts on the edge of the wood. At certain points the line was not more than one thousand yards from the outer ramparts of Le Quesnoy.

In the evening of the 24th October, the Second Brigade was relieved in line by the Rifle Brigade. In hard fighting during the next few days, the latter brigade substantially improved the position on the divisional front, and established additional posts. Pending the resumption of the advance, the divisional sector was re-organised.

On the morning of the 24th, the First Brigade had marched to Solesmes, 2nd Wellington moving first at 7 a.m. The route was through Beauvois, Cambresis, Bevillers, Quievy and Fontaine-au-Tertre—the roads good, and the weather fine. In Solesmes, the billets were in some rather "shell-shocked" houses. However, there was an abundance of straw and other supplies lying about, and by dark everyone was comfortable. Solesmes must have been a fair-sized town, albeit now somewhat battered about. Here about one thousand inhabitants had been left behind by the retreating enemy.

Col. W. H. Cunningham, D.S.O., and Capt. J. T. Dallinger, M.C., were now to leave the Second Battalion, under orders to return to New Zealand on tour of duty. On the march to Solesmes, the battalion marched past the Colonel and so took leave of its tried and trusty commander, who had for long borne the heat and burden of the day. The command of the 2nd Battalion was now assumed by Major H. E.

McKinnon, M.C., and Lieut. S. A. Murrell took over from Capt. Dallinger the duties of adjutant.

Although daily expecting orders, both battalions were to remain at Solesmes for more than a week. On the Sunday, many of our men attended a Roman Catholic service in the Solesmes Church, the Vicar-General of Cambrai, through an interpreter, expressing the gratitude of the inhabitants at their deliverance from the Germans.

By the 28th, the advance on the Corps front had been temporarily suspended. The Rifle Brigade continued to hold the line on the New Zealand Divisional front, west and north-west of Le Quesnoy.

It was now the lull before the storm. A great deal of cleaning-up work was done by everyone; a certain amount of training was done and frequent use was made of the baths at Marou.

Towards the end of October, Capt. M. Urquhart, M.C., who had only just returned from New Zealand, took up duties as second in command of his old battalion, the 2nd. About the middle of October, Capt. F. S. Varnham, M.C., who, for some months, had been adjutant of the 1st Battalion, was appointed Staff Captain to the First Brigade, and Lieut. A. R. Blennerhassett was appointed acting-adjutant in his stead. About the same time, Lieut. H. E. Blennerhassett was appointed acting-Quartermaster of the 1st Battalion, taking over the duties from 2nd Lieut. A. D. Price, M.C., M.M., who was about to return to New Zealand on duty.

Participation in the advance was not long to be delayed, for, on the 1st November, warning orders were received outlining the operation to be carried out by the New Zealand Division at Le Quesnoy and east of that town, and battalion, company commanders and scouts were already reconnoitring the routes to the assembly positions. The following day, Brigade orders were received for the operation at Le Quesnoy. The whole operation was now discussed by battalion commanders with their company commanders and plans formed. It was Sunday, and, after Church Parade in the morning, all preparations were made for the advance.

THE WELLINGTON REGIMENT

About four o'clock in the afternoon, both battalions marched out from Solesmes, 1st Wellington's band playing us out of the town. The civilians turned out in numbers to see us move off. The march was a slow and tiring one, accomplished in drizzling rain and over a rather bad route. The assembly positions were at last reached, and we settled down in bivouacs north-east of Beaudignies for the night, having a meal from the cookers before turning in.

CHAPTER LI.

Le Quesnoy—Villereau—Potelle—Rhonelle River – Herbignies — Le Carnoy — Le Quesnoy Falls to the Rifle Brigade—We Push Through Mormal Forest —Sarioton Road—Major H. E. McKinnon is Killed —Relief by 2nd Brigade—Back to Villereau—Our Captures.

THE role allotted to the New Zealand Division was, in conjunction with the 37th Division on the right, and the 62nd Division of the VI. Corps on the left, to attack and establish a line from the western edge of the Mormal Forest northwards through the more distant outskirts of Herbignies to the cross roads at Tous Vents. This involved an advance of nearly four miles from the Division's present line, the capture of Le Quesnoy, and of the ground two and a half miles beyond its eastern rampart.

The civil population was still in Le Quesnoy, and the bombardment of the town was quite out of the question. Without artillery assistance, a frontal attack was impossible. It was arranged, therefore, to envelop Le Quesnoy from the flanks. The plan for the attack on the 4th November, was decided upon as follows:—

(1) 5.30 a.m. 1st, 2nd and 4th Battalions of the Rifle Brigade were to capture the railway and envelop the western side of Le Quesnoy.

(2) 7.29 a.m. The 3rd Battalion of the Rifle Brigade and 1st Auckland were to establish positions beyond the eastern ramparts of the town.

(3) 8.56 a.m. 1st and 2nd Wellington were to pass through the Rifle Brigade north of the town, and strike south-east. At about the same

time, the 3rd Battalion of the Rifle Brigade would advance on the south of the town. When these converging movements met, the First Brigade would take over the whole front, leaving the Rifle Brigade free to mop up Le Quesnoy.

(4) 10.20 a.m. The First Brigade would continue the advance to the final objectives, and should the enemy weaken, patrols were to be pushed forward some 3000 yards.

Ample artillery support was to be provided for the operation.

Rain had set in over-night, but at about 3 o'clock in the morning it cleared. Dawn broke fine, but later a thick mist came over, to clear later in the morning, and give way to a fine sunny day. Punctually at 5.30 a.m., our guns and mortars crashed down a strong barrage. The Rifle Brigade at once pressed forward towards its objectives. At some points stout resistance was encountered, which was not overcome without fierce fighting. At other points, the Rifle Brigade established its line with inconsiderable trouble. All along the New Zealand Division's front, the first objectives were reached up to time, large numbers of prisoners being taken, and dozens of machine-guns falling into our hands.

South of Le Quesnoy the Third Rifles now moved forward, while, shortly afterwards, north of the town, 1st Auckland in touch with the 62nd Division, continued the encircling movement. By 8.30 a.m., the Aucklanders had cleared Ramponeau. First Auckland had under fifty casualties, yet captured some three hundred prisoners and fifty machine-guns.

First and Second Wellington made ready to move shortly after 6 o'clock from the bivouacs near Beaudignies to their assembly positions in the sunken Orsinval road. There was a fair amount of shelling along the Precheltes River and the railway line and at the assembly positions, and the dense fog, which had rapidly come over, and the smoke barrage round Le Quesnoy, made the march rather difficult. However, by 8 a.m. both Wellington battalions were in position. As they lay here, Lieut. A. R. Blennerhassett, Adjutant of the 1st Battalion, was killed and Lieut. P. H. G. Bennett (Scout Officer) wounded.

A few minutes later, both battalions left their assembly positions and started to move forward to the line occupied by 1st Auckland preparatory to launching the attack upon their own objectives. At 8.56 a.m., 1st and 2nd Wellington moved to the attack, 1st Wellington on the right, 2nd Wellington on the left. As Wellington went forward, the Aucklanders turned to the right, and faced Le Quesnoy, linking up with the Rifle Brigade. The town was being rapidly surrounded.

1st Wellington found little resistance to its advance. There was some fighting on the Villereau Road, and at one point where an enemy machine-gun gave trouble, Sergeant R. Charteris rushed the post single handed, put the gun out of action, and captured the crew. In most cases, the enemy, although in considerable strength, seemed content to withdraw more quickly than our troops could advance.

The 2nd Battalion, moving through the woods on the steep Rhonelle bank, encountered little opposition. A small party of 2nd Battalion signallers under Lance-Corporal J. H. Griffiths came upon three 77 m.m. guns of the enemy still in action. Such a chance was too good to miss. The signallers promptly dropped their wire, and charged the guns. They captured the guns and took two of the enemy prisoners, the others making good their escape. In Villereau, the 2nd Battalion found some fifty civilians and also came upon a party of the enemy (two officers and twenty-two men).

By 9.25 a.m., both battalions were upon their first objectives, and Wellington-West Coast Company, under Captain E. White (who behaved throughout with fearless dash and determination) then extended the 1st Battalion's right to the southern boundary occupied by the Third Rifles. The First Brigade was now ready to push on to its final objectives.

·Although our line was well over a mile beyond the town, there was as yet no sign of the capitulation of Le Quesnoy, nor was there to be for several hours longer.

THE WELLINGTON REGIMENT

At 10.20 a.m., the advance was resumed, 1st and 2nd Wellington moving forward along the whole New Zealand Front in touch with the troops on either flank. A section of Otago Mounted Rifles was now attached to 2nd Wellington, and a section of Third Hussars to 1st Wellington. One of 1st Wellington's companies bore too much to a flank, and Lieut. A. J. Nimmo, commanding Ruahine Company, in support, immediately sent a platoon forward to fill the gap. The enemy was now thoroughly disorganised and demoralised. Potelle was taken in our stride. Then passing through the woods on either side of the railway and along the banks of the Rhonelle River, where they captured guns, limbers and horses, 1st Wellington entered and cleared Herbignies. Many Germans had fled into cellars; but few escaped Sergeant H. O. D. Clark and his men. A platoon under Sergeant S. Board captured nearly 200 prisoners and 10 machine-guns. Sergeant F. Baker, M.M., Sergeant I. G. Short, Lance-Corporal F. Lang (who hacked his way through a hedge to surprise an enemy machine-gun), and Private W. G. Vial, who captured two machine-gun posts in succession, were only some of those to rush enemy machine-guns.

At Herbignies and elsewhere, the released inhabitants pressed coffee, milk and fruit upon us. Before mid-day, our objectives had everywhere been reached. The casualties had been extremely light, probably because the attack was delivered from a flank. During the attack, 1st Battalion Headquarters had been established successively at Ramponeau (where a Hun Aid Post was taken over, the M.O. in charge handing over his revolver with old-fashioned courtesy to our C.O.) Potelle Chateau and on southern edge of Herbignies, while the 2nd Battalion's were first at St. Sepulchre, afterwards moving forward to Ferme de Lion (that night).

On the left flank, 2nd Wellington patrols had early passed Le Carnoy, where a party under Company Sergeant-Major J. H. Foster, coming under heavy fire from a house, rushed and captured two machine-guns. Scouts, indeed, went almost as far as Le Grand Sart. By the time the main advance was continued, however, the enemy had filtered back

THE WELLINGTON REGIMENT

and little progress could be made in the daylight against obstinate machine-gun fire from the left flank, although on the right we were more successful and reached the western edge of Mormal Forest. Private L. G. Loveday pushed forward into the Wood, and followed a road into a clearing more than a mile from the front line. On returning, he saw a party of seven of the enemy. Loveday shot three, and took the other four, including two officers, prisoners. First Wellington's patrols, pushing through the forest, encountered no opposition, except from a cavalry patrol, which Private A. D. Anderson fired on and dispersed, four dead horses, and two prisoners being left behind.

Many notable acts of gallantry were performed by all ranks that day. Near Villereau, Lieut. J. Courtney was in command of a leading platoon of the 2nd Battalion. When the advance was held up, he personally reconnoitred forward, and then led a party against a machine-gun, the capture of which undoubtedly saved many casualties. When an enemy machine-gun threatened to check his platoon, Lieut. W. S. Brown, M.M., with the 2nd Battalion, attacked the gun, capturing it and killing the crew. Again, near Villereau, he similarly overcame machine-gun resistance. During the operation, his work was brilliant and led in great measure to the capture of several field guns. Private F. J. Nettleingham had shown marked courage and initiative when his platoon had come under very heavy machine-gun fire near Pont de la Louette. He pushed on ahead, located the enemy gun, and forced its crew to abandon the gun. Then rushing alone into the trench, he took some fifteen German prisoners. His prompt courageous action saved many casualties.

Lieut. C. B. Lepper, in command of Taranaki Company (1st Battalion), had supervised the advance of that company over difficult country, and then very ably directed the mopping up operations and the clearing of posts. Many other brave deeds by men of all ranks must perforce go urecorded.

Even after Le Quesnoy was completely encircled, and our line established well beyond it, the enemy garrison still held out, and frustrated the efforts of the Rifle Brigade,

THE WELLINGTON REGIMENT

whose special mission it was to bring about its fall. Le Quesnoy with its moat and ramparts formed an extraordinarily strong defensive position, and the Rifle Brigade was confronted with an entirely novel situation. Once the investment of the town had been completed, clearly its fall was only a matter of time.

About 9 o'clock in the morning, a small party from the 4th Rifles had gained a precarious footing on the fortifications; but, on attempting to scale the inner bastion, the officer commanding and one of the men had both been shot through the head and killed instantly. Further progress for the time being was out of the question. Before noon, the Rifle Brigade sent several of its prisoners into the town to explain the hopelessness of the garrison's situation, and to invite surrender. Nothing came of these overtures. Late in the afternoon, one of our aeroplanes dropped into the town a message in German of which the following is a translation.

"To the Commander of the Garrison of Le Quesnoy.

The position of Le Quesnoy is now completely surrounded. Our troops are far east of the town. You are therefore requested to surrender with your garrison. The garrison will be treated as honourable prisoners of war.

The Commander of the British Troops."

During the afternoon, the 4th Battalion Rifle Brigade, made a further attempt. After reconnaissances made by several parties, that Battalion's efforts were to be crowned with success. About 4 o'clock in the afternoon, a small party with a ladder scaled the ramparts. The advent of this party caused a panic amongst the defenders, who met them not with machine-gun fire, but with a jabbering of German.

It was not long before the remainder of the 4th Battalion Rifle Brigade were swarming up the ladder. Within a quarter of an hour, the 2nd Battalion Rifle Brigade marched in at the Valenciennes Gate.

Early in the evening of the 4th, 1st and 2nd Wellington were ordered to push further forward to the Sarioton Road. Under a light barrage, Hawkes Bay Company of the 1st

Battalion pushed through Mormal Forest, two platoons being led by Lieut. (Acting-Captain) C. G. Stewart, who displayed great coolness and initiative. One post only of the enemy was encountered by the 1st Battalion, and this was dealt with effectively. The 2nd Battalion, with Wellington-West Coast Company and Ruahine Company leading, continued the advance, and, by 1.30 a.m., they had reached the Sarioton Road, Taranaki Company wheeling to the left to form a defensive flank. The operation was entirely successful, the enemy having withdrawn, albeit only a few hours before. During this operation, while 2nd Battalion Headquarters were moving forward to an advanced position, Major H. E. McKinnon, M.C., commanding the 2nd Battalion, and his adjutant, Lieutenant S. A. Murrell, were killed by an enemy shell.

What bad luck it was to go right through only to be struck down when everyone knew the War was won, and Germany's capitulation but a matter of hours. McKinnon was one of the original platoon commanders of Wellington-West Coast Company in the Main Body. He took part in the whole of the Gallipoli Campaign; was at the landing at Anzac; saw those few days of stiff fighting at Cape Helles; was one of the very few to cross the "Daisy Patch" and survive.

On the Somme of 1916, in command of Wellington-West Coast Company in the 2nd Battalion, McKinnon again did gallant service, which was recognised a few months later by the award to him of the Military Cross. At Messines, McKinnon again led Wellington-West Coast Company and, a few weeks later, at La Basse Ville, he displayed conspicuous courage and skill in the command of that company for which he received a bar to the Military Cross. At Passchendaele, at the capture of Gravenstafel on 4th October, McKinnon, went over as liaison officer with the English Brigade on our left. Early in 1918, came those shattering German attacks to be countered by our Armies and followed by the smashing of the Hindenburg Line. Apart from a few short weeks of rest in England, McKinnon was with the Regiment all the time. And now, the last time his old battalion ever engaged the enemy, Lieut.-Col. H. E. McKinnon, now its commander, was struck down. McKinnon would have been the first to say "C'est la guerre."

Thus died a man than whom few served his Country in War so long, or so well.

Before 6 o'clock the following morning (5th November) the Second Brigade passed through our front line to exploit the success gained by the First Brigade. During the morning, rain set in, and as the Second Brigade had pushed well ahead, 1st Wellington was withdrawn to the shelter of the buildings on the eastern edge of Herbignies. In the afternoon, both Wellington Battalions marched back in heavy rain to Villereau, the 1st Battalion making its headquarters the Old Mill. Here, Captain M. Urquhart, M.C., took over command of the 2nd Battalion from Capt. D. S. Columb, who had taken charge on the death of Major McKinnon.

During this, the final engagement of the War, the 1st Battalion had had two officers (Lieut. (Acting Capt.) A. R. Blennerhassett and Lieut. Quilliam and seven other ranks killed and two officers and 20 other ranks wounded. The casualties in the 2nd Battalion were 3 officers (Major H. E. McKinnon, Lieut. S. A. Murrell and Lieut. H. D. Banks killed) and 58 other ranks. The 1st Battalion had taken, it was estimated, 1000 prisoners, while in guns and material, it had captured 45 field guns, 11 limbers, 14 horses, 7 trench mortars, 2 wagons, 60 machine-guns, 1 water cart, 2 small carts and 100 rifles. The capture of the 2nd Battalion were:—prisoners, 15 officers and 414 other ranks, 33 field guns, 33 machine-guns, 5 trench mortars, 1 team of artillery horses, 1 chestnut hack, 7 wagons.

On the 6th, Major (temp. Lieut-Col.) H. E. McKinnon M.C. (Acting Commanding Officer 2nd Battalion), Lieut. S. A. Murrell (Adjutant 2nd Battalion) and Lieut. A. R. Blennerhassett (Adjutant 1st Battalion), Lieut. H. D. Banks (2nd Battalion) and Lieut. C. W. Quilliam and several men of 2nd Wellington, all of whom had been killed in action on the 4th, were buried in Le Quesnoy Cemetery with military honours. The funeral ceremony was conducted by the Rev. Mortimer Jones (1st Battalion), Rev. G. T. Brown (2nd Battalion) and Rev. Segreif (formerly 3rd Battalion). The Brigadier and Brigade Major attended the funeral, and the commanding officers, company commanders and twelve men per company from both battalions. After the service, a firing party from 2nd Wellington fired three volleys.

CHAPTER LII.

Solesmes — Beauvois — The Armistice — Preparing for the March to the Rhine.

DURING the next few days not a great deal was done, we cleaned up our billets and buried the enemy dead in our area. The weather which had been showery, now turned fine and frosty. "B" teams marched from Beauvois and rejoined the battalions. Major. W. F. Narbey arrived back from England and took command of the 2nd Battalion. 2nd Lieut. C. G. Stewart was appointed acting-adjutant of the 1st Battalion, while Lieut. D. Cowan became adjutant of the 2nd Battalion.

On the 10th November, the 1st Brigade was ordered to move to Solesmes. In the morning, 1st and 2nd Wellington held a combined church service. Early in the afternoon, both battalions marched out of Villereau via Beaudignies-Romeries to Solesmes, going into billets there in Rue de L'Abbaye. Early on the 11th, both battalions left Solesmes for Beauvois. At about half past nine in the morning during the march, the news was made known that the Armistice with Germany had been signed, and would take effect at 11 o'clock that morning. The news was received very quietly. There was no demonstration. Deep down in everyone's mind, there was no doubt a feeling of profound relief and of profound thankfulness.

First Wellington were marching through Quievy at 11 a.m. (Armistice hour) and the band struck up the familiar strains of "Bonnie Dundee."

Both battalions arrived at Beauvois shortly after midday. Billets there were good, all companies having plenty of

THE WELLINGTON REGIMENT

accommodation. The 1st Battalion was in some good buildings around the junction of the Cambrai Road and the main street of Beauvois, with its transport in a ruined factory.

On the 13th, General Russell met all the officers of the Division and explained the proposed demobilisation orders and the educational scheme. He also stated that the New Zealand Division would form part of the Army of Occupation that was to proceed to the River Rhine. The following morning, both battalions attended the General Thanksgiving Service of the whole division.

On Sunday, the 17th, a Combined Church Service of the 1st and 2nd Battalions of the Regiment was held in the Divisional Theatre. During the afternoon, 2nd Wellington played 2nd Auckland at football. On the 18th, there was a slight fall of snow. In the morning, both battalions took part in a divisional route march. 1st Wellington was the leading battalion, followed by 2nd Wellington. In the afternoon, the officers of the 1st Battalion played football against a combined fifteen from the squadron of the Royal Air Force and a Scotch Battalion, our team winning 18 to nil.

A good deal of time was now given to ceremonial drill, and both battalions were being made spick and span for the move to the Rhine. Some route marching was done, and a good deal of football played. In the first round of the New Zealand Division's Senior Rugby Competition, 1st Wellington defeated 2nd Otago, while our 2nd Battalion went under to a team from the divisional train after a hard fought game.

The 2nd Battalion was now to lose its popular R.M.O., for Captain W. F. Currie, who had been with it so long was now transferred to the Second Field Ambulance, Captain Rowley taking his place.

Major (Temporary Lieut.-Col.) F. K. Turnbull, D.S.O., M.C., O.C. 1st Battalion was now promoted Lieutenant-Colonel. Major W. F. Narbey, commanding the 2nd Battalion, was now promoted Temporary Acting Lieut.-Col. and Capt. M. Urquhart, M.C., Temporary Acting Major. Lieut. H. H. Mackrell, M.M., so long Sergeant Major of Hawkes Bay Company in the 2nd Battalion, and now returned from Eng-

THE WELLINGTON REGIMENT

land with his commission, was appointed Assistant-adjutant in his old battalion.

There were many now in both battalions to receive awards, who for long had borne the heat and burden of the day. C.S.M. W. H. James had been acting as Company Sergeant Major of Taranaki Company's 1st Battalion from 17th September to 11th November—a period during which his batttalion was on several occasions engaged in heavy fighting. He had always shown conspicuous gallantry, particularly in Briastre on the 11th and 12th October, when his company suffered severe casualties, and at Le Quesnoy, when he did fine reconnaissance work. Sergt. S. Gaston, too, had done good work for the 1st Battalion. During the period from 17th September to 11th November, on many occasions, he had taken charge of ration and supply waggons when it was necessary to deliver stores under heavy shell and machine-gun fire and had always set a splendid example. Sergt. T. Muir had served as transport Sergeant to the 2nd Battalion and had been present during all active operations throughout 1918, and had at all times displayed marked courage and had never once failed to deliver a single load of either ammunition, water or food. Then there was C.S.M. R. A. Boyd, who had had long service with Hawkes Bay Company (2nd Battalon) and had, on more than one occasion, shown conspicuous gallantry and devotion to duty. Both in the line and out his gallantry, ability and initiative had always been a fine example. Then too, there was Sergt. J. Tannahill. During an attack near Beaumont Hamel on 30th March he had shown splendid leadership as a platoon Sergeant. In the consolidation of the captured position, under heavy machine-gun and rifle fire, his coolness and courage had spurred on and inspired his men. Then for the rest of the year his work both as platoon Sergeant and Q.M.S. had been consistently excellent.

CHAPTER LIII.

The March to the Rhine—Verviers—We Cross the German Frontier — The Journey Completed by Train—Cologne — Leichlingen—Longenfeld—Christmas 1918—Demobilisation.

ON the morning of the 27th November, orders were received that the New Zealand Division would commence a move to Charleroi on the following day. The day was spent in preparing for the march. In the evening, the orders were altered, and we were not to move until the 29th. The New Zealand Division was now to become part of the II. Army, and the move to Charleroi was to bring us into the II. Army area.

On the 29th, the first day's march en route for Charleroi was commenced. Both Wellington battalions started before 7 o'clock in the morning. The dress was full marching order with felt hats. Blankets were carried by the transport. The 1st Battalion marched as far as Haussy via Bevillers-Quievy-Fontaine-au-Tertre Farm-Solesmes. The 2nd Battalion covered twelve miles reaching Vendignies before noon. On the following day, the march was continued, 1st Wellington proceeding to Wagnies-le-Grand via St. Martin-Bermerian, while the 2nd Battalion reached Wagnies-le-Petit.

We shall not follow the Regiment all the way to the German frontier; but a list of the places at which we were billetted on the march is given in Appendix "A."

On the march to Lobbes, we crossed the French-Belgian border. The inhabitants of the liberated provinces received us most cordially. The windows of the town were placarded with posters welcoming the British troops. We stayed at

THE WELLINGTON REGIMENT

Lobbes, two days and the 2nd Battalion's Band became extremely popular. It played selections which were greatly appreciated by the inhabitants, so much so, that, on our marching out, they collected at various points along the thickly populated route and pleaded for music.

At Tamines, our men had a good welcome, as, indeed, everywhere. While at Isnes and Spy, many of them took the opportunity of visiting the fortress city of Namur. At Spy one company of the 2nd Battalion was billetted in the Municipal Theatre.

By the 13th December, the Regiment had marched one hundred and seven miles, and was now in the Anthiet area. Here a halt was made for four days, mainly because boots were in such urgent need of repair and replacement that we could hardly have continued the march. In Petit Wanze, the little village where the 2nd Battalion was billetted, two dances were given during our stay. From here also, large numbers had leave to go to Huy.

The march to Jemeppe was a particularly interesting one along the banks of the Meuse. The valley of the Meuse is very thickly populated and the inhabitants lined the route giving us a most cordial reception. Here, general leave was granted to Liege—thirty-five minutes' journey by train. In Jemeppe itself, a concert was given by the civil population in honour of the troops. Shortly after leaving Jemeppe, we crossed the Meuse and passed the Fort d'Embourg. It was a stiff pull up the hill leading to and past d'Embourg.

By the 19th December, we had reached Verviers. Here we had a most enthusiastic welcome from the inhabitants, who lined the streets in thousands. It was hard indeed to get through the crowd. In Verviers, there was general leave. The local morning paper was eulogistic in our praise.

On the 20th, the frontier was crossed. The inhabitants of Verviers gave us a most enthusiastic send off, and it was almost impossible for the band to play, as the people insisted on giving our gallant makers of music a proper farewell. To the strains of "Bonnie Dundee", the Regiment marched briskly into Germany.

THE WELLINGTON REGIMENT

On the following day, both battalions entrained at Herbesthal station. At the station, a hot tea and biscuits were served by the Y.M.C.A. After a journey of about five hours, we arrived at Ehrenfeld station, near Cologne. Here tea was again served by the Y.M.C.A., and we marched off in fighting order to our destinations, the 1st Battalion to Leichlingen, and the 2nd Battalion to Longenfeld. The route followed was via Cologne-Mulheim-Weisdorf-Opladen. The Rhine was crossed by the famous Bridge of Boats, and the bands played the regimental march from bank to bank. The inhabitants seemed to take our entry as a matter of course. After detraining, it had been a sixteen miles march. The distance marched from Beauvois to the entraining station had been about 159 miles, and these additional 16 miles, made a total of 175 miles actually marched.

The Regiment was not long in settling down in billets. Both battalions had to supply a number of guards, piquets and patrols. The behaviour of the German inhabitants was very orderly and large numbers used to assemble to see guard mounting.

Dinner on Christmas Day was hardly up to expectations. The 2nd Battalion had to postpone its official dinner on account of non-arrival of the turkeys. However, there was plum pudding, and an issue of beer. The 1st Battalion had its officers' mess in Tannenhoff Hotel, while Baron von Eppinghoven's residence provided the mess for the officers of the 2nd Battalion.

Leave to Cologne was now freely granted, and nearly everyone made the most of his opportunity of seeing that city.

The 26th December, marked the beginning of the end of the Regiment in the field, for on that day, Lieut. Farrington and 56 other ranks left the 1st Battalion on return to New Zealand, to be followed the following day by Capt. B. H. Morison and seven 1914 and twenty-five 1915 class men from the 2nd Battalion. A very enthusiastic send off was given them.

THE WELLINGTON REGIMENT

Demobilisation now set in apace, and drafts left for England every few days.

During January, the weather was for the most part fine, but cold. The education classes were in full swing; but both battalions found time to play a good deal of football.

On the 17th, H.R.H The Prince of Wales visited both battalions. He spoke to nearly all the officers and chatted with many of the men.

By the end of January, the ranks had been so depleted by demobilisation, that it was decided to amalgamate both battalions, and, accordingly, on the 5th February, the 2nd Battalion marched from Longenfeld to Leichlingen, and a composite Wellington Battalion was organised under Lieut.-Col. F. K. Turnbull, D.S.O., M.C., with Major M. Urquhart, M.C., second in command, and Lieut. D. Cowan, adjutant. We may well take leave of the Regiment there.

> "Ten thousand glorious actions that might claim
> Triumphant laurels and immortal fame,
> Comprised in crowds of glorious actions lie,
> And troops of heroes undistinguished die."

THE WELLINGTON REGIMENT

Casualties (Death only) in Theatres.

THEATRE	Killed in Action Officers	Killed in Action Other Ranks	Died of Wounds Officers	Died of Wounds Other Ranks	Died of Sickness Officers	Died of Sickness Other Ranks	Died of Other Causes Officers	Died of Other Causes Other Ranks	Totals Officers	Totals Other Ranks	GRAND TOTALS
France ...	43	1094	13	383	3	29	3	14	62	1520	1582
Gallipoli ..	13	436	2	80	...	30	...	...	15	546	561
Egypt	...	...	...	...	...	7	...	...	...	7	7
Other Theatres, at Sea, in England, etc. etc.	1	...	...	...	1	31	3	7	5	38	43
Totals. ...	57	1530	15	463	4	97	6	21	82	2111	
Grand Totals	1587		478		101		27		.2193		

Honours and Awards.

The rank shown is the rank held at the time of the award.

The Victoria Cross.

11795 CPL. LESLIE WILTON ANDREW.

For conspicuous bravery when in charge of a small party in an attack on the enemy's position. His objective was a machine-gun post, which had been located in an isolated building. On leading his men forward, he encountered unexpectedly a machine-gun post, which was holding up the advance of another company; he immediately attacked, capturing the machine-gun and killing several of the crew. He then continued the attack on the machine-gun post, which had been his original objective. He displayed great skill and determination in his disposition, finally capturing the post, killing several of the enemy and putting the remainder to flight. Corporal Andrew's conduct throughout was unexampled for cool daring, initiative and fine leadership, and his magnificent example was a great stimulant to his comrades.

10/2950 SGT. JOHN GILROY GRANT.

For conspicuous bravery and devotion to duty near Bancourt on the 1st September, 1918, when Sergeant in command of a platoon forming part of the leading waves of the battalion attacking the high ground to the east of Bancourt. On reaching the crest, it was found that a line of five enemy machine-gun posts offered a serious obstacle to further advance. Under point blank fire, however, the company advanced against these posts. Sergeant Grant, closely followed by a comrade, rushed forward ahead of his platoon and with great dash and bravery entered the centre post, demoralizing the garrison and enabling the men of his platoon to mop up the position. In the same manner he then rushed the post on the left, and the remaining posts were quickly occupied by his company. Throughout the whole operation on this and the two previous days, Sergeant Grant displayed coolness, determination and valour of the highest order, and set a splendid example to all.

Companion of the Order of the Bath.

Brig.-Gen. Hart, H. E., C.M.G., D.S.O.

Companion of the Order of St. Michael and St. George.

Brig.-Gen. Hart, H. E., C.B., D.S.O.

Distinguished Service Order.

Lieut.-Col. Cook, C. F. D.
Lieut.-Col. Cunningham, W. H.
Brig.-Gen. Hart, H. E.
Major Turnbull, F. K., M.C.
Lieut.-Col. Weston, C. H.

THE WELLINGTON REGIMENT

Officer of Most Excellent Order of the British Empire.

Capt. Muir, A. S. (Temp. Major)
Capt. Oram, H.
Capt. Riddiford, R. E. W.
Capt. Treadwell, C. A. L.

Member of Most Excellent Order of the British Empire.

Capt. Kirk, J. R.
Lieut. Burdekin, C. B.
Lieut. Noseda, P. R.
Capt. Porteous, L. V.

Military Cross.

Lt. Ashby, F. E. (Temp. Capt.)
2nd Lieut. Barton, G. A. A.
2nd Lieut. Brown, W. S.
Lieut. Burge, W. R.
2nd Lieut. Cooke, W. B., M.M.
2nd Lieut. Cornwall, F. C.
Lieut. Courtney, J.
Lieut. Crawford, T. H.
Capt. Crosse, H. E.
Lieut. Curham, D. W. (Temp. Capt.)
Lieut. Dallinger, J. T.
2nd Lieut. Dixon, L. M.
Lieut. Fowler, W. K.
2nd Lieut. Galloway, M. S
2nd Lieut. Guthrie, S. G.
2nd Lieut. Hollis, R. V.
Capt. Hume, G. H.
Lieut.-Col. Jardine, L. H.
Capt. Keir, J.
Lieut. King, T. L. R.
Lieut. Lee, C. E.
Lieut. Lepper, C. B.
2nd Lieut. Little, N. F.
2nd Lieut. McIsaac, A. R.
Capt. McKinnon, H. E.
Capt. McLean, W. H.
2nd Lieut. McSaveney, G.
Lieut. Malone, E. L.
Lieut. Melles, A. G.
Capt. Morgan, F. H. E.
2nd Lieut. Morison, D. G. H. B.
2nd Lieut. Nicol, R. K.
Lieut. Nimmo, A. J. (Temp. Capt.)
2nd Lieut. Okey, R. L.
2nd Lieut. Pennefather, S. S., D.C.M.
2nd Lieut. Pettitt, H.
2nd Lieut. Pott, G. F.
2nd Lieut. Price, A. D.
Capt. Rauch, J. N.
Rev. Richards, R.
2nd Lieut. Riddiford, R. E. W.
Lieut. Robinson, C. G. H.
Capt. Rose, J. M.
Lieut. Simmonds, H.
Lieut. Thomas, J. T.
Lieut. Turnbull, F. K.
Capt. Urquhart, M.
Capt. Varnham, F. S.
Chap. Capt. Walls, C.
2nd Lieut. Ward, T. L.
Capt. White, A. T.
Lieut. Wood, R.
Capt. Wrightson, R. W.

Bar to Military Cross.

Lieut. Ashby, F. E., M.C.
Lieut. Burge, W. R., M.C. (Temp. Capt.)
2nd Lieut. Hollis, R. V., M.C.
Capt. McKinnon, H. E., M.C.
Lieut. Melles, A. G., M.C.

THE WELLINGTON REGIMENT

Distinguished Conduct Medal.

14456	Sgt. Baker, F.	47439	Pte. Lang, F.
10/1731	Pte. Barker, C. R.	16560	Pte. Lee, J. A.
10/4448	Pte. Barr, K.	14651	Sgt. Lewis, W. J.
10/274	Cpl. Bennett, P. H. G.	10/1282	Sgt. Macaskill, M.
28078	Sgt. Blundell, E. K.	11/1570	C.S.M. McKean, W.
20290	W.O. 2, Board, S.	10/2228	Pte. Mahoney, F.
10/3199	C.S.M. Boyd, R. A.	10/2235	Sgt. Menzies, C. E.
10207	Cpl. Bradley, A.	7/1121	Sgt. Muir, T.
10/2876	Cpl. Bullock, W. W.	29449	Pte. Murphy, D.
10/2542	L.-Cpl. Carins, L. T. (Temp. Cpl.)	7/2291	Sgt. Murray, W.
13733	C.Q.M.S. Clark, H. O. D.	47458	L.-Cpl. Nettleingham, F. J.
10/3519	Cpl. Cooksley, W. E., M.M.	10/904	Cpl. Notton, A.
10/2901	Sgt. Corkill, R.	10/1307	Pte. O'Connor, F.
31230	Cpl. Crocker, T. R.	10/2732	Cpl. Paterson, A.
33314	Pte. Dallard, C. J.	10/1318	Sgt. Pennefather, S. S.
10/1466	Sgt. Devery, C. N.	10/902	Sgt. Potter, R. C.
11/1271	Cpl. Dibble, S. T., M.M.	53414	Pte. Richmond, T. M. E.
10/3878	L.-Sgt. Foot, S. C.	31353	L.-Cpl. Ritchie, L. R.
22238	Sgt. Forde, M. J.	10/3994	Pte. Ryan, J. E.
26085	W.O. 2 C.S.M. Foster, J. H.	10/1331	L.-Cpl. Scarfe, E. R. F.
10/213	C.S.M. Frost, W. E.	30408	Pte. Sheriff, W.
10/1240	Sgt. Gaston, S.	30650	Sgt. Short, J. D.
9/1556	Cpl. Gilbert, H. P.	10/4576	Pte. Smith, A.
10/2492	Sgt. Goldingham, K. A.	10/1674	Pte. Swan, J. W.
52995	L.-Cpl. Greenbank, L.	10/2778	Sgt. Tannahill, J.
38690	Cpl. Griffiths, J. H.	65612	L.-Cpl. Vial, W. G.
10/4115	Sgt. Heaton, F.	29513	Pte. Thomson, R.
28139	L.-Cpl. Hill, C. T.	10/2379	Sgt. Tunley, F. C.
10/1861	C.S.M. James, W. H.	10/4215	Pte. Vestey, M.
59391	Pte. Lanauze, E.	12/960	Sgt. (Temp. C.S.W.) Ward, M.

Bar to Distinguished Conduct Medal.

10/3878 Sgt. Foot, S. C., D.C.M.

Military Medal.

10/3166	Pte. Adsett, G.	33508	Sgt. Beacock, J. A.
10205	Pte. Alexander, R.	41720	Pte. Beaufort, F. E.
23784	Pte. Anderson, A. D.	10/2855	L.-Sgt. Beck, M.
10/3826	Cpl. Anderson, V. G.	20285	Pte. Belbin, F. A.
10/4048	Sgt. Andrew, J. J.	10/2523	Cpl. Bell, W. D.
52923	Pte. Andrew, W.	10/3832	L.-Cpl. Billing, E. A.
29335	Pte. Andrews, A.	11780	Cpl. Bird, A. F.
10/3468	Sgt. Angus, R.	15672	Pte. Black, E. L.
45810	Pte. Atkinson, E. W.	23790	L.-Cpl. Black, H. McL.
14556	Cpl. Baker, F.	11805	Cpl. Blake, J. R.
38645	L.-Cpl. Ball, W. E.	24/976	Pte. Blakemore, H. B.
11/2299	Pte. Barber, F. C.	10/3493	L.-Sgt. Borlase, W.
31212	Pte. Bargh, C.	63284	Pte. Borrie, D.
10/3476	Cpl. Bargh, W.	6/2488	L.-Sgt. Boyce, T.
41734	Pte. Baty, J. A.	11/2646	Sgt. Brandt, H. J.

THE WELLINGTON REGIMENT

MILITARY MEDAL—continued.

44437	Pte. Brialey, E. S.	10/3552	Pte. Frost, E. W. J.
10/2873	Pte. Brown, G. A.	23820	L.-Cpl. Fuller, E. G.
33511	Pte. Brown, T.	10/2151	Pte. Geange, T.
8/1943	Pte. Brown, W. S.	31996	Pte. Gerrand, J. F.
34504	Pte. Buchanan, G. H.	10/362	Sgt. Gilshnan, S. E.
69442	Pte. Buckeridge, E.	10/360	Pte. Golding, S. W.
13588	Pte. Bullick, T.	9/1558	L.-Cpl. Gordon, C. J.
24/701	Pte. Burke, J. A.	10/1068	Cpl. Gordon, P. A.
10/2878	Cpl. Burnley, L. A. G.	10/2429	Pte. Gray, W. A.
62499	Pte. Burns, S. R.	10/1504	Cpl. Griffin, M.
13/2417	Pte. Burnside, R. J.	30375	L.-Cpl. Haldane, W. J.
22304	L.-Cpl. Butler, A. J.	10/575	L.-Cpl. Hall, A.
14386	Pte. Butterworth, J. S.	31261	Pte. Hamlin, K. W.
61529	Pte. Byrne, N.	31262	L.-Cpl. Hammersley, J. M.
13513	Pte. Cameron, K.		
12694	Pte. Campbell, R.	10/3579	Cpl. Hampton, H. R.
10/4073	L.-Cpl. Chapman, W. C.	10/3581	L.-Cpl. Hannan, W. C.
10/2886	Sgt. Chappell, F. E.	10/2953	L.-Cpl. Hansen, C. W.
11840	Sgt. Charteris, R.	70738	L.-Cpl. Hanson, F. M. H.
15700	Pte. Chirnside, T.		
38121	Pte. Clark, J. W.	10/1250	Cpl. Hardy, J. H.
31233	Pte. Cleland, T. B.	24/1388	Pte. Harris, F. C.
56558	Pte. Closey, F. W.	15717	Pte. Hart, G. H. C.
10/2556	Pte. Collin, B. A.	10/2960	Cpl. Harvey, R. A.
10/314	Sgt. Collis, F.	10/2961	Sgt. Hatton, R.
10/303	Pte. Connell, C. W. (Died since discharge.)	33647	L.-Sgt. Hesse, B.
		38697	Pte. Henderson, A. R.
14587	Pte. Cooke, H.	20525	Pte. Henderson, E.
10/3519	Cpl. Cooksley, W. E.	10/3292	L.-Cpl. Henson, J. H. H.
10/3520	Pte. Coombes, A. N.	39533	Pte. Hinds, C.
10/3521	Pte. Coombes, J. A.	10/3296	Sgt. Holmes, W. A.
11623	L.-Cpl. Cowie, G. M.	61645	Pte. Hopkins, C.
10/2565	Pte. Creed, S. G.	10/3601	Pte. Howatson, A. S.
10/3230	Cpl. Crutchley, L.	57089	Pte. Hudson, R.
10/308	Sgt. Curran, T. M. J.	14638	Pte. Ilton, W. E.
22326	L.-Cpl. Cuthill, R. J.	14642	Pte. Irvine, J.
41763	Pte. Dabner, H.	41562	Pte. Jackson, R. M.
41758	L.-Cpl. Dawbin, H. J.	10/4130	Pte. Jacques, W. H.
30562	Pte. Dillon, A. H.	10/2658	Sgt. Jenkins, D. A.
11/1271	Pte. Dibble, S. T.	15732	L.-Sgt. Jensen, A. R.
10/3159	Sgt. Dinnie, C. H.	39823	Pte. Jensen, E.
31965	Cpl. Dodds, J. T. K.	10/1865	Sgt. Johansen, W. L.
10/2921	Pte. Donovan, C. A.	15733	Pte. Johnson, A. E.
13745	L.-Cpl. Dunford, D. J.	10/793	Cpl. Johnson, H. R.
38001	Pte. Edwards, E. E.	10/3921	Pte. Johnson, J.
10/2596	Sgt. Elliott, W. C. D.	10/3614	L.-Cpl. Johnson, O. H.
14600	L.-Cpl. Evans, W. A.	31293	L.-Cpl. Johnston, E. C.
11/367	Cpl. Fernadez, J.	11/2134	Pte. Jones, D.
57212	Pte. Finn, H. McL.	23838	L.-Cpl. Jones, S. W.
10/2932	Sgt. Finucane, E. M.	25534	Pte. Jopp, J. A.
11/1546	Pte. Fitzgerald, J.	28351	Sgt. Kasper, H. L.
10/2937	L.-Cpl. Fly, M. H.	22998	Pte. Kindberg, A.
25503	Pte. Fowler, S. J. E.	10/3317	L.-Cpl. King, E.
10/2139	L.-Sgt. Francis, W. A.	31302	Pte. Knight, N. R.
10/1239	Sgt. Fraser, D.	10/3320	Pte. Lamb, J. B.
5/767	Cpl. Fraser, J. D.	29031	Pte. Lamb, S.

THE WELLINGTON REGIMENT

MILITARY MEDAL—continued.

61312	Pte. Larkins, H.	20404	Cpl. O'Donnell, H. D.
28168	Pte. Larsen, D. H.	24/1454	Pte. Orr, N.
20173	Pte. Law, N. H.	10/4162	Pte. Otto, W. E.
40020	Pte. Lee, G. J.	9/1599	Cpl. Ovenden, W. B.
10/868	Sgt. Lepper, C. B.	10/1943	Cpl. Overend, W.
14651	L.-Cpl. Lewis, W. J.	12464	Pte. Park, A.
20370	Cpl. Linn, E. J.	10/2275	Pte. Paynter, W. H.
23004	Pte. Lord, C. C.	32055	Pte. Peart, F. W.
10/3938	Pte. Loveday, L. V. G.	40047	L.-Cpl. Petersen, E. P
12/3080	Pte. Lovelock, F.	30636	L.-Cpl. Phaup, T. W.
10/3328	Pte. Low, J. C.	10/1952	Sgt. Pilkington, U.
10/2211	Sgt. Luff, T. R.	23600	Pte. Pirrit, D. A.
19/3638	Pte. Lymer, E.		(Temp. Cpl.)
9/1588	Pte. McCarthy, J. P.	10/3371	L-Cpl. Poots, R.
49157	Pte. McClenaghan, W. T.	8/2100	Pte. Potter, J.
		10/1051	Sgt. Price, A. D.
20392	Cpl. McCracken, J.	2/1815	Cpl. Price, H. G.
22272	L.-Cpl. McCrostie, D. C.	10/3706	Pte. Priest, J. W.
13/3058	Cpl. McCully, A.	14147	Pte. Purcell, A.
11909	Pte. McElligott, J.	28918	L.-Cpl. Quennin, B. G.
10/3008	Cpl. McFarlane, H. M.	12474	Pte. Ramsey, W. E.
24/1435	Pte. McGonagle, D. L.	10/2288	Pte. Randell, P. L.
10/3011	Sgt. McKay, G. R.	33442	Pte. Raynor, C. W.
11/1570	Cpl. McKean, W.	47643	Pte. Rees, W. B.
33396	Sgt. MacKenzie, K.	53067	Pte. Reid, A. E.
65077	Pte. McLellan, A.	23/2526	Pte. Randall, W. S.
10/2693	Cpl. McLelland, W. H.	10/2292	Cpl. Renner, C.
10/3022	Pte. McOnio, G.	10/601	Sgt. Rennie, L. J.
12240	Pte. McPhee, J.	10/3715	L.-Cpl. Revell, E. J.
10/1894	L.-Cpl. Macguire, T. F.	10/3068	L.-Sgt. Richardson, F. G.
22262	Pte. Macklam, A.		
10/817	Sgt. Mackrell, H. H.	49263	Pte. Richardson, T.
13701	Sgt. Mair, A. D.	10/3719	Pte. Rickard, E.
28176	Pte. Matthews, C.	31353	L.-Cpl. Ritchie, L. R.
12427	L.-Cpl. May, W. H.	10/151	Cpl. Roach, G. H.
10/4142	Pte. Metcalfe, M.	23875	L.-Cpl. Robson, J.
24/1426	Sgt. Millar, J.	9/1510	Pte. Rogers, H. F.
32029	Pte. Mitchell, C. C. A.	599978	Pte. Ross, M.
23848	L.-Cpl. Moffitt, W.	23879	Pte. Rossiter, A. A.
11785	Pte. Morgan, C. M.	23/2083	Pte. Ruane, A. T.
42155	Pte. Morris, C. S.	39103	Pte. Rusbridge, H. W.
10/3957	Pte. Morris, P.	10903	L.-Cpl. Ruston, P.
10/2250	Sgt. Moss, J. C.	10/2384	Pte. Schoch, J. B.
51055	L.-Cpl. Moyes, D.	10/518	Sgt. Sciascia, C.
20397	Pte. Needham, D. G.	29496	Pte. Scothern, G. J
11920	Pte. Newell, D. W.	63426	Pte. Scott, J. D.
10/593	Sgt. Nicholas, L. R. (Died since discharge.)	10/2469	Cpl. Scott, W. E.
		29505	L.-Cpl. Sheen, W.
29460	Pte. Nicholls, J. C.	10/3737	Pte. Sims, A. F.
29458	Cpl. Nicholls, T. H.	65468	Pte. Smith, A. G. T.
31337	Pte. Nicholson, M.	10/2765	Pte. Smith, A. J.
10/4159	Pte. Nielsen, M.	13713	Cpl. Smith, H. B.
64113	Pte Nielsen, R. W. E.	15792	Cpl. Smylie, A.
25/220	Sgt. Nilsson, E. I.*	11/1370	Pte. Stedman, A. J.
10281	Cpl. Northe, R. P.	15793	Pte. Still, A. E. (Died since discharge.)
62623	Pte. O'Connor, R. J.		

341

THE WELLINGTON REGIMENT

MILITARY MEDAL—continued.

25962	L.-Cpl. Strahan, T. A.	40410	Pte. Watson, J. A.
10/3095	Cpl. Stuart, D. M.	31386	Pte. Wildsmith, C. T.
11976	Pte. Tait, G. A. G.	28252	Pte. Wiley, H. F.
6/369	Sgt. Thomason, H. H.	23908	Sgt. Wilkie, P. D.
44535	L.-Cpl. Thomson, C.	55877	Pte. Williams, F. J.
10/3760	Sgt. Tod, A. N.	15825	Pte. Willis, H. J.
10/2782	Cpl. Tott, F. G.	10/605	L.-Sgt. Wilson, A. M. de L.
10/4210	Cpl. Trebes, W.		
10/3113	Pte. Trueman, F. L.	10/766	C.S.M. Wood, R. (now 2nd Lieut.)
23/1918	Cpl. Tuke, E. A.		
7/1794	Pte. Turnbull, A.	17/221	Pte. Worthington, L E. J.
28241	Pte. Ure, R. J.		
16015	Pte. Venning, S. J.	10129	L.-Cpl. Wright, A.
15811	Pte. Verran, J. S.	10/4219	Pte. Wright, F.
14704	Pte. Ward, G. A.	10/1711	Pte. Wright, R. F.
10/2787	Pte. Ware, W. G. C.	47495	L.-Cpl. Zeinert, A.
10/674	Sgt. Wasley, W. A.		

Bar to Military Medal.

41734	Cpl. Baty, J. A., M.M.	10/1068	Sgt. Gordon, P. A., M.M.
10/2885	L.-Sgt. Beck, M., M.M.		
12694	Pte. Campbell, R., M.M.	20173	Pte. Law, N. H., M.M.
3/85	Cpl. Carruthers, W., M.M.	10/2787	Pte. Ware, W. G. C., M.M.

Meritorious Service Medal.

10/2874	Pte. Brown, W. E.	10/4415	C.Q.M.S. Maynard, F. C.
10/1427	S.-Sgt. Burdekin, C. B.		
15/136	A.-S.-Sgt. Cameron, J. C.	30609	Sgt. Menzies, G. H.
		10/1920	C.Q.M.S. Miller, W.
10/3446	Sgt. Carrig, T.	10/1293	S.M. Mitchell, C.
10/2048	S.S.M. Castle, S. J.	7/1121	Cpl. Muir, T., D.C.M.
10/1449	Q.M.S. Cooper, M.	10/1066	Sgt. Norman, C.
10/5000	S.M. Davis, D.	10/190	S.S.M. O'Dowd, T. E.
10/1105	Sgt. Edwards, H. T. C.	15/2049A	S.-Sgt. Parsons, R. W. G.
12364	Sgt. Eriksen, E.		
25/177	Pte. Findlay, E. A. (now L.-Cpl.)	11942	Sgt. Quirk, W. J.
		15/139A	S.-Sgt. Rose, D. E. L.
10/600	Sgt. Griffin, G. H.	22498	Pte. Sammons, W. A.
10/15	Sgt. Hawthorne, V. H.	10/3394	Pte. Spicer A. T.
10/2641	Pte. Herbert, E. J.	10/2009	C.S.M. Toye, D. A. W.
10/3671	Pte. McGrath, C. J.	10/192	Sgt. Tresider, A. L.
		10/59	Sgt. Tuohy, J.

Mentioned in Despatches.

10/734	Cpl. Arnold, A. C.	10/262	C.S.M. Bick, H. A. (Temp. S.-Q.M.S.)
10/750	2nd. Lieut. Arthur, N. A		
		23070	Lieut. Blennerhassett, A. R. (Acting Capt.)
10/3476	L.-Cpl. Bargh, W.		
10/1731	Pte. Barker, C. R.	13/11	Lieut. Boscawen, H. T.
10/274	L.-Cpl. Bennett, P. H. G.	23/1564	C.S.M. Bowie, J. H.
		13866	Cpl. Boylen, P.

THE WELLINGTON REGIMENT

MENTIONED IN DESPATCHES—continued.

10/2081	Sgt. Broderick, N. A.	10/1039	Lt.-Col. Malone, W. G. (twice).
10/3203	Sgt. Burgess, C. G.	30609	Sgt. Menzies, G. H.
22599	Capt. Cade, J. R.	10/663	Lieut. Morison, B. H., M.C. (temp. Capt.)
10/706	Pte. Carbines, A. V.		
10/2546	2nd. Lieut. Chamberlain, N. F.	10/2481	Capt. Muir, A. S. (twice).
10/2886	Cpl. Chappell, F. E.	10/658	Major Narbey, W. F.
10/603	2nd Lieut. Chaytor, F. C.	10/1109	Pte. Neale, J.
10/543	Major Cook, C. F. D., D.S.O. (twice).	45894	Sgt. Nicholson, A. J.
		12/3913	Major Oram, H.
10/1450	Capt. Cooper, W. S.	10/909	Cpl. O'Shannessy, J. P.
10/474	Lieut. Cousins, E. G.	27105	Pte. Oliver, W. T.
10/659	Major Cox, E. P.	8/263	Lieut. Pollock, W.
10/2565	Pte. Creed, S. G.	10/910	Lieut. Preston, A. H.
10/729	Pte. Crone, C.	15/76	S.M. Prideaux, F.
10/1085	Lt.-Col. Cunningham, W. H. (three times).	18703	Pte. Primrose, H. L.
		10/1623	T.-Sgt. Quinlan, A.
10/3530	Pte. Dean, A. E.	10/778	Pte. Reid, J. R.
10/3159	Sgt. Dinnie, C. H.	23/2526	Pte. Rendall, W. S., M.M.
10/966	Cpl. Duncan, A. G.		
10/1105	Pte. Edwards, H. T. C. (Acting Sgt.)	9/1623	Lieut. Riddiford, R. E. W., M.C. (twice).
15/8	Lt.-Col. Esson, J. J., C.M.G.	24/1800	Cpl. Ronaldson, A. C.
		10/692	Capt. Rose, J. M.
10/2135	Major Fletcher, W. H.	10/3144	Major Ross, F. (killed in action).
10/2142	Sgt. Freeman, R.		
8/1474	Sgt. Gilling, A.	10/2482	Capt. Scott, R. F. C.
10/1242	C.Q.M.S. Goldup, J. M.	10/2469	Pte. Scott, E.
13750	Cpl. Gordon, W. P.	15/161	C.S.M. Selby, R.
10/3579	Pte. Hampton, H. R.	10/3148	Lieut. Sheldon, H. J. D.
10/1074	Capt. Harston, E. S.		
10/133	Lt.-Col. Hart, H. E., D.S.O. (four times).		Major Short, J. L.
		41235	Capt. Skelley, P. W. (Died of wounds.)
4/1164	2nd. Lieut. Hastedt, B. C.		
		12/460	Sgt. Sparke, S. T.
10/723	Pte. Hayden, H. E.	10/487	S.-Sgt. Swan, C. S.
40700	Sgt. Hendry, H.	10/1674	Pte. Swan, J. W.
46909	Capt. Herbert, L. T.	8/3133	Lieut. Treadwell, C. A. L.
23747	Lt.-Col. Holderness, H.		
10/824	C.S.M. Johnson, A.	10/131	Capt. Turnbull, F. K., M.C. (three times).
10/392	Pte. Johnston, S.		
19213	Capt. Jones, W. H.	10/660	Capt. Urquhart, M.
10/395	Lieut. Jackson, J. K. E.	10/2015	Capt. Varnham, F. S.
15/18	Capt. Kettle, D., M.C.	10/3424	Sgt. Wells, C. M.
10/411	Sgt. Kitto, A.	10/2478	Lt.-Col. Weston, C. H.
20173	Pte. Law, N. H.	11/2005	Lieut. White, A. T.
10/987	Cpl. Little, E.	6/775	2nd. Lieut. Williams, A. J.
10/18	Capt. McColl, A. B. (Killed in action.)		
		14711	L.-Sgt. Wilson, A. W.
10/135	Major McKinnon, H. E.	10/76	Q.M.S. Williams, T. H.
10/3806	Capt. McLean, W. H., M.C.	10/75	Lieut. Wilson, E. R.
		10/1372	Capt. Wrightson, R. W.
10/2228	Pte. Mahoney, F.		

THE WELLINGTON REGIMENT

The names of the following were brought to the notice of the Secretary of State for War for valuable services at Home towards the successful conduct of the War:

Pte. Gaffney, T.
Major Gambrill, R. F.
W.O. 2 Harris, H. W.
Cpl. Henderson, F. G.
2nd. Lieut. Hill, W. S.

Sgt. Kay, L. V.
S.S.M. O'Dowd, T. E.
2nd. Lieut. Pettit, H., M.C.
Capt. Porteous, L. V., M.B.E.

Foreign Decorations.

Medaille Militaire (French).

10/3530	Pte. Dean, A. E.
11/55	Sgt. Gurzell, J.

Croix de Guerre (French).

10/213	C.S.M. Frost, W. E.
10/133	T.B.-Gen. Hart, H. E.
15/18	Major Kettle, D., M.C.
10/658	Major Narbey, W. F.
10/692	Capt. Rose, J. M., M.C.

Medaille d'Honneur (Avec Glaves).

10/2048	S.S.M. Castle, S. J.	1/409	Pte. Sim, W. J. (en Bronze).
30609	Sgt. Menzies, G. H.		
1/175	Sgt. Robertson, J. H. (en Vermeil).	1/43	Sgt. Watson, R. McK. (en Bronze).

Croix de Guerre (Belgian).

10/2399	Sgt. Affleck, E.	10/196	Sgt. Law, A. E.
10/2841	Sgt. Andreassen, T. A.	10/450	L.-Cpl. McChesney, H. J.
13588	L.-Cpl. Bullick, T., M.M.		
49881	Pte. Farquhar, G. R.	11909	Pte. McElligott, J.
10/1507	Sgt. Gunnell, A. J.	10/2782	Sgt. Tott, F. G.

Serbian Gold Medal.

10/626	Pte. Duffill, G.
10/500	Pte. Pederson, E.

THE WELLINGTON REGIMENT

Order of St. Stanislaus, 3rd Class (Russian).
10/1085   Lt.-Col. Cunningham, W. H.

Order of Danilo, 5th Class (Montenegrian).
10/660   Capt. Urquhart, M.

Italian Bronze Medal.
10/3424   Sgt. Wells, C. M

Mentioned in Army Corps Routine Orders.
10/626   Pte. Duffill, G.
10/127   2nd. Lieut. Grace, T. M. P.
10/1674   Pte. Swan, J. W.

THE WELLINGTON REGIMENT

Nominal Roll of Honour of Members of the Regiment who died while serving with the New Zealand Expeditionary Force during the Great War:

Reg. No.	Rank.	Name.	Date death.	Cause.	Place.
18207	2/Lt.	Ackhurst, George	4-10-17	K in A	France
5/1388A	Pte.	Adams, Reginald L.	16- 9-16	K in A	France
16740	Pte.	Adams, Victor H.	17- 7-17	K in A	France
37959	Pte.	Adamson, Alex. J.	4-10-17	K in A	France
54798	Pte.	Addis, John F.	4-11-18	K in A	France
23/1924	Pte.	Ahern, Joseph	31- 8-18	K in A	France
39510	Pte.	Aitchison, F. W. D.	22-10-17	K in A	France
10/956	L/Sgt.	Aitken, Gordon	8- 8-15	K in A	Gallipoli
10/1391A	W/O.2.	Aitken, John	8- 8-15	K in A	Gallipoli
10/1392A	Pte.	Alabaster, Edward H.	21- 4-17	K in A	France
10/2510	Pte.	Aldridge, Ailbe	19- 9-16	D of W	France
10/1393	Pte.	Aldridge, Francis E.	27- 9-16	D of W	France
10/2834	L/Cpl.	Alexander, Charles	16- 9-16	K in A	France
10/3824	Pte.	Alexander, Eric D.	14-12-17	K in A	France
10/205	Pte.	Alexander, William A.	23- 8-15	D of W	Malta ex Gal.
10/4047	Pte.	Algie, Robert	19-11-16	D of W	France
30500	Pte.	Allardice, Henry J.	4-10-17	K in A	France
8/3462	Pte.	Allaway, Albert E.	3- 6-16	K in A	France
10/2056	Pte.	Allen, Edward L.	16- 9-16	K in A	France
23774	Pte.	Allen, Frederick A.	2-10-16	K in A	France
10/3805	Pte.	Allen, Frederick A.	19-11-16	D of W	U.K. ex F"ce.
42007	Pte.	Allen, Stanley	4-10-17	K in A	France
10/2512	Pte.	Allgood, William	25- 6-17	K in A	France
10288	L/Cpl.	Allington, William G.	4-10-17	K in A	France
47384	Pte.	Ambrose, Albert T.	1-10-18	D of W	France
26/1562	Pte.	Ambrose, Charles W.	25-10-17	D of W	France
63991	Pte.	Ambury, Raymond J.	30- 8-18	K in A	France
9/1522	T/Sgt.	Amos, Philip M. M.	7- 5-18	K in A	France
10/398	Pte.	Amos, William H. J.	8- 8-15	K in A	Gallipoli
10/878	Pte.	Amundsen, Ralph	8- 5-15	K in A	Gallipoli
10/2840	Pte.	Andersen, Robert	27- 9-16	K in A	France
30501	Pte.	Anderson, Bertie T.	24-10-17	D of W	France
10/2514	Pte.	Anderson, Gordon D.	3- 7-16	K in A	France
30335	Pte.	Anderson, Herbert J. L.	4-10-17	K in A	France
10/665	Cpl.	Anderson, John F.	8- 8-15	D of W	Gallipoli
35153	Pte.	Anderson, Thomas R.	4-10-17	K in A	France
52552	Pte.	Anderson, William	5- 4-18	K in A	France
31202	Pte.	Anderson, William	16- 7-17	D of W	France

THE WELLINGTON REGIMENT

Reg. No.	Rank.	Name.	Date death.	Cause.	Place.
10/2060	Pte.	Andersen, Charles L. R.	8- 8-15	K in A	Gallipoli
52057	Pte.	Andrew, Charles	26-11-17	K in A	France
10/1397A	Pte.	Andrew, John	8- 8-15	K in A	Gallipoli
10/2842	Pte.	Andrewes, Leonard C.	8- 6-17	K in A	France
10/477	L/Cpl.	Andrews, Hugh D.	16- 9-16	K in A	France
33500	Pte.	Andrews, Thomas	13- 6-17	K in A	France
10/1175	Pte.	Annabell, Fred. F.	27- 4-15	K in A	Gallipoli
10/3469	Pte.	Ånstis, Norman E.	5- 8-16	D of W	U.K. ex F'ce.
10/3828	Pte.	Apted, Albert	4-10-17	K in A	France
61485	Pte.	Archer, Charles R.	30- 8-18	K in A	France
10/959A	Pte.	Argrave, George	8- 8-15	K in A	Gallipoli
10/1398A	Pte.	Arguile, Clarence	8- 8-15	K in A	Gallipoli
10/1399A	Pte.	Argyle, Leonard C.	8- 8-15	K in A	Gallipoli
10/1400A	Pte.	Argyle, Percival	8- 8-15	K in A	Gallipoli
40275	Pte.	Armer, Keith	27- 7-17	K in A	France
10/478	Pte.	Armstrong, L. C.	9- 5-15	D of W	At sea ex Gal.
10/1727	Pte.	Armstrong, Martin	8- 8-15	K in A	Gallipoli
52358	Pte.	Arnaboldi, Philip G.	15-10-17	K in A	France
10/1069	Cpl.	Arnold, Harry	27- 4-15	K in A	Gallipoli
13/2410	L/Cpl.	Arnott, William P.	31- 7-17	K in A	France
50978	Pte.	Arrowsmith, Alfred	14-12-17	K in A	France
10/792	Pte.	Arthur, Hedley C.	7- 8-15	Disease	Gib. ex Gal.
33274	Pte.	Ash, Henry E.	4-10-17	K in A	France
10/1401B	Pte.	Ashman, Thomas G.	1-10-15	D of W	Turkey ex Gallipoli
23780	Pte.	Ashworth, Ernest	2-10-16	K in A	France
10/1402	Pte.	Ashworth, Robert	8- 8-15	K in A	Gallipoli
11/2022	L/Cpl.	Astbury, Eric D.	9- 6-17	K in A	France
10/1176	Pte.	Aston, Eardley H.	16- 9-16	K in A	France
10/179	Pte.	Attwood, Edward B.	8- 8-15	K in A	Gallipoli
10/1178	Cpl.	Auld, Robert W.	26- 8-15	D of W	Egypt ex Gallipoli
10/3175	Pte.	Austin, Horace	5-10-17	D of W	France
10/2518	Pte.	Bacon, Thomas R.	15- 8-16	K in A	France
17744	Pte.	Bailey, Leonard W.	31- 7-17	K in A	France
10/3177	Pte.	Bailey, William E.	28-11-17	K in A	France
10/716	Pte.	Baily, Ronald H.	24- 9-15	D of W	U.K. ex Gal.
10/1404	Pte.	Bain, James	5- 8-15	Sickness	At Sea ex Gallipoli
10/1730	Lt.	Bain, John S.	8- 8-15	K in A	Gallipoli
10/198	L/Sgt.	Baines, Arthur	8- 8-15	K in A	Gallipoli
24/1587	Pte.	Baker, Arthur	20- 9-16	K in A	France
10/288	Pte.	Baker, Cecil F.	8- 8-15	K in A	Gallipoli
5/513A	Pte.	Baker, Frederick G.	21-10-17	K in A	France

THE WELLINGTON REGIMENT

Reg. No.	Rank.	Name.	Date death.	Cause.	Place.
10/3178	Pte.	Baker, Henry J.	2-10-16	K in A	France
10/2846	Pte.	Baker, Montrose A.	12-10-16	D of W	U.K. ex F"ce.
10/2847	L/Sgt.	Baldwin, Stanley	21- 8-17	K in A	France
23/1545	L/Cpl.	Ballard, Frank E.	28- 7-16	K in A	France
29351	Pte.	Ballinger, Thomas E.	23- 6-17	K in A	France
10/1405	Pte.	Banks, Arthur G.	15- 8-15	D of W	Gallipoli
33098	Lt.	Banks, Henry D.	4-11-19	K in A	France
10/2849	Pte.	Banks, Harold V.	1- 2-18	K in A	France
42013	Pte.	Bannatyne, Charles E.	20-12-17	K in A	France
10/167	Pte.	Bannerman, E. I.	29- 4-15	K in A	Gallipoli
14557	Pte.	Bannister, Alex. M.	6-11-19	Disease	N.Z. ex F"ce.
14558	Pte.	Bannister, Stanley M.	20- 6-17	D of W	France
10/2404	Sgt.	Barber, James	14- 6-16	Accd. K.	France
12/3908	Pte.	Barber, Thomas E.	17- 9-16	K in A	France
7/1175	Pte.	Barber, Valentine J.	14- 7-16	K in A	France
12/2207	Sgt.	Barlow, Alfred	11-10-18	K in A	France
10/3180	Pte.	Barlow, John B.	29-11-17	K in A	France
10/1408	Pte.	Barnby, Henry	8- 8-15	K in A	Gallipoli
33503	Cpl.	Barnes, Harry F.	17-10-17	D of W	France
45811	Pte.	Barnes, John	4-10-17	K in A	France
10/1733	Pte.	Barnes, Victor J.	8- 8-15	K in A	Gallipoli
11/1405	Pte.	Barnett, Herbert E.	10- 6-17	K in A	France
10/2664	Pte.	Barns, Daniel	24-10-17	D of W	France
51299	Pte.	Barriball, A. E. C.	12-10-18	K in A	France
10/2852	L/Cpl.	Barter, James H.	3- 8-18	Disease	U.K.
49138	Pte.	Bartlett, Stan. A.	27- 3-18	K in A	France
10277	Pte.	Barton, Frank A. J.	31- 7-17	K in A	France
41723	Pte.	Barton, Harry C.	1- 8-17	K in A	France
15661	Pte.	Bartosh, Richard A.	2- 5-17	K in A	France
29339	Pte.	Barugh, John	24- 8-18	K in A	France
56529	Pte.	Bate, Thomas	16-10-18	D of W	U.K. ex F"ce.
10/3846	Pte.	Batley, Norman P.	10- 7-16	K in A	France
10/2067	Sgt.	Battison, Walter	28- 9-16	K in A	France
10/275	Pte.	Baxter, Bernard E.	29- 4-15	K in A	Gallipoli
10/278	Pte.	Baxter, Edgar T.	8- 8-15	K in A	Gallipoli
10/1736	L/Cpl.	Bayler, Frank W.	8- 8-15	K in A	Gallipoli
10/2068	Pte.	Bayne, George A.	8- 8-15	K in A	Gallipoli
10/44	Pte.	Bayne, James	4- 9-15	K in A	Gallipoli
31943	Pte.	Beach, Edward	26- 7-17	K in A	France
10/3181	Pte.	Beach, Harold L.	16- 9-16	D of W	France
10/1410	Pte.	Bealing, Francis W.	8- 8-15	K in A	Gallipoli
10/1411	Pte.	Beard, Charles	8- 8-15	K in A	Gallipoli
39741	Pte.	Beattie, Charles L.	7- 8-17	D of W	France
47844	Pte.	Beattie, Phillip E.	27- 3-18	K in A	France
11801	Pte.	Beattie, Robert A.	14- 9-16	K in A	France

THE WELLINGTON REGIMENT

Reg. No.	Rank.	Name.	Date death.	Cause.	Place.
10/2853	Pte.	Beatty, Arthur	30- 3-18	K in A	France
23788	Pte.	Beauchamp, P. F. W.	6- 2-19	Disease	U.K.
10/2855	Sgt.	Beck, Matthias (M.M. and Bar)	4-10-17	K in A	France
36941	Pte.	Beech, John T.	10- 8-17	K in A	France
10/2069	Pte.	Behrent, Walter H.	8- 8-15	K in A	Gallipoli
10/2070	Pte.	Bell, Cameron	27- 9-16	K in A	France
10/125	Pte.	Bell, Henry G. T.	8- 5-15	K in A	Gallipoli
38646	Pte.	Bell, Richard	27- 3-18	K in A	France
10/636	Pte.	Bell, Roy C.	17- 6-15	Disease	Australia ex Gallipol
14562	L/Cpl.	Benington, H. S.	31- 7-17	K in A	France
10/123	Pte.	Bennell, Robert T.	8- 8-15	K in A	Gallipoli
14372	Pte.	Bennet, Charles E.	26-10-16	K in A	France
19/13	Pte.	Bennett, Henry	10-10-18	Disease	N.Z. ex F"ce.
49664	Pte.	Bennett, William B.	20-12-17	K in A	France
10/2071	Pte.	Benson, Isaac R.	8- 8-15	K in A	Gallipoli
10/1740	Pte.	Bentley, Edgar N.	31- 7-17	K in A	France
10/3482	Sgt.	Benton, Joseph L.	1-10-18	D of W	France
10/649	Pte.	Beresford, W. R.	8- 8-15	K in A	Gallipoli
29352	Pte.	Bern, James R.	4-10-17	K in A	France
10/783	L/Sgt.	Bernard, Arthur C.	8- 8-15	K in A	Gallipoli
47393	Pte.	Berry, Charles R.	1-10-18	K in A	France
21143	Sgt.	Berry, William J. V.	31- 7-17	K in A	France
10/3188	Pte.	Bertaud, Harold I.	16- 9-16	K in A	France
20288	Pte.	Best, Frederick J.	24- 8-18	D of W	France
14374	Pte.	Best, James	31- 7-17	K in A	France
10/1417	Pte.	Bethune, Roderick	9- 5-15	D of W	At sea ex Gallipoli
15671	Pte.	Betteley, Fred.	5- 4-18	K in A	France
10/1742	Pte.	Bickens, Henry F.	8- 8-15	K in A	Gallipoli
10/132	2/Lt.	Bicknell, Cyril A.	23- 6-16	Injuries	France
13/3003	Pte.	Biddick, George J.	28- 9-16	K in A	France
59304	Pte.	Biddle, Walter E.	20-12-17	K in A	France
44691	Pte.	Bidgood, Andrew	4-10-17	K in A	France
41713	Pte.	Bidmead, John V.	30- 3-18	K in A	France
11619	Pte.	Biggs, Bertie	4-10-17	K in A	France
10/755	Pte.	Biggs, William H.	8- 8-15	K in A	Gallipoli
72614	Pte.	Billesden, John W.	4-11-18	K in A	France
10/3832	L/Cpl.	Billing, E. A. (M.M.)	12- 4-18	D of W	France
59305	Pte.	Birbeck, John R. S.	28-12-17	K in A	France
2/1138	Pte.	Birnie, Charles	25- 8-17	D of W	France
10/304	Pte.	Bissett, G. F. McG.	27- 4-15	K in A	Gallipoli
28612	T. L/Sgt.	Bjermquist, C. H.	4-10-17	K in A	France
10208	Cpl.	Black, Alfred R.	30- 3-18	K in A	France

THE WELLINGTON REGIMENT

Reg. No.	Rank.	Name.	Date death.	Cause.	Place.
19109	Pte.	Black, Fred. R.	5- 4-17	Disease	U.K. ex F"ce.
10150	Sgt.	Black, Harry	29- 3-18	D of W	France
31214	Pte.	Black, Hugh R.	7- 6-17	K in A	France
10/3488	Pte.	Black, John	11-10-16	D of W	U.K. ex F"ce.
1/528	Sgt.	Black, John W.	4-10-17	K in A	France
15673	Pte.	Black, Sydney M.	26- 8-18	K in A	France
10/280	Pte.	Black, William	2-10-15	Disease	Malta ex Gallipoli
14747	Pte.	Black, William	21- 2-17	K in A	France
10/2075	Pte.	Blackburn, Samuel A.	16- 9-16	K in A	France
10291	Pte.	Blackmore, Arthur	8- 8-15	K in A	Gallipoli
10/680	Pte.	Blackstock, Irving	24- 4-15	K in A	Gallipoli
28420	Pte.	Blain, Edward	3- 7-17	D of W	France
10/1746	Pte.	Blake, Arthur S.	4-10-17	K in A	France
10/808	Cpl.	Blake, Phillip	8- 8-15	K in A	Gallipoli
10/1420	Pte.	Blake, Thomas M.	·8- 8-15	K in A	Gallipoli.
24/976	Pte.	Blakemore, H. B. (M.M.)	4-10-17	K in A	France
10304	Pte.	Blaramberg, C. D.	10-12-16	K in A	France
23070	(Lt.) (A/Cap.)	Blennerhassett, A. R. (M.I.D.)	4-11-18	K in A	France
48160	Pte.	Body, Frank	27- 3-18	K in A	France
48432	Pte.	Boggs, Joseph W.	27- 2-20	Accd. K.	N.Z.
13723	Pte.	Bogun, Charles P.	18- 4-18	D of W	France
10/1024	2/Lt.	Bollinger, George W.	10- 6-17	D of W	France
45630	Pte.	Bolstad, John A.	4-10-17	K in A	France
10/1116	Sgt/Mjr.	Bonar, Archibald J. M.	28- 4-15	K in A	Gallipoli
10/3839	Pte.	Booth, William	15- 6-16	K in A	France
41733	Pte.	Booth, Willie	22- 7-18	K in A	France
10/3195	Pte.	Borthwick, John R.	7- 6-17	K in A	France
13/11	Capt.	Boscawen, Hugh T.	4-10-17	K in A	France
31940	Pte.	Bosse, Albert	31- 7-17	K in A	France
10/2866	Pte.	Bosworth, William	27- 9-16	K in A	France
61507	Pte.	Bougen, John	1- 9-18	D of W	France
10/4439	W.O.1	Bould, Charles W.H.	27- 9-16	K in A	France
10/4056	Pte.	Boult, Charles	15-10-16	D of W	France
10/943	Pte.	Bourgeous, Arthur	8- 8-15	K in A	Gallipoli
10/3196	Pte.	Bouttell, John A.	8- 6-17	K in A	France
50009	Pte.	Bouvett, Albert	14-11-17	Disease	France
52565	Pte.	Bowden, Alfred H. F.	9-10-18	D of W	France
33509	Pte.	Bowden, Edward J.	6-10-17	D of W	France
10/645	Cpl.	Bowden, Keble R.	8- 5-15	K in A	Gallipoli
22683	Pte.	Bowden, William R. H.	17- 6-17	K in A	France
65333	Pte.	Bowen, Robert C. B.	29- 9-18	D of W	France
37963	Pte.	Bowers, Charles W.	17-10-17	K in A	France

THE WELLINGTON REGIMENT

Reg. No.	Rank.	Name.	Date death.	Cause.	Place.
61509	Pte.	Bowie, Henry J.	29- 9-18	K in A	France
10/1421	Pte.	Bowker, George A.	8- 8-15	K in A	Gallipoli
10/2077	L/Cpl.	Bowles, Edmond	12-10-18	K in A	France
13/3133	Pte.	Boyle, Claude	15- 9-16	K in A	France
33289	Pte.	Bracken, William J.	13- 9-18	K in A	France
29345	Pte.	Bradley, Victor S.	18- 6-17	K in A	France
23/1566	Pte.	Bradley, William G.	12- 7-16	D of W	France
52370	Pte.	Brame, Albert V.	24- 8-18	D of W	France
45815	Pte.	Brandon, Leonard V.	13- 9-18	K in A	France
50993	Pte.	Brannigan, Edward	14- 5-18	D of W	France
10/1749	Pte.	Breach, Edward	2- 9-15	D of W	Egypt ex Gallipoli
10/2078	Pte.	Breen, James J.	8- 8-15	K in A	Gallipoli
10/277	Pte.	Brettargh, Ronald O.	8- 8-15	K in A	Gallipoli
23/1570	Pte.	Brew, Percival S.	2-10-16	K in A	France
10/2079	Pte.	Brewer, Charles T.	8- 8-15	K in A	Gallipoli
10/950	Pte.	Brewer, James W.	8- 8-15	K in A	Gallipoli
10/1423	Pte.	Brierley, Fred.	8- 8-15	K in A	Gallipoli
10/1073	Sgt.	Brimer, Cyril T.	23- 9-16	K in A	France
50995	Pte.	Brinkman, Norman H.	24- 8-18	K in A	France
61515	Pte.	Bristow, George H.	18-10-18	K in A	France
10/969	L/Sgt.	Britten, Vivian R.	8- 8-15	K in A	Gallipoli
69758	Pte.	Broadhead, Ben.	13- 8-18	K in A	France
10/2488	Sgt.	Brodie, Gordon	24-11-15	K in A	Gallipoli
10/3201	T/Cpl.	Brodribb, Fred. J.	16- 9-16	K in A	France
10/295	Cpl.	Brokker, Alfred E.	20- 4-17	D of W	France
15677	Pte.	Brooking, Arnold W.	5-11-18	D of W	France
10/273	Pte.	Broome, Harry E. M.	10- 5-15	K in A	Gallipoli
30339	Pte.	Brough, Julian P.	4-10-17	K in A	France
10/3841	Pte.	Brough, William	28- 9-16	K in A	France
10/806	Pte.	Brown, Alan	7- 5-15	K in A	Gallipoli
64004	Pte.	Brown, Albert	24- 8-18	K in A	France
10/2083	Pte.	Brown, David B.	4-10-17	K in A	France
38114	Pte.	Brown, David T.	12- 6-17	D of W	France
10/662	Pte.	Brown, Frank R.	26- 4-15	K in A	Gallipoli
10/4065	Pte.	Brown, Frank R.	3-10-16	K in A	France
10/1192	Pte.	Brown, Herbert W.	8- 5-15	K in A	Gallipoli
10/2084	Pte.	Brown, James P.	8- 8-15	K in A	Gallipoli
63287	Pte.	Brown, John	30- 9-18	K in A	France
10/283	Pte.	Brown, John Love	8- 5-15	K in A	Gallipoli
2/1424A	Pte.	Brown, John M.	28- 8-15	Disease	Malta ex Gallipoli
39749	Pte.	Brown, Michael	17- 8-17	K in A	France
38112	Pte.	Brown, Reginald E.	4-10-17	K in A	France
22226	Sgt.	Brown, William G. N.	20-10-18	Disease	U.K.

THE WELLINGTON REGIMENT

Reg. No.	Rank.	Name.	Date death.	Cause.	Place.
10/4067	Pte.	Brown, William R.	17- 7-18	Disease	France
54826	Pte.	Bruce, Daniel L.	18-11-17	K in A	France
10/1426	Pte.	Bruce, David	8- 8-15	K in A	Gallipoli
28082	Pte.	Bruce, William	1-10-18	K in A	France
10/2536	Pte.	Bruen, Austin H.	10-11-15	K in A	Gallipoli
29341	Pte.	Brunt, Arthur	30- 3-18	K in A	France
10/298	Pte.	Bryant, Hedley	10- 5-15	D of W	Gallipoli
9/2155	Pte.	Bryce, Hamish T.	20- 9-16	K in A	France
10/2875	Pte.	Buchan, James	16- 9-16	K in A	France
14383	Pte.	Bullen, Thomas J.	31-10-16	D of W	France
13588	L/Cpl.	Bullick, T. (M.M.) C.D.G. (Belgian)	29 -9-18	K in A	France
10/2876	Cpl.	Bullock, Walter W. (D.C.M.)	4-10-17	K in A	France
10/3844	Pte.	Bunyan, John	3- 7-16	K in A	France
67516	Pte.	Burgess, Charles D.	14-10-18	K in A	France
10/16	L/Cpl.	Burgess, Charles W.	29- 4-15	K in A	Gallipoli
12/3570	Pte.	Burgess, Claude E.	11- 7-16	D of W	France
28072	Pte.	Burgess, Thomas J.	24- 8-18	K in A	France
10/3833	Pte.	Burkitt, Frank E.	12- 6-16	K in A	France
11810	Pte.	Burn, Gordon S.	27- 3-18	D of W	France
10/540	L/Cpl.	Burns, Allan C.	8- 8-15	K in A	Gallipoli
10/805	Pte.	Burr, Gordon	8- 8-15	K in A	Gallipoli
23/88	Pte.	Burr, James	16- 9-16	D of W	France
10/1671	Pte.	Burridge, Richard S.	8- 8-15	K in A	Gallipoli
44440	Pte.	Burrow, Robert	17-12-17	K in A	France
10/862	Cpl.	Burrows, John H.	8- 8-15	K in A	Gallipoli
10/1764	Pte.	Bussell, James	17-10-16	Disease	Turkey ex Gallipoli
10/2089	L/Cpl.	Butcher, Albert	16- 9-16	K in A	France
10/297	Pte.	Butcher, Joseph	15- 8-15	D of W	Egypt ex Gallipoli
10/4069	Pte.	Butler, Daniel D. D.	29- 6-16	K in A	France
38655	Pte.	Butler, Joseph C. T.	27- 3-18	K in A	France
47620	Pte.	Butler, Joseph T.	4-10-17	K in A	France
54420	Cpl.	Butler, L. A. G. J.	26- 8-18	K in A	France
10/1429	Pte.	Butler, Richard P.	1-10-16	K in A	France
10/276	Pte.	Butler, William J. I.	8- 8-15	K in A	Gallipoli
14386	Pte.	Butterworth, J. S. (M.M.)	29- 9-18	D of W	France
28100	Pte.	Calcinai, Alfred B.	26- 7-17	D of W	France
31220	Pte.	Calder, Willie B.	8- 6-17	K in A	France
59465	Pte.	Callaghan, C. H. L.	11-10-18	K in A	France
23141	Pte.	Callaghan, Claude	29- 9-16	K in A	France
37972	Pte.	Callaghan, Edward	4-10-17	K in A	France

THE WELLINGTON REGIMENT

Reg. No.	Rank.	Name.	Date death.	Cause.	Place.
1/9	Pte.	Cameron, Harry J.	18- 7-18	K in A	France
33514	Pte.	Cameron, James	31- 3-18	D of W	France
28099	Pte.	Cammock, Frank H.	14-10-17	K in A	France
X 10/1060	L/Cpl.	Cammock, William R.	16- 8-15	D of W	Malta ex Gallipoli
10/802	Pte.	Campbell, Archibald	10- 8-15	D of W	At Sea ex Gallipoli
10/1203	L/Sgt.	Campbell, Ernest W.	8- 8-15	K in A	Gallipoli
13294	L/Cpl.	Campbell, George C.	21- 6-17	D of W	France
10/310	L/Cpl.	Campbell, James	8- 5-15	K in A	Gallipoli
10/1201	Pte.	Campbell, John	8- 8-15	K in A	Gallipoli
10/1028	Pte.	Campbell, John A.	14-12-14	Disease	Egypt
62129	Pte.	Campbell, M. McL.	30- 3-18	K in A	France
10/1202	Pte.	Campbell, William	13- 9-15	Disease	Egypt ex Gallipoli
10/3850	Pte.	Campbell, William A.	23- 9-16	D of W	France
31165	Pte.	Cannell, Hugh N.	2-10-18	K in A	France
29358	Pte.	Capstick, Arthur A.	8-10-17	D of W	France
10/706	Pte.	Carbines, Arthur V. (M.I.D.)	8- 8-15	K in A	Gallipoli
6/3959	2/Lt.	Carey, Cyril F.	7-11-16	D of Injs. (accidental)	U.K.
23755	Pte.	Carey, Elija J.	14-10-16	D of W	France
10/740	2/Lt.	Cargo, James R.	3- 6-15	K in A	Gallipoli
30349	L/Cpl.	Carley, Sydney E.	4-10-17	K in A	France
33110	Pte.	Carmody, James	4-10-17	K in A	France
10/2387	Pte.	Carpenter, George S.	8- 8-15	K in A	Gallipoli
10/1156	Pte.	Carr, Edward J.	30- 4-15	D of W	At Sea ex Gallipoli
15685	Pte.	Carr, Percy R.	9- 6-17	K in A	France
15686	Pte.	Carrington, Bernard	31- 7-17	K in A	France
22492	Pte.	Carroll, John	21- 2-17	K in A	France
3/85	2/Lt.	Carruthers, Walter (M.M. & Bar)	29- 9-18	K in A	France
61357	Pte.	Carswell, George A.	16- 5-18	K in A	France
10/142	Pte.	Carswell, Norman E.	8- 5-15	K in A	Gallipoli
33298	Pte.	Carter, Albert B.	4-10-17	K in A	France
24529	Pte.	Carter, Charles	16- 9-16	K in A	France
10/2098	Pte.	Carter, Felix	8- 8-15	K in A	Gallipoli
15687	Pte.	Carter, Herbert	41- 7-17	K in A	France
10/1435	Pte.	Carter, John	8- 8-15	K in A	Gallipoli
65653	Pte.	Cartwright, Archie L.	1-10-18	D of W	France
51556	Pte.	Cassidy, Samuel R.	30- 3-18	K in A	France
17/382	Pte.	Caswell, William	23- 6-17	K in A	France
10/3216	L/Cpl.	Cattell, Sam.	20- 7-16	D of W	France

THE WELLINGTON REGIMENT

Reg. No.	Rank.	Name.	Date death.	Cause.	Place.
10/3503	Pte.	Cattermole, James	13-10-16	D of W	France
24/1615	Pte.	Chambers, Harry	16- 9-16	K in A	France
11828	Pte.	Chambers, James F.	15- 9-16	K in A	France
10/1439	Pte.	Chapman, Frank T.	7- 5-15	K in A	Gallipoli
10/3505	T/Cpl.	Chapman, Frederick	2- 4-17	D of W	France
10/709	Pte.	Chapman, Fred. O.	11- 7-15	D of W	Egypt ex Gallipoli
69464	Pte.	Chapman, James W.	30- 9-18	K in A	France
10/2411	Pte.	Chapman, Sydney P.	8- 8-15	K in A	Gallipoli
28094	L/Cpl.	Chard, Albert H.	1-10-18	K in A	France
10/1440	Pte.	Charles, Edward H.	8- 8-15	K in A	Gallipoli
10/845	L/Cpl.	Charleston, Alex. A.	16- 9-16	K in A	France
39758	Pte.	Charlesworth, George	12- 8-18	Disease	U.K.
10/2547	Pte.	Charman, William H.	16- 9-16	K in A	France
10/1773	Sgt.	Chatfield, Joseph	20- 7-18	D of W	France
10/237	Pte.	Chinnery, Daniel C.	8- 5-15	K in A	Gallipoli
10/3508	Pte.	Chisnall, Richard W.	3- 7-16	K in A	France
10/1206	Pte.	Christensen, A. O.	20- 7-15	Disease	At Sea ex Gallipoli
23763	L/Cpl.	Christensen, A. R.	9- 6-17	D of W	France
10/2548	Pte.	Christiansen, G. W. F.	23- 5-18	K in A	France
61218	Pte.	Christie, Alexander	16-10-18	D of W	France
15691	Pte.	Christie, Anderson	14-12-17	K in A	France
10/765	Pte.	Christie, Augustus	1- 6-17	D of W	France
44455	Pte.	Christieson, William J.	4-10-17	D of W	France
10/719	Cpl.	Claffey, Joseph	15- 5-15	D of W	Egypt ex Gallipoli
28323	Pte.	Claffey, Patrick J.	4-10-17	K in A	France
10/3217	Pte.	Clague, William A.	8- 6-17	K in A	France
28429	Pte.	Clapham, Harry C.	16- 3-18	Disease	France
10/2367	Lt.	Clark, Alexander J.	13- 8-15	K in A	Gallipoli
32818	Pte.	Clark, Daniel S.	18- 7-17	K in A	France
10/1775	Pte.	Clark, Ernest W.	26- 8-15	D of W	Egypt ex Gallipoli
51688	Pte.	Clark, George	26-10-17	D of W	France
10/3857	Pte.	Clark, Ian C.	16- 9-16	K in A	France
10/2103	Pte.	Clark, James	16- 5-17	Disease	U.K. ex Gal.
10/2890	Pte.	Clark, James D.	16- 9-16	K in A	France
49292	Pte.	Clark, Percy N.	30- 3-18	K in A	France
10/1132	L/Cpl.	Clark, Samuel G.	8- 8-15	K in A	Gallipoli
37768	Pte.	Clark, Sydney	17-10-17	D of W	France
51300	Pte.	Clark, Willie H.	21- 4-18	D of W	France
28616	2/Lt.	Clarke, Ernest	24- 8-18	K in A	France
52576	Pte.	Claxton, Albert P. J.	1- 9-18	K in A	France
11/2308	Pte.	Clay, Blakeman J.	16- 9-16	K in A	France

THE WELLINGTON REGIMENT

Reg. No.	Rank.	Name.	Date death.	Cause.	Place.
14757	Pte.	Cleary, Sidney	31- 7-17	D of W	France
31222	Pte.	Clegg, James Elias	27- 7-17	D of W	France
9/1413	L/Cpl.	Clemens, Herbert J.	11-10-18	K in A	France
51005	Pte.	Clement, Mark	20-10-17	K in A	France
10/977	Pte.	Clement, Sydney G.	8- 8-15	K in A	Gallipoli
17697	L/Cpl.	Cliff, James E.	7- 7-18	Disease	At Sea ex Gallipoli
33520	Pte.	Clifford, Leslie James	4-10-17	K in A	France
69466	Pte.	Close, Frank	4-11-18	K in A	France
31958	Pte.	Cobeldick, Eric W.	26- 7-17	K in A	France
10/313	Pte.	Cochrane, Albert D.	8- 8-15	K in A	Gallipoli
25817	Pte.	Codd, Albert C.	18-10-17	D of W	France
28093	Pte.	Codd, Herbert H.	7- 6-17	K in A	France
15696	Pte.	Codd, William E.	15- 8-17	K in A	France
10/842	L/Cpl.	Cogar, Charles L.	8- 8-15	K in A	Gallipoli
10/843	Pte.	Cogar, Richard	5- 6-15	K in A	Gallipoli
41741	Pte.	Cole, Arthur	12- 6-18	Disease	U.K. ex F"ce.
10/931	Sgt.	Cole, Charles H.	30- 7-15	K in A	Gallipoli
11832	Pte.	Cole, Rex	8- 2-18	K in A	France
31953	Pte.	Coleman, Cecil	12-10-17	D of W	France
10/1778	Pte.	Coleman, Charles	8- 8-15	K in A	Gallipoli
26/1574	Pte.	Coles, James	1-10-18	K in A	France
10/1446	Pte.	Colhoun, Albert	8- 8-15	K in A	Gallipoli
47622	Pte.	Collett, Charles W.	25- 8-18	K in A	France
59326	Pte.	Collier, William	11- 8-18	K in A	France
6/2492	Pte.	Collin, Rupert	16- 9-16	K in A	France
10/2893	Pte.	Collinson, Robert W.	8- 6-17	K in A	France
10/3221	Cpl.	Comeskey, James	29- 7-18	Accd. K	France
10/2894	Pte.	Comeskey, Peter L. C.	16- 9-16	K in A	France
10/317	L/Cpl.	Comyns, Claude L.	25- 9-15	Accd. K	N.Z.
29360	Pte.	Connell, Alfred H.	4-10-17	K in A	France
10/3223	Pte.	Connell, Henry J.	9- 7-16	Accd. K.	France
10/3517	Pte.	Connolly, John	3- 9-18	D of W	France
47405	Pte.	Connolly, Patrick	29- 8-18	K in A	France
10/1948	Pte.	Connolly, Robert H.	8- 8-15	K in A	Gallipoli
51106	Pte.	Connor, John	2- 4-18	K in A	France
10/4077	Pte.	Conwell, Robert	1- 3-17	D of W	France
10/543	Lt.-Col.	Cook, Charles F. D. (D.S.O., M.I.D.) (2)	2- 5-18	Disease	U.K.
13/3014	Pte.	Cook, Graham W.	11- 7-16	D of W	France
10/1006	L/Cpl.	Cook, Henry G.	7- 6-17	K in A	France
47407	Pte.	Cook, James J.	4-12-17	K in A	France
10/2896	Pte.	Cook, Robert J.	22- 5-16	D of W	France
13738	L/Cpl.	Coombe, Reginald T.	24- 8-18	K in A	France
10/1215	Sgt.	Coonan, John T.	8- 8-15	K in A	Gallipoli

THE WELLINGTON REGIMENT

Reg. No.	Rank.	Name.	Date death.	Cause.	Place.
10/380A	Pte.	Cooper, Albert G.	26-12-14	Disease	Egypt
11837	L/Cpl.	Cooper, Arthur	27- 3-18	D of W	France
54471	Pte.	Cooper, Douglas H.	30- 9-18	K in A	France
10/1448	Pte.	Cooper, Ernest	8- 8-15	K in A	Gallipoli
8/1438	Pte.	Cooper, John H.	1-10-16	K in A	France
10/1780	Pte.	Cooper, Victor W.	8- 8-15	K in A	Gallipoli
10/666	Cpl.	Copeland, William J.	2- 5-15	K in A	Gallipoli
15694	Pte.	Corbett, Albert	23- 6-17	K in A	France
20305	L/Cpl.	Corbett, Robert S.	1-10-18	D of W	France
33521	Pte.	Corcoran, Thomas	30-11-17	D of W.	France
11/407	Pte.	Corlett, Alfred H.	8- 8-15	K in A	Gallipoli
10/2562	Sgt.	Corlett, Arthur B.	11- 8-16	K in A	France
10/307	Pte.	Corlett, Franklin	8- 8-15	K in A	Gallipoli
24/1003	Pte.	Corsar, Charles S.	19- 5-16	Accd. K	France
52582	Pte.	Coster, Alfred C. C.	30- 3-18	K in A	France
12355	Pte.	Courtney, Eugene L.	29- 9-16	D of W	France
10/116	Lt.	Cowan, Andrew R.	15- 5-15	D of W	At Sea ex Gallipoli
20971	Pte.	Cowan, James L.	8- 6-17	D of W	France
10/3809	2/Lt.	Cowie, Alfred C.	2-10-16	K in A	France
10/1216	Pte.	Cowley, James	8- 8-15	K in A	Gallipoli
11839	Pte.	Cowling, Frank W.	10-12-16	K in A	France
10/173	Pte.	Cox, George T.	14- 5-15	D of W	At Sea ex Gallipoli
41430	2/Lt.	Cox, Norman D.	31- 8-18	K in A	France
10/2903	Pte.	Coxhead, David	17- 9-16	K in A	France
29363	Pte.	Coxhead, George	17-11-18	Disease	N.Z.
25/1699	Pte.	Cox-Smith, Stephen	4-10-16	D of W	France
10/2108	Pte.	Craig, George	31-10-15	Disease	N..Z ex Gal.
10186	Pte.	Craig, James	30- 9-16	K in A	France
10/2563	Pte.	Cranney, Augustin J.	29-11-17	K in A	France
8/3225	Cpl.	Crannitch, John	1- 8-17	D of W	France
10/2564	Pte.	Cranswick, Thomas B.	7- 6-17	K in A	France
23803	Pte.	Crawford, Hugh M.	4- 5-17	D of W	France
13426	Pte.	Crawford, James	19- 9-16	K in A	France
10/3226	Pte.	Crawford, James T.	19- 3-19	Disease	Germany after Armistice
10/2908	Sgt.	Crawford, L. J. B. C.	12-10-18	K in A	France
10/3445	Pte.	Creamer, Robert H.	8- 6-17	K in A	France
12974	Pte.	Creaney, Mark O.	4-10-17	K in A	France
10/2567	Pte.	Cress, Leonard J.	17- 9-16	D of W	France
45829	Pte.	Cresswell, Edward G.	29-11-17	K in A	France
10/1783	Pte.	Crocombe, Walter	8- 8-15	K in A	Gallipol
10/3227	L/Cpl.	Crofskey, John	23- 6-17	K in A	France

356

THE WELLINGTON REGIMENT

Reg. No.	Rank.	Name.	Date death.	Cause.	Place.
10/3158	Cpl.	Crombie, Fred. W.	7- 6-17	K in A	France
10/718	Cpl.	Crompton, Thomas S.	5- 3-17	K in A	France
10/729	Pte.	Crone, C. (M.I.D.)	8- 8-15	K in A	Gallipoli
51696	Pte.	Cronin, Edward J.	3- 4-18	K in A	France
14589	Pte.	Crosbie, Andrew	26- 6-17	K in A	France
33313	Pte.	Crossman, Edwin L.	13- 9-18	K in A	France
26998	Cpl.	Crothers, Fred. C.	4-11-18	D of W	France
46121	Pte.	Crouch, Frank	4-10-17	K in A	France
9/1537	Pte.	Crowley, Michael	3-10-16	D of W	France
10/2390	Cpl.	Crowther, Albert S.	21-10-17	D of W	France
10/3869	Pte.	Cruickshank, William	14-12-16	Acc. In.	France
23807	Pte.	Crump, Ernest F.	24-11-16	K in A	France
23/1962	Pte.	Cumming, Greig	3- 7-16	K in A	France
10/306	Pte.	Cummins, Colin G.	8- 8-15	K in A	Gallipoli
10/1460	L/Sgt.	Cunningham, D.	22- 6-17	D of W	France
18/2571	Pte.	Cunningham, L. J.	2-12-15	Disease	At Sea ex Mudros
24/1633	Cpl.	Curran, Clifford H.	13- 9-16	K in A	France
10/3526	Pte.	Currie, Arthur	7- 6-17	K in A	France
10/2572	Pte.	Currie, George C.	5- 6-16	D of W	France
61227	Pte.	Currie, James	23- 8-18	K in A	France
10/3870	Cpl.	Currie, Walter	4-10-17	K in A	France
31231	Pte.	Curry, Albert B.	17-10-17	D of W	France
10/3232	Pte.	Curtis, Norman H. E.	29- 9-16	K in A	France
28091	Cpl.	Cuthbert, John	31- 7-17	K in A	France
10/3233	Pte.	Cutten, George	11- 3-18	Disease	At Sea on route to N.Z.
64031	Pte.	Dalzell, Alex. G.	27- 5-19	Disease	U.K.
10/2398	Pte.	Daniel, Robert J.	8- 8-15	K in A	Gallipoli
10/1787	Pte.	Darville, Percy L.	28- 6-15	K in A	Gallipoli
12358	Pte.	D'Ath, Cuthbert	10- 6-17	D of W	France
10/2417	Pte.	Davidson, Joseph H.	8- 8-15	K in A	Gallipoli
10/882	L/Cpl.	Davidson, Karl N.	16- 9-16	D of W	France
10/1124	2/Lt.	Davidson, Thomas A.	8- 8-15	K in A	Gallipoli
10/2578	Pte.	Davidson, William A.	8-12-15	D of W	Egypt ex Gallipoli
10/664	Pte.	Davidson, William P.	31- 8-15	D of W	Gallipoli
16/2916	Pte.	Davies, James	2- 8-17	D of W	France
10/334	Pte.	Davies, William	8- 8-15	K in A	Gallipoli
10/2112	Pte.	Davis, Fred. A.	8- 8-15	K in A	Gallipoli
10/1044	Sgt.	Davis, Llewelyn T.	5- 9-15	D of W	Gallipoli
13430	Cpl.	Davis, Sydney G.	27- 7-17	K in A	France
10/1222	Pte.	Davis, Thomas	8- 5-15	K in A	Gallipoli
10/2114	Pte.	Davy, Nelson	8- 8-15	K in A	Gallipoli
27734	Pte.	Dawe, Thomas W. E.	5-10-18	D of W	France

THE WELLINGTON REGIMENT

Reg. No.	Rank.	Name.	Date death.	Cause.	Place.
10/1790	Pte.	Dawson, Basil F.	8- 8-15	K in A	Gallipoli
10/2583	T/Sgt.	Dawson, James W.	25- 9-16	K in A	France
20309	Pte.	Dawson, Samuel J.	4-10-17	K in A	France
10/1464	Pte.	Day, Robert J.	10- 5-15	D of W	At Sea ex Gallipoli
47623	Pte.	Daysh, William E.	24- 8-18	K in A	France
10/1465	Pte.	Dellow, John	8- 8-15	K in A	Gallipoli
38358	L/Cpl.	Dempsey, Earnest H.	24-11-17	K in A	France
28620	Pte.	Dempster, Thomas D.	4-10-17	K in A	France
10/621	Cpl.	Demsey, George D.	8- 8-15	K in A	Gallipoli
10/2418	Pte.	Dennehy, B. J.	3- 7-16	K in A	France
10/633	Pte.	Denny, Richard J.	8- 8-15	K in A	Gallipoli
61560	Pte.	Denton, Ernest H.	13- 9-18	K in A	France
36741	Pte.	Depree, John G.	24- 8-18	K in A	France
10/1467	Pte.	Dew, Arthur L.	8- 8-15	K in A	Gallipoli
5/332	Pte.	Deverson, Bertie G.	16- 9-16	K in A	France
23810	Pte.	Dewar, Davidson B.	11-12-16	D of W	France
13428	Pte.	Dewar, Ernest	15- 9-16	K in A	France
11844	L/Cpl.	Diamond, Herbert A.	22-10-17	K in A	France
51018	Pte.	Dickie, John D.	5- 4-18	K in A	France
10/1468	Pte.	Dickson, Donald McK.	18- 7-15	K in A	Gallipoli
59874	Pte.	Diggleman, Otto	4-11-18	D of W	U.K. ex F"ce.
20311	L/Cpl.	Dillon, William A.	4-10-17	K in A	France
20117	Pte.	Dimond, Harry	1- 8-17	K in A	France
28106	Pte.	Dixon, James A.	20- 6-17	D of W	France
7/2376	L/Cpl.	Doak, David J. W.	30- 3-18	D of W	France
27666	Pte.	Doak, Stephen	4-10-17	K in A	France
10/1470	Pte.	Dobbie, Reg. H. V.	8- 8-15	K in A	Gallipoli
10/3240	T/L.S.	Dobbyn, Joseph L.	2-10-16	K in A	France
10/3807	Lt.	Dobson, Reg. H.	18- 9-16	K in A	France
28109	Pte.	Dodunski, Paul	4-10-17	K in A	France
23812	Pte.	Doherty, Adam T.	7- 6-17	K in A	France
32788	Cpl.	Doig, James	4-10-17	K in A	France
28111	L/Cpl.	Donald, William K.	15- 6-17	D of W	France
10/1795	Pte.	Donkin, William S.	8- ·8-15	K in A	Gallipoli
36956	Pte.	Donne, John A.	7- 7-17	D of W	France
10/2588	Pte.	Donnelly, Francis P.	2-10-16	K in A	France
10/157	Pte.	Donnelly, George J.	8- 5-15	K in A	Gallipoli
19128	Cpl.	Doran, Edmund J.	2- 9-18	D of W	France
51020	Pte.	Doran, Fred. A.	20-10-17	K in A	France
23/1375	Pte.	Doria, Leonard J.	8- 6-17	K in A	France
10/2589	Pte.	Dorset, David A.	26- 9-16	K in A	France
10/326	Pte.	Dorsett, Charles H.	9- 5-15	D of W	Gallipoli
24353	2/Lt.	Doughty, William T.	31- 7-17	K in A	France
10/4502	Pte.	Douglas, James	17- 9-16	K in A	France

THE WELLINGTON REGIMENT

Reg. No.	Rank.	Name.	Date death.	Cause.	Place.
29750	Pte.	Douglas, William	6- 4-18	D of W	France
10/2826	Cpl.	Downard, Sam. C. G.	23- 7-16	D of W	France
10/2119	Sgt.	Downing, Albert J.	8- 8-15	K in A	Gallipoli
10/2582	Pte.	Dowson, Tom	27- 9-16	K in A	France
31239	Pte.	Dowthwaite, Henry A.	31- 7-17	K in A	France
25489	Pte.	Doyle, Arthur E.	8- 6-17	K in A	France
25/21	2/Lt.	Doyle, Henry T.	10-10-18	Drowned At Sea	
52972	Pte.	Driscoll, Thomas	27- 3-18	K in A	France
10/580	Pte.	Driver, Thomas	8- 8-15	K in A	Gallipoli
29377	Pte.	Druitt, Alfred	4-10-17	K in A	France
10/1473	Pte.	Drummond, Robert	19- 9-16	D of W	France
70760	Pte.	Dudley, W. A. De V.	9-11-18	D of W	U.K. ex F
10/626	Pte.	Duffill, George (Serbian Gold Medal)	4-10-17	K in A	France
10/1801	Pte.	Duggan, Clarence K.	8- 8-15	K in A	Gallipoli
33525	Pte.	Duggan, James	30- 3-18	K in A	France
10/4090	Pte.	Duller, Arthur L.	25- 9-16	K in A	France
10/1802	Pte.	Dunbar, Alex. C.	8- 8-15	K in A	Gallipoli
10/236	Pte.	Dunbar, Robert	8- 6-17	K in A	France
10/966	Cpl.	Duncan, Alex. G. (M.I.D.)	7- 8-15	K in A	Gallipoli
10/3247	Pte.	Dunlop, Matthew A.	15- 9-16	K in A	France
18587	Pte.	Dunn, Alexander J.	6- 8-17	D of W	France
24/1032	Pte.	Dunn, Allan	4-10-17	K in A	France
10/594	Pte.	Dunn, John R.	8- 8-15	K in A	Gallipoli
10/328	Pte.	Dunn, Robert C.	8- 8-15	K in A	Gallipoli
10/113	Pte.	Dunnage, Robert G.	8- 5-15	K in A	Gallipoli
61578	Pte.	Dunne, Jock D.	24- 8-18	K in A	France
38803	Pte.	Dunne, William P.	23-10-17	K in A	France
37998	Pte.	Durose, Harold	23- 4-18	D of W	France
10/330	L/Sgt.	Dust, Gilbert F.	8- 5-15	K in A	Gallipoli
10/1229	Pte.	Dustin, Claude	16- 5-15	K in A	Gallipoli
27248	Pte.	Duval, William	11- 2-18	K in A	France
10/2593	Pte.	Dyett, Arthur F.	23-10-16	Injuries	France
11850	Pte.	Dyke, William H.	3-10-16	K in A	France
33527	Pte.	Eagleson, Robert	30- 8-18	K in A	France
61579	Pte.	Eames, Leslie J.	4- 5-18	K in A	France
10/340	Pte.	Earles, Robert W.	9- 5-15	K in A	Gallipoli
10/1232	Pte.	Earley, Edward J.	8- 8-15	K in A	Gallipoli
10/1231	Pte.	Earley, William	8- 5-15	K in A	Gallipoli
22957	Pte.	Earp, Harry	2- 1-18	K in A	France
33147	Pte.	Eden, James A.	9- 9-18	D of W	France
10/335	Sgt.	Edwards, John H.	30- 9-18	K in A	France
10/1475	Pte.	Edwards, John H.	8- 8-15	K in A	Gallipoli

THE WELLINGTON REGIMENT

Reg. No.	Rank.	Name.	Date death.	Cause.	Place.
59196	Pte.	Edwards, Joseph H.	1-10-18	K in A	France
44461	Pte.	Eiffe, John K.	4-10-17	K in A	France
11852	L/Sgt.	Elcock, Sidney J.	4-11-18	K in A	France
10/2124	Pte.	Ellaby, Cecil A.	8- 8-15	K in A	Gallipoli
10/962	Pte.	Ellery, Cecil T.	4- 5-15	K in A	Gallipoli
10/1476	Pte.	Ellingham, Claude	8- 8-15	K in A	Gallipoli
22490	Pte.	Elliott, Norman L.	8- 6-17	K in A	France
10/1234	Pte.	Elliott, William	15- 5-15	D of W	Egypt ex Gallipoli
10/2925	Cpl.	Elliott, William H. M.	3-10-17	D of W	France
10/2127	L/Cpl.	Ellis, Alfred G.	16- 9-16	D of W	France
10/2129	Pte.	Elmes, John E.	18-11-15	D of W	At Sea ex Gallipoli
17/51	Pte.	Elrick, John	14- 7-16	K in A	France
9/1555	Pte.	Garrard-Elsworth, E. G.	1-10-16	K in. A	France
38792	Pte.	Elton, Charles E. S.	15- 9-18	Disease	U.K. ex F'ce.
10/337	Cpl.	Enright, Percy	8- 8-15	K in A	Gallipoli
52398	Pte.	Ernest, David	3- 4-18	K in A	France
23751	2/Lt.	Esam, Stanley O.	16- 9-16	K in A	France
22567	Pte.	Esselborn, W. R. L.	4-10-17	K in A	France
10/1805	Pte.	Eustace, Alfred	21- 8-15	D of W	At Sea ex Gallipoli
51561	Pte.	Evans, Robert E.	12- 9-18	D of W	France
14600	L/Cpl.	Evans, Walter A. (M.M.)	3-10-18	K in A	France
36166	Pte.	Evans, William J.	25- 8-18	K in A	France
10/2597	Pte.	Evers-Swindell, Fred.	4-10-17	K in A	France
10/3875	Pte.	Ewing, Alexandra	16- 9-16	K in A	France
61585	Pte.	Ewing, John C. L.	24- 8-18	K in A	France
28003	Pte.	Exell, Benjamin	5-10-17	D of W	France
21237	Pte.	Fair, Bertram R.	20- 4-17	K in A	France
33531	Pte.	Fair, Richard A.	4-10-17	K in A	France
20131	Pte.	Falconer, James J.	8- 6-17	K in A	France
10/777	Pte.	Falconer, William C.	8- 8-15	K in A	Gallipoli
23817	Pte.	Farmer, Reuben A.	4-10-17	K in A	France
5/1483A	Pte.	Farrell, William F.	20-10-17	K in A	France
10/50	Pte.	Fayen, Louis W.	8- 5-15	K in A	Gallipoli
10/704	Pte.	Fearon, Henry G.	8- 8-15	K in A	Gallipoli
29381	Pte.	Feek, Gordon S.	30- 3-18	K in A	France
10/2816	Lt.	Fell, Gerald H.	7- 6-17	K in A	France
52075	Pte.	Fenemor, Edwin J.	1- 9-18	K in A	France
39788	Pte.	Ferguson, David	24-10-17	K in A	France
28119	Pte.	Ferguson, John A.	4-10-17	K in A	France
46984	Pte.	Ferris, Robert A.	4-11-18	K in A	France

THE WELLINGTON REGIMENT

Reg. No.	Rank.	Name.	Date death.	Cause.	Place.
11857	Pte.	Fever, Harold J.	1-10-16	D of W	France
10/347	Pte.	Field, Henry G.	8- 8-15	K in A	Gallipoli
19136	Pte.	Fife, Douglas A.	22- 6-17	K in A	France
39789	Pte.	Fill, Henry V.	4-10-17	K in A	France
10/344	Pte.	Findlay, Matthew	19- 5-16	D of W	U.K. ex Gallipoli
29383	Pte.	Finlay, Andrew C.	8- 6-17	K in A	France
33532	Pte.	Finlay, George R.	4-10-17	K in A	France
10/2602	Pte.	Finlayson, Robert L.	30- 7-18	D of W	France
10/1166	Pte.	Fisher, Edward H.	29- 4-15	K in A	Gallipoli
10/628	L/Cpl.	Fisher, George J.	2-10-16	K in A	France
47871	Pte.	Fitzell, Robert T.	14- 4-18	K in A	France
52402	Pte.	Fitzgerald, C. F.	21-10-17	K in A	France
11/1546	Pte.	Fitzgerald, John (M.M.)	2-10-16	K in A	France
10/2604	Pte.	Fitzgerald, Joseph	30- 8-18	K in A	France
31247	Pte.	Fitzmaurice, H. S.	7- 6-17	K in A	France
39577	Pte.	Fitzsimons, E. J. P.	9- 8-17	D of W	France
10/2935	Cpl.	Flavell, Carleton	7- 6-17	K in A	France
32511	Pte.	Fleming, William G.	18- 8-17	K in A	France
10/1812	Pte.	Fletcher, Herbert	8- 8-15	K in A	Gallipoli
10/3798	Pte.	Fletcher, Samuel	14-10-16	D of W	France
5/244A	2/Lt.	Flood, John W.	8-11-18	D of W	France
10/1157	Pte.	Flynn, Robert S.	8- 8-15	K in A	Gallipoli
10/2136	L/Cpl.	Fogarty, Thomas J.	16- 9-16	K in A	France
10/1813	L/Cpl.	Foley, John C. T.	17- 7-15	K in A	Gallipoli
37796	Pte.	Forbes, Colin	26-11-18	Disease	U.K.
11/475	Pte.	Ford, Charles A.	28- 9-16	K in A	France
38679	Pte.	Forde, Norman A.	3-10-17	K in A	France
64051	Pte.	Forster, George	1-10-18	K in A	France
10/1054	L/Cpl.	Forsyth, Archibald J.	29- 4-15	K in A	Gallipoli
10/2607	Pte.	Foster, Alfred J.	17- 9-16	K in A	France
10/3258	Pte.	Foster, Alfred M.	10- 6-17	D of W	France
10/1815	Pte.	Foster, Francis J.	17- 9-16	K in A	France
52405	Pte.	Fowler, William	5- 4-18	K in A	France
10/2137	Pte.	Fox, George D.	8- 6-17	K in A	France
25504	Pte.	Fox, James	11- 4-18	K in A	France
24532	Pte.	Fox, Thomas	16- 9-16	K in A	France
10/3880	Pte.	Frampton, Albert E.	6-10-16	D of W	U.K. ex F"ce.
11/1314	Pte.	Francis, Frederick W.	31- 7-17	K in A	France
10/2138	Pte.	Francis, Gilbert B.	13-11-15	D of Dis.	Malta ex Gallipoli
10/2139	L/Sgt.	Francis, William A. (M.M.)	7- 5-17	K in A	France
10/1169	Capt.	Frandi, Ateo	Between May 6 & 10, 1915	K in A	Gallipoli

THE WELLINGTON REGIMENT

Reg. No.	Rank.	Name.	Date death.	Cause.	Place.
38005	Pte.	Frank, Karl W.	16- 8-17	D of W	France
10/4424	Pte.	Franklin, Lovel W. H.	15- 9-16	K in A	France
37191	Pte.	Franklin, Samuel W.	31-10-17	Disease	France
33344	Pte.	Franklyn, Henry W.	10-10-17	D of W	France
10/1817	Pte.	Fraser, Arthur J.	8- 8-15	K in A	Gallipoli
51033	Pte.	Fraser, Donald	17-10-18	Disease	N.Z.
31251	Pte.	Fraser, Douglas	8- 6-17	K in A	France
10/957	Pte.	Fraser, Kinnear G.	27- 4-15	K in A	Gallipoli
10/252	Pte.	Fraser, Malcolm	8- 8-15	K in A	Gallipoli
28120	Pte.	Freeman, Charles H. C.	3- 5-17	K in A	France
47418	Pte.	Freeman, John	4-10-17	K in A	France
10/1489	Pte.	Freeman, Joseph A.	8- 8-15	K in A	Gallipoli
36965	Pte.	Freeman, Norman	5-10-17	D of W	France
10/2142	Sgt.	Freeman, R. (M.I.D.)	22- 5-18	K in A	France
8/2596	Pte.	Frew, David H.	7- 6-17	K in A	France
10/263	Pte.	Friis, Franklyn	21- 9-16	D of W	France
10/213	W.O. 11	Frost, W. E. (D.C.M.) (Croix-de-Guerre, French)	17- 8-16	D of W	France
10/1072	Sgt.	Fryday, Edward John	12- 5-15	D of W	Egypt ex Gallipoli
12/2550	Sgt.	Fulcher, Harry E.	4-10-17	K in A	France
12/4529	Cpl.	Funke, Harold H.	27- 3-18	K in A	France
10/3883	Pte.	Furze, Claude N.	18- 9-16	K in A	France
10/3884	Pte.	Furze, James H.	16- 9-16	K in A	France
44470	Pte.	Gage, Charles	4-10-17	D of W	France
10/3263	Pte.	Galbraith, Robert	16- 9-16	K in A	France
10/2147	Pte.	Galloway, Robert	8- 8-15	K in A	Gallipoli
29387	L/Cpl.	Gandy, William F.	4-10-17	K in A	France
31993	Pte.	Garaway, Frank D.	26- 7-17	K in A	France
10/923	Pte.	Gardner, Alfred	8- 8-15	K in A	Gallipoli
10/1820	Pte.	Garland, William J.	1- 9-15	Disease	At Sea ex Mudros
64053	Pte.	Garven, George J.	24- 8-18	K in A	France
41780	Pte.	Gaskell, Ephraim	11-10-18	K in A	France
56586	Pte.	Gaskell, Norman	11-11-18	Disease	U.K.
10/573	Pte.	Gaskin, Herbert H.	8- 6-15	D of W	Egypt ex Gallipoli
24425	Pte.	George, Frank W.	4-10-17	K in A	France
31254	Pte.	Gerrard, Thomas	13- 8-18	D of W	France
30573	Pte.	Geyger, Leon	2- 5-18	D of W	France
10/2943	L/Cpl.	Gibb, George A.	11- 2-17	K in A	France
15712	Pte.	Gibbons, Arnold W. R.	31-10-16	K in A	France
10/91A	Pte.	Gibbons, Austin	20- 9-16	D of W	France

THE WELLINGTON REGIMENT

Reg. No.	Rank.	Name.	Date death.	Cause.	Place.
17/303	L/Cpl.	Gibbons, Walter J.	30- 9-16	K in A	France
12380	Pte.	Gibbs, Arthur C. G.	2-10-16	K in A	France
10/2945	Pte.	Gibbs, Joseph	17- 9-16	D of W	France
11767	Lt.	Gibbs, Walter G.	26- 9-18	D of W	France
11858	Pte.	Giblin, Percy	3- 9-18	D of W	France
38010	Pte.	Gibson, Llywelyn G.	4-11-18	K in A	France
23824	Pte.	Gibson, Percy N.	19- 4-17	K in A	France
24/1663	Pte.	Giddens, John T.	2-10-16	K in A	France
10/1822	Pte.	Gifford, Robert	8- 8-15	K in A	Gallipoli
10/3562	Sgt.	Gilchrist, Hugh	30- 5-16	D of W	France
11864	Pte.	Gilchrist, William H.	17- 9-16	D of W	France
45852	Pte.	Gill, David Roy	30- 9-18	K in A	France
10/2617	Cpl.	Gill, William J.	19- 5-18	K in A	France
10/3265	Pte.	Gillies, Duncan	14- 6-16	K in A	France
38151	Pte.	Gillies, Walter	9-10-17	D of W	France
39525	Cpl.	Gilligan, James F.	4- 5-18	K in A	France
25508	Pte.	Gisborne, Henry	4-10-17	K in A	France
10/3813	Pte.	Given, John E.	16- 9-16	K in A	France
44468	Pte.	Given, William	4-10-17	K in A	France
10/1825	Pte.	Glasgow, John M.	8- 8-15	K in A	Gallipoli
28460	Pte.	Glendinning, John	27- 3-18	K in A	France
10/2368	Pte.	Glenny, George H.	25- 9-15	Disease	Mudros ex Gallipoli
49889	Pte.	Glover, John S.	11-10-18	K in A	France
3/498	L/Cpl.	Goddard, Douglas	26-11-16	K in A	France
59354	Pte.	Godfrey, Frazil E.	12-10-18	K in A	France
10/4459	Pte.	Godfrey, Joseph F. W.	22- 7-16	D of W	France
1/279	Pte.	Godsell, Amos W.	7- 6-17	K in A	France
10341	L/Cpl.	Goldsmith, Fred.	22-10-17	K in A	France
51035	Pte.	Goldsmith, Fred. P.	7- 2-18	K in A	France
10/2159	Pte.	Goldstone, William	8- 8-15	K in A	Gallipoli
71394	Pte.	Gooding, Arthur J.	22-11-18	D of W	France
10/1495	Pte.	Goodwin, Charles	8- 8-15	K in A	Gallipoli
10/3889	Pte.	Goodwin, Walter E.	4-10-17	K in A	France
10/1496	Pte.	Gordon, George A.	2- 8-15	K in A	Gallipoli
29390	Pte.	Gordon, Robert	10- 6-17	D of W	France
10/2392	Pte.	Gosling, John T.	8- 8-15	K in A	Gallipoli
10/4460	Pte.	Gould, Frank	20- 9-16	K in A	France
33539	Pte.	Gould, John E.	4-10-17	K in A	France
48493	Pte.	Goulstone, John W.	30- 3-18	K in A	France
59358	Pte.	Gourlay, Albert J.	1-11-18	D of W	U.K. ex F"ce.
28464	Pte.	Gowland, Wilfred	21-10-17	K in A	France
10/127	2/Lt.	Grace, Thomas M. P.	8- 8-15	K in A	Gallipoli
10/366	Pte.	Graham, Alex. H.	1- 5-15	K in A	Gallipoli
10/3570	Pte.	Graham, Frederick	29-10-16	K in A	France

THE WELLINGTON REGIMENT

Reg. No.	Rank.	Name.	Date death.	Cause.	Place.
10/261	Pte.	Graham, Hugh	28- 5-15	K in A	Gallipoli
10/1829	Pte.	Graham, John	8- 8-15	K in A	Gallipoli
24006	Pte.	Granger, Claude A.	1-10-17	D of W	France
31838	Pte.	Grant, Arnold E.	27- 3-18	K in A	France
10/2163	Pte.	Grant, Charles K.	8- 8-15	K in A	Gallipoli
22428	Pte.	Grant, Robert	31- 7-17	K in A	France
46988	Pte.	Gray, Alex. R.	1- 9-18	K in A	France
10/361	Pte.	Gray, Douglas W.	8- 5-15	K in A	Gallipoli
10/357	2/Lt.	Gray, James H.	9- 5-15	D of W	At Sea ex Gallipoli
20332	Pte.	Gray, Percy S.	29-11-17	K in A	France
10/1498	Pte.	Gray, W. A. (M.M.)	1- 4-18	K in A	Gallipoli
10/2429	Sgt.	Gray, W. A. (M.M.)	1- 4-18	K in A	France
23/1649	Pte.	Green, Albert J.	14- 7-16	D of W	U.K. ex F'ce.
49813	Pte.	Green, Fred. L.	14-12-17	K in A	France
51040	Pte.	Greenaway, Finlay	31- 8-18	D of W	France
10/833	Pte.	Greene, Jasper A.	16- 9-16	K in A	France
59362	Pte.	Greenwell, John	27- 8-18	D of W	France
48494	Pte.	Greenwood, Joseph E.	30- 3-18	K in A	France
10/3137	Pte.	Greig, Robert W.	1- 6-16	K in A	France
10/2626	Pte.	Greig, William	16- 9-16	K in A	France
10/3315	Pte.	Grennell, Richard P.	28- 4-16	D of Sickness, France	
10/735	Pte.	Grey, John	2-12-17	K in A	France
10/1504	Sgt.	Griffin, Martin (M.M.)	12-10-18	K in A	France
29393	Pte.	Griffiths, Alfred V.	21-10-17	K in A	France
10/1505	Pte.	Griffiths, Richard	8- 8-15	K in A	Gallipoli
10/883	Cpl.	Griffiths, Sidney J.	15- 8-15	D of W	Egypt ex Gallipoli
10/354	Pte.	Griffiths, William J.	30- 4-15	D of W	At Sea ex Gallipoli
10/721	Pte.	Grimmer, Frank W.	10- 8-15	D of W	At Sea ex Gallipoli
10/4108	Pte.	Grooby, Henry A.	16- 9-16	K in A	France
42092	Pte.	Grundy, William T.	26-11-17	D of W	France
15714	L/Cpl.	Guest, John	18- 4-18	D of W	France
10/3576	L/Cpl.	Guilford, Cecil	4- 5-18	D of W	France
10/364	Sgt.	Gunn, William A.	30- 4-15	D of W	At Sea ex Gallipoli
45859	Pte.	Hacket, Lawrence	4-10-17	K in A	France
10/3276	Pte.	Haddon, Eustace F.	13-10-17	D of W	France
10/1831	Sgt.	Hadfield, Frederic W.	30- 8-18	K in A	France
10/610	Pte.	Hagenson, Alfred	13- 7-15	K in A	Gallipoli
10/368	Sgt.	Haines, Lance H.	8- 8-15	K in A	Gallipoli
10/218	Pte.	Haining, William	8- 5-15	K in A	Gallipoli
10/371	L/Cpl.	Hales, Howard W.	16- 9-16	K in A	France

THE WELLINGTON REGIMENT

Reg. No.	Rank.	Name.	Date death.	Cause.	Place.
39589	Pte.	Hales, Wilfred F.	15- 6-17	D of W	France
31263	Pte.	Haliday, Edward A. R.	8- 6-17	K in A	France
23/2195	Sgt.	Hall, Arthur T.	4-10-17	K in A	France
68330	Pte.	Hall, Francis	4-11-18	K in A	France
39802	Pte.	Hall, George	4-10-17	K in A	France
61290	Pte.	Hall, Hugh	13- 9-18	K in A	France
6/245	Pte.	Hall, Jack	1-12-17	K in A	France
49814	Pte.	Hall, John	24-11-17	K in A	France
10/3278	Pte.	Hall, Reynolds	17- 9-16	K in A	France
10/401	L/Cpl.	Hall, Stacey M.	16- 9-16	K in A	France
31259	Pte.	Hall, Thomas B.	7- 6-17	K in A	France
10/651	Cpl.	Hall, Vincent J. B.	2- 6-15	D of W	Egypt ex Gallipoli
33356	Pte.	Hall, William J.	21- 7-17	K in A	France
13438	Pte.	Hallett, James T.	8- 6-17	K in A	France
47425	Pte.	Hallgarth, Albert J.	14-12-17	K in A	France
44481	Pte.	Hambling, H. L. E.	28- 2-18	D of W	U.K. ex F"ce.
10/3915	Pte.	Hamblyn, Henry John	3-10-16	K in A	France
10/3894	Pte.	Hamblyn, James E.	27- 7-17	K in A	France
25517	Pte.	Hamblyn, Thomas D.	8- 6-17	K in A	France
25516	Pte.	Hamblyn, William C.	8- 6-17	K in A	France
11/1803	Pte.	Hamilton, Albert S.	3- 4-18	D of W	France
10/4464	Pte.	Hamilton, David	8-10-16	D of W	France
10/3578	L/Sgt.	Hamilton, John M.	5- 6-16	K in A	France
39527	Pte.	Hamilton, Noel	27- 3-18	D of W	France
10/2952	Pte.	Hamilton, William	4- 5-18	K in A	France
65390	Pte.	Hampton, William H.	13- 9-18	K in A	France
52419	Pte.	Handley, Thomas	3- 4-18	K in A	France
10/3580	Pte.	Hanify, Godfrey P.	16- 9-16	K in A	France
61274	Pte.	Hanlon, Bertie A. M.	21- 9-18	D of W	France
11/194	Pte.	Hannett, Arthur A.	11-10-16	D of W	France
10/2953	Cpl.	Hansen, C. W. (M.M.)	4-10-17	K in A	France
10/73	Pte.	Hansen, Charles	8- 5-15	K in A	Gallipoli
41797	Pte.	Hansen, David	31- 8-18	D of W	France
25868	Pte.	Hansen, Viggo	8- 6-17	K in A	France
10/637	Cpl.	Hansford, W. W.	5-10-17	D of W	France
23767	Pte.	Hansen, Clarence J.	31- 7-17	D of W	France
10/1510	Pte.	Happer, Thomas	6- 6-15	K in A	Gallipoli
10/1511	Pte.	Harding, Alfred H.	8- 8-15	K in A	Gallipoli
10/738	Pte.	Harding, Alfred R. F.	26- 4-15	K in A	Gallipoli
64059	Pte.	Hardy, Harry	24- 8-18	K in A	France
10/1834	Pte.	Hardy, Joe	8- 8-15	K in A	Gallipoli
15716	Pte.	Hardy, Lancelot	26- 7-17	K in A	France
61291	Pte.	Hare, Robert	22- 5-18	D of W	France
31267	Pte.	Harkness, Alex. D.	16- 8-18	D of W	France

THE WELLINGTON REGIMENT

Reg. No.	Rank.	Name.	Date death.	Cause.	Place.
24365	2nd Lt.	Harle, Douglas A.	4-10-17	K in A	France
10/2430	Pte.	Harlen, Percy	14-11-15	Disease	Mudros ex Gallipoli
10/4114	Pte.	Harmell, Anton F.	27- 9-16	K in A	France
29401	Pte.	Harnett, Francis J.	8- 6-17	K in A	France
8/397	Pte.	Harnett, James	16- 9-16	D of W	France
14545	2/Lt.	Harper, Arthur H. S.	9-12-16	Disease	France
62057	Pte.	Harre, William	11-10-18	K in A	France
10/598	Pte.	Harris, Alexander	8- 8-15	K in A	Gallipoli
11871	Pte.	Harris, Allen R.	24- 8-18	K in A	France
10/881	Sgt.	Harris, Ernest J.	12-11-16	D of W	France
10/372	Pte.	Harris, Frank A.	8- 8-15	K in A	Gallipoli
24/1388	Pte.	Harris, Frederick C. (M.M.)	14- 1-18	Disease	U.K.
31268	Pte.	Harris, George E.	8- 8-17	K in A	France
10/2955	Pte.	Harris, James	21-10-17	K in A	France
10/1515	Pte.	Harris, John H.	15- 9-15	D of W	Egypt ex Gallipoli
48716	Pte.	Harris, Martin E. L.	24- 8-18	K in A	France
10/377	Pte.	Harris, Stephen A.	8- 8-15	K in A	Gallipoli
24618	Pte.	Harris, William H.	8- 6-17	K in A	France
20339	Pte.	Harrison, Arthur D.	31- 7-17	K in A	France
39806	Pte.	Harrison, Frank	10- 8-17	K in A	France
48024	Pte.	Harrison, James H.	14- 9-18	K in A	France
10/3898	Pte.	Harrold, William H.	31- 7-17	K in A	France
10231	Pte.	Hart, Harold L.	16- 9-16	K in A	France
33359	Pte.	Hart, Henry E.	13- 6-17	D of W	France
10/3286	Pte.	Hart, Samuel R.	15- 9-16	K in A	France
64204	Pte.	Hartland, Jack W.	4-11-18	K in A	France
10/1837	Pte.	Hartley, John	30- 7-15	K in A	Gallipoli
63151	Pte.	Hartsonge, Jeremiah	1-10-18	K in A	France
20341	Pte.	Harvey, Charles G.	20- 4-17	K in A	France
29400	Pte.	Harvey, Claude	1- 8-17	D of W	France
10/859	Sgt.	Harvey, Jack L.	8- 8-15	K in A	Gallipoli
10/2959	Sgt.	Harvey, James	29-11-17	K in A	France
10/2960	Cpl.	Harvey, Robert A.	7-10-17	D of W	France
10036	Pte.	Harvey, William C. G.	9-10-17	D of W	France
10/2175	Cpl.	Harvey, William H.	14- 8-15	D of W	Mudros ex Gallipoli
13761	Pte.	Harwood, Herbert R.	8- 6-17	K in A	France
10/3900	Pte.	Haslett, George	27- 3-18	K in A	France
5/447	L/Cpl.	Hastie, William E.	18- 5-18	D of W	France
10/1520	Pte.	Hastings, John E.	16- 9-16	K in A	France
20342	Pte.	Hatcher, Thomas W.	30- 9-17	D of W	France
65661	Pte.	Hawes, George W.	11-10-18	K in A	France

THE WELLINGTON REGIMENT

Reg. No.	Rank.	Name.	Date death.	Cause.	Place.
10/2962	Pte.	Hawke, Ernest H.	20- 7-16	K in A	France
12198	Pte.	Hawke, Harold P.	31- 7-17	K in A	France
12391	L/Cpl.	Hawkes, Herbert A.	4-10-17	D of W	France
10/4122	Pte.	Hawley, John	27- 9-16	K in A	France
10/2178	Pte.	Hay, Gordon G.	8- 8-15	K in A	Gallipoli
68570	Pte.	Hay, Henry	22- 9-18	D of W	U.K. ex F"ce.
10345	Pte.	Hay, James	27- 9-16	K in A	France
10/714	L/Cpl.	Hayden, Bill	18- 8-15	D of W	At Sea ex Gallipoli
10/723	Pte.	Hayden, H. E. (M.I.D.)	26- 4-15	K in A	Gallipoli
10/1841	Pte.	Hayes, John J.	5- 3-17	K in A	France
58528	Pte.	Hays, Frederick	16- 5-18	K in A	France
10/1255	Pte.	Hayward, Charles	8- 8-15	K in A	Gallipoli
28141	Pte.	Hazell, Frank E.	24- 8-17	D of W	France
10/3288	Pte.	Headifen, Leonard	22- 6-17	D of W	France
14622	Pte.	Heal, Alfred C.	4-10-17	K in A	France
10/470	Cpl.	Heald, Gilbert	27- 6-15	K in A	Gallipoli
10/989	Pte.	Heale, Walter G.	8- 8-15	K in A	Gallipoli
10/900	Pte.	Heathcote, Herbert H.	7- 6-17	K in A	France
10/1521	Pte.	Heather, Douglas W.	7- 7-15	Disease	At Sea ex Gallipoli
29402	Pte.	Hebden, Percy	5-10-18	D of W	France
27655	Pte.	Hende, Peter B.	8- 6-17	K in A	France
10/1844	Pte.	Henderson, Alexander	4- 9-15	D of W	Egypt ex Gallipoli
14623	Pte.	Henderson, C. W.	16-11-16	K in A	France
10/2179	Pte.	Henderson, Edward G.	15- 8-15	D of W	At Sea ex Gallipoli
15721	Pte.	Henderson, G. T. A.	8-10-17	D of W	France
10/2369	Lt.	Henderson, George W.	24- 6-16	Injuries Ac. bomb explosion	France
23831	Pte.	Henderson, Thomas	2-10-16	K in A	France
1/037	Pte.	Henneker, George J.	12- 1-18	K in A	France
10/1847	Pte.	Hennessy, Charles M.	14- 8-15	Disease	At Sea ex Gallipoli
10/2967	L/Cpl.	Henry, Malcolm R.	16- 9-16	K in A	France
51165	Pte.	Henzler, Robert	24- 8-18	K in A	France
15723	Pte.	Herbert, Edward L.	16-11-16	K in A	France
39811	Pte.	Hercock, Reg. C.	13- 9-18	K in A	France
36865	Pte.	Herman, William	4-10-17	K in A	France
38703	Pte.	Hesketh, Ernest J.	1- 8-17	K in A	France
23832	Pte.	Heys, James H.	4-10-17	K in A	France
10/604	Pte.	Hiatt, Samuel J. R.	30- 7-15	K in A	Gallipoli
4/1128	Sgt.	Hickson, Arnold C.	7- 6-17	K in A	France

THE WELLINGTON REGIMENT

Reg. No.	Rank.	Name.	Date death.	Cause.	Place.
18164	Pte.	Hickson, Clarence H.	30- 9-18	K in A	France
51255	Pte.	Higgie, Collin L.	2- 4-18	D of W	France
10/3293	Pte.	Higginbottom, Willie	7- 9-18	D of W	France
53012	Pte.	Higgins, James	11- 4-18	K in A	France
10/1375	Sgt.	Higgott, William T.	9- 5-15	K in A	Gallipoli
59898	Pte.	Hill, Alexander	14- 4-18	K in A	France
10/172	Pte.	Hill, Louis W.	29- 4-15	K in A	Gallipoli
15724	Pte.	Hill, Percy	27- 7-17	D of W	France
10/374	Pte.	Hill, Reginald I.	8- 8-15	K in A	Gallipoli
10233	Pte.	Hill, William C.	27- 9-16	K in A	France
10/3906	Cpl.	Hilliar, Charles J.	23-10-17	K in A	France
28046	2/Lt.	Hindlesmith, Arthur	1-10-18	D of W	France
14627	Pte.	Hirst, Thomas R.	31- 7-17	K in A	France
53016	Pte.	Hishon, Daniel	4- 5-18	K in A	France
53015	Pte.	Hislop, Albert J.	23- 1-20	Disease	N.Z.
14629	Pte.	Hitchman, Hugh J. C.	1- 8-17	K in A	France
10/3596	Pte.	Hoare, Alexander J.	15- 9-16	K in A	France
38160	Pte.	Hobbs, James	13-10-18	D of W	France
44280	Pte.	Hobbs, Oswald	31- 8-18	K in A	France
22249	Pte.	Hodge, Harry	31- 7-17	K in A	France
10/3908	Pte.	Hodgson, Henry F.	16- 9-16	K in A	France
47826	Pte.	Hodgson, John H.	21-12-17	D of W	France
39813	Pte.	Hodgson, Sidney B.	4-10-17	K in A	France
72659	Pte.	Hogan, William M.	30- 9-18	Accd. K Bomb	France
10/2970	Pte.	Hogg, James L.	29- 6-16	K in A	France
52425	Pte.	Hogg, John A.	14- 4-18	K in A	France
28135	Pte.	Holdstock, William L.	3- 1-18	D of W	France
10/2648	Sgt.	Holland, Percy R.	4- 2-17	D of W	France
69407	Pte.	Hollins, Walter	1- 9-18	K in A	France
10/595	Pte.	Holmes, Arthur W.	29- 4-15	K in A	Gallipoli
31278	Pte.	Holmes, Harry V.	31- 7-17	K in A	France
10/1075	Pte.	Holmes, Reuben V.	8- 8-15	K in A	Gallipoli
10/3296	Sgt.	Holmes, W. A. (M.M.)	3-10-16	D of W	France
39534	Pte.	Holz, Allan	13- 6-17	K in A	France
39535	Pte.	Holz, Ernest J. J.	13- 6-17	K in A	France
10/831	Pte.	Honnor, Edwin H.	16- 9-16	K in A	France
10/3297	Pte.	Hooper, Alex. J.	16- 9-16	D of W	France
36866	Pte.	Hope, Robert	14- 6-17	K in A	France
10/471	Pte.	Hopkins, Robert G.	8- 8-15	K in A	Gallipoli
10/2508	2/Lt.	Hopkirk, William S.	1- 6-16	K in A	France
23/786	Pte.	Hopping, Bertram F.	3- 7-16	K in A	France
61648	Pte.	Horne, John	12-10-18	K in A	France
10/2971	Pte.	Hornsby, John F.	17- 9-16	D of W	France
10/2650	Pte.	Hornsby, Robert	7-11-15	Disease	Mudros

THE WELLINGTON REGIMENT

Reg. No.	Rank.	Name.	Date death.	Cause.	Place.
10/2651	Pte.	Horsman, William E.	2-12-15	K in A	Gallipoli
53494	Pte.	Howard, Frank S.	30- 8-18	K in A	France
1/384	2/Lt.	Howard, Frederick	8- 6-17	K in A	France
10351	Cpl.	Howard, Harold	4-10-17	K in A	France
10/2973	Pte.	Howell, Albert E.	25- 9-16	K in A	France
74051	Pte.	Howell, Noah A.	4-11-18	K in A	France
10/2654	Pte.	Hudson, Francis C.	16- 9-16	K in A	France
10/727	Cpl.	Hudson, Thomas H.	18- 5-16	Disease	U.K.
10/3602	Pte.	Hughes, Fred	5- 5-17	D of W	France
10/7	Lt.	Hugo, Laurance W. A.	27- 4-15	K in A	Gallipoli
10142	Pte.	Hull, Henry V.	1-10-18	K in A	France
10/1263	Pte.	Hulme, James	22- 8-15	Disease	Malta ex Gal.
59379	Pte.	Hume, Patrick J.	13- 9-18	K in A	France
20351	Pte.	Hume, Samuel S.	7- 6-17	K in A	France
28136	Pte.	Humphries, W. L.	23- 6-17	K in A	France
13/3038	Pte.	Hunn, Henry	23- 9-16	D of W	France
7/1627	Cpl.	Hunt, George W.	27- 7-17	K in A	France
10/32	Pte.	Hunt, Klein	8- 8-15	K in A	Gallipoli
38026	Pte.	Hunter, Andrew	16- 4-18	D of W	France
10/2436	Pte.	Hunter, James	8- 8-15	K in A	Gallipoli
49153	Pte.	Hunter, John J.	4-11-18	K in A	France
10/1855	Pte.	Hunter, William M.	8- 8-15	K in A	Gallipoli
38705	Pte.	Hunter, William T.	18- 7-18	D of W	France
41800	Pte.	Hurley, Daniel	4-10-17	K in A	France
10/2977	Pte.	Hurley, William	4-10-17	K in A	France
22803	Sgt.	Hurst, Chris. J.	6-11-18	D of W	France
10/2978	Pte.	Hurst, Thomas H.	18- 9-16	D of W	France
10/3603	Pte.	Hutchinson, C. L.	16- 9-16	K in A	France
52612	Pte.	Hutchison, John A.	28- 1-18	K in A	France
10/1857	Pte.	Hutton, Frank R.	8- 8-15	K in A	Gallipoli
12/4198	Pte.	Huxtable, Henry	27- 7-17	K in A	France
10/3605	L/Sgt.	Ibbotson, Herbert	31- 7-17	K in A	France
10/3917	Pte.	Inglis, John R.	14-12-17	K in A	France
33548	Pte.	Ingram, Eric J.	4-10-17	K in A	France
10/889	Cpl.	Ireland, Ernest J.	7- 5-15	K in A	Gallipoli
10/1534	Pte.	Ireland, Joseph	8- 8-15	K in A	Gallipoli
10/1098	Pte.	Ireland, William A.	10- 8-15	K in A	Gallipoli
61652	Pte.	Irvine, James	20- 3-19	Disease	France
10/624	Pte.	Irving, Eric C.	29- 4-15	K in A	Gallipoli
27656	Pte.	Irving, Walter J.	5- 6-17	K in A	France
47892	Pte.	Irwin, James	8- 5-18	D of W	France
56605	Pte.	Irwin, Walter D.	29- 8-18	K in A	France
23835	Pte.	Jack, Andrew	20- 7-17	D of W	France

THE WELLINGTON REGIMENT

Reg. No.	Rank.	Name.	Date death.	Cause.	Place.
25532	Pte.	Jackson, Ewan A.	23- 6-17	K in A	France
10/394	Pte.	Jackson, Henry G.	8- 8-15	K in A	Gallipoli
10/395	Lt.	Jackson, John K. E. (M.I.D.)	28- 3-18	D of W	France
30593	L/Cpl.	Jacobson, Ernest R.	4-10-17	K in A	France
10/1535	Pte.	Jagerhorn, George	23- 3-16	Disease	N.Z.
10/1267	Pte.	Jakes, William	10- 7-15	Disease	Lemnos
19096	Pte.	James, David	7- 6-17	K in A	France
10/1860	Pte.	James, George A.	1- 8-15	D of W	At Sea ex Gallipoli
10/3918	Pte.	James, Leslie	16- 9-16	K in A	France
10/137	L/Cpl.	Jameson, Ian D.	8- 5-15	K in A	Gallipoli
10/676	Pte.	Jamison, William	8- 8-15	K in A	Gallipoli
39822	Pte.	Jardine, Thomas	6-10-17	D of W	France
28148	Pte.	Jarrett, William	25- 8-18	Disease	U.K.
8/2956	Cpl.	Jeffries, Ralph S. C. (M.M.)	4-10-17	K in A	France
10/1537	Pte.	Jeffs, Thomas	8- 8-15	K in A	Gallipoli
1/205	Sgt.	Jenkinson, Horace E.	18-10-17	D of W	France
10/136	Pte.	Jennings, Edgar McI.	3- 8-15	K in A	Gallipoli
27903	Pte.	Jensen, Christoffer	27- 3-18	K in A	France
39823	Pte.	Jensen, Ernest (M.M.)	4-11-18	K in A	France
10/2193	Pte.	Jessop, William H.	8- 8-15	K in A	Gallipoli
33554	Pte.	Johanson, Walter O.	4-10-17	K in A	France
10/1865	Sgt.	Johanson, William L. (M.M.)	8- 6-17	K in A	France
10/3307	L/Cpl.	Johns, Percival G.	29- 1-18	K in A	France
15733	Pte.	Johnson, Albert E. (M.M.)	4-10-17	K in A	France
10/1268	Pte.	Johnson, Arthur R.	8- 8-15	K in A	Gallipoli
53026	Pte.	Johnson, Frank W.	17- 9-18	D of W	France
31291	Sgt.	Johnson, George A.	13- 9-18	K in A	France
10/4125	Pte.	Johnson, Nilander	16- 9-16	K in A	France
9/1186	Pte.	Johnson, Walter	20-10-17	K in A	France
10173	Pte.	Johnston, Albert	30- 8-18	K in A	France
31293	L/Cpl.	Johnston, Edward C. (M.M.)	3- 4-18	K in A	France
24/1403	Pte.	Johnston, Stanley C.	2-10-16	K in A	France
10/2981	Pte.	Johnstone, Albert E.	27- 6-16	K in A	France
16/538	Mjr.	Jones, Albert E. M.	11-10-17	D of W	France
11/325	Pte.	Jones, Arthur B.	31-10-16	D of W	France
38711	Pte.	Jones, Bertie Alma	4-10-17	K in A	France
10/4127	Pte.	Jones, Cyril B.	16- 9-16	K in A	France
10/3311	Pte.	Jones, Ernest A.	16- 9-16	K in A	France
23837	Pte.	Jones, Frederick G.	3-10-17	K in A	France

THE WELLINGTON REGIMENT

Reg. No.	Rank.	Name.	Date death.	Cause.	Place.
25165	Pte.	Jones, Henry E.	7- 6-17	K in A	France
10/3312	Pte.	Jones, Henry M.	16- 9-16	K in A	France
10/3615	L/Cpl.	Jones, James W.	14- 9-16	K in A	France
29413	Pte.	Jones, Richard W.	9- 6-17	K in A	France
14644	Cpl.	Jones, Robert	24- 3-19	Disease	N.Z.
10/826	Pte.	Jones, Thomas B. S.	8- 8-15	K in A	Gallipoli
10/396	Pte.	Jones, Walter	8- 5-15	K in A	Gallipoli
10/3616	Pte.	Jones, William	16- 4-18	K in A	France
25534	Cpl.	Jopp, James A. (M.M.)	29- 8-18	K in A	France
28151	Pte.	Jordan, John R.	4-10-17	K in A	France
11486	Pte.	Jordan, Noel L.	2-10-16	K in A	France
69494	Pte.	Joyce, Patrick J.	1-10-18	K in A	France
38033	Pte.	Joyner, Arthur	4-10-17	K in A	France
38713	Pte.	Joynt, Charles H.	31- 7-17	K in A	France
10/235	Cpl.	Juno, George	8- 8-15	K in A	Gallipoli
33383	Pte.	Jury, Alfred W.	4-10-17	K in A	France
20360	Pte.	Karalus, Fred. S.	9- 6-17	D of W	France
10/1867	Pte.	Kauter, William	8- 8-15	K in A	Gallipoli
10/193	Cpl.	Kay, Benjamin	8- 5-15	K in A	Gallipoli
10355	Pte.	Kean, John	8- 6-17	K in A	France
10/1868	Pte.	Kearney, Richard	19- 9-16	D of W	France
10/874	Pte.	Keasberry, John C.	28- 4-15	K in A	Gallipoli
40336	Pte.	Kehoe, William	24-10-17	K in A	France
24/1406	Pte.	Keightley, Frank	14- 9-16	K in A	France
30100	Capt.	Keir, John (M.C.)	23-10-17	K in A	France
11/1543	Pte.	Keith, John	8- 8-15	K in A	Gallipoli
10235	Pte.	Kelliher, William	10-12-16	D of W	France
38034	Pte.	Kells, Herbert H.	21- 5-18	D of W	France
10/3620	Pte.	Kelly, Cecil W.	15- 9-16	K in A	France
10/2986	Pte.	Kelly, Gilbert G.	26- 9-16	K in A	France
28157	Pte.	Kelly, John	4-10-17	K in A	France
28158	Pte.	Kelly, Martin	21-10-17	K in A	France
10/3314	Pte.	Kelly, Michael	3- 7-16	K in A	France
14999	Pte.	Kelly, Thomas B.	4-10-17	K in A	France
10/1117	Pte.	Kemshed, Frank M.	19- 8-17	D of W	France
10/585	Sgt.	Kendle, George R.	27- 4-15	K in A	Gallipoli
38035	Pte.	Kendrick, Edward J.	1- 9-18	K in A	France
10/767	Pte.	Kennedy, Clyde	7- 8-15	K in A	Gallipoli
25542	Pte.	Kennedy, Tom C.	31- 7-17	K in A	France
63167	Pte.	Kennelly, Charles H.	12-10-18	D of W	France
24/1264	Pte.	Kenny, Ernest G. B.	14- 6-16	K in A	France
10/3316	Pte.	Kent, Charles J.	28- 7-16	K in A	France
52619	Pte.	Kent, James J.	12- 2-18	D of W	France
10/403	Cpl.	Ker, Douglas	27- 4-15	K in A	Gallipoli

THE WELLINGTON REGIMENT

Reg. No.	Rank.	Name.	Date death.	Cause.	Place.
10/1546	Pte.	Kewley, Alfred	14- 5-15	D of W	At Sea ex Gallipoli
41822	Pte.	Keys, George E.	4-10-17	K in A	France
10/3622	Pte.	Kilbride, William G.	19- 8-17	D of W	France
10/2197	Pte.	Kimberley, Ernest H.	15- 8-16	K in A	France
9/1881	Pte.	King, Cyril V.	3- 7-16	K in A	France
27696	2/Lt.	King, Lancel L.	4-10-17	K in A	France
33560	Pte.	King, William	4-10-17	K in A	France
10/1873	Pte.	Kingdon, Roy R.	16- 6-15	K in A	Gallipoli
69244	Pte.	Kinsella, Peter T.	20- 2-19	Disease	U.K.
11774	2/Lt.	Kinvig, James G.	31- 7-17	K in A	France
10/1550	Pte.	Kirk, Charles E.	23-10-15	Drowned at Salonika Torpedoed	
20362	Pte.	Kirkland, John	15- 6-17	D of W	France
8/4435	2/Lt.	Kirkley, Wilfred	17- 9-16	K in A	France
36984	Pte.	Kitchingham, Charles	11- 7-17	K in A	France
57401	Pte.	Klein, John W.	11-10-18	K in A	France
10/3319	Pte.	Klenner, John	4-10-17	K in A	France
36985	Pte.	Knight, Edgar S.	14- 6-17	K in A	France
31302	Cpl.	Knight, Norman R. (M.M.)	16- 4-18	K in A	France
59918	Pte.	Knott, Joseph C.	30- 8-18	K in A	France
48515	Pte.	Knowles, Francis W.	4-10-17	K in A	France
20363	Cpl.	Knowles, Herbert R.	14-12-17	K in A	France
10/1275	Pte.	Knyvett, Edmund C.	16-17- 9-16	K in A	France
32021	Pte.	Lack, John R.	23- 8-17	K in A	France
20364	Pte.	Laidlaw, James S.	7- 6-17	K in A	France
42843	Pte.	Lamb, Alfred D.	20- 2-19	Disease	France after Armistice.
29420	Pte.	Lamb, Alfred J.	4-10-17	K in A	France
25547	Pte.	Lamberg, Charles J. G.	30- 9-17	K in A	France
10/3929	Pte.	Lampard, James	16- 9-16	K in A	France
10/3321	Pte.	Lane, Harold H.	17- 6-16	D of W	France
10/3931	Pte.	Langdon, Charles	15- 9-16	K in A	France
44495	Pte.	Langdon, Robert L.	11- 2-18	K in A	France
44492	Pte.	Langdon, Robert W.	4-10-17	K in A	France
10/3930	Pte.	Langley, David	19-10-17	Disease	France
10/48	Pte.	Langley, Ernest	27- 4-15	K in A	Gallipoli
10/107	Pte.	Larkin, Leonard	8- 8-15	K in A	Gallipoli.
48341	Pte.	Larking, Frank C.	4-11-18	K in A	France
10/1557	Pte.	Larsen, Fritjof	8- 8-15	K in A	Gallipoli
10360	T. L/Sgt.	Larsen, Harry	29- 8-18	K in A	France
10/822	Sgt.	Lascelles, D. R. B.	8- 8-15	K in A	Gallipoli

THE WELLINGTON REGIMENT

Reg. No.	Rank.	Name.	Date death.	Cause.	Place.
10/3627	L/Cpl.	Lassen, Godfrey	2-10-16	K in A	France
38041	Pte.	Latham, Wilfred J. R.	12-10-18	K in A	France
28160	L/Cpl.	Law, George E.	4- 1-18	D of W	U.K. ex F"ce.
45872	Pte.	Lawrence, E. W. H.	6-11-17	D of W	U.K. ex F"ce.
10/1880	Pte.	Lawrence, Thomas G.	8- 8-15	K in A	Gallipoli
10/2671	Cpl.	Lawson, Clifford P.	30- 3-18	K in A	France
10/177	Pte.	Lawton, Walter V.	8- 8-15	K in A	Gallipoli
30114	Lt.	Lee, Clarence E. (M.C.)	26- 8-18	K in A	France
10/1559	Sgt.	Lee, Harold A. G.	17- 6-15	K in A	Gallipoli
10/1882	Pte.	Leeks, Cedric W.	8- 8-15	K in A	Gallipoli
38809	Pte.	Lees, John E. L.	31- 8-18	K in A	France
39833	Pte.	Lehndorf, Arthur R.	4-10-17	K in A	France
11889	Pte.	Leith, Alex. Craig	28- 9-16	K in A	France
10/2206	Pte.	Lennox, Harry	15- 9-16	K in A	France
10/1561	Pte.	Leonard, Albert J.	14- 8-15	D of W	At Sea ex Gallipoli
11059	Pte.	Leslie, James	4-10-17	D of W	France
10/3936	Pte.	Leslie, John W.	2/3- 7-16	K in A	France
10/2675	Cpl.	Lever, Wallace	20- 7-16	D of W	France
10/416	Pte.	Levien, Victor N.	8- 8-15	K in A	Gallipoli
29422	Pte.	Lewin, John	28-10-17	D of W	France
29423	Pte.	Lewis, Andrew J.	29- 3-18	K in A	France
10/1279	Pte.	Lewis, Edmund K.	16- 5-15	K in A	Gallipoli
27673	Pte.	Lewis, Lionel	4- 6-17	D of W	France
55118	Pte.	Lewis, Thomas J.H.	26- 8-18	D of W	France
10/2208	Pte.	Lewis, Watkin E.	8- 8-15	K in A	Gallipoli
10/1884	Pte.	Liddington, Sam. J.	24- 8-15	D of W	At Sea ex Gallipoli
45874	Pte.	Liddle, Herbert	29- 9-18	K in A	France
20368	L/Cpl.	Liddy, Thomas J.	14-12-17	K in A	France
20369	Pte.	Lilly, Clarence H.	8- 6-17	K in A	France
10/1885	Pte.	Lima, Frank	7- 8-15	K in A	Gallipoli
15737	Pte.	Limpus, Percy	7- 6-17	D of W	France
10/2998	Pte.	Lindop, Walter H.	17- 9-16	D of W	France
33390	Pte.	Lippett, Albert H.	18- 6-17	K in A	France
10/2209	Pte.	Lister, Frank	27- 1-18	K in A	France
10/104	Pte.	Little, Walter	8- 8-15	K in A	Gallipoli
47597	Pte.	Little, William	4- 9-18	D of W	France
10/535	Pte.	Loach, George W.	8- 8-15	K in A	Gallipoli
10/2677	Pte.	Loader, Eric L.	22- 9-16	D of W	France
10/420	Sgt.	Lochhead, John A.	8- 8-15	K in A	Gallipoli
10/1087	Pte.	Lockett, Robert L. B.	8- 8-15	K in A	Gallipoli
48230	Pte.	Looney, James	14-12-17	K in A	France
10/747	L/Cpl.	Looney, Wilfred G.	26- 4-15	K in A	Gallipoli

THE WELLINGTON REGIMENT

Reg. No.	Rank.	Name.	Date death.	Cause.	Place.
15739	L/Cpl.	Lord, Norman C.	14-12-17	K in A	France
33564	Pte.	Lord, Sidney W.	17-10-17	K in A	France
10/2210	Pte.	Lorenzen, Wilfred E.	8- 8-15	K in A	Gallipoli
12421	Pte.	Loughman, Daniel P.	7- 6-17	K in A	France
38721	Pte.	Love, Cecil	4-10-17	K in A	France
48522	Pte.	Low, Edward Q.	13-10-18	D of W	France
10/244	Pte.	Low, Robert M.	17- 5-15	D of W	Egypt ex Gallipoli
64084	Pte.	Lowson, Albert L.	2-10-18	K in A	France
11892	L/Cpl.	Lucas, George R.	30- 3-18	D of W	France
10/3941	Pte.	Luck, William H.	31- 8-16	D of W	U.K. ex F"ce.
10/3637	L/Cpl.	Lugg. Albert H.	26- 6-17	K in A	France
13/3047	Pte.	Lunham, Thomas	21-10-16	K in A	France
29428	Pte.	Lyford, George H.	4-10-17	K in A	France
10/606	Pte.	Lynch, Henry K.	8- 8-15	K in A	Gallipoli
10/1563	Pte.	Lynch, Owen E.	8- 8-15	K in A	Gallipoli
12422	Pte.	Lynch, William	2-10-16	K in A	France
40339	Pte.	Lynskey, Patrick W.	31- 7-17	D of W	France
10/2680	Pte.	McAllister, Peter G.	4-10-17	K in A	France
10/4505	Sgt.	McArthur, Alfred A.	2/3- 7-16	K in A	France
10/1581	Pte.	McArthur, John	9- 5-15	D of W	Gallipoli
10/964	Pte.	McCarthy, Justin F.	8- 5-15	K in A	Gallipoli
47451	Pte.	McCaughern, Thomas	8- 5-18	K in A	France
13349	Pte.	McCaw, Thomas J.	21-12-17	D of W	At Sea on route N.Z. ex France
37000	Pte.	McClure, John B.	12- 6-17	K in A	France
23/1747	Cpl.	McClymont, James	12- 9-18	D of W	France
10/18	Capt.	McColl, Alex. B. (M.I.D.)	2- 7-16	K in A	France
32042	Pte.	McConnell, Robert	19- 6-17	K in A	France
24428	Pte.	McConvill, John H.	31- 5-18	K in A	France
24/853	Pte.	McCorkill, John	30- 8-18	D of W	France
33576	Pte.	McCormick, David J.	4- 5-18	K in A	France
10/2216	Pte.	McCormick, William	11- 8-15	K in A	Gallipoli
24034	Pte.	McCowen, Richard O.	4-10-17	K in A	France
10/1888	Pte.	McCulloch, William	8- 8-15	K in A	Gallipoli
10/1890	Pte.	McDiarmid, William O.	7- 4-16	Declared Missing believed Dead U.K.	
10/1089	W.O.1	McDonald Alex.	27- 4-15	K in A	Gallipoli
28626	Pte.	MacDonald, Alex.	21-10-17	K in A	France
10/13	Pte.	McDonald, Charles C.	15- 9-16	K in A	France
10/433	L/Cpl.	McDonald, Charles V.	8- 5-15	K in A	Gallipoli

THE WELLINGTON REGIMENT

Reg. No.	Rank.	Name.	Date death.	Cause.	Place.
64101	Pte.	McDonald, Donald H.	30- 8-18	K in A	France
33416	Pte.	McDonald, Hector S.	4-10-17	K in A	France
45876	Pte.	Macdonald, Horatio A.	27- 3-18	K in A	France
29452	Pte.	McDonald, John	10- 4-19	D of W	N.Z. ex F'ce.
59946	Pte.	McDonald, John A.	5- 5-18	D of W	France
14668	Pte.	McDonald, John F.	2- 8-17	K in A	France
10/1891	Pte.	McDonald, Kenneth	12-11-15	K in A	Gallipoli
10/242	Pte.	Macdonald, Kenneth	8- 8-15	K in A	Gallipoli
33578	L/Cpl.	McDonald, Murdoch A.	1- 9-18	K in A	France
10/3668	L/Cpl.	McDonald, Noel	4-10-17	K in A	France
10/2685	Pte.	McDowell, Charles N.	22-10-17	K in A	France
24/2049	Pte.	McEvoy, Owen	15- 9-16	K in A	France
10/2830	Pte.	McEwan, Roy	15- 5-16	K in A	France
25283	L/Cpl.	McEwan, William	8- 6-17	K in A	France
19167	Pte.	McEwen, Stanley H.	7- 6-17	K in A	France
33579	Pte.	McFarlane, David J.	8- 7-17	K in A	France
49833	Pte.	McFarlane, Reginald	28-11-17	K in A	France
10/1584	Pte.	McFarlane, Robert G.	8- 8-15	K in A	Gallipoli
10/1146	Pte.	McFarlane, William V.	8- 8-15	K in A	Gallipoli
33417	Pte.	McGhie, Arnold J.	16- 7-19	Injuries (suicide)	N.Z.
10/3660	Pte.	MacGibbon, Henry J.	19- 9-16	K in A	France
52439	L/Cpl.	McGill, David	20-12-17	K in A	France
24/1727	Pte.	McGillivray, Donald	14- 9-16	K in A	France
10/1115	W.O. 1	McGlade, Matthew	26- 4-15	K in A	Gallipoli
10/695	Pte.	McGonagle, Cyril	8- 6-17	K in A	France
59424	Pte.	McGonagle, Daniel	12-10-18	K in A	France
10/3670	Pte.	McGoverne, Ernest G.	3- 7-16	K in A	France
39867	Pte.	McGrath, Charles	14- 6-17	K in A	France
14139	Pte.	McGrath, John	11- 6-17	D of W	France
10/1586	Pte.	McGree, Patrick J.	8- 8-15	K in A	Gallipoli
10/4480	Pte.	McGuire, Edmund	6-10-17	D of W	France
37851	Pte.	McHale, William H.	3-10-17	K in A	France
3/700	2/Lt.	McHardie, Cyril J.	22- 5-18	K in A	France
22430	Pte.	MacInnes, Archie	20- 8-17	K in A	France
29967	Pte.	McIntosh, Robert	30- 8-18	K in A	France
15754	Pte.	McIntyre, Alexander	24- 8-18	K in A	France
10/2687	Pte.	McIntyre, Donald J.	26- 9-16	K in A	France
10/3673	Sgt.	McKay, Andrew	13- 9-18	K in A	France
36473	L/Cpl.	McKay, Charles D.	4-10-17	K in A	France
10/1897	Pte.	McKay, Eric G.	8- 8-15	K in A	Gallipoli
10/3012	Pte.	McKay, John	28- 9-16	D of W	France
24382	Sgt.	Mackay, John C.	21- 6-17	K in A	France
12445	L/Cpl.	McKay, John W.	10- 6-17	K in A	France
23/847	Pte.	McKegney, Hugh	7- 6-17	K in A	France

375

THE WELLINGTON REGIMENT

Reg. No.	Rank.	Name.	Date death.	Cause.	Place.
32043	Pte.	McKelvey, Daniel A.	19- 6-17	D of W	France
10/67	Pte.	McKenzie, David	27- 4-15	K in A	Gallipoli
11918	Pte.	McKenzie, Edward W.	22-10-17	K in A	France
11/1351	Pte.	McKenzie, George	29- 9-16	K in A	France
10/549	Pte.	McKenzie, Henry	8- 8-15	K in A	Gallipoli
25146	Pte.	McKenzie, John M.	19-10-16	D of W	France
24/1711	T. Cpl.	McKenzie, Neil L.	4- 7-16	D of W	France
19087	Lt.	McKenzie, Seaforth W.	26- 1-18	Accd. K (Aeroplane)	France
44619	Pte.	McKenzie, William L.	4-10-17	K in A	France
65420	Pte.	Mackenzie, William S.	12-10-18	K in A	France
24671	Pte.	McKey, Michael D. C.	8- 6-17	K in A	France
24/2245	Pte.	Mackie, Raymond T.	11-11-16	D of W	France
47568	Pte.	McKinna, William J.	28- 3-18	D of W	France
10/2225	Pte.	McKinnon, Alex. D.	31- 8-15	Disease	Egypt
10/135	Mjr.	McKinnon, Hugh E. (M.C. & Bar, M.I.D.)	4-11-18	K in A	France
32528	Pte.	McKinnon, Malcolm	1- 8-17	K in A	France
40155	2nd. Lt.	MacLachlan, Ninian	27- 8-16	K in A	France
6/2224	Cpl.	MacLachlan, Peter	31- 7-17	D of W	France
38058	Pte.	McLaren, James H.	2- 8-17	D of W	France
10/922	Pte.	McLauchlan, Alex. R.	8- 8-15	K in A	Gallipoli
10/3966	Sgt.	McLaughlan, Francis	4-10-17	K in A	France
10/1591	Pte.	McLaughlan, James	8- 8-15	K in A	Gallipoli
10/2692	Pte.	McLaughlan, John	15- 9-16	K in A	France
12/4233	Pte.	McLaughlan, William	16- 9-16	K in A	France
37004	Pte.	McLaughlin, Edmund	23-10-17	Disease	France
39548	Pte.	McLaughlin, Edward	4-10-17	K in A	France
10/3675	L/Cpl.	McLaughlin, John J.	7- 6-17	D of W	France
10/4481	Cpl.	Maclean, Clarence	27- 3-18	K in A	France
30624	Pte.	McLean, Donald	29- 3-18	D of W	France
69509	Pte.	McLean, William J.	2- 9-18	D of W	France
29454	Pte.	McLeay, Ian McK.	7- 6-17	K in A	France
26/1767	Pte.	McLeod, Alexander	17- 8-17	D of W	U.K. ex F"ce.
41853	Pte.	McLeod, John L.	5-10-17	D of W	France
10/3677	Pte.	McLeod, Murdoch T.	16- 9-16	D of W	France
39580	Pte.	Macleod, Robert B.	15-12-17	D of W	France
10/1079	Capt.	McLernon, Leslie S.	8- 8-15	K in A	Gallipoli
10/3679	Cpl.	McMillan, Fred. T.	4- 4-18	K in A	France
10/814	Pte.	McMillan, Herbert	29- 4-15	D of W	At Sea ex Gallipoli
10/1592	Pte.	MacMillan, James	20- 7-17	K in A	France
40350	Pte.	McMillan, James F.	5-10-17	D of W	France
20372	L/Cpl.	Macmillan, K. P. H.	14-12-17	K in A	France
10/2371	Capt.	Macmorran, James	30- 8-18	K in A	France

THE WELLINGTON REGIMENT

Reg. No.	Rank.	Name.	Date death.	Cause.	Place.
10/472	Pte.	McMurray, Wilfred L.	8- 5-15	K in A	Gallipoli
10/819	Pte.	McNabb, Cyril	30- 4-15	K in A	Gallipoli
10/830	Pte.	McNabb, Roy A.	16- 5-15	K in A	Gallipoli
29456	Pte.	McNamara, Clive J.	8- 6-17	K in A	France
10/463	Pte.	McNeil, William	8- 8-15	K in A	Gallipoli
48253	Pte.	McNeill, John	1-10-18	K in A	France
10/2697	Pte.	McNickel, Thomas F.	22-11-15	D of W	Egypt ex Gallipoli
10/37	L/Cpl.	McPhee, Duncan	8- 5-15	K in A	Gallipoli
12240	Pte.	McPhee, John (M.M.)	9-10-17	K in A	France
39872	L/Cpl.	McQueen, Robert H.	11- 4-13	K in A	France
10369	Pte.	MacRae, Alexander	1-10-16	K in A	France
54942	Pte.	McRae, Donald	20-12-17	K in A	France
33588	Sgt.	McRae, Donald Alex.	13- 9-18	D of W	France
10/3342	L/Cpl.	McRae, Hugh	30- 3-18	K in A	France
13/3056	Pte.	McWhirter, Frank	9- 7-16	K in A	France
5/1562A	Pte.	McWilliam, James	21- 9-16	D of W	France
39843	Pte.	Maberly, Harold E.	5-10-17	D of W	France
10/1399	Pte.	Mace, Henry A.	28-7-17	D of W	France
69405	Pte.	Mace, Stanley D.	31- 8-18	D of W	France
38051	Pte.	Maddock, Richard J.	14- 5-18	K in A	France
42151	Pte.	Madsen, Charles O. C.	4-10-17	K in A	France
14026	2/Lt.	Magnusson, Oscar	4-10-17	K in A	France
10/2228	L/Cpl.	Mahoney, Frank (D.C.M. & M.I.D.)	21- 8-17	K in A	France
10/439	Pte.	Mailman, Alfred C.	27- 4-15	K in A	Gallipoli
10/423	L/Sgt.	Maliman, Victor	8- 8-15	K in A	Gallipoli
10/1901	Pte.	Main, James	22- 9-15	D of W	U.K ex Gal.
20373	Pte.	Main, Stephen R.	8- 6-17	K in A	France
26425	Pte.	Maisey, Leonard	31- 8-18	K in A	France
20374	Pte.	Major, Arthur M.	31- 7-17	D of W	France
10/2497	2/Lt.	Makin, Joseph	30- 9-18	K in A	France
10/1564	Pte.	Maller, John P.	5- 9-15	D of W	U.K. ex Gal.
11/699	Lt.	Malone, Edmond L. (M.C.)	6- 4-18	D of W	France
10/1039	L/Col.	Malone, William G. (M.I.D.) (2)	8- 8-15	K in A	Gallipoli
69252	Pte.	Maloney, Timothy F.	12-10-18	K in A	France
10/4137	Pte.	Manning, Walter J.	18- 9-16	K in A	France
10/2498	Sgt.	Manoy, Reginald L.	16- 9-16	K in A	France
10/427	Pte.	Mansfield, William W.	8- 8-15	K in A	Gallipoli
10/725	Pte.	Marett, Robert	29- 6-16	K in A	France
11/2147	T/Cpl.	Marfell, Frank	16-11-16	K in A	France
30607	Pte.	Marquet, Albert O.	23-10-17	D of W	France
52630	Pte.	Marr, John A.	29- 7-18	D of Disease	U.K. ex F'ce.

THE WELLINGTON REGIMENT

Reg. No.	Rank.	Name.	Date death.	Cause.	Place.
10/1904	Pte.	Marra, George H.	8- 8-15	K in A	Gallipoli
30606	L/Cpl.	Marris, Robert C.	4-10-17	K in A	France
24387	2/Lt.	Marsden, Harry U. F.	4-10-17	K in A	France
18580	2/Lt.	Marsden, Joseph S.	4-10-17	K in A	France
11/1828	Pte.	Marsh, Howard E.	20- 6-17	K in A	France
10/3345	Pte.	Marshall, Bernard	4- 2-17	D of W	France
10/1288	Cpl.	Marshall, James	7- 8-15	K in A	Gallipoli
7/1874	Pte.	Marshall, Patrick O'C.	12- 7-17	Disease	N.Z.
11/897	Pte.	Marshall, William P.	22- 7-18	K in A	France
10/1001	Pte.	Marter, Clarence	20- 8-15	D of W	Egypt ex Gallipoli
10/2232	L/Cpl.	Martin, Arthur W.	16- 9-16	K in A	France
39850	Pte.	Martin, Charles F.	4-10-17	K in A	France
10/3644	Pte.	Martin, Frederick	2-10-16	D of W	France
10/2233	Pte.	Martin, Harry H.	8- 8-15	K in A	Gallipoli
10/1567	Pte.	Martin, Michael D.	8- 8-15	K in A	Gallipoli
10/402	Pte.	Martin, Ranald L. H.	8- 8-15	K in A	Gallipoli
10/2004	Pte.	Martin, Thomas H.	8- 8-15	K in A	Gallipoli
10/1909	Pte.	Martin, William John	8- 8-15	K in A	Gallipoli
10/1376	Cpl.	Maru, Charles W.	4- 5-18	D of W	France
10/230	Pte.	Mason, Ernest	8- 8-15	K in A	Gallipoli
51178	Pte.	Mason, Fred	28-11-17	K in A	France
38052	Pte.	Mason, James F.	21-10-17	K in A	France
10/204	Pte.	Mason, Leonard	21- 6-15	D of W	At Sea ex Gallipoli
10/4138	Pte.	Mason, Leslie M.	4-11-18	K in A	France
47447	Pte.	Masters, Charles G.	24- 8-18	D of W	France
10/1910	Pte.	Masters, Herbert V.	8- 8-15	K in A	Gallipoli
10/1290	Pte.	Matear, Robert	29- 4-15	K in A	Gallipoli
10/1133	Pte.	Mather, Athal B. W.	27- 9-15	D of W	Egypt ex Gallipoli
10/3645	Pte.	Matheson, John	3- 7-16	K in A	France
10/3646	L/Sgt.	Mathews, John D.	4-10-17	K in A	France
10/447	Pte.	Matthew, Samuel D.	5-12-16	D of W	U.K. ex F'ce.
40348	Pte.	Maunder, Alfred R.	25- 4-13	K in A	France
44554	Pte.	Maunder, Roger E.	31- 8-18	K in A	France
29438	Pte.	Maxwell, David	8- 6-17	K in A	France
10/3946	Pte.	May, Frederick	4-10-17	K in A	France
10/1914	Pte.	Mearns, Enoch A.	8- 8-15	K in A	Gallipoli
11896	Pte.	Meek, Edward P.	19- 2-19	Disease	U.K.
10/3950	Pte.	Meeman, Harry C.	14- 9-16	K in A	France
10/1915	Pte.	Mellor, Arthur F.	8- 8-15	K in A	Gallipoli
10/1916	L/Cpl.	Mellor, Clement	8- 8-15	K in A	Gallipoli
10/1082	Lt.	Menteath, C. B. S.	6/10- 5-15	K in A	Gallipoli
10/2236	Pte.	Mercer, Basil E.	8- 8-15	K in A	Gallipoli

THE WELLINGTON REGIMENT

Reg. No.	Rank.	Name.	Date death.	Cause.	Place.
24/1746	Pte.	Mercer, Sydney	25- 9-16	D of W	France
49160	Pte.	Merritt, Fred. H.	6- 5-18	K in A	France
6/4577	2/Lt.	Meuli, Lorenz W.	16- 9-16	K in A	France
10/629	Pte.	Midgley, James	16- 9-16	K in A	France
31314	Pte.	Miers, Ernest W.	23- 6-17	K in A	France
10/3954	Pte.	Miller, Harry	20-10-16	K in A	France
33569	Pte.	Miller, Jack S.	27- 7-17	D of W	France
10/1570	L/Cpl.	Miller, William F. S.	27- 9-16	K in A	France
10/465	Pte.	Milligan, Edward N.	25- 4-15	K in A	Gallipoli
28627	Cpl.	Millington, William B.	4-10-17	K in A	France
41838	Pte.	Mills, George J.	4-10-17	D of W	France
10/442	L/Cpl.	Mills, John E.	29- 4-15	K in A	Gallipoli
10/816	Pte.	Mills, Percy	8- 8-15	K in A	Gallipoli
23847	Pte.	Mills, Thomas G.	2-10-16	D of W	France
29442	Pte.	Milne, Douglas	9- 6-17	D of W	France
45886	Pte.	Milne, Francis	4-10-17	K in A	France
13667	Pte.	Milne, Garnett	28- 9-16	K in A	France
10/1921	Pte.	Milne, James	8- 8-15	K in A	Gallipoli
10/1922	Pte.	Milroy, Robert	8- 8-15	K in A	Gallipoli
31319	Pte.	Minihan, James P.	22-12-17	D of W	U.K. ex F'ce.
10/1923	Cpl.	Minnell, Horace	8- 8-15	K in A	Gallipoli
42156	Pte.	Misson, George W.	22-10-18	Died cause not stated	Germany ex France
23/2039	Pte.	Mitchell, Herbert W. A.	4-10-17	K in A	France
10/801	Pte.	Mitchell, John S.	8- 8-15	K in A	Gallipoli
31317	Pte.	Mitchell, Joseph	17- 6-17	K in A	France
2/435	Pte.	Mitchell, Leslie	22-10-16	D of W	France
26750	Cpl.	Mitchell, Ross E. L.	2- 8-17	K in A	France
10/1572	Pte.	Mitchell, Thomas S.	8- 8-15	K in A	Gallipoli
11903	Pte.	Mitchell, Valentine P.	31- 3-18	D of W	France
10/1173	Pte.	Moffat, Harry	7- 8-15	K in A	Gallipoli
10/3034	Sgt.	Moffatt, George	4-10-17	K in A	France
14657	Pte.	Moffett, Arthur G.	3- 5-17	K in A	France
28177	Pte.	Moffett, Thomas	7- 6-17	K in A	France
14837	Pte.	Moloney, James	8- 6-17	K in A	France
19158	Pte.	Monaghan, Harry	1- 8-17	D of W	France
10/3035	Pte.	Monahan, John J.	25- 9-17	D of W	U.K. ex F'ce.
10/459	Pte.	Monk, Bernard H.	7- 5-15	K in A	Gallipoli
10/1125	Cpl.	Monteith, Sydney B.	6- 6-15	D of W	Gallipoli
32693	Pte.	Moody, David S.	4-10-17	K in A	France
23215	Pte.	Moody, Oliver J.	30-10-16	K in A	France
10/3352	Pte.	Mooney, Alexander O.	13- 9-16	K in A	France
10/456	Pte.	Moore, Frank H.	29- 4-15	K in A	Gallipoli
11076	Pte.	Moore, Joseph W.	8- 6-17	K in A	France
10/1925	Pte.	Moore, Stanley G.	8- 8-15	K in A	Gallipoli

THE WELLINGTON REGIMENT

Reg. No.	Rank.	Name.	Date death.	Cause.	Place.
12224	Pte.	Moore, William	31- 7-17	K in A	France
10/1926	Pte.	Moore, William J.	10- 8-15	K in A	Gallipoli
11505	Pte.	Moosman, Lewis J.	1-10-16	K in A	France
10/3640	Capt.	Morgan, Fred. H. E. (M.C.)	22- 7-18	D of W	U.K. ex F"ce.
10/3037	L/Cpl.	Morgan, Harry C.	4-10-17	K in A	France
31323	Pte.	Morgan, Thomas	4- 6-17	K in A	France
24/1755	Pte.	Morris, Eric V. J.	31- 7-16	K in A	France
10/3653	Sgt.	Morris, Gerald W.	23- 6-17	K in A	France
45538	Pte.	Morris, John	15-12-17	D of W	France
10/1574	Pte.	Morris, Norman	8- 8-15	K in A	Gallipoli
15751	Pte.	Morris, Thomas	6-10-17	D of W	France
10/1007	Pte.	Morrison, Edwin D. R.	28- 4-15	K in A	Gallipoli
31320	Pte.	Morrison, Evan W.	5- 4-18	D of W	France
20386	Pte.	Morrow, John	4-10-17	K in A	France
24763	L/Cpl.	Mortland, William J.	31- 7-17	K in A	France
20387	L/Cpl.	Mosen, Walter G.	29- 9-18	K in A	France
31324	Pte.	Mott, Thomas T.	27- 7-17	K in A	France
28175	Pte.	Mowat, Herbert G.	4- 6-17	D of Disease	France
10/3353	Cpl.	Moy, Robert E.	21- 8-17	D of W	France
10/641	Pte.	Muhleisen, Frederick	29- 4-15	K in A	Gallipoli
10/1047	Pte.	Muir, Harold I.	29- 6-16	K in A	France
10/751	Pte.	Mulcahy, John	8- 8-15	K in A	Gallipoli
10/3655	Pte.	Mulcahy, Patrick	16- 9-16	K in A	France
16919	Pte.	Muldrew, William J.	24- 8-18	K in A	France
10/825	Pte.	Mulholland, W. J.	9- 5-15	K in A	Gallipoli
30615	Pte.	Mullins, Michael F.	5-11-17	D of W	France
13459	Pte.	Mullins, Thomas	15- 9-16	K in A	France
10/784	L/Sgt.	Mulley, Martin W.	27- 4-15	K in A	Gallipoli
12227	Pte.	Munro, Charles	6- 5-18	K in A	France
10/1930	Lt.	Munro, Kenneth	3- 7-16	K in A	France
10/435	Cpl.	Murdoch, Sidney	8- 8-15	K in A	Gallipoli
24/1760	Sgt.	Murnane, Laurance J.	23- 7-17	D of W	France
10/1579	Pte.	Murphy, James	8- 8-15	K in A	Gallipoli
45892	Pte.	Murphy, James P.	22-10-17	K in A	France
24/2046	Pte.	Murphy, John	31- 7-17	K in A	France
14659	Pte.	Murray, William	4- 6-17	D of W	France
33413	Pte.	Murray, William D.	31- 7-17	K in A	France
1/557	A/Capt.	Murrell, Sydney A.	4-11-18	K in A	France
10/2713	L/Cpl.	Mutton, Charles T.	7- 6-17	K in A	France
10/1931	Pte.	Myers, Ewart G.	8- 8-15	K in A	Gallipoli
10/1000	Pte.	Myhill, Robert	10- 5-15	D of W	Gallipoli
11089	Pte.	Nash, Francis	11- 2-17	K in A	France

THE WELLINGTON REGIMENT

Reg. No.	Rank.	Name.	Date death.	Cause.	Place.
23/1761	Sgt.	Neal, Alfred	23- 4-18	D of W	France
23/1762	Sgt.	Neal, Ernest	4-10-17	K in A	France
23/1763	T/L-Sgt.	Neal, George	30- 1-18	K in A	France
39551	Pte.	Neilsen, Alfred	4-11-18	K in A	France
10/1933	Pte.	Nelson, Edward	8- 8-15	K. in A	Gallipoli
31333	Pte.	Nelson, Thomas	8- 6-17	K in A	France
33425	Pte.	Nelson, William G.	16- 6-17	K in A	France
10/468	Cpl.	Nesbit, Alfred	8- 8-15	K in A	Gallipoli ?
33427	Pte.	Ness, Thomas J. J.	31- 7-17	K in A	France
10/437	Pte.	Newcombe, C. E. H.	8- 8-15	K in A	Gallipoli '
11/1940	L/Cpl.	Newlove, Leighton L.	13- 6-17	D of W	France
10/3041	Pte.	Newman, Frederick G.	27- 9-16	K in A	France
30629	Pte.	Newman, Wilfred C.	4-10-17	K in A	France
30630	Pte.	Newman, William T.	10- 2-18	D of W	France
13463	Pte.	Newport, Allan	1-10-16	K in A	France
10/928	Pte.	Newson, Thomas J.	13- 9-15	D of W	Malta ex Gallipoli
10/708	Pte.	Newton, Howard	2- 5-15	D of W	Egypt ex Gallipoli
65157	Pte.	Neylon, John J.	30- 9-18	K in A	France
30631	L/Cpl.	Nias, George W.	4-10-17	K in A	France
10/1595	Pte.	Niccolls, Owen S.	8- 8-15	K in A	Gallipoli '
24/2548	Sgt.	Nicholl, Joseph A.	4-10-17	K in A	France
23/2055	Pte.	Nicholls, Ernest	2-10-16	K in A	France
12/609	L/Cpl.	Nicholls, George H.	8- 6-17	K in A	France
10203	Pte.	Nicholls, Ilbert E. A.	16- 9-16	K in A	France
10/913	Pte.	Nicholson, George	3- 6-16	K in A	France
59432	L/Cpl.	Nicholson, Peter	25- 8-18	D of W	France
10/932	Pte.	Nickels, Arthur	8- 8-15	K in A	Gallipoli
24/1765	Pte.	Nicklin, Alfred	5-10-17	K in A	France
25168	Pte.	Nickolls, Frederick C.	7- 6-17	K in A	France
9/1474	Pte.	Nicol, George A.	4-10-17	K in A	France
10/2499	Lt.	Nicol, Robert A.	5- 8-18	K in A	Persia
29461	Pte.	Nield, Cyril W.	4-10-17	K in A	France
64113	Pte.	Nielsen, Rasmus W. E.	14- 8-19	Injuries (Suicide gun shot wounds)	N.Z.
10/992	Pte.	Nielsen, William A.	7- 5-15	K in A	Gallipoli
53060	Pte.	Nix, Roy	24- 8-18	K in A	France
11/2348	Pte.	Norman, Edward L. F.	27- 7-17	D of W	France
11/1944	Pte.	Norris, Fred. L.	3- 6-16	K in A	France
25572	Pte.	Norris, John H. M.	8- 6-17	D of W	France
10/996	Cpl.	Northey, Samuel	8- 8-15	K in A	Gallipoli
10/3355	L/Cpl.	Northover, L. W.	22-10-17	K in A	France

THE WELLINGTON REGIMENT

Reg. No.	Rank.	Name.	Date death.	Cause.	Place.
65440	Pte.	Nutsey, Charles	30- 8-18	K in A	France
10/1600	Pte.	O'Brien, Henry	27- 4-15	K in A	Gallipoli
25573	Pte.	O'Brien, John	4-10-17	K in A	France
10/1937	Pte.	O'Brien, Michael	7- 6-17	K in A	France
10/1938	Pte.	O'Callaghan, D. W.	8- 8-15	K in A	Gallipoli
10/3688	Pte.	O'Connor, George P.	29- 9-16	K in A	France
29462	Pte.	O'Connor, Michael F.	9- 6-17	K in A	France
10/2261	Pte.	O'Connor, Richard	3- 7-16	K in A	France
10/1603	Cpl.	O'Connor, Timothy	27- 7-17	K in A	France
30396	Pte.	O'Gorman, Thomas	4/6-10-17	K in A	France
61748	Pte.	O'Grady, Daniel F.	13- 9-18	K in A	France
63062	Pte.	O'Halloran, A.	24- 8-18	K in A	France
10/112	Pte.	O'Keeffe, John	30- 4-15	D of W	At Sea ex Gallipoli
10/2458	Pte.	O'Leary, Jeremiah C.	24- 8-18	K in A	France
10/96	Sgt.	O'Neale, Arthur B.	27- 4-15	K in A	Gallipoli
51187	Pte.	O'Neill, Bernard	20-12-17	K in A	France
10/1605	Pte.	O'Neill, Richard	19- 8-15	D of W	Egypt ex Gallipoli
10/3045	Pte.	O'Reilly, Francis C.	23- 7-17	K in A	France
22507	Pte.	O'Reilly, Michael	9-12-17	D of W	France
10/95	Pte.	O'Shea George A.	11- 1-16	Disease	Egypt
72579	Pte.	O'Shea, James M.	23-10-18	Disease	France
40752	2/Lt.	O'Sullivan, Leo D.	24- 8-18	D of W	France
39875	Pte.	Oakley, Robert	25- 7-17	D of W	France
18696	Sgt.	Ogden, Thomas	16- 5-18	K in A	France
23/2524	Pte.	Okey, Alfred J.	4- 6-16	K in A	France
10/3356	Pte.	Okey, Lionel G.	15- 9-16	K in A	France
10/761	Lt.	Okey, Royden L. (M.C.)	30- 9-18	K in A	France
10/737	Sgt.	Okey, Sydney M.	8- 8-15	K in A	Gallipoli
10/3968	Pte.	Old, Edgar	7- 6-17	K in A	France
10/1940	L/Sgt.	Old, Harold	3- 4-18	D of W	France
10/3822	L/Cpl.	Old, Harry A.	8- 6-17	K in A	France
10/2459	Pte.	Oliver, Budge W.	15- 8-15	K in A	Gallipoli
10/98	Pte.	Oliver, Edward J.	8- 8-15	K in A	Gallipoli
11925	Pte.	Oliver, Richard A.	8- 6-17	K in A	France
10/97	L/Cpl.	Oliver, Thomas	16- 9-16	D of W	France
8/4196	Pte.	Olsen, Ingolf E.	19- 9-16	K in A	France
32051	L/Cpl.	Olsen, Peter William	4-10-17	K in A	France
42180	Pte.	Olson, Albert A.	4-10-17	K in A	France
10/3692	Sgt.	Ordish, Alfred W.	16- 9-16	K in A	France
38062	Pte.	Orr, James	29- 7-17	K in A	France
42174	Pte.	Osborne, Charles P.	4-10-17	K in A	France

THE WELLINGTON REGIMENT

Reg. No.	Rank.	Name.	Date death.	Cause.	Place.
10/3038	L/Cpl.	Otto, Norman C.	25- 9-16	K in A	France
24/1767	Pte.	Overend, William T.	9- 6-16	D of W	France
10/1944	Pte.	Owens, Peter J.	8- 8-15	K in A	Gallipoli
10/461	Pte.	Oxley, Thomas	8- 8-15	K in A	Gallipoli
23238	Pte.	Packard, Alfred R.	31- 7-17	K in A	France
45903	Pte.	Padden, Patrick	4-10-17	K in A	France
10/3694	Pte.	Paget, Samuel F.	4-10-17	K in A	France
32534	Cpl.	Paine, Herbert W. G.	16- 5-18	K in A	France
10/28	Sgt.	Pallant, Donald K.	8- 5-15	K in A	Gallipoli
39878	Pte.	Palmer, Alexander C.	30- 9-18	K in A	France
10/496	Pte.	Palmer, Hector V.	29- 4-15	K in A	Gallipoli
10/1609	Pte.	Panton, Joseph L.	19- 8-15	Disease	Egypt ex Gallipoli
22603	Lt.	Park, Victor H.	4- 3-19	Disease	France
10/1034	Pte.	Parker, Albert J.	8- 8-15	K in A	Gallipoli
23/2061	Pte.	Parker, Claude	15- 9-16	K in A	France
10/2729	Pte.	Parker, Edgar M.	9-10-16	D of W	France
10/3050	Pte.	Parker, Edward L. C.	20-10-16	D of W	France
10049	Pte.	Parker, Samuel C.	17- 9-16	K in A	France
20408	Pte.	Parkes, Charles	31- 7-17	K in A	France
10/1061	Pte.	Parkinson, R. W.	23- 7-15	Disease	Mudros ex Gallipoli
10/2270	Sgt.	Parkinson, Walter H.	9- 6-17	K in A	France
10/4167	Pte.	Parkyn, Richard	16- 9-16	K in A	France
33941	Pte.	Parmenter, Jack	15-10-17	K in A	France
10/2730	L/Sgt.	Parr, Thomas A.	4-10-17	K in A	France
10/785	Sgt.	Parrington, Hugh M.	25- 8-15	Disease	Egypt ex Gallipoli
38064	Pte.	Parsons, Albert E.	5- 2-19	Disease	Germany
38741	Pte.	Parsons, John G. W.	20- 7-17	K in A	France
10/1309	Cpl.	Parsons, Reginald	8- 8-15	K in A	Gallipoli
10/876	Pte.	Pascoe, Charles H.	1- 8-16	K in A	France
38069	L/Cpl.	Patching, James A.	12-10-18	K in A	France
56846	Pte.	Paterson, Douglas	7- 9-18	D of W	France
10/3699	Pte.	Paterson, William H.	8- 6-17	K in A	France
61764	Pte.	Patterson, Albert	30- 8-18	K in A	France
10/1310	Pte.	Patterson, William H.	8- 8-15	K in A	Gallipoli
11/1208	Cpl.	Pattison, Herbert C.	23- 3-18	Accd. K (At musketry practice)	France
23760	L/Cpl.	Paul, James C.	8- 6-17	K in A	France
10/2274	2/Lt.	Paul, Sydney V.	23-10-17	K in A	France
52645	Pte.	Payn, John F.	3-10-18	K in A	France
10/619	Pte.	Payne, George	8- 5-15	K in A	Gallipoli

THE WELLINGTON REGIMENT

Reg. No.	Rank.	Name.	Date death.	Cause.	Place.
10/2500	Sgt.	Pearce, Arthur H.	23-10-17	K in A	France
46143	Pte.	Pearce, Owen D.	13- 5-18	D of W	France
45908	Pte.	Pearce, Harold C.	19-10-17	D of W	France
10/1612	Cpl.	Pearson, Charles E.	29- 1-18	D of W	France
10/2802	Pte.	Pearson, Gordon G.	22-10-15	Disease	Lemnos
10/3974	Pte.	Pearson, Thomas	10- 7-16	K in A	France
23093	Pte.	Peat, George W.	8- 7-17	K in A	France
45909	Pte.	Pedder, Mervyn H.	12-10-18	K in A	France
15767	L/Cpl.	Pedersen, Einer	30- 8-18	K in A	France
11930	Pte.	Pedersen, Karl B. K.	8- 6-18	D of W	France
38742	Sgt.	Pelley, George W.	1- 9-18	D of W	France
38743	Pte.	Pelley, Thomas H.	15-11-18	Disease	N.Z.
10/1613	Pte.	Penney, John G.	8- 8-15	K in A	Gallipoli
10/4487	L/Cpl.	Penny, Walter B.	4-10-17	K in A	France
10/1614	Pte.	Pepper, James J.	8- 8-15	K in A	Gallipoli
31343	Pte.	Percival, Henry R.	30- 8-18	K in A	France
10/1053	2/Lt.	Percy, Frank	15- 8-16	D of W	France
10/63	Pte.	Percy, Henry S.	8- 8-15	K in A	Gallipoli
30603	Pte.	Percy, Leigh C. F.	29- 8-18	K in A	France
10/1616	Pte.	Perie, Joseph G.	8- 8-15	K in A	Gallipoli
28200	Pte.	Perkins, Frank G.	13-10-17	D of W	France
10/908	Cpl.	Persse, John G.	8- 8-15	K in A	Gallipoli
10/195	Pte.	Persson, Martin A.	8- 8-15	K in A	Gallipoli
14674	Pte.	Peters, Albert E.	7- 2-17	K in A	France
10/579	Pte.	Peters, Maitland H.	11- 6-15	K in A	Gallipoli
11932	Pte.	Peters, Richard	11-11-16	K in A	France
38065	Pte.	Petersen, Timis F.	4-10-17	K in A	France
13/3229	Pte.	Peterson, Fred. C.	27- 3-18	K in A	France
14477	Pte.	Petherick, Walter V.	12- 8-17	D of W	France
10/3056	Pte.	Phelps, James	27- 9-16	K in A	France
11105	Pte.	Philips, Malcolm	28- 9-16	K in A	France
64121	Pte.	Phillips, Benjamin S.	1-10-18	K in A	France
16577	Pte.	Phillips, Cecil	9- 6-17	D of W	France
10/499	Pte.	Phillips, Charles E.	27- 4-15	K in A	Gallipoli
10/1319	Pte.	Phillips, George	8- 8-15	K in A	Gallipoli
10/3368	Pte.	Phillips, William J.	29- 6-16	K in A	France
10/1033	Pte.	Pickard, John H. T.	30- 4-15	D of W	At Sea ex Gallipoli
52546	Pte.	Pidgeon, Robert	24- 8-18	K in A	France
10/3057	Pte.	Pidwell, Henry H.	16- 9-16	K in A	France
24/2073	Pte.	Pierce, Daniel W.	7- 6-17	K in A	France
10/2735	Pte.	Pine, George A.	27- 9-16	K in A	France
10/920	Pte.	Pitt, George P.: about	16- 5-17	K in A	Gallipoli
27185	Sgt.	Player, Ernest N.	16-10-17	D of W	U.K. ex F"ce.
10/39	Pte.	Playle, Stanley E.	16- 9-16	K in A	France

THE WELLINGTON REGIMENT

Reg. No.	Rank.	Name.	Date death.	Cause.	Place.
10/3982	Pte.	Pollard, Norman A.	4-10-17	K in A	France
28199	L/Cpl.	Pooley, Reginald E.	4-10-17	D of W	France
10/3058	Cpl.	Poole, Albert W. G.	4-10-17	K in A	France
30637	Pte.	Porteous, William T.	4-10-17	K in A	France
15771	Pte.	Porter, George R.	7- 7-17	D of W	France
10/3983	Pte.	Potroz, Augustus	17- 9-16	D of W	France
10/467	L/Cpl.	Potter, John	4- 9-18	D of W	France
10/1142	Pte.	Potts, John K.	8- 8-15	K in A	Gallipoli
20228	Pte.	Powell, Peter C. McE.	29- 8-18	K in A	France
33603	Pte.	Powell, Thomas H.	4-10-17	K in A	France
10/1621	Pte.	Power, Augustus	8- 8-15	K in A	Gallipoli
10/3984	Pte.	Power, Thomas E.	4-10-17	K in A	France
15772	L/Cpl.	Preshaw, Harold H.	31- 7-17	K in A	France
29477	Pte.	Preston, John	7- 6-17	K in A	France
10/2738	Pte.	Preston, John	24- 3-17	K in A	France
20415	Pte.	Preston, William C.	10-12-16	K in A	France
10/1170	Pte.	Price, William C.	8- 5-15	K in A	Gallipoli
33438	Pte.	Prichard, Robert	31- 7-18	Disease	France
10/1621	Pte.	Prideaux, Thomas P.	27- 4-15	K in A	Gallipoli
10/907	Pte.	Priest, Andrew J.	27- 4-15	K in A	Gallipoli
10/4175	Cpl.	Priest, George	27- 7-17	K in A	France
10/93	Pte.	Prior, Morton C.	29- 4-15	K in A	Gallipoli
37013	Pte.	Pulford, Ernest W.	24-10-18	D of W	France
10/219	Pte.	Pull, Frederick S.	29- 4-15	K in A	Gallipoli
47463	Pte.	Pullen, Vivian R.	4- 8-19	Disease	N.Z.
27794	Pte.	Purcell, Robert	16-11-17	Accd. K	U.K. (Run over by motor bus)
10/3061	Pte.	Pye, Wilfred O.	8- 8-16	Disease	France
10/3985	Pte.	Pyn, John A.	3- 8-16	D of W	France
11940	Pte.	Quarterman, Fred. C.	15- 9-16	K in A	France
24/2555	Pte.	Quealy, Thomas	3- 6-17	D of W	France
10/2284	Pte.	Quick, William B. A.	10-12-16	K in A	France
10/3708	Pte.	Quickenden, T. G.	15- 9-16	K in A	France
60294	2/Lt.	Quillan, Cecil W.	4-11-18	K in A	France
10/2285	L/Cpl.	Quilliam, Reg. P.	3- 8-16	K in A	France
33439	Pte.	Quin, Arthur H.	30- 8-18	K in A	France
36487	L/Cpl.	Radford, Lester R.	4-10-17	K in A	France
20418	Pte.	Rae, Alfred W.	1- 8-17	D of W	France
10/1624	Pte.	Randall, Joseph	21- 8-15	Disease	Malta ex Mudros
24/1787	Pte.	Ratcliffe, Ernest	4-10-17	K in A	France
10/776	Pte.	Rauch, Walter J.	8- 8-15	K in A	Gallipoli

THE WELLINGTON REGIMENT

Reg. No.	Rank.	Name.	Date death.	Cause.	Place.
10/1323	Pte.	Rawlings, Herbert	17- 9-16	K in A	France
47465	Pte.	Raynor, Walter H.	9- 2-18	D of W	France
10/4490	Pte.	Reader, Charles W.	19-12-16	D of W	France
10/1959	Pte.	Reardon, Herbert	8- 8-15	K in A	Gallipoli
12330	L/Cpl.	Redmond, William J.	9- 6-17	D of W	France
41891	Pte.	Redstone, Bernard E.	4-10-17	K in A	France
44868	Pte.	Reece, Arthur	4-10-17	K in A	France
10/3712	Pte.	Reeves, Charles	30- 7-16	D of W	France
10/3064	Pte.	Reid, Alexander	26- 9-16	D of W	France
55868	Pte.	Reid, Frank F.	16- 8-18	K in A	France
39893	Pte.	Reid, Gavin	5-10-17	K in A	France
10/3713	Pte.	Reid, George	6- 4-17	D of W	France
31350	Pte.	Reid, James	7- 6-17	K in A	France
10/1626	Pte.	Reilly, John	8- 8-15	K in A	Gallipoli
42203	Pte.	Reilly, Phillip	4-10-17	D of W	France
10/209	Pte.	Reisima, Robert R.	9- 5-15	K in A	Gallipoli
10/1084	Pte.	Remnant, Joseph S.	10- 3-15	Disease	Australia en route N.Z. ex Egypt
10/2745	Pte.	Renton, George	17- 9-16	K in A	France
10/1627	Sgt.	Renwick, Harold	18- 7-17	D of W	France
33607	Pte.	Reynard, Frank	27-11-17	K in A	France
10/3066	Pte.	Reynish, Roger C.	30-11-17	K in A	France
10/3067	Pte.	Reynish, Thomas H.	30- 9-17	Injuries (Suicide by shooting)	France
10/353	Pte.	Reynolds, Samuel	16- 5-15	K in A	Gallipoli
28631	Pte.	Rhodes, Ernest W.	23- 7-17	K in A	France
40131	Pte.	Rice, Leslie C.	3- 2-18	D of W	France
38071	Pte.	Rice, Patrick J.	14-12-17	K in A	France
10/181	T/Cpl.	Richards, Charles H.	2- 8-17	K in A	France
11945	Cpl.	Richards, Frank H.	19- 4-18	D of W	France
10/2746	Pte.	Richards, Godfrey	4- 2-17	D of W	France
10/1962	Pte.	Richards, Herbert E.	7- 8-15	K in A	Gallipoli
10/2747	Pte.	Richards, Roy F.	20-11-15	K in A	Gallipoli
11786	Pte.	Richardson, Claude M.	12-11-16	D of W	France
10/3068	Sgt.	Richardson, Frank G. (M.M.)	31- 8-18	K in A	France
25593	Pte.	Richardson, L. C.	12- 4-18	D of W	France
38794	Pte.	Richardson, Michael	4-10-17	K in A	France
10/1327	Sgt.	Richardson, T. G. A.	13- 7-16	Disease	N.Z.
68322	Pte.	Ricketts, Leslie S.	11-10-18	K in A	France
9/1623	Capt.	Riddiford, Richard (O.B.E., M.C., M.I.D. twice)	10- 2-19	Disease	U.K.
32067	Pte.	Riddle, Ewing S.	4-11-18	K in A	France
38218	Pte.	Rigby, Edward	4-11-18	K in A	France

THE WELLINGTON REGIMENT

Reg. No.	Rank.	Name.	Date death.	Cause.	Place.
25317	Pte.	Riley, George	31- 7-17	K in A	France
10/1964	Pte.	Rimmer, Thomas A.	8- 8-15	K in A	Gallipoli
10/2295	Pte.	Ringrow, Frank	8- 8-15	K in A	Gallipoli
33610	L/Cpl.	Rintoul, Richard W. P.	7-10-17	D of W	France
10/3721	Cpl.	Rising, Henry N.	27- 7-17	K in A	France
23/2078	Pte.	Ritchie, John	15- 9-16	K in A	France
47468	Pte.	Ritchie, John	8- 2-18	K in A	France
24/1306	2/Lt.	Robbie, George A.	22- 7-17	K in A	France
23/905	Pte.	Roberts, Frederick J.	21-10-16	D of W	France
61785	Pte.	Roberts, John M.	2- 9-18	D of W	France
10/1632	Pte.	Roberts, Owen H.	26- 5-15	D of W	Malta ex Gal.
12261	Pte.	Roberts, Sam	27- 9-16	D of W	France
10/503	Pte.	Roberts, Sydney	27- 4-15	K in A	Gallipoli
12076	Pte.	Robertson, Albert E.	31- 8-18	K in A	France
10/2749	L/Cpl.	Robertson, Albert W.	22- 6-16	K in A	France
33611	Pte.	Robertson, Charles S.	29- 9-18	K in A	France
37054	Pte.	Robertson, Douglas L.	27- 3-18	K in A	France
10/2463	Cpl.	Robertson, Arch. J.	15- 6-17	D of W	France
10/509	Pte.	Robinson, Arthur G.	8-·8-15	K in A	Gallipoli
29485	Pte.	Robinson, Claud	26- 6-17	K in A	France
32066	Pte.	Robinson, Francis J. C.	7- 6-17	K in A	France
10/3379	Pte.	Robinson, Joseph T.	10- 6-16	D of W	France
10/2464	Pte.	Robinson, Richard	8- 8-15	K in A	Gallipoli
30161	L/Cpl.	Robinson, Roy G.	30- 3-18	K in A	France
47833	Pte.	Robinson, Thomas S.	8- 1-18	D of W	U.K. ex F"ce.
10/1634	Pte.	Robinson, Thomas W.	8- 8-15	K in A	Gallipoli
26008	Cpl.	Robinson, Will. H. M.	7- 8-17	K in A	France
10/4182	L/Cpl.	Robson, James	17- 9-18	D of W	France
10/1052	L/Cpl.	Robson, Robert C.	29- 4-15	D of W	At Sea ex Gallipoli
24/1798	Cpl.	Rodgers, Harry	4-10-17	K in A	France
10/733	T/Cpl.	Rogers, Charles A.	25- 9-16	K in A	France
39898	Pte.	Rogers, David	21- 8-17	D of W	U.K. ex F"ce.
38750	Pte.	Rogers, George H.	3-10-17	K in A	France
51578	Pte.	Rogers, Samuel G.	29- 9-18	K in A	France
15778	L/Cpl.	Roil, Raymond J.	24- 8-18	D of W	France
10/2299	Pte.	Ronaldson, Ernest B.	8- 8-15	K in A	Gallipoli
15779	Pte.	Rook, Percy A.	11- 2-18	K in A	France
39899	Pte.	Rose, Charles H.	13- 9-18	K in A	France
9/2221	Pte.	Rose, Owen A.	16- 9-16	K in A	France
10/52	Pte.	Rose, Sydney	8- 5-15	K in A	Gallipoli
51070	Pte.	Rose, William A.	13-10-17	K in A	France
10/2751	Pte.	Rose, William V.	3- 9-15	Disease	At Sea en route Egypt
10/92	L/Sgt.	Rosenfeldt, A. B. P.	8- 5-15	K in A	Gallipoli

THE WELLINGTON REGIMENT

Reg. No.	Rank.	Name.	Date death.	Cause.	Place.
10/2300	Pte.	Rosie, Donald W.	16- 9-16	K in A	France
14868	Pte.	Ross, Alfred W.	3/4-10-17	D of W	France
11/1738	L/Cpl.	Ross, Davis A.	2- 4-17	K in A	France
10/3144	Mjr.	Ross, Fleming (M.I.D.)	18- 9-16	K in A	France
12263	Pte.	Ross, Hugh L.	1- 8-17	K in A	France
10/508	Pte.	Ross, James	8- 8-15	K in A	Gallipoli
10/3075	Pte.	Ross, Munro W. N.	16- 9-16	K in A	France
27140	Pte.	Ross, Roderick	20-12-17	D of W	U.K. ex F'ce.
23879	Pte.	Rossiter, Albert A. (M.M.)	23- 3-18	Accd. K	France (Shot at Musketry practice)
45918	Pte.	Rowe, William Charles	4-10-17	K in A	France
69523	Pte.	Rowland, Ernest D. N.	1- 9-18	K in A	France
10/505	Pte.	Rowley, Norman S.	27- 7-15	Disease	At Sea ex Gallipoli
10/4491	Pte.	Royal, James	10-11-18	Disease	U.K.
59461	Pte.	Ruddle, Joseph	13- 9-18	K in A	France
10/502	L/Sgt.	Rule, Frank J.	26- 5-15	D of W	Egypt ex Gallipoli
10/1972	Pte.	Rundle, Fred. G.	25- 1-17	D of W	U.K. ex F'ce.
24/1802	Pte.	Rush, William H.	5-10-16	D of W	France
10/1973	Pte.	Russell, George G.	8- 8-15	K in A	Gallipoli
56660	Pte.	Russell, James R.	24- 8-18	K in A	France
10/1643	Pte.	Russell, Joseph	14-12-18	Disease	U.K.
10/2306	Pte.	Russell, Richard J.	8- 8-15	K in A	Gallipoli
10/3728	Pte.	Rutherford, H. S.	31- 7-17	D of W	France
28542	Pte.	Ryan, David W.	19- 6-17	K in A	France
10/702	Pte.	Ryan, Denis	8- 5-15	K in A	Gallipoli
29492	Pte.	Ryan, Joseph	7- 6-17	K in A	France
10/486	L/Sgt.	Ryan, Patrick W.	16- 9-16	K in A	France
10/919	Sgt.	Ryder, William	29-11-17	D of W	France
14871	Pte.	Sabin, John N.	21-10-17	K in A	France
21163	Pte.	Saint, Stanley A. A.	31- 7-17	K in A	France
10/3078	Pte.	Sally, John	4-10-17	K in A	France
66227	A/Capt.	Salmond, William G.	9- 7-18	K in A	France
10056	Pte.	Sanderson, William	2-10-16	K in A	France
17854	Pte.	Sattler, Charles L.	30-10-16	K in A	France
24/333	Pte.	Saunders, Hubert M.	16- 8-17	D of W	France
25323	Pte.	Saunders, Mark	4-10-17	K in A	France
10/1329	Pte.	Saunders, Thomas	29- 4-15	K in A	Gallipoli
24/1807	Cpl.	Savage, Albert	25- 8-18	K in A	France
11/2219	Pte.	Sawyer, Arthur H.	21- 9-16	D of W	France
10/3387	Pte.	Saywell, George N.	17-10-17	K in A	France

THE WELLINGTON REGIMENT

Reg. No.	Rank.	Name.	Date death.	Cause.	Place.
12483	Pte.	Saywell, Roy W.	23-10-16	D of W	France
10/4194	Pte.	Scarlett, Joseph B.	28- 9-16	K in A	France
62643	Pte.	Schischka, Martin J.	30- 8-18	K in A	France
24/1922	Pte.	Schmidt, George H.	4- 6-16	D of W	France
10/2384	Pte.	Schoch, John B. (M.M.)	28- 9-16	D of W	France
10/1022	Pte.	Schofield, Hiram	27- 4-15	K in A	Gallipoli
10/1645	Pte.	Schofield, Joe W.	8- 8-15	K in A	Gallipoli
10/525	Pte.	Schulz, Herbert A.	29- 4-15	K in A	Gallipoli
10/518	Sgt.	Sciascia, Charles	1- 8-17	K in A	France
38075	L/Cpl.	Scott, Arthur M.	20- 8-17	K in A	France
13820	Pte.	Scott, Daniel C.	22-10-17	D of W	France
10/2482	Capt.	Scott, Robert F. C. (M.I.D.)	9- 6-17	D of W	France
42412	Pte.	Scrugham, William W.	31- 8-18	K in A	France
10/2309	Pte.	Scrutton, Ernest J.	8- 8-15	K in A	Gallipoli
10/1647	Pte.	Seagrave, Ambrose	7- 6-17	K in A	France
12485	Pte.	Semmens, Arthur B.	30- 8-18	K in A	France
33616	Pte.	Serpell, Percy C.	9- 7-17	D of W	France
10/1978	Pte.	Sewell, Edgar	8- 8-15	K in A	Gallipoli
10/224	Pte.	Sewell, James W.	29- 4-15	K in A	Gallipoli
38228	Pte.	Seymour, Felix	4-10-17	K in A	France
10/1333	Pte.	Seymour, William	8- 5-15	K in A	Gallipoli
10/1979	Pte.	Shackleford, Harold	17- 9-16	K in A	France
10/528	Pte.	Shadlow, Stephen	29- 4-15	K in A	Gallipoli
10/1649	Cpl.	Shakeshaft, Alfred	24-10-17	K in A	France
11955	Pte.	Shannon, Ronald L.	5- 6-17	D of W	France
23897	Sgt.	Sharp, James H.	1-10-17	K in A	France
8/2312	Pte.	Sharpe, Sydney A.	31- 7-17	K in A	France
10/1980	Pte.	Shaw, Alexander	8- 8-15	K in A	Gallipoli
23/2528	Pte.	Shaw, William	14- 9-16	K in A	France
27701	Pte.	Shea, John H.	11- 6-17	D of W	France
29971	Pte.	Shearer, Charles H.	8- 6-17	D of W	France
61810	Pte.	Sheed, William R.	27- 3-18	K in A	France
11957	Pte.	Sheehan, John	16- 3-18	Disease	France
10/1981	Pte.	Sheerin, James	8- 8-15	K in A	Gallipoli
10/3872	Pte.	Shefford, James	8- 6-17	K in A	France
10/1653	Pte.	Sheldon, John J. W.	8- 8-15	K in A	Gallipoli
25598	Pte.	Shepherd, Orr	7- 6-17	K in A	France
31726	L/Cpl.	Sheppard, Thomas C.	12-10-18	K in A	France
46146	Pte.	Sherlock, Percy J.	11-10-18	K in A	France
45926	Pte.	Sherlock, Robert	1-10-18	K in A	France
10/3735	L/Cpl.	Sherret, John A.	14- 9-16	K in A	France
10/1014	Pte.	Sherwood, John C.	17-12-15	D of W	At Sea ex Gallipoli

THE WELLINGTON REGIMENT

Reg. No.	Rank.	Name.	Date death.	Cause.	Place.
33456	Pte.	Sherwood, Sidney H.	4-10-17	K in A	France
20434	Pte.	Shield, Ronald C.	8- 6-17	K in A	France
10/89	Sgt.	Shields, Philip F.	16- 9-16	K in A	France
32991	Pte.	Shirley, Thomas O.	16- 8-17	D of In. (Lewis Gun Accd.)	France
10/563	Cpl.	Shoebridge, Albert J.	5- 8-19	D of W and sickness	N.Z. ex Gal.
10/1982	Pte.	Shoemark, James C.	8- 8-15	K in A	Gallipoli
31358	Cpl.	Short, Hughie T.	25- 8-18	K in A	France
10/1160	Pte.	Short, Leslie H.	8- 8-15	K in A	Gallipoli
59467	Pte.	Shotter, William J.	9- 3-19	D of W	U.K. ex F'ce.
30410	Cpl.	Shrimpton, Arthur V.	15- 6-17	D of W	France
38077	Pte.	Shrimpton, Stanley M.	31- 7-17	K in A	France
49849	Pte.	Siegel, Charles C.	30- 3-18	K in A	France
10/1655	Pte.	Siegel, John A.	8- 8-15	K in A	Gallipoli
10/87	Sgt.	Sievers, Gerald	8- 8-15	K in A	Gallipoli
30649	Pte.	Sievers, Louis W.	30-11-17	K in A	France
44239	Pte.	Signal, William C.	1-10-18	K in A	France
12488	Pte.	Sim, Albert J.	12-10-18	K in A	France
10/1983	Pte.	Sim, Walter L.	8- 8-15	K in A	Gallipoli
28221	Pte.	Simmons, Emanuel	6- 6-17	K in A	France
10/690	Pte.	Simpson, Alan L.	11- 6-15	D of W	Gallipoli
10/941	Pte.	Simpson, Bethel J.	17- 3-15	Disease	Egypt
10/1985	Pte.	Simpson, Claude E.	8- 8-15	K in A	Gallipoli
39903	Pte.	Simpson, Joseph	31- 7-17	K in A	France
10/1986	Pte.	Simpson, William	15- 8-15	K in A	Gallipoli
29501	Pte.	Simson, Charles	4- 7-17	D of W	U.K. ex F"ce.
23/2088	Pte.	Simson, Fred. G. O.	11- 6-17	D of W	France
10/203	L/Cpl.	Simson, Sydney	16- 9-16	K in A	France
10/2501	Sgt.	Skeet, Ernest	2- 7-16	K in A	France
23/2089	Pte.	Skellon, Tom H.	21- 9-16	D of W	France
33460	Pte.	Slight, Cecil H.	23- 8-17	K in A	France
47003	Pte.	Sly, Ernest L.	4-10-17	K in A	France
10/202	Sgt.	Smale, Henry T.	8- 5-15	K in A	Gallipoli
15791	Pte.	Smith, Albert E.	31- 7-17	K in A	France
10/3999	Pte.	Smith, Albert V.	16- 9-16	K in A	France
10/3801	Pte.	Smith, Alexander H.	22- 7-16	K in A	France
10/2767	Pte.	Smith, Frank	16- 9-16	K in A	France
13534	L/Cpl.	Smith, George F.	27- 3-18	K in A	France
59789	Pte.	Smith, Harold McD.	19- 9-18	D of W	France
10/1037	Pte.	Smith, James W.	2- 5-15	K in A	Gallipoli
10/1340	Pte.	Smith, John E.	16- 5-15	K in A	Gallipoli
10/534	Pte.	Smith, John H.	6- 5-15	D of W	At Sea ex Gallipoli
59471	Pte.	Smith, John P.	28- 4-18	D of W	France

THE WELLINGTON REGIMENT

Reg. No.	Rank.	Name.	Date death.	Cause.	Place.
10/1164	Pte.	Smith, Sydney C. P.	10- 4-16	Disease	Egypt
10/698	Pte.	Smith, Thomas D. D.	3- 7-16	K in A	France
10/1342	Pte.	Smith, Walter R.	8- 5-15	K in A	Gallipoli
10/2315	Pte.	Smith, Thomas W.	8- 8-15	K in A	Gallipoli
10/1991	Pte.	Smith, Wilfred C.	8-10-17	D of W	France
13477	Pte.	Smith, William C.	1- 7-17	D of W	France
10/789	Sgt.	Smyth, Ernest O.	28- 8-15	D of W	Egypt ex Gallipoli
54405	Pte.	Smyth, Wilfred E.	2-11-19	Disease	N.Z. ex F'ce.
10/2768	Pte.	Snaddon, Frank	11- 7-16	D of W	France
10/3087	T/Cpl.	Snell, Edward D.	30- 6-16	D of W	France
52656	Pte.	Soal, Louis O.	25- 8-18	K in A	France
10/877	Sgt.	Sole, Leslie P.	9- 5-15	D of W	At Sea ex Gallipoli
10/812	Sgt.	Sole, Reginald G.	8- 8-15	K in A	Gallipoli
49850	Pte.	Somers, John	29- 9-18	K in A	France
10/1343	T/Sgt.	Somerton, James	3- 8-16	D of W	France
20441	Pte.	Sorrenson, William M.	31- 7-17	K in A	France
10/523	L/Cpl.	Souness, Neil	4-10-17	K in A	France
52481	Pte.	Soutar, Philip R. W.	20-12-17	K in A	France
65067	Pte.	South, Sidney C.	1- 9-18	K in A	France
61822	Pte.	Sowerby, Fred. H.	27- 7-18	K in A	France
30655	Pte.	Spaccesi, Antonie	4-10-17	K in A	France
38081	Pte.	Sparkes, Ernest P.	6- 5-18	K in A	France
38080	Pte.	Spicer, Percy D.	1-12-17	K in A	France
23/1821	Pte.	Spillane, William	22- 9-16	K in A	France
10/2396	Pte.	Spooner, Edward J.	8- 8-15	K in A	Gallipoli
10/854	Sgt.	Spratt, Walter	8- 8-15	K in A	Gallipoli
10/782	Sgt.	Squire, Alan R.	8- 8-15	K in A	Gallipoli
22527	2/Lt.	Stables, Robert H.	18-10-17	D of W	France
42228	Pte.	Standen, Sydney	22-10-17	K in A	France
10/1725	Cpl.	Stanley, Thomas	3- 4-17	K in A	France
36490	Pte.	Stark, William Y.	21- 7-17	K in A	France
28220	Pte.	Steffert, Neville E.	27- 7-17	K in A	France
24/1489	Pte.	Stent, Richard	3- 7-16	K in A	France
10/1345	Pte.	Stephens, Arthur F. N.	8- 8-15	K in A	Gallipoli
11/1973	Pte.	Stephens, Edward	15- 9-16	K in A	France
10/1346	Pte.	Steven, John	8- 5-15	K in A	Gallipoli
10/4203	Pte.	Stevens, Arthur	16- 9-16	K in A	France
10/2322	Cpl.	Stevens, James	11-10-18	K in A	France
39561	Pte.	Stevens, John L.	31- 7-17	K in A	France
10/4492	Pte.	Stevens, Neil J.	31- 8-18	D of W	France
10/2772	Pte.	Stevenson, Claude	7- 6-17	K in A	France
10/998	Sgt.	Stevenson, Hugh K.	7- 6-17	K in A	France
10/4190	Pte.	Stewart, Alexander	28- 6-17	D of W	France

THE WELLINGTON REGIMENT

Reg. No.	Rank.	Name.	Date death.	Cause.	Place.
48581	Pte.	Stewart, Arthur E.	5-10-17	D of W	France
10/201	Pte.	Stewart, David	4- 7-15	Disease	Mudros ex Gallipoli
8/2482	Pte.	Stewart, David R.	21- 9-16	K in A	France
10/2323	Pte.	Stewart, Ernest O.	27-12-15	Disease	Mudros ex Gallipoli
60004	Pte.	Stewart, George C.	1-10-18	K in A	France
10/3092	Pte.	Stewart, Jack C.	19- 3-17	Disease	U.K. ex F"ce.
60002	Pte.	Stewart, James	12-10-18	K in A	France
11/1978	Pte.	Stewart, John	16- 9-16	K in A	France
39909	Pte.	Stewart, Thomas	10- 7-17	K in A	France
10/1663	Pte.	Stewart, William	8- 8-15	K in A	Gallipoli
28215	Pte.	Still, John H.	14-12-17	K in A	France
10/3747	T/Sgt.	Stirrat, Alex. G.	16- 9-16	K in A	France
46087	Pte.	Stitt, Alexander M.	1- 9-18	D of W	France
10/530	Pte.	Stock, George	8- 8-15	K in A	Gallipoli
30658	Pte.	Stockham, Thomas W.	4-10-17	K in A	France
10/1666	Pte.	Stokes, James F.	8- 8-15	K in A	Gallipoli
10/2775	Pte.	Stokes, John E.	14- 1-17	K in A	France
10/2325	Pte.	Stokes, Sydney H.	8- 8-15	K in A	Gallipoli
72994	Pte.	Stone, Thomas R.	8-11-18	Disease	France
25611	Pte.	Stott, James T.	9- 6-17	D of W	France
10/3748	Pte.	Stowers, Robert S.	16- 9-16	K in A	France
10/2822	2/Lt.	Strack, Karl J.	4-10-17	K in A	France
15794	L/Cpl.	Stratton, William J.	4-10-17	K in A	France
11/2489	Pte.	Street, Charles E.	14- 6-16	Disease	France
41169	Pte.	Stringfellow, George	5-10-17	D of W	France
10/1670	Pte.	Stroud, Sidney E.	8- 8-15	K in A	Gallipoli
10/947	T/Cpl.	Struthers, Andrew	8- 6-17	K in A	France
10/3096	Pte.	Stubbs, Pearson	11- 6-17	D of W	France
10/168	Pte.	Studley, Arthur	8- 8-15	K in A	Gallipoli
28227	Pte.	Stumbles, Albert	4-10-17	K in A	France
29508	Pte.	Sturch, Edward J.	8- 6-17	K in A	France
10/1671	Pte.	Style, Herbert H.	8- 8-15	K in A	Gallipoli
53085	Pte.	Sullivan, Cornelius	1-10-18	K in A	France
10/3097	Pte.	Sullivan, James	30- 8-18	D of W	France
23/2100	Pte.	Sullivan, John B.	31- 5-16	K in A	France
35181	Pte.	Sullivan, Thomas	5-10-17	D of W	France
65472	Pte.	Summers, Charles	31- 8-18	K in A	France
10/1673	Pte.	Sutherland, Peter J.	8- 8-15	K in A	Gallipoli
18121	Pte.	Sutherland, Will. C.	22- 7-17	D of W	France
10/2777	L/Cpl.	Sutton, Enoch	8- 6-17	K in A	France
10/488	Pte.	Svenson, Charles	8- 8-15	K in A	Gallipoli
10/1674	Pte.	Swan, James W. (D.C.M., M.I.D.)	16- 9-16	K in A	France

THE WELLINGTON REGIMENT

Reg. No.	Rank.	Name.	Date death.	Cause.	Place.
59481	Pte.	Swannick, Abraham	8- 8-18	D of In.	France (Accd. bomb expl.)
10/758	Pte.	Swindlehurst, F. R.	8- 8-15	K in A	Gallipoli
10061	Pte.	Swinney, John	20- 9-16	D of W	France
10/1163	Pte.	Sykes, Cyril G.	8- 8-15	K in A	Gallipoli
28229	Pte.	Sykes, James	31- 7-17	K in A	France
13481	Pte.	Sylvester, Will. A.	4-10-17	K in A	France
31369	Pte.	Symes, Francis E.	30- 3-18	K in A	France
15797	Cpl.	Symons, Arthur	27- 3-18	K in A	France
24/2106	Pte.	Symons, Benjamin	27- 6-17	K in A	France
10/2832	Cpl.	Talbot, Percy G. A.	16- 9-16	K in A	France
10/2778	Sgt.	Tannahill, John (D.C.M.)	30- 9-18	K in A	France
25613	Pte.	Tanner, Frederick A.	16- 4-18	K in A	France
10/797	Pte.	Tanner, William H.	8- 8-15	K in A	Gallipoli
10/1678	Pte.	Tansley, Ivan	8- 8-15	K in A	Gallipoli
67721	Pte.	Tansley, John A. L.	3-10-18	D of W	France
51792	Pte.	Tapp, George E.	14-11-17	K in A	France
10/1679	Pte.	Tate, Charles D.	18- 7-15	D of W	At Sea ex Gallipoli
10/246	L/Cpl.	Tattle, Philip G.	29- 4-15	K in A	Gallipoli
33476	Pte.	Taucher, Rupert S.	24-11-17	K in A	France
10/1681	Lt.	Tayler, George W.	8- 8-15	K in A	Gallipoli
10/3404	T/Cpl.	Taylor, Alan G. G.	3-10-16	K in A	France
10/611	Pte.	Taylor, Alexander N.	8- 8-15	K in A	Gallipoli
46150	Pte.	Taylor, Alexander W.	4-10-17	K in A	France
10/2331	L/Cpl.	Taylor, Archibald	8- 8-15	K in A	Gallipoli
33477	Pte.	Taylor, Claude E.	4-10-17	K in A	France
10/3755	Pte.	Taylor, Edward C.	15- 9-16	K in A	France
10/2334	Pte.	Taylor, Gilbert R.	8- 8-15	K in A	Gallipoli
15801	Pte.	Taylor, Harold E.	31- 7-17	K in A	France
10/948	Cpl.	Brooke-Taylor, H. R.	16- 9-16	K in A	France
52112	Pte.	Taylor, John B. E.	3-10-18	K in A	France
11/2492	Pte.	Taylor, Leslie F. C.	2-12-18	Accd. K	France (Run over by motor lorry)
10/4043	Pte.	Taylor, Lionel G.	9- 7-16	K in A	France
34172	Pte.	Taylor, Orton C.	4-10-17	K in A	France
8/2738	L/Cpl.	Taylor, Reginald	20- 6-17	K in A	France
10/3756	Pte.	Taylor, Robert	16- 9-16	K in A	France
28233	Pte.	Taylor, Robert	31- 7-17	K in A	France
10/83	Pte.	Taylor, Thomas L.	14-12-17	K in A	France
49852	Pte.	Temperley, Arnold H.	3- 8-18	Drowned at Sea en route U.K. from France	

THE WELLINGTON REGIMENT

Reg. No.	Rank.	Name.	Date death.	Cause.	Place.
28235	Pte.	Terlich, Joseph	20- 8-17	K in A	France
44536	Pte.	Terry, Percy E.	4-10-17	K in A	France
10/1682	T/Cpl.	Thaxter, Lawrence P.	15-10-16	K in A	France
10/1351	Pte.	Thaxter, William	8- 8-15	K in A	Gallipoli
10/3138	Pte.	Thomas, Alban	21-11-15	D of W	Gallipoli
10/537	Pte.	Thomas, George V.	8- 5-15	K in A	Gallipoli
39913	Pte.	Thomas, Harold S.	24- 8-18	K in A	France
10/2005	Pte.	Thomas, Hugh F.	8- 8-15	K in A	Gallipoli
64169	Pte.	Thomas, Joseph P.	26- 7-18	K in A	France
10/1038	L/Cpl.	Thomas, Rupert J.	8- 8-15	K in A	Gallipoli
52113	Pte.	Thomason, Alfred R.	31- 8-18	K in A	France
10/57	Pte.	Thompson, Charles W.	8- 8-15	K in A	Gallipoli
23/1216	Pte.	Thompson, Henry W.	20-10-17	K in A	France
39919	Pte.	Thompson, James I.	16-11-17	K in A	France
15803	Cpl.	Thompson, Mark W.	5-10-17	K in A	France
10/3808	2/Lt.	Thomson, Alister McL.	17- 6-16	K in A	France
44535	Cpl.	Thomson, Colin (M.M.)	4-11-18	K in A	France
10/2338	Pte.	Thomson, Harold J.	8- 8-15	K in A	Gallipoli
63237	Pte.	Thorn, William A.	14- 9-18	D of W	France
42230	Pte.	Thornton, George A.	6-12-17	D of W	France
11971	Pte.	Thrupp, Ernest	8- 6-17	K in A	France
10/3409	Pte.	Thrupp, G. E.	14- 6-16	K in A	France
20457	Pte.	Thrush, Edward W.	8- 6-17	K in A	France
10/1545	Pte.	Thurlow, William H.	8- 8-15	K in A	Gallipoli
10/1354	Pte.	Thurlow, William J.	1- 5-15	K in A	Gallipoli
12513	Pte.	Tobin, Frank O.	17- 7-17	D of W	France
14713	Cpl.	Todd, George G.	1- 8-18	K in A	France
31376	L/Cpl.	Todd, Harry P.	21-10-17	K in A	France
53094	Pte.	Todd, Samuel E.	29- 8-18	K in A	France
37020	Pte.	Todd, Victor	4-10-17	K in A	France
44537	Pte.	Todd-Strachan, D. D.	9-11-18	Disease	N.Z.
10/1012	Pte.	Tohill, Albert J.	19- 8-15	D of W	Egypt ex Gallipoli
10/251	Pte.	Toomer, Harold J.	10- 5-15	D of W	At Sea ex Gallipoli
10/3415	Pte.	Toomey, Patrick	12- 8-16	K in A	France
10/3112	Pte.	Toon, Clifford	16- 9-16	K in A	France
10/4013	Pte.	Topp, Kaj	20- 7-16	K in A	France
12514	Pte.	Tosswill, William W.	4-10-17	K in A	France
45934	Pte.	Trainor, Peter J.	22- 4-18	K in A	France
10/527	Pte.	Travers, George	8- 8-15	K in A	Gallipoli
10/591	Pte.	Traynor, James	8- 5-15	K in A	Gallipoli
10/1686	Pte.	Tremayne, A. E.	8-8-15	K in A	Gallipoli
10/2480	Capt.	Tremewan, Hugh S.	16- 9-16	D of W	France
52055	Pte.	Tucker, Edwin A.	30- 8-18	K in A	France

THE WELLINGTON REGIMENT

Reg. No.	Rank.	Name.	Date death.	Cause.	Place.
10/899	Pte.	Tucker, Harry E.	15- 6-18	Disease	U.K.
32097	Pte.	Tucker, Thomas H.	26- 7-17	K in A	France
24/1557	Pte.	Tunks, Wilfred D.	4-10-17	K in A	France
13140	Pte.	Turchie, Joseph	6- 4-18	D of W	France
24/1218	Pte.	Turner, Arthur H.	14- 6-17	D of W	France
10/1357	Pte.	Turner, Arthur M.	11- 5-15	D of W	At Sea ex Gallipoli
9/2237	Sgt.	Turner, David	5- 8-17	D of W	France
10/249	Pte.	Turrell, Arthur G.	9- 8-15	K in A	Gallipoli
20462	Pte.	Tuson, James	30- 3-18	K in A	France
7/2323	Cpl.	Twisleton, Ronald B.	4-10-17	K in A	France
15808	Pte.	Twomey, Hugh M.	1-10-18	K in A	France
40391	Pte.	Tye, William R.	21- 8-17	K in A	France
11980	Pte.	Ulyatt, Sydney M.	28- 9-16	K in A	France
28242	Cpl.	Ure, William H.	4-10-17	K in A	France
28243	Pte.	Ustallo, Carl	31- 7-17	K in A	France
15809	Sgt.	Uzzell, Benjamin	13- 9-13	K in A	France
10/1358	Pte.	Varcoe, Wesley E.	8- 5-15	K in A	Gallipoli
11/833	Cpl.	Vaughan, Oswald de W.	4-10-17	K in A	France
10/773	Pte.	Velvin, Errol J.	13- 6-15	D of W	Gallipoli
10/2346	Pte.	Vickers, Edward W.	25- 8-15	Disease	Malta ex Gal.
10/898	Pte.	Vickers, Frank L.	8- 8-15	K in A	Gallipoli
6/2309	Pte.	Vine, William L.	23- 6-17	K in A	France
10/2014	Pte.	Virtue, William E.	8- 8-15	K in A	Gallipoli
10/1687	Pte.	Vyner, Arthur W.	16- 9-16	K in A	France
12517	Pte.	Waby, Benjamin	7- 6-17	K in A	France
10/1485	Pte.	Wade, David	3- 7-15	D of W	Malta ex Gal.
10/3116	Pte.	Wain, Stephen	23- 6-16	K in A	France
10/2016	Pte.	Wainwright, Fred.	8- 8-15	K in A	Gallipoli
10/2347	Pte.	Wake, Hereward L.	8- 8-15	K in A	Gallipoli
6/1746	Pte.	Wakelin, John	16- 9-16	K in A	France
38774	Pte.	Wakerley, James A.	23- 7-17	K in A	France
10/78	Pte.	Waldie, Robert B.	8- 8-15	K in A	Gallipoli
33482	Pte.	Wale, Roy A.	4-10-17	K in A	France
49949	Pte.	Walker, Andrew	14-12-17	K in A	France
10/2017	Pte.	Walker, Frank E.	8- 8-15	K in A	Gallipoli
39568	Pte.	Walker, James	1- 8-17	K in A	France
17738	Pte.	Wallace, George	30- 3-18	K in A	France
10/1690	Pte.	Wallace, John R.	8- 8-15	K in A	Gallipoli
10/1081	L/Cpl.	Wallace, Samuel W.	10- 8-15	D of W	Gallipoli
31382	Pte.	Wallace, Thomas	20-10-17	K in A	France
48592	Pte.	Wallbank, William	24- 8-18	K in A	France

THE WELLINGTON REGIMENT

Reg. No.	Rank.	Name.	Date death.	Cause.	Place.
10/2020	Pte.	Walsh, Patrick J.	8- 8-15	K in A	Gallipoli
10/4018	Pte.	Walsh, Robert E.	27- 9-16	K in A	France
10/3423	Pte.	Ward, Charles K.	27- 7-17	K in A	France
33483	Pte.	Ward, Charles R.	4-10-17	K in A	France
13490	Pte.	Ward, Edward	2-11-17	Disease	France
60020	Pte.	Ward, Frank	17- 4-18	D of W	France
10/187	Pte.	Ward, George A.	23- 5-15	D of W	At Sea ex Gallipoli
36704	Pte.	Ward, George H.	4-10-17	K in A	France
10/2021	Pte.	Ward, Henry J.	8- 8-15	K in A	Gallipoli
20471	Pte.	Ward, Reuben O.	8- 6-17	K in A	France
45938	Pte.	Warner, Harry	4-10-17	K in A	France
10/613	W.O.2	Warnock, Thomas L.	15- 9-16	K in A	France
44810	Pte.	Warren, Robert A.	31- 8-18	K in A	France
20472	Pte.	Wasley, Alfred T.	31- 8-18	D of W	France
38092	Pte.	Waterman, Archibald	21- 8-17	D of W	France
19230	Pte.	Waters, John H.	15- 1-17	K in A	France
10/3119	Pte.	Watmore, George F.	12- 7-16	K in A	France
56114	Pte.	Watson, John E.	5-11-18	Disease	France
10/991	Pte.	Watson, William J.	26- 7-16	K in A	France
10/3771	L/Cpl.	Watters, Alexander	27- 3-18	K in A	France
10/2024	Pte.	Weavers, Leslie G.	28- 8-15	D of W	Egypt ex Gallipoli
10/2025	Pte.	Webb, Daniel	8- 8-15	K in A	Gallipoli
51091	Pte.	Webb, Edward D.	1- 9-18	K in A	France
10/1021	Lt.	Webb, Ernest J. H.	17-11-14	Injuries	Colombo en route Egypt (Accd. on Troopship)
39920	Pte.	Webb, Thomas C.	4-10-17	K in A	France
61862	Pte.	Webster, Charles W.	1-10-18	K in A	France
10/2029	2/Lt.	Wells, Ewart L.	8- 8-15	K in A	Gallipoli
10/4496	Pte.	Wenck, A. J. D.	24- 9-16	D of W	France
61867	Pte.	Westh, Phillip A.	12-10-18	K in A	France
61919	Pte.	Westray, George A.	1-10-18	D of W	France
13841	Pte.	Whelan, William	31- 7-17	K in A	France
10/1698	Pte.	Whichelo, Hubert M.	8- 8-15	K in A	Gallipoli
10/154	T/L-Sgt.	Whishaw, Harry G.	3- 7-16	K in A	France
10/1138	Pte.	Whitaker, James H.	8- 8-15	K in A	Gallipoli
64184	Pte.	White, Alexander E.	26- 8-18	K in A	France
10/4144	Pte.	White, Daniel P.	16- 9-16	K in A	France
10/3444	L/Sgt.	White, Godfrey D.	27- 4-18	D of W	France
64185	Pte.	White, Leo O.	4-11-18	K in A	France
7/2578	L/Cpl.	White, Norman C.	4-10-17	K in A	France
10/4022	Pte.	White, Norman G.	9- 8-16	D of W	U.K. ex F'ce.
63981	Pte.	White, Reg. R.	31- 8-18	D of W	France

THE WELLINGTON REGIMENT

Reg. No.	Rank.	Name.	Date death.	Cause.	Place.
36506	Pte.	White, Ronald H.	3- 9-17	Disease	France
23/2115	Pte.	White, Ronald W.	14- 9-16	K in A	France
28567	L/Cpl.	White, Thomas E.	31- 7-17	D of W	France
25626	Pte.	White, William	29- 9-18	K in A	France
23907	Pte.	Whitehorn, Sam. H.	1-12-17	K in A	France
10/3123	Pte.	Whitelaw, Eric R.	5-10-17	D of W	France
10/4495	Pte.	Whiteley, Harry	19- 9-16	K in A	France
15059	Pte.	Whiteman, George	31-7-17	K in A	France
10/2033	Pte.	Whiteman, Walter T.	8- 8-15	K in A	Gallipoli
53723	Pte.	Whiting, Albert C. H.	20-12-17	K in A	France
10/2504	Pte.	Whitmore, Thomas H.	10-11-15	Disease	Mudros
10/569	Pte.	Whitta, Fred. V.	29- 4-15	K in A	Gallipoli
10/746	L/Cpl.	Whittington, H. K.	8- 8-15	K in A	Gallipoli
47491	Pte.	Whitwell, Beaumont	4-10-17	K in A	France
10/77	Pte.	Whyman, Fred. C.	2- 7-16	K in A	France
44541	Pte.	Whyte, Walter	12-10-17	K in A	France
15821	Cpl.	Widt, Christian S.	1- 9-18	K in A	France
37041	Pte.	Wightman, Percy	10- 7-17	D of W	France
10/3429	Pte.	Wilkie, David H.	4-10-17	K in A	France
61871	Pte.	Wilkins, George	31- 8-18	K in A	France
13381	Pte.	Wilkinson, Carroll J.	12-10-18	K in A	France
5/213	Pte.	Wilkinson, John F.	12-10-18	K in A	France
24747	Pte.	Willacy, James	1- 8-17	D of W	France
7/1535	Pte.	Williams, Albert H.	20- 9-16	D of W	France
6/775	Lt.	Williams, Alfred J. (M.I.D.)	1-10-18	K in A	France
33488	Pte.	Williams, Arthur	2- 8-17	K in A	France
10/2035	Sgt.	Williams, Arthur C.	8- 8-15	K in A	Gallipoli
10/2473	Pte.	Williams, Bertram V.	8- 6-17	K in A	France
38095	Pte.	Williams, Daniel L.	2- 1-18	D of W	U.K. ex F'ce.
10/3125	Pte.	Williams, Leslie J.	16- 9-16	K in A	France
10/576	Pte.	Williams, Noel	7- 7-15	Disease	Mudros ex Gallipoli
55003	Pte.	Williams, Norman V.	6- 4-18	K in A	France
10/210	Pte.	Williams, Oliver	29- 4-15	K in A	Gallipoli
10/1705	Pte.	Williams, William S.	8- 8-15	K in A	Gallipoli
14898	Cpl.	Williamson, Matthew	4-11-18	K in A	France
10/3432	Pte.	Williamson, Peter	15- 3-18	Disease	France
30415	L/Cpl.	Wills, Leslie J.	4-10-17	K in A	France
30681	L/Cpl.	Wilson, Arthur	13- 9-18	K in A	France
10/238	Pte.	Wilson, Carson	8- 8-15	K in A	Gallipoli
11985	Pte.	Wilson, Charles	27- 9-16	K in A	France
11/1092	L/Cpl.	Wilson, Dave	23- 9-16	K in A	France
10/732	Pte.	Wilson, Donald S.	17- 8-15	D of W	At Sea ex Gallipoli

THE WELLINGTON REGIMENT

Reg. No.	Rank.	Name.	Date death.	Cause.	Place.
10/75	Lt.	Wilson, Edmund R. (M.I.D.)	27- 4-15	K in A	Gallipoli
10/4217	Pte.	Wilson, Herbert	2-10-16	K in A	France
36714	Pte.	Wilson, Hugh	4-10-17	K in A	France
10/2037	Pte.	Wilson, James G.	8- 8-15	K in A	Gallipoli
10/3433	Pte.	Wilson, John A.	21- 2-17	K in A	France
40416	Pte.	Wilson, Michael	4-10-17	K in A	France
10/3783	Pte.	Wilson, Percy C.	12- 6-16	D of W	France
39570	Pte.	Wilson, Peter J.	4-10-17	K in A	France
16023	Pte.	Wilson, Richard	7- 6-17	K in A	France
65165	Pte.	Wilson, Richard J.	30- 9-18	K in A	France
10/3127	Pte.	Wilson, Robert	25- 9-16	D of W	France
10/2039	Pte.	Wilson, Thomas L.	8- 8-15	K in A	Gallipoli
10/1328	Pte.	Wilson, Walter	7- 6-17	K in A	France
10/541	L/Cpl.	Winter, Adrian	29- 4-15	K in A	Gallipoli
10/524	W.O.1	Winter, William H.	8- 8-15	K in A	Gallipoli
55006	Pte.	Wolstenholme, Roland	2- 8-18	D of W	France
12525	L/Cpl.	Wood, Finlay C.	5- 4-18	K in A	France
38787	Pte.	Wood, Joseph E.	1- 8-17	K in A	France
10/554	Pte.	Wood, Norman H.	8- 5-15	K in A	Gallipoli
10/897	Pte.	Wood, Percy	8- 8-15	K in A	Gallipoli
10/3132	Pte.	Wood, Thomas	16- 9-16	K in A	France
38247	L/Cpl.	Woodford, Joseph E.	11- 7-17	K in A	France
10/2364	Pte.	Woodger, John	8- 8-15	K in A	France
10/4218	Pte.	Woodley, Andrew	22- 9-16	D of W	U.K. ex F"ce
10/1110	L/Cpl.	Woods, William	8- 8-15	K in A	Gallipoli
42250	Pte.	Woodward, Walter	24- 8-18	K in A	France
10/2381	Pte.	Worley, Robin J.	28- 8-15	D of W	Malta ex Gal.
48604	Pte.	Wright, Ernest M.	30- 9-18	D of W	France
41920	L/Cpl.	Wright, George H.	15- 8-18	K in A	France
10/165	L/Cpl.	Wright, John	8- 5-15	K in A	Gallipoli
25629	Pte.	Wright, Thomas	1- 8-17	D of W	France
10/4220	Pte.	Wyber, Isaac	5-10-17	D of W	France
10/2795	L/Cpl.	Yearbury, G. D.	2-10-16	K in A	France
17849	Pte.	York, Henry M.	7- 6-17	K in A	France
1/11	2/Lt.	Young, Albert V.	1- 5-17	K in A	France
16035	Pte.	Young, Alfred C.	8- 6-17	K in A	France
10/2476	Pte.	Young, James A.	16- 9-16	K in A	France

Appendix "A."

The places at which the 1st and 2nd Battalions of the Wellington Regiment were billetted on their march of over 150 miles from Beauvois to the German frontier.

Date.		1st Battalion.	2nd Battalion.
Nov.	28	Beauvois	Beauvois
,,	29	Haussy	Vendignies
,,	30	Wagnies-le-Grand	Wagnies-le- Petit
Dec.	1	} St. Waast	Pissotau
,,	2		
,,	3	Louvroil Area	Louvroil Area
,,	4	Jeaumont	Marpent
,,	5	} Lobbes	Lobbes
,,	6		
,,	7	Marchienne-au-Pont	Dampremy
,,	8	Tamines	Tamines
,,	9	} Isnes	Spy
,,	10		
,,	11	Daussonlx	Villers-lez-Heest
,,	12	Pontillas	Petit Waret
,,	13	} Anthiet	Petit Wanze
,,	14		
,,	15		
,,	16		
,,	17	Jemeppe	Jemeppe
,,	18	Gomze Andoument	Beaufays
,,	19	Verviers	Verviers

PRINTED BY
FERGUSON & OSBORN LTD.,
202 LAMBTON QUAY,
WELLINGTON, N.Z.